Home Truths About Domestic Violence

D0220264

While men's violence to women is an everyday, culturally supported activity, this Reader demonstrates that men's violence can be curtailed and that women and children can be assisted effectively; that state policies and provision can be improved; and that women can actively participate in the resolution of their difficulties. Bringing together new work and key papers, *Home Truths About Domestic Violence* provides a comprehensive overview and up-to-date account of the progress so far and identifies what still needs to be done. Areas covered include:

- women's experience of violence
- children's experience of violence
- personal experiences of the justice system
- state policies on violence in the US and UK
- educational programmes and initiatives to combat violence.

This substantial Reader makes a significant contribution to the understanding of domestic violence from both a policy and a practice perspective. Together with its companion volume, *Home Truths About Child Sexual Abuse*, it provides an in-depth resource for a wide range of teachers, students and professionals, highlighting the diverse and complex dimensions of the problem of domestic violence.

Jalna Hanmer is Professor of Women's Studies at the International Centre for the Study of Violence and Abuse, University of Sunderland. **Catherine Itzin** is Research Professor in Social Work and Social Policy and Co-Director of the International Centre for the Study of Violence and Abuse, University of Sunderland.

Also available

Home Truths About Child Sexual Abuse
Influencing policy and practice – A reader
Edited by Catherine Itzin
Routledge 2000: 460pp

The prevention of child sexual abuse means stopping abusers abusing. How can this be achieved?

> '[In] this hard hitting book . . . Professor Itzin . . . questions the efficacy of current child protection and child sexual abuse prevention policies in stopping . . . ordinary men's abuse of their own and other people's children . . . She is clearly trying to change things for children in the future.'
>
> Anne Bannister, *Community Care*

Hardback   0-415-15261-5   £55
Paperback   0-415-15262-3   £18.99

Home Truths About Domestic Violence

Feminist influences on policy and practice
A reader

**Edited by Jalna Hanmer and
Catherine Itzin**

With Sheila Quaid and
Debra Wigglesworth

London and New York

First published 2000
by Routledge
11 New Fetter Lane, London EC4P 4EE

Simultaneously published in the USA and Canada
by Routledge
29 West 35th Street, New York, NY 10001

Routledge is an imprint of the Taylor & Francis Group

Typeset in Goudy by Wearset, Boldon, Tyne and Wear
Printed and bound in Great Britain by Biddles Ltd, Guildford and King's
Lynn

British Library Cataloguing in Publication Data
A catalogue record for this book is available from the British Library

Library of Congress Cataloging in Publication Data

Home truths about domestic violence : feminist influences on policy and
practice : a reader / edited by Jalna Hanmer and Catherine Itzin with
Sheila Quaid and Debra Wigglesworth.
     p. cm.
  Includes bibliographical references and index.
  1. Family violence. 2. Victims of family violence – Services for.
  I. Hanmer, Jalna. II. Itzin, Catherine, 1944–

HV6626 .H64 2001
362.82'92–dc21

                                                              00–046454

ISBN 0–415–24156–1 hbk
ISBN 0–415–24157–X pbk

Dedication

To women on the front line of violence in the home whose struggles against violent men inform every page.

Contents

Illustrations

Figures

Tables

Contributors

David Adams, Ed. D., is co-founder and Program and Research Director of Emerge, the first counselling programme in the US for men who abuse women. His articles about men who batter and intervention programmes have been published in numerous books and journals.

Jackie Barron is a freelance researcher currently working for Women's Aid Federation England (WAFE) and the National Autistic Society. Author of *Not Worth the Paper . . .?* (1990) and co-author of *Councillors in Crisis* (1991).

Kate Cavanagh, Ph.D., is a lecturer in Social Work in the Department of Social Policy and Social Work at Glasgow University, Scotland. She is an activist, practitioner and researcher. Kate is co-editor of *Working With Men: Feminism in Social Work* (1997).

Thangam Debbonaire provides training, consultancy and research on domestic violence to UK organisations. She was National Children's Officer for the Women's Aid England (1991–7) and co-author of *Domestic Violence and Child Protection: A Practitioner's Guide* (2000).

R. Emerson Dobash is Professor of Social Research in the Department of Applied Social Sciences at the University of Manchester, and a co-director of the Violence Research Centre. Amongst co-authored books, numerous government reports, journal and anthology articles is *Rethinking Violence Against Women* (1999).

Russell P. Dobash is Professor of Criminology in the Department of Applied Social Sciences at the University of Manchester and co-director of the Violence Research Centre. Amongst co-authored books, numerous government reports, journal and anthology articles is *Changing Violent Men* (2000).

Evelyn Gillan is Co-Director and founding member of the Zero Tolerance Charitable Trust. A qualified social worker, she has worked primarily in equalities campaigning, including the Women's Unit, Edinburgh District Council, as Campaigns and Promotions Officer from 1985–93.

Sue Griffiths, Ph.D., researches and teaches on the MA, Violence, Abuse and Gender Relations at Leeds Metropolitan University. She is an evaluator of the West Yorkshire Police Vulnerable Victims Project and a member of the campaign group, Justice for Women.

Gill Hague is a founder member of the University of Bristol Domestic Violence Research Group which conducts national and international studies. She has produced many publications on domestic violence and regards herself as an activist as well as an academic.

Jalna Hanmer is Professor of Women's Studies, International Centre for the Study of Violence and Abuse, University of Sunderland. She is currently evaluating the West Yorkshire Police Vulnerable Victims Project. Books she has co-authored and other publications include *Arresting Evidence: Domestic Violence and Repeat Victimisation* (1999).

Nicola Harwin is Director of the Women's Aid Federation England. She has developed policy and services, campaigned and researched for 25 years. Nicola is also an author and trainer in the field of domestic violence and a member of the Women's National Commission.

Marianne Hester is Professor of Sociology and Social Policy at the University of Sunderland, where she co-directs the International Centre for the Study of Violence and Abuse. She has researched many aspects of violence and abuse, including domestic violence and children.

Catherine Itzin, Ph.D., is Research Professor in Social Work and Social Policy and co-director of the International Centre for the Study of Violence and Abuse at the University of Sunderland. She has edited *Home Truths About Child Sexual Abuse: Influencing Policy and Practice* (2000), the companion volume to this Reader.

Davina James-Hanman is the Greater London Domestic Violence Project Coordinator. She has worked in the field of domestic violence for over a decade in the capacities of advocate, campaigner, conference organiser, crisis counsellor, policy officer, project manager, refuge worker, researcher, trainer and writer.

Liz Kelly is Professor in Sexualised Violence. She works at the Child and Woman Abuse Studies Unit, University of North London, which has completed 20 research projects. In activism, spanning 27 years, she was involved in founding a refuge and rape crisis line.

Helena Kennedy, QC, is a criminal barrister, having acted in many leading British cases including the Brighton Bombing Trial and the Guildford Four Appeal. She is Chair of the British Council, Chair of the Human Genetics Commission and a Labour Peer since 1997.

Sue Lees is Professor of Women's Studies at the University of North London. Her publications include *Losing Out* (1996), *Carnal Knowledge: Rape on Trial*

(1997), *Ruling Passions: Sexual Violence, Reputation and the Law* (1997), *Policing Sexual Assault* (1999).

Ruth Lewis, Ph.D., is a lecturer in the Department of Social Policy at the University of Newcastle. With Rebecca and Russell Dobash and Kate Cavanagh, she is currently completing the first national study of homicide in Britain.

Ellen Malos is a founder member of the Domestic Violence Research Group at the University of Bristol. She has been a women's movement activist since the 1960s. Her many publications include *The Politics of Housework* (1995), and (with Gill Hague) *Domestic Violence: Action for Change* (1998).

Amina Mama is Professor of Gender and Development at the University of Cape Town in South Africa. Her publications include *The Hidden Struggle: Statutory and Voluntary Sector Responses to Violence Against Black Women in the Home* (1989).

Coral McDonnell, a founder of the Duluth Domestic Abuse Intervention Project (DAIP), has contributed to DAIP programme development and publications for 18 years, facilitated groups for women charged with domestic assault, and was involved in the production of a manual co-ordinating community responses to domestic violence.

Caroline McGee is a research officer with the NSPCC and author of *Childhood Experiences of Domestic Violence* (2000). Her main research interests are violence against children and women, surviving trauma and involving children in research.

Jayne Mooney, Ph.D., is a Senior Lecturer in Criminology and Gender Studies, Middlesex University. Research interests include violence against women, methodology, deprivation and crime. She has authored *The Miranda Crime and Community Survey* (1993) and *The North London Domestic Violence Survey* (1994).

Rebecca Morley, School of Sociology and Social Policy, University of Nottingham, is principal investigator on a study of the impact of changing housing policy on women's vulnerability to domestic violence funded by the Violence Research Programme, Economic and Social Research Council.

Audrey Mullender is Professor of Social Work and Director of the Centre for the Study of Safety and Well-being at the University of Warwick. She has produced over 100 publications, including three books on domestic violence, and was until recently editor of the *British Journal of Social Work*.

Pragna Patel, a long-standing member of Southall Black Sisters, founded the SBS centre in 1982 and, with others, Women Against Fundamentalism. Her current work includes casework, co-ordinating the Zoora Shah campaign, and organising SBS's 21st anniversary celebrations.

Ellen L. Pence, Ph.D., is a founder of the Domestic Abuse Intervention Project (DAIP) in Duluth, Minnesota, and co-author of *Educational Groups for Men*

Who Batter: The Duluth Model (1993) (see Appendix 2), and *Coordinated Community Responses to Domestic Violence: Lessons from the Duluth Model* (1999).

Sheila Quaid is Senior Lecturer in Sociology and subject leader for Gender Studies at the University of Sunderland. She is currently researching lesbian identity and reproductive rights for a doctoral thesis, entitled 'Lesbian Motherhood: Processes of Inclusion and Exclusion'.

Elaine Samson is Co-Director and a founding member of the Zero Tolerance Charitable Trust. When Women's Officer on Edinburgh District Council, 1992–5, she was part of the creative team that implemented the Zero Tolerance campaign locally. She continues to develop Zero Tolerance campaigns.

Debra Wigglesworth is a Ph.D. candidate and researcher at the International Centre for the Study of Violence and Abuse, University of Sunderland. She is currently working on the Home Office evaluation of the West Yorkshire Police Vulnerable Victims Project.

Acknowledgements

We would like to thank our publisher, and particularly our editor Edwina Welham, for their support, patience and commitment to seeing this book, together with its companion volume *Home Truths about Child Sexual Abuse*, into print in the year 2000.

Copyright acknowledgements

All chapters are © the contributors. Grateful acknowledgement for permission to reproduce the following previously published material.

Chapter 1 is reproduced with permission from J. Hanmer 'Out of Control: Men, Violence and Family Life', in Popay, J., Hearn, J. and Edwards, J. (eds) (1998) *Men, Gender Divisions and Welfare*, London: Routledge, pp. 128–46.

Chapter 10 is reproduced with permission from P. Patel, 'Third Wave Feminism and Black Women's Activism' in Mirza, H. S. (ed.) (1998) *Black British Feminism*, London: Routledge, pp. 255–68.

Chapter 14 is reproduced with permission from M. Pence and C. McDonnell, 'Developing Policies and Protocols', in Shepard, M. F. and Pence, E. L. (1998) *Coordinating Community Responses to Domestic Violence: Lessons from Duluth and Beyond*, Thousand Oaks, CA: Sage, pp. 41–64.

The tables in Chapter 18 are derived from J. Hanmer, S. Griffiths and D. Jerwood (1999) *Arresting Evidence: Domestic Violence and Repeat Victimisation*, Home Office Police Research Series Paper 104. Reprinted with permission.

The posters in Chapter 19 and on the cover are reproduced with permission of the Zero Tolerance Charitable Trust.

Appendix 1 is reprinted with permission from N. Harwin (1998) 'Families Without Fear: Women's Aid Agenda for Action on Domestic Violence' Bristol: Women's Aid Federation England.

Introduction

Prevention, provision and protection

Jalna Hanmer and Catherine Itzin

This book is a Reader on violence against women and their children from known men. The aim is to present the way in which violence against women is theorised, and how research and activism have led to a gradual shift in understanding and responses to women who are abused and the men who abuse them, including diversities of race, class and ethnicity. Research provides evidence for change; it is formative in the development of theory and practice and underpins the implementation and evaluation of change programmes. This Reader has gathered evidence-based material demonstrating how feminist and feminist-influenced research, alongside women's demands for change and the provision of alternative services, assist the incorporation into Government policy of feminist ideas and responses to violence against women and their children. What remains to be done is identified and based on what is known about men's violence.

Change requires new conceptual frameworks. The major feminist contributions have been to define and to evidence male violence as fundamental to the social control of women, to identify coercive male domination and abuses of women in the home as problems of importance, and to place this violence on the world-wide agenda of social change. Women's movements have been, and are, driving forces for change. By effectively assisting women and their children, male violence is challenged and this provides a new starting point for conceptual and practice-oriented developments. While men's violence is an everyday, culturally supported activity, this Reader demonstrates that men's violence can be curtailed and that women and children can be assisted effectively; that state policies and provision can be improved; and that women actively participate in the resolution of their difficulties.

This Reader presents both new and previously published work. It is divided into five sections.

Chapters 1–4: women's experiences of violence from known men in the home

In Chapter 1, Jalna Hanmer examines social processes that sustain violence against women. The analysis is based on interviews with 60 women living in refuges and the community, half of whom were of Asian origin, and half were white with roots in the locality of the study. From experiential accounts of 'devastating relationships with men', Hanmer examines the structuring of hierarchy and privilege within families, the advantages that come from being male, and sons, husbands and fathers, and how benefits associated with these social statuses are extracted and enforced through men's use of violence and the collusion of families and others.

In Chapter 2, Jayne Mooney presents the findings of a 1993 study of domestic violence in North London. A random sample of 1000 women and men was methodologically designed to overcome some of the known limitations of victimisation surveys. It involved a complex three-stage programme of interviewer-administered questionnaires, the use of vignettes to explore men's attitudes and behaviour, self-completion questionnaires for women and in-depth interviews. Using this gender-sensitive methodology produced 'hidden figures' of domestic violence incidence and prevalence as defined by the women who experienced it and the men who perpetrated it.

In Chapter 3, Amina Mama reports on the findings of a study of black women's experience of domestic violence conducted in the 1980s and carried out in London, with over 100 women contacted through Women's Aid and community organisations. It also involved interviews with housing, social and legal organisations and with workers at 18 Women's Aid refuges. The study found that while all women experience hardship in seeking to leave abusive men, the effects of racism makes the situation worse for black women.

In Chapter 4, Sue Lees analyses marital rape cases heard at the Court of Appeal between 1991 and 1995, and reports on findings from a study conducted in 1993 with 100 women who experienced rape. Although guidelines to encourage judges to give longer sentences for rapists were issued in the late 1980s, and the marital rape exemption was abolished in 1991, Lees found that marital rape was still not treated as seriously by the English judiciary as rape by strangers or acquaintances, and that the sentence in 50 per cent of rape cases was reduced on appeal. She explores the reasons judges treat marital rape as less serious and considers the research evidence linking marital rape and murder.

Chapters 5–7: children's experiences of violence in the home

In Chapter 5, Caroline McGee reports on a qualitative research study into the domestic violence experiences of children and their mothers and services to support and protect children. Carried out for the NSPCC and built on McGee's experience of working with children in local authority care and with Women's Aid, this study involved interviews with 54 children and 47 mothers. Child interviews were designed to be suitable for three age groups: 5–8 year olds, 8–11 year olds and teenagers. The chapter includes an overview of social services, housing, health, education and the police as perceived by domestic violence survivors, and the views of children and their mothers on how their needs can best be met and services improved.

In Chapter 6, Marianne Hester reports on how a collaboration between feminist researchers and an NSPCC team led to a positive impact on the team's work with abused children who had lived with domestic violence. The project involved interviews with the NSPCC team, analysis of case files and some observation of practice. The chapter outlines how, through a process of defining and identifying domestic issues, these were incorporated and integrated into the work with abused children. The project led to a greater understanding and visibility of the links between child abuse and domestic violence, and to a wider application of safety measures for both children and their mothers.

In Chapter 7, Gill Hague, Audrey Mullender, Liz Kelly, Ellen Malos, with Thangam Debbonaire and in partnership with the National Women's Aid Federation of England, report on research on work with children in refuges. The study investigated the contribution of children's workers to practice with children and examined the impacts of domestic violence on children and their mothers. They present the history and developments in work with children in refuges, including employment, training and organisational issues, the impact of racism and of legislation, and recent general developments in the awareness of children's issues and domestic violence.

Chapters 8–10: experiences of women who fight back

In Chapter 8, Sue Griffiths examines the role of anger to develop a theoretical understanding of women's agency. From interviews with 18 women, eight of whom faced criminal charges for killing or injuring their violent male partners, she examines how women's violence – including lethal violence – occurs simultaneously with domestic violence victimisation. She develops a new way of looking at women's responses to repeated domestic violence, conceptualising the repertoire of active responses used by victimised women as progressing from reaction to resolution to resistance. She reviews the lack of connection between women's angered responses and success in using the defence of provocation and recommends a new defence to murder.

Chapter 9 is based on an interview with Helena Kennedy, QC by Catherine Itzin, about the criminal justice system's response to women who have killed their violent partners. It draws on the cases of Sara Thornton, Kiranjit Ahluwalia and Emma Humphreys, all of whom achieved high public profiles as campaigners fighting for their release from life sentences. All three sustained years of violence and abuse from male partners and killed in their attempts to stop this violence. Kennedy finds that most women kill in desperation, in self-defence, or in the defence of their children. In the interview she discusses gender bias in the legal system and the need for a different defence for women who kill, based on self-preservation.

In Chapter 10, Pragna Patel describes the origins and work of Southall Black Sisters in providing support and services for Asian women victims of domestic violence, in the context of her own experience as an Asian woman. She describes the growth of a politics of resistance against the racism she experienced in Britain because she was the 'wrong colour', and injustices she experienced because she was the 'wrong gender'. Her chapter is about the intersectionality of gender, race and class as she has witnessed and experienced it. She contributes an analysis of the state, the family, religious and ethnic communities in maintaining gendered power relations by permitting violence against women.

Chapters 11–13: influencing state policies on violence against women from known men

In Chapter 11, R. Emerson and Russell P. Dobash examine major developments around woman abuse in Britain and the USA. They discuss innovation and change in conceptualising violence against women and effecting change within the institutions of the state, identify the problem as violence against women and, through interviews with women and men, examine the differences between men's and women's experiences and use of violence, including homicide. They describe the world-wide activist responses to violence against women, discuss the importance of housing, and the limits of social change.

In Chapter 12, Nicola Harwin and Jackie Barron explain the role of Women's Aid in addressing domestic violence; examine the implications for women and their children of recent legislative and policy initiatives; and discuss outstanding issues and future directions. They describe the founding principles, service provision, and support given to women and children through Women's Aid from the start of the second wave of the women's liberation movement in the 1970s. They discuss specific civil and criminal laws, and their impact on women and children, government action on domestic violence, multi-agency initiatives, and conclude that there is still a long way to go.

In Chapter 13, Rebecca Morley discusses the housing needs of women experiencing domestic violence and the importance of a strong independent refuge movement if women are to achieve their human right to live free of violence. She examines and evaluates legislation, policy and practice responses of local and central government to abused women's need for social housing. The chapter includes early findings from a study funded by the Violence Initiative of the Economic and Social Research Council. The study is evaluating the impact of changing housing policy on women's vulnerability to violence through questionnaire surveys of all refuge groups and case studies in four housing authorities.

Chapters 14–15: partnership approaches by statutory and voluntary sector agencies

In Chapter 14, Ellen Pence and Cora McDonnell describe the development and implementation of the Domestic Abuse Intervention Project (DAIP) in Duluth, Minnesota, known world-wide as the 'Duluth Model'. It is a programme based on negotiating agreements with community agencies in an inter-agency approach with two aims: ensuring the safety of the domestic violence victim and holding perpetrators responsible and accountable for their violence. In this chapter they set out the lessons learned during two decades of policy development in Duluth and provide guidance on best practice.

In Chapter 15, Davina James Hanman describes the development of domestic violence fora in the UK. She argues that inter-agency approaches are the best and possibly the only way to meet the needs of women and children experiencing domestic violence who, research has shown, will make between five and twelve agency contacts before obtaining the assistance they require. She describes the 1995 Governmental Inter-Agency Circular on Domestic Violence, the current influence on statutory duties of the Crime and Disorder Act (1998) requiring local authorities and police to work together to reduce crime, and findings from research on effective partnership working.

Chapters 16–19: decreasing the violence of men

In Chapter 16, Russell P. and R. Emerson Dobash, Kate Cavanagh and Ruth Lewis discuss the impact and effectiveness of criminal justice interventions in domestic violence, therapeutic and pro-feminist programmes, and the findings of a three-year research evaluation of two Scottish programmes. New instruments were designed to measure change in men's violent behaviour and interviews and postal questionnaires obtained women's views on changes in their partners' use of violence. The authors recommend a combination of criminal justice system interventions and court-mandated abuser programmes based on the principles of the Duluth and the Emerge models in the USA.

In Chapter 17, David Adams describes Emerge, the world's first intervention programme for men who are violent to their women partners. The principles underlying it, influenced by the women's movement, are based on an understanding of domestic violence as a crime against women, the belief that men should be educated to accept complete responsibility for their violence and to learn non-violent and non-coercive behaviour. Adams presents the programme, its evaluation, and the lessons learned about the nature of men's violence against women and what can be done about it.

In Chapter 18, Hanmer and Griffiths describe the implementation and evaluation of a new strategic approach and model for policing domestic violence to reduce repeat offending by men and to ensure the safety of women. Domestic violence offenders differ greatly in that only a minority require repeat police attendance, and an operational programme with incrementally increasing interventions, systematically applied, reduces their number. This operational programme improved the consistency and effectiveness of policing domestic violence through pro-active early interventions and intensified responses to men who persistently abuse women.

In Chapter 19, Evelyn Gillan and Elaine Samson describe the Zero Tolerance Charitable Trust's history, activities and their evaluation. They describe public education media and poster campaign initiatives to raise awareness and to communicate the message that men, not women, are responsible for male viol-ence expressed as rape, child sexual abuse and domestic violence, and present survey results of young people's attitudes to violence. Zero Tolerance developed the concept of the 'three Ps' – prevention, provision, and protection – and these three ideas, the prevention of violence, the provision of support, and legal protection, now provide a basic framework for Government policy.

Chapter 20: the influence of feminism on domestic violence policy and practice

In Chapter 20, Catherine Itzin draws on the material in the Reader to discuss what is known about men's violence against women. She summarises and com-ments on varying definitions of domestic violence and their impact on preva-lence data, the power relations of domestic violence, the knowledge about violent men gained from women and from men's programmes, and how the gen-dering of the language of domestic violence can make men more visible in public policy and professional practice. She argues that recognising domestic violence as a 'men-thing' is crucial to the success of domestic violence preven-tion at the level of the state, just as it is at the level of the individual.

Appendix 1 is *Families Without Fear: the Women's Aid Agenda for Action on Domestic Violence* with recommendations for a national strategy. This Women's Aid Federation England (WAFE) document, located here alongside current government policy, sets the agenda for the next phase of government policy development.

Appendix 2 is the Duluth Domestic Abuse Intervention Project Power and Control Wheel.

Part I

Women's experiences of violence from known men in the home

1 Domestic violence and gender relations

Contexts and connections[1]

Jalna Hanmer

Violence against women is not diminishing in frequency or intensity, even though violence from men to women began to be recognized as a major social problem over 20 years ago (Parliamentary Select Committee 1975). The experiences of women, the frequency of abusive behaviour from men, and the responses of professionals are drawn upon to provide frameworks for policy and interventions (Dobash and Dobash 1980; see also Chapter 11; Hanmer and Saunders 1984; 1993; Mooney 1993 (see Chapter 2); Mirlees-Black *et al.* 1996). Over the past two decades considerable effort has gone into providing women and their children with effective assistance, although this remains, for the most part, patchy and partial.[2] Resistance to identifying violence against women as crime, as serious, as worthy of agency intervention, has been examined in health, housing, social services and policing services (Binney *et al.* 1981; Borkowski *et al.* 1983; Maynard 1985; Edwards 1989; Hague and Malos 1993; Hanmer and Saunders 1993; Hanmer 1995; Hague *et al.* 1995). Resistance by informal contacts, and the actions taken by the women and men involved, has received less attention.[3]

This chapter examines social processes that sustain violence against women. The focus is on the different responses women and men experience from the many others who are part of the social context in which violence against women takes place. The analysis is derived from interviews held with 60 women living in refuges and in the community, with first languages of English, Punjabi and Urdu, and from agency personnel with whom they had contact.[4] Half of the women interviewed have personal or family origins from the Asian sub-continent, primarily Pakistan, but also Bangladesh and India. The remaining 30 women are not completely homogenous in terms of personal and family origins, but almost all are white and see their origins as within the area of interview.

Women's accounts of their lives provide information on how hierarchy and privilege is structured within families, how cultural boundaries apply to men and women, how individual women negotiate within and move beyond culturally and socially prescribed limits on their behaviour, and how individual men maintain their socially superior position without altering their behaviour. The analysis focuses on the areas of struggle between women, men, families and others, how these develop over time, and the strategies women and men adopt in order to achieve their desired outcomes. In these interviews women describe their partner's relationships with members of his family of origin, with her and the children, with his and her friends, with work colleagues, and with other women. As with women, men's strategies involve relationships with his family, her family, his, her and their children, his friends, her friends, other women and other men. Families, friends and acquaintances may actively or passively support, even encourage, or restrain men in their violence. Agencies too, participate in these processes.

Whatever their 'race', 'ethnicity' or 'culture', women experiencing violence have in common devastating relationships with men (see Chapter 3). All the women interviewed live in a web of relationships bound by family and culture in which expectations of correct behaviour for women and men differ substantially. When confronted with repeated violence, women describe how family members and others intervene in women's lives and how women attempt to use networks of family and friends to mitigate, if not resolve, problems with their men.[5] Women's accounts demonstrate that men from varied cultural and ethnic groups have in common cultural and family advantages that come from being male, from being sons, husbands and fathers.

These dynamics raise a number of key questions around difference and commonality and, when considering violence, call into question the use of 'race' or 'ethnicity' and their associated 'cultures' as dominant markers of sameness and variation in experience. There are many differences between the women interviewed in this study, but these cannot be placed neatly into the categories 'race', 'ethnicity' or even 'culture', when focusing on violence and the responses of women, men, the larger family and other informal relationships and groups. Differences often thought of as major, such as the type of marriage entered into by women and men, do not produce fundamentally different gendered experiences of violence.

Amongst the 60 women interviewed there are three types of marriage characterized by two factors: who arranged the marriage, and kinship. Marriages arranged by families may be between those related by kinship, in particular first cousins, or between those who are not kin; or marriage may be arranged by the individual marriage partners. These differences are important to the lives of men and women, but domination, control and violence towards women and children occur whatever the preferred form of marriage and, whatever the preferred form of marriage, families and others attempt to mediate relationships characterized by violence. The pattern of marriage within white British society, which is seen as freely entered into by both parties and based solely on personal choice, seems no more likely to produce marriages free of violence than those arranged between either family members or strangers. Women and men who live together without marriage may also have relationships characterized by violence.

Others do act to restrain a husband and/or other family members who may be abusing an individual woman. While these interventions may work for some women, these interviews are with women for whom individual and family modes of intervention are not effective. These ineffectual interventions suggest that, for men, other cultural values can take precedence. The most basic factor constituting the cultural framework that either fully or partially legitimates home-based violence by men against women is that the boundaries specifying correct behaviour for women are not those that bind men to society and cultures, however diverse cultures may be in other ways. Men stand outside community and family accountability as understood by and applied to women.

These differential values and boundaries are the subject of this chapter. The accounts of women expose the advantages men experience as males in the roles of sons, husbands and fathers. The chapter describes women's perceptions of the feelings men express about women and children, how this affects women's feelings about themselves and the relationship, and their subsequent responses. The intangible and tangible benefits men gain from the abuse of women are described. Women's experiences of the responses of others to the violence, to women, children and men then follows. The acceptability of violence has shifting boundaries and men vary their strategies when women begin to leave. Leaving is a process that can occur over a brief to a very long time period.

Advantages men experience as males, sons, husbands and fathers

Men gain many advantages as males, sons, husbands/cohabitees and fathers, and these advantages are interrelated. A man's status as son is an aspect of his behaviour as husband and father. His status as husband is an aspect of his behaviour as father, and all three statuses are predicated on being male. Men's statuses are cumulative from son to husband to father. This is seen more clearly with men living in extended families, as they have daily interaction with parents, siblings and other family members, than with men living in nuclear families where contact with the wider family is less frequent. The general principle of status interrelatedness, however, still applies. The cumulative statuses of men are reinforced by public policy and its implementation. For example, men retain considerable authority over women and children upon divorce or relationship break-up, through residence and contact orders and their threat, and through non-intervention by the criminal justice system in their continued violence to and harassment of women.

The advantages men gain from violence have been known for some time, with both service provision to women and research demonstrating certain key elements (Hearn 1995). However, these elements are usually described as forms of women's oppression, rather than personal and social benefits to men. In order to develop an analysis that incorporates the actions of others, it is necessary to bring the man on to centre stage. He is both a primary force in the construction of social life characterized by degradation, humiliation and personal harm, and the upholder of deeply held cultural values which make it very difficult to effectively intervene in his violence. Women describe major benefits gained by men through the use of violence.

Violence and the expression of feelings

Men express many feelings through violence and their feelings may determine their actions. Men may enjoy inflicting violence. 'The more violence he did to me, the more happy he would be.' 'After he had hit me, he would say, "Sit here in front of me, if I see any tears in your eyes then see what happens." Then he would say, "Laugh and talk to me".' This form of behaviour may also involve children (see Chapters 5 and 6). In a long session of violence, 'he slapped her [the child] and she became unconscious. He said [to the wife/mother], "You hit her; if you hit her you'll save yourself."' And he continued to abuse her until she did. Knowledge of this type of personal behaviour is well documented in the study of war and political regimes in which torture and genocide are part of the social process, but it has yet to be incorporated into family studies.

A more frequently met pattern of emotional response is to hold women responsible for the men's feelings. 'If I were to say to him like a couple of days after he'd hit me, my head's still hurting me, he'd say, "It will fucking hurt in a minute. What have I told you, don't keep starting. You always start me off. You're the one who fucking always winds me up. It's all your fault."' Women may respond by accepting responsibility for his feelings: 'And in the end I got to believing it was my fault.' Once in a domestic situation of recurring violence, women seek explanations for the abuse they suffer and self-blame is a widespread initial, if not long-term, way of understanding his behaviour.

A further development is to re-interpret his violence as caring for her. One form this takes is to re-create the man as a baby. His 'baby self' becomes the love object:

> He is happy with me; he does love me; he doesn't want no one else to get my feelings. He is like a baby to me because I've seen him upset and I know the way he feels and he's come to me for help. I know he does need me and he's nobody else to turn to.

Another way to interpret violence as caring is to perceive threats and fear of death as proof of the strength of the man's positive feelings.

> He is so jealous I've even been accused of knocking about with his own dad! That's how jealous he is, but he's really caring with it as well. There is no way on earth he wants anyone else to have me, no way. That's because he cares. If I ever left him he'd literally kill me.

When women interpret violence in this way, then leaving him can feel like a betrayal: 'Now I feel as though I've let him down.' Emotional conflict may delay or inhibit women leaving. Women may leave temporarily as the conflict of feelings generated by leaving becomes too intense for them to remain away. Women can experience deep conflict; for example, one woman did not want to lose her highly controlling husband. He rarely allowed her to leave the house, but now that her eldest child had reached the mandatory school age he had to be taken to school, otherwise she feared the children would be taken from her by social services. Women who permanently leave violent men move beyond taking responsibility for the feelings of men. Women who permanently leave recognize the feelings of men in relation to violence as negative. It may take women some time before they begin to re-interpret the expression of his feelings in this way.

When men demonstrate an obvious lack of interest in the abused woman through relationships with other women or demonstrate a lack of concern for their children, women more easily recognize the feelings of men in relation to violence as negative. Men from Asian origins may have white women as sexual partners while being married to women brought into England as wives. This causes great unhappiness to women who said, for example, that their husband would take the white girlfriend out in the car, but never themselves, or that they brought their white girlfriend into the home, expecting the wife to cook and serve as if the other woman occupied her place within the marriage. White women, too, were expected to put up with other women: 'he used to make me leave the house at the weekends so he could bring his girlfriend to stay.' These patterns of behaviour went along with jealousy so that 'If I were walking anywhere I had to look straight ahead'. Or women could be commanded to keep their heads down: 'I weren't allowed to look this way or that way'. Men saw themselves as in control of their own lives and as having the right to have extramarital or other cohabitant relationships at the same time. One man explained to the woman he was abusing why he behaved as he did in this way: 'I'm my own boss.'

Pregnancy and having children can result in strong negative feelings for some men, with violence beginning at this point. This too can be an aspect of sexuality. For example, 'He said, "You're not a woman, you're finished." He said to me, "After bearing a child, the woman is no longer a woman."' The strength of negative feelings generated in men with pregnancy and childbirth may be expressed as wish for the child's death. 'When pregnant, he hated me, he hated her. He said, "I hope you lose it, I hope it dies."' This child was seriously ill in hospital and when pressed to come and see her, he sent a message saying, 'No, I hope she fucking drops dead'.

While men gain status as fathers as well as sons and husbands, not all men want women to have children, or to have a particular child. Women can undergo abortion in order to meet the demands of the man with whom they live. Once children are born, men may use violence and threats as ways to get rid of them, particularly when a child is the result of an earlier relationship. A man may begin a relationship by expressing interest in a woman's existing children, but once he is taken into the woman's household his behaviour can become abusive. Woman may decide to send a child to its natural father or allow the child to be taken into the care of the local authority as a way of maintaining marital harmony. The anguish and contradictory feelings then experienced by women may lead to repeated attempts to leave men who are both step-fathers to children from her previous relationship, and biological fathers of subsequent children borne by the woman.

Servitude and financial exploitation

Women's domestic labour is essential for maintaining family life and is an important aspect of their existence as wives. The movement from 'normal' demands to excessive is a matter of degree. One Asian woman in an extended family said, 'They didn't think anything of me. They didn't think "she is part of the household also", but like a servant all day cleaning, washing clothes, doing everyone's ironing, putting it away. All day doing the work.'

Women from all cultural groups have their money taken from them. This begins with dowry or wages and moves on to child benefit and other state welfare entitlements. The man may give her no money, and all household bills including food for her and the children must come from her income, whether wages or welfare. Both white and Asian women can be forced to leave home because of lack of food for themselves and their children. When women do not know that the state will provide a minimum to ensure life, as with some recently arrived Asian women, they may leave home, regarding themselves lucky for not having died through starvation as a result of the extended family ceasing to feed them.

Cultural values, boundaries and social processes: responses to violence against women and children

Other family members, friends and acquaintances respond to these types of behaviour from men to women and children in contradictory ways. The responses of others are frequently characterized by alternating behaviours as support moves between the woman and the man. Thus a son may be told to stop hitting his wife when directly observed, to which he may nor may not respond, while his parents may demand that she apologize for upsetting him when she has been badly beaten on another occasion, but it has not been seen by them. Interventions may be ambiguous and erratic, as family members are pulled this way and that by competing and contradictory values, views and feelings.

One way this ambiguity can be expressed is when a family member assists a woman to leave and later, which can be within days, informs the husband of where she is. Once out of danger the more profound value of maintaining men's access to their wives predominates. Another is the fact that directly observed violence can generate an immediate intervention to that specific situation. In the heat of the moment the wider issues of why this is happening and what the appropriate response of the wife should be to ensure her husband does not beat her are not of immediate relevance. While directly viewed violent attacks are more likely to result in raising the more general issue of appropriate behaviour between women and men in family life, unseen but verbally recounted attacks may also have this impact on other members of a woman's family and friends. On occasion in-laws may intervene as well as her family of origin. However, non-intervention in violence from husbands to wives may occur when it is directly seen as well as when unseen. One white woman said, 'Friends came around and saw from the beginning. He smacked me in front of them, saying, "Oh shut up, you're getting on my nerves." They got up and walked out saying they can't get involved.'

She may be told to accede to his demands, whatever these may be. No demand may be too excessive so, for example, one Asian woman was told by her in-laws to agree to his second marriage to a white woman and to her joining the household. To refuse was to bring violence upon herself, understandable in the eyes of other family members. Further, her refusal to obey provided a justification for not intervening. Family members may tire of intervening with the man, particularly when the more general aim of maintaining the man's access to his wife is predominant. Another Asian woman said, 'It was getting that when he hit me, my dad didn't even do anything about it.' This woman was expected to obey her husband as a way of obtaining marital harmony.

Women described how men's violence against children is responded to in the same ways by others. As discussed earlier, pregnancy and/or the birth of children can trigger violence, and can also escalate and extend violence from men in all cultural groups. For example, a young white woman found that, with late pregnancy, her problem turned from arguments to violent attacks. After the birth of her daughter he also began to assault the child. He would come home, wake the infant to say 'hello', and when she began to cry he would smack her to make her go to sleep. Because her family and in-laws did not live with them, they did not see the assaults on the infant and therefore could remain unaware. Although they knew about the assaults on the woman, no one asked about the child. Lack of awareness is not innocent, it contains a social value, that of non-intervention. His superior status as son, husband and father not only makes knowledge of his abuse unwelcome, it serves as a protective force or shield.

The relative lack of value of females may be directly expressed. For example, one young Asian woman from Pakistan, who married into an Asian family in Britain, found that her abuse moved from verbal to physical with the birth of her daughter. The family would intervene by removing the daughter when she was being directly assaulted and by remonstrating with her husband for assaulting the baby. The family explained the abuse of the baby as 'daughters are loans' and the continued abuse of the woman by 'once you have a girl, all the rest will be girls'.

Cultural values, boundaries and social processes: responses to violent men

The cultural boundaries of family and community accountability for men incorporate privileging male over female. Men as head of households have the role of maintaining family hierarchies and of ensuring that women and children recognize and respond to the authority vested in sons, husbands and fathers. Men can both protect social hierarchies within the extended family and be protected from criticism.

Sons may be expected to ensure the dominance of their mothers and fathers in relation to the daughter-in-law. For example one Asian woman was beaten because she verbally contradicted her mother-in-law. 'He said, "You can't say anything. Whatever my mother says, that is right. It's not that you are right, you are not right. You are wrong."' This also happens to other women. A white woman was beaten because her mother-in-law objected to her refusal to allow her grandson to have something from a shop. When this was relayed to her son, he 'came in and went bloody mad, hitting me and saying, "Don't fucking speak to him like that again and don't do this and don't do that."'

In turn men are to be protected from others finding out about their behaviour towards their wives and children. When interventions from family members fail to be effective or non-intervention is the strategic response of others, self-interest may eventually surface. He may be told to treat her better because more problems may ensue if he does not; that is, serious injury or death, which would adversely affect the family as a whole. Families, and abused women too, may actively participate in protecting men; so, for example, if the police are looking for a man or wanting information that may lead to his arrest and prosecution, no help is given. 'I said, "I'm not going to get him arrested."'

When women cannot be trusted to keep silent about violence, other family members, in both white and Asian families, may assist their violent male relative. Women may be kept within the home or under surveillance at all times when they leave the home or others call at the house. When external contacts are absolutely necessary, such as visits to the doctor, women will be accompanied. If a stay in hospital is necessary – for example, for childbirth – then the extended family may become particularly solicitous and kindly as well as warning the woman to say nothing about her husband and his behaviour. These strategies are effective and, at the very least, postpone outside intervention.

Women's independence may be restricted. 'I wasn't allowed to go up to town without one of his family. I had to go around to his sister's and say, "Oh, are you coming up to town?"' Alternatively, the restrictions on women's movements outside the home can be so extreme that women never leave the house without their partners. These experiences of white women are not simple parallels with the situation of Asian women who are kept indoors within the extended family home, as the cultural justifications for this practice do not exist in the same way within white British society. Asian women, however, can be so tightly supervised that they are never allowed to speak to visitors to the home, including other family members, for fear they will disclose the abuse.

Gaining and maintaining control over women also involves using children. Men may abduct children if women leave or start civil law actions to gain contact with children in order to find out where she has gone or to have access to her so that the abuse can continue. This occurs even when men have seriously damaged the relationship with children or when they have never previously expressed any interest in the children. Both contact and residence orders can be made in favour of men who have violently abused both women and the children, although these may also be refused by family courts. The use of the civil courts in this way prolongs the emotional agony for women and children who are seeking to re-establish a life free from violence (Hester and Radford 1996). Contact visits by men often mean leaving the children at their mother's or another relative's home. When his family express little or no interest in the children, and he is not seeking contact as a way of trying to return to the marital home or to further attack her, his visits can become erratic and then cease.

Men obviously understand the boundaries that define their privilege and can be irate when these are challenged. A white woman said:

> I had all his boot marks in my back. His sister went mad like and when he came from work she said, 'What are you playing at? Have you seen her back?' He told her to mind her own business and it was nothing to do with her. It was our problem and we'd sort it out. And then he went mad at me for showing her my back. I weren't allowed to talk about it. I weren't allowed to cry.

Shifting boundaries of acceptable violence

Cultural values governing the boundaries of acceptable violence are not static. Gradations of violent behaviour may become acceptable or unacceptable to others as time passes. The cultural boundaries that are threatened with transgression remain intact if values shift to accommodate a wider range of behaviour from the husband/father. Acceptance of violence to wives and children can increase over time, if family and the interventions of others to limit violence from the husband/father are not successful. Family dynamics may also shift in contradictory ways. For example, as violence increased for one Asian woman, the extended family became more polarized. Over time both efforts to intervene with her husband on her behalf and positive responses to her decreased. Her husband's negative evaluation and behaviour towards her and the child became increasingly acceptable to all but one member of the family, another low-status woman who risked her personal security in helping this woman obtain effective assistance outside the family. This help was offered in secrecy and had to remain undisclosed to protect the quality of life of this second woman as she breached the cultural boundaries of hierarchy and privilege that governed this family's life.

There are other reasons why acceptance of violence to wives and children increases over time. Families may make little or no effort to intervene to protect their daughter and sister. A British-born Asian woman experienced a growing acceptance of violence and restrictions on her from her family once her husband had joined her from Pakistan. Married at 15 years of age in Pakistan, she returned to England a few months later and was allowed to work, to control her own money, to wear Western clothes, and to go out with friends and workmates. When her husband joined her several years later upon receiving his visa from British immigration, her life became progressively more restricted and ultimately she was not allowed to work, to have access to any money, to wear Western dress or to go out, and her family became progressively more tolerant of his abuse of her and her young daughter. This young woman was married to her mother's brother's son and not to her father's brother's son, although one was eligible. 'My mum didn't want to be proven that she's wrong [about insisting on this match] and my dad didn't want to prove to his relations that yes, he listened to his wife' [rather than pursue the culturally preferred patrilineal first-cousin marriage between the children of brothers].

If the values of others do not shift towards greater toleration of violence and the further enmeshing of women in the relationship, then the cultural boundaries of hierarchy and privilege may be transgressed and the husband/father deprived of his wife and child. This requires the woman to want to end the relationship and often for at least one other to support and to help her, although leaving can be delayed if agency staff are obstructive (Hanmer 1995). Then actions around children in the civil courts may permit male-dominated family hierarchy and male privilege to be restored. Through residence and contact orders the hierarchical order between the ex-husband and the ex-wife and children can be re-established. This is a very commonplace outcome (Hester and Radford 1996).

For example, one white woman with a child by her boyfriend feared leaving as he always threatened he would take the child. Even though he had children by his wife, with whom he still lived, and other girlfriends, when she turned to the police for help she was told she could not take the child from the home nor, although the house was in her name only, would the police remove him from the premises. The local social services disagreed with this interpretation of the law and told her she could leave with her child. After leaving he assaulted those who helped her and criminally damaged several family properties. After arrest by the police, no further action was taken in relation to these crimes. The DSS gave the boyfriend the refuge address, although the policy is to not do this, and the court welfare officer supported contact even though he continued to be violent on access. While it may seem strange that this woman feared leaving because he would take the child, her fears were not that unreasonable given this outcome.

Statutory agencies may also force women to make a choice between their husband and their children. With the birth of a child, violence creates new conflicts of values. Women may be required by others to transgress either the boundaries of being a wife or of being a mother. Women may respond by giving up one or more children in order to prioritize the man, or alternatively providing for their children can lead women to transgress the boundaries of family and marriage hierarchies. Amongst the 60 women interviewed, the forced choice, with and without agency involvement, between their children and their husband/father/boyfriend often led to their permanently leaving violent men.

Men's strategies when women leave

After violent attacks or when women leave, men frequently utilize several strategies simultaneously in response. These include tears, apologies and expressions of a desire for the relationship to continue. 'When I left he comes down and says, "I'm really sorry, please come back." He would cry.' Men could enlist the help of others. 'He would get his sisters to phone me up.' As well as continuing violence, another strategy is threats to the woman's personal security and to that of her children: 'he would threaten to take the children off me.' These strategies might accompany or supplant trying to shift the blame: 'He would try to twist it so that he was justified to do what he did. If I hadn't made him jealous that night it wouldn't have happened.'

When the limits to his acceptable use of violence are reached, various strategies are used by men to reinstate themselves with family and friends. One way to deflect attention from having gone too far is for the husband/father to turn himself into a victim. This is accomplished through self-injury. For example, one white woman rushed to her in-laws on having been seriously assaulted by their son. 'I thought, they're going to see this time, what he had done.' His mother who previously refused to believe her son was assaulting his wife now accepted it and turned to help her. He took a drug overdose the same night and when he returned to the home of his mother and father he asked his wife, 'Don't you feel sorry for me?'

With persistent repeated violence, men may refuse to let women leave. This is a serious problem as violence to women is likely to increase at the time she indicates an intention to end the relationship, or if she does leave without his knowledge and he finds her new home. But when women succeed in leaving, men often form another relationship and have further children continuing the pattern of violence and control. 'He's got a little daughter and apparently he's got fed up of her as well. She's left him a few times because I think he's got violent with her.'

While most women who leave violent men recount multiple ways men try to keep them from going, not all men seek to retain their wives. A small proportion are violent as a way of encouraging women to leave. 'He'd got his girlfriend in the family way, and he just wanted to get rid of me. He used to fetch her over when I was at my mum's, and take her into my bed.' Whether the aim is to retain or replace a woman, violence can be a strategy.

Conclusion

These 60 interviews demonstrate that in the last analysis, while there may be objections, the reality is that men can place their affections, loyalties, income and time elsewhere and still maintain their position as son, husband and father in the eyes of others. The reverse situation is not possible for a woman. She owes him affection, loyalty, income/money and time, expressed as both physical and emotional labour. Women who place their affections, loyalties, income and time elsewhere are inevitably defined by others as bad wives and mothers, against whom social sanctions must and will be introduced and enforced. Violence against women and their children demonstrates that these basic requirements of the good wife need not be reciprocated for a man to be seen as a good enough husband and father. Although not all women are equally affected, there is a clear double standard in operation that, regardless of their cultural group, impacts on women to the advantage of the men with whom they live.

In all cultural and ethnic groups husbands have cultural and family advantages that come both from being male and from their roles as sons, husbands and fathers. This may partly explain why men are often so loath to give up the women and children they abuse. They lose the gendered social advantages gained by being a husband and father and have only those of being male and a son to fall back upon. When women establish themselves as single parents, men who are not immediately moving on to another woman become single and itinerant, a lowly social position especially as men age. To be head of a nuclear family, or married within an extended family, carries considerable power and status for the male in the wider community.

The maintenance of family hierarchy and male privilege within the family group conflicts with interventions to control violence against women and children. Prioritizing men, their needs, wants and desires means tolerating behaviours that would not be permitted from lower-status members of the family group, namely, women and children. Women share the values that sustain this basic social organization, as do other family members, friends, acquaintances and often formal agency personnel (Hanmer 1995). The primary modes for handling the conflict that arises between the valuing of non-violent behaviour towards wives and children and the valuing of men in hierarchically organized family group relations are to not know or, if knowledge is inevitable, to view the matter as private. If knowledge is inescapable then the wife may be expected to control her husband through her behaviour, and/or to accede to his demands, or to view his behaviour as appropriate. The point of these strategies adopted by others outside the marital pair is to avoid making a value judgement on his behaviour and to avoid the need to intervene, thus leaving intact values supporting gendered family hierarchies.

This is, however, a terrain of cultural conflict, with the boundaries of family hierarchy and privilege being transgressed by others outside the marital or cohabiting pair and by the women themselves, frequently ambivalently, and sometimes without question, and in ever-increasing numbers. These others include family members, friends, acquaintances and formal agency personnel. The view that women and children are not required to live in violent relationships appears to be gaining social support, but at the same time traditional family values are being increasingly promoted. The conflict of values observed among individuals within families is paralleled by wider social pronouncements on family values by government and other public figures in the 1990s, and by increasing governmental actions to restrict state benefits to one-parent, i.e. women-headed families (Harne and Radford 1994).

Transgression can be experienced as being given back half a life or as a new beginning. Some women have the pleasure of face-to-face confrontations in which men cannot retaliate. One man saw his ex-wife whilst in the company of his new girlfriend whom he wanted to impress. The ex-wife said:

> I don't care what you do now. I don't care if you go and die somewhere. I've got my baby, and that's all I want. I don't want you. I don't want your family. I don't need you and I don't need your family either. Why don't you go and catch a disease and die of it?

This woman also had the pleasure of telling his new girlfriend that he would be hitting her soon too. These experiences are relatively rare compared with their opposite, where women live in fear of being found or continue to be harassed and assaulted and may even fear death.

While leaving may be difficult and take some years to achieve, in the end the decision can be easy. 'I just got up one morning and I thought, "Oh fuck this, I'm going." So I went around to my sister's and got in touch with Women's Aid.' Leaving can be hard, and can raise ambivalent emotions, 'The moment I sat in the [police] car I thought, "This is wrong." Because of him I have to leave my mum, my dad, my brothers and sisters.' Women's problems do not cease on the point of leaving, as the continuing support of men by families, friends, acquaintances can be joined by that of agencies, particularly at the point of leaving. There can be a lack of awareness or minimising of the importance of home-based violence in the lives of women and children amongst agency staff who share the same cultural values and ambivalence about men in families as women's families, friends and other acquaintances.[6]

Out-of-control men, however, can be feared. Media representation and public opinion lurch between the binary opposition of kind and caring son, husband, father and that of sex fiend, beast, violent hooligan or dangerous criminal (Hanmer and Saunders 1993). Although women are in the greatest danger from men with whom they live, out-of-control men are portrayed and understood as 'other' or unlike those whom we know. To demand social responsibility for men in families is to reverse this understanding, but to do so will challenge the uniquely privileged position of men in families. Creating similar expectations for men and women in relation to appropriate behaviour in family life[7] inevitably involves a loss of social and personal privileges for men. This would be a major social transformation. We should not be surprised that after 25 years of women's campaigning and direct services to women this remains a demand yet to be achieved.

Notes

1 Originally published as 'Out of Control: Men, Violence and Family Life' in Popay, J., Hearn, J. and Edwards, J. (eds) *Men, Gender Divisions and Welfare*, London: Routledge, pp. 128–46.

2   Direct services to women began with the provision of refuges through Women's Aid groups in 1971. Refuges provide accommodation for women and their children who leave violent situations, and there are national associations in England, Northern Ireland, Scotland and Wales. Rape Crisis help lines and other services, and Incest Survivor groups are also provided by women for women.

3   Paula Wilcox (1996) *Social Support and Women Leaving Violent Relationships*, Ph.D. thesis, University of Bradford, explores the informal support available to, and needed by, women who have been re-housed as a result of violence from the men with whom they previously lived.

4   This research, Violence and the Stress-Coping Process; Project 1, was funded through the Economic and Social Research Council's Initiative on the Management of Personal Welfare, 1991–3 (L206252003).

5   This analysis assumes women want to alter the relationship and believe they need the help of others to do so. One of the 60 women interviewed did not conform to this pattern. She believed others could not help her or him and that she had to do it herself. She did not intend to leave the relationship, but used the refuge from time to time for temporary relief as changes in his behaviour were too slow. Although the statutory authorities were only just beginning to become aware of her, the conflict she experienced between her desire to continue the relationship and the possibility that her children might be taken from her drove her into the refuge on this particular occasion.

6   For example, in a comment on Panorama's Princess Diana interview, the psychologist Oliver James said:

> What I find worrying is that, throughout her interview, Diana will have encouraged a lot of discontented women to blame a man or their relationship instead of seeing that they have problems. A lot of these women will make a tragic mistake, divorce and destroy their children's lives, as a result of what Diana has said. One would have liked her to have thought more widely and offered that insight to the nation.
>
> (Walk 1995: 4)

7   For example, a woman who, by leaving for a holiday before her ex-cohabitee appeared to look after the children, took a chance that he could turn up as promised. She was jailed for a year when he did not. Judge Wickham said, 'What you did was a serious crime against your children, putting your personal pleasure before their welfare. You took a chance, good mothers don't take such chances.' Although seen as a good mother, this did not mitigate her offence. The judge took the view that, 'if you are not punished for leaving your children there will be a widespread sense of outrage that justice has not been done and a real risk that someone else will take the law into his or her own hands'. There was, of course, no criticism of or charges against the ex-cohabitee and father (*The Independent*, 15 November 1995: 5).

References

Binney, V., Harkell, G. and Nixon, J. (1981) *Leaving Violent Men*, London: National Women's Aid Federation.

Borkowski, M., Murch, M. and Walker, V. (1983) *Marital Violence: The Community Response*, London: Tavistock.

Dobash, R. E. and Dobash, R. (1980) *Violence Against Wives: The Case Against the Patriarchy*, Shepton Mallet: Open Books.

Edwards, S. (1989) *Policing 'Domestic' Violence: Women, the Law and the State*, London: Sage.

Hague, G. and Malos, E. (1993) *Domestic Violence: Action for Change*, Cheltenham: New Clarion Press.

Hague, G., Malos, E. and Dear, W. (1995) *Against Domestic Violence: Inter-agency Initiatives*, Bristol School for Advanced Urban Studies, University of Bristol.

Hanmer, J. (1995) *Policy Development and Implementation Seminars: Patterns of Agency Contact with Women*, Research Paper No. 12, Research Unit on Violence, Abuse and Gender Relations, University of Bradford.

Hanmer, J. and Saunders, S. (1984) *Well-Founded Fear: A Community Study of Violence to Women*, London: Hutchinson.

Hanmer, J. and Saunders, S. (1993) *Women, Violence and Crime Prevention*, Aldershot: Avebury.

Harne, L. and Radford, J. (1994) 'Reinstating patriarchy: the politics of the family and the new legislations', in Mullender, A. and Money, R. (eds) *Children Living with Domestic Violence*, London: Birch and Whiting, pp. 68–85.

Hearn, J. (1995) *Policy Development and Implementation Seminars: Patterns of Agency Contacts with Men Who Have Been Violent to Known Women*, Research Paper No. 13, Research Unit on Violence, Abuse and Gender Relations, University of Bradford.

Hester, M. and Radford, L. (1996) 'Contractions and compromises: the impact of the Children's Act on women's and children's safety', in Hester, M., Kelly, L. and Radford, J. (eds) *Women, Violence and Male Power*, Buckingham: Open University Press, pp. 81–98.

Independent, The (1995) 'Mother of three jailed in home-alone case', 15 November: 5.

Maynard, M. (1985) 'The response of social workers to domestic violence', in Pahl, J. (ed.) *Private Violence and Public Policy: The Needs of Battered Women and the Response of the Public Services*, London: Routledge & Kegan Paul, pp. 125–41.

Mirlees-Black, C., Mayhew, P. and Percy, A. (1996) *The 1996 British Crime Survey England and Wales*, London: Home Office Statistical Bulletin.

Mooney, J. (1993) *The Hidden Figure: Domestic Violence in North London*, London: Middlesex University (London, Islington Police and Crime Prevention Unit).

Parliamentary Select Committee on Violence in the Family (1975) Vol. I Report (together with the proceedings of the committee), Vol. II Evidence, Vol. III, Appendices, London: HMSO.

Walk, P. (1995) 'Feminist guru who made up Diana's mind', The News Review, *The Sunday Times*, 31 December.

Wilcox, P. (1996) *Social Support and Women Leaving Violent Relationships*, Ph.D. thesis, University of Bradford.

2 Revealing the hidden figure of domestic violence

Jayne Mooney

Domestic violence has, since the 1970s, been increasingly recognised as a serious social problem. There is, of course, a great deal of historical evidence to show that women have always suffered violence from their husbands and partners (see Martin 1976; Tomes 1978; Dobash and Dobash 1979; Freeman 1979; Smith 1989; Clarke 1992; Doggett 1992; see Chapter 11). However, it is a problem that has only become publicly evident at times when there has been a strong feminist movement, enabling the collective organisation against its occurrence (Freeman 1979; Brokowski et al. 1983; Wilson 1983). Thus, it was an issue for first wave feminists at the end of the nineteenth century, as it is for this generation of feminists (Cobbe 1904). Today, programmes on television or the radio or an article written about the subject are far more common. Domestic violence has become a priority issue for many local authorities and police divisions in Great Britain.

Despite current concern, domestic violence has been recognised as an area which needs more detailed and in-depth research, particularly on the general population (Smith 1989). The true extent of domestic violence is generally agreed to be an unknown quantity. Many commentators consider it to have one of the highest hidden figures of any crime (Dobash and Dobash 1979; Hanmer and Stanko 1985; Worrall and Pease 1986; British Medical Association 1998). Figures derived from agencies such as the police and women's refuges are necessarily selective and encompass only a small proportion of victims. It is well documented that police figures suffer from the problem of the 'hidden figure of crime'; that is, the non-reporting of crime to the police by the public and the failure of the police to record crime that is reported. Agency figures represent merely the 'tip of the iceberg' and in some cases, for instance those derived from women's refuges, point more to the limited availability of such resources rather than the overall extent of the problem. Both the reasons for the lack of reporting and its variation by subgroup are subject to speculation.

Victimisation surveys, which typically involve asking a sample of the population about crimes which have been committed against them in the previous year, have, both on a national level (Hough and Mayhew 1983; Chambers and Tombs 1984; Hough and Mayhew 1985; Mayhew et al. 1989; Kinsey and

Anderson 1992; Mayhew *et al.* 1993; Mirrlees-Black *et al.* 1996) and a local level (for example, Kinsey 1985; Jones *et al.* 1986; Lea *et al.* 1986; Painter *et al.* 1989; Crawford *et al.* 1990; Painter *et al.* 1990), made a considerable contribution to the knowledge of the hidden figure of many crimes, the social and geographical patterning of problems, the potential levels of demand and the degree of satisfaction with the relevant agencies. Although they have their own hidden figure of non-response, this is greatly reduced when compared to police statistics. In the area of domestic violence, victimisation surveys are seen to have severe limitations. The researchers themselves frequently recognise the figures to be under-representative and there are doubts as to whether mass surveys covering the whole gamut of crime have the sensitivity to pick up on all but a fraction of the actual incidence of domestic violence. Levels of non-reporting are thought to be considerable for various reasons: fear of reprisals (the perpetrator may be near to the interview situation), embarrassment, psychological blocking, and so on (Walklate 1989). Domestic violence is often unknown to anyone outside the immediate family and it is unlikely that a victim will choose to reveal her experiences to an uninterested interviewer, a stranger, standing on the doorstep with a clipboard. Thus incidence figures uncovered by such surveys are low, for example, three per cent in the Merseyside Crime Survey (Kinsey 1985), eight per cent in the Second Islington Crime Survey (Crawford *et al.* 1990), three per cent in the 1995 British Crime Survey (Mirrlees-Black *et al.* 1996).

Research by feminists, in contrast, has pointed to much higher figures (for example, the path-breaking work of Jalna Hanmer and Sheila Saunders (1984) and Ruth Hall and Women Against Rape (1985)). Feminists have also been aware of the profound methodological inadequacies of conventional surveys, most notably in terms of defining what actually constitutes domestic violence (see Kelly 1988), and have employed more sensitive research strategies (for example, with respect to interviewing techniques and the use of self-complete questionnaires (Bains 1987; McGibbon *et al.* 1989). Unfortunately, this body of work has been restricted by a lack of funding and has come under criticism for the use of too small or biased sampling methods which prevent the results from being generalised to the population as a whole (MacLean 1985; Jones *et al.* 1986).

It has been suggested that the on-going lack of authoritative statistics on domestic violence ultimately serves to limit the ability to take preventative or remedial action to alleviate the problem (London Strategic Policy Unit 1986; Smith 1989). The North London Domestic Violence Survey was developed in response to the need for better information on the extent of domestic violence in the general population. It builds on feminist research insights and couples this with a random survey large enough to make cross-tabulations by age, class and ethnicity. The North London Domestic Violence Survey is the largest survey focused solely on domestic violence to take place in Great Britain. This chapter details the method used and presents key findings.

Defining domestic violence

In researching domestic violence, the first issue that needs to be confronted is that of definition. There has been a lack of consistency between researchers, policy makers, members of the public and so on, over the relationships and types of behaviour that should be included under the rubric of 'domestic violence' and considerable debate over whether the term should be used at all (see, for example, Bograd 1988; Smith 1989; DeKeseredy and Hinch 1991; Kashani and Allan 1998).

With respect to relationships, 'domestic' can quite clearly be referring to violence that occurs in the context of marriage or co-habitation between heterosexual partners, between siblings, between parent and child, and in gay and lesbian cohabiting relationships. It can, in addition, be used to cover pre-domestic relationships, for example, dating relationships, and post-domestic relationships as in the case of ex-partners who are no longer living together. Domestic violence has been the term most favoured in policy-making areas because it is seen as covering all domestic relationships (Smith 1989; British Medical Association 1998). Many commentators have, however, argued for more specific terminology for, although domestic violence may be useful as a contrast to 'stranger violence', and serves to highlight the fact that a large amount of violence occurs in domestic relationships, its generality is not helpful with regard to theoretical or policy concerns. It is necessary to identify the specific relationships involved, as each type may involve different factors and have different needs which will have to be matched by specific policies. More importantly, as feminist researchers have pointed out, domestic violence is a gender-neutral term and as such fails to clarify who is the victim and who is the perpetrator, masking the fact that, in heterosexual relationships, women are most frequently subjected to violence by men. It is for this reason that various researchers have preferred to use terms such as 'wife battering', 'wife abuse' or 'woman abuse' in order to emphasise on whom the violence is directed (e.g. Bograd 1988; DeKeseredy and Hinch 1991). Edwards (1989) and Walklate (1992a, 1995b) have in their work enclosed 'domestic' in inverted commas to acknowledge its problematic character, particularly in the light of the controversial research of the Family Research Laboratory of the University of New Hampshire, USA, which denies the gender dimensions to this subject (Straus *et al.* 1981; Straus and Gelles 1986; 1988).[1]

In this project the gendered nature of much domestic violence is emphasised and I have tried to be as specific as possible in clarifying the relationships involved. The term 'domestic violence' is retained for convenience purposes only as information was collected on violence in a wide range of relationships including parent and child, between siblings, against women in dating relationships and against men. The primary focus was, however, on violence perpetrated on women by husbands or boyfriends, including ex-husbands and ex-boyfriends.

The second problem of definition relates to 'violence': what is it that constitutes violence? This has two levels: how the different researchers define violence and the various definitions that women themselves make. Different rates of domestic violence will be calculated depending on the yardstick the researcher uses. Is a shove, for example, domestic violence or not? What is the status of threats of violence or mental cruelty? Some researchers have preferred to confine their attention mainly to physical behaviour. Bograd, for example, in *Feminist Perspectives on Wife Abuse*, states that:

> Wife abuse is defined in this volume as the use of *physical force* by a man against his intimate cohabiting partner.... Violence may qualitatively change the nature of intimate relationships, even if they were characterised previously by the presence of severe psychological abuse. Violence threatens the physical safety and bodily integrity of the woman, and intensifies and changes the meanings of threats and humiliation (My emphasis) (1988: 12).

Gelles and Cornell[2] – although presenting a different theoretical position to Bograd – likewise restrict their definition, arguing that, 'from a practical point of view, lumping all forms of malevolence and harm-doing together may muddy the waters so much that it might be impossible to determine what causes abuse' (1985: 23–4). The implication is that physical violence is worse than psychological abuse/mental cruelty. Walker (1979) reported in her study that most of the women described verbal humiliation as their worst experience of battering, irrespective of whether physical violence had been used. The North London Domestic Violence Survey started from the premise that mental cruelty, threats, sexual abuse, physical violence and any other form of controlling behaviour used against a woman by her husband or boyfriend are all domestic violence, and as such are serious and merit individual investigation; this has been reflected in the questions asked. It was made clear throughout exactly what definition was being used with respect to the various categories of domestic violence and the different rates which result from any given definition. Respondents vary in similar ways to researchers in defining what constitutes 'real' violence (see Kelly 1988). Some respondents will define a push or shove as physical violence, whereas others will not. The values held by the respondent are likely to be affected by their gender, age, ethnicity, class and education. For this reason the very first question in the self-complete questionnaire (Stage two of the research) established women's definitions of violence and subsequent questions were based on separating out the incidence of the various forms of domestic violence. Qualitative interviews were also incorporated into the project to examine in more depth how women define their experiences.

The method used to research domestic violence

The method used in the survey was essentially a variation of the victimisation survey, adapted to try to deal with the specific problems involved in researching domestic violence, for example, those of definition, fear of reprisals and embarrassment.

Given the sensitive nature of this research, great care was taken over the selection of the interviewing team. All were chosen for their understanding of and commitment to the problem of domestic violence. The majority of the interviewers were highly experienced, having worked on previous surveys. Six interviewers were recruited from the minority groups represented in the study area; of these, five could speak some of the relevant community languages. All received intensive training and information on the help available to those experiencing domestic violence. They were monitored in the field by a field-work supervisor with counselling and social work experience.

A major feature of the interviewing brief was to interview respondents on their own. This was to try to ensure that the respondent did not feel inhibited, and that neither their safety nor that of the interviewer was compromised in any way. All respondents received Help-Line cards which featured the telephone numbers of a wide range of agencies. My intention was to avoid the 'interview and run' style that has characterised many surveys. I wanted to ensure that, should the need arise, support was available (see Radford 1987).

The importance of back-up support was highlighted in one of the pilot studies when a 65-year-old woman told an interviewer about her experience of being raped over 40 years ago by her husband's friend. The interviewer was the first person she had informed and she was clearly still affected by the experience, particularly as her husband had remained in frequent contact with the man concerned. As a result the interviewer, at her request, put her in touch with a local counselling service which she found a great help ('a relief to be able to talk about it after so long'). The interviewer also made several follow-up visits. In a project of this nature it is essential that relevant support services are available locally and willing to take on any referrals from the survey.

The survey was local[3] in focus yet large; 1000 individuals were interviewed in an area of North London which has a wide age range and is mixed both in terms of ethnicity and class. Thus just under one-half of the population were from England, Scotland and Wales, and there were substantial Irish and African Caribbean populations as well as those of Cypriot, Asian and African origin. The survey location was a typical inner city area where, although housing tenure was predominantly council tenants, there has been a considerable process of gentrification with one in five houses being owner-occupied.

Stage one

Stage one of the survey was conducted along the lines of the traditional victimisation survey method. An interviewer-administered questionnaire was used and included questions on avoidance behaviour, victimisation and policing. The questionnaire was constructed so that the more general questions relating to crime were asked first, thus providing a useful lead-in to the questions on more 'sensitive' issues. Where possible, open-ended questions were included to let respondents 'speak for themselves' about their experiences. This general questionnaire was administered to 571 women and 429 men.

One of the aims of this stage of the study was to generate data on the attitudes of men to domestic violence, so a section of the questionnaire was directed at male respondents only. This was included in order to move away from the conventional research emphasis on women alone; it is, after all, men not women who largely perpetrate violence on women and as such we should provide some focus on their behaviour, its motivation and likely cause. Vignettes were used detailing where in a 'conflict' situation, men could see themselves as using violence. Dobash and Dobash have suggested that, 'the four main sources of conflict leading to violent attacks are men's possessiveness and jealousy, men's expectations concerning women's domestic work, men's sense of the right to punish "their" women for perceived wrongdoing, and the importance to men of maintaining or exercising their position of authority' (1992: 4) and it was this that I tried to reflect in designing the 'conflict' situations. The 'conflict' situations included quarrels over domestic arrangements, childcare, infidelity and so on. For example, one of the vignettes asked men whether they would use violence in a situation in which their partner was 'nagging' them. This approach was supplemented by male self-report questions on actual violence. Men were asked if they had ever hit their partner in any of the 'conflict' situations. Obviously if you ask men directly if they had hit their partner, they will reply 'no', but if you present them with a 'conflict' situation it was conjectured that this might elicit a more honest and greater response rate.[4] Whilst even with this approach, some men may see their violence as not 'severe' enough to mention, or feel it is not relevant if it occurred outside the scope of the 'conflict' situation or may simply lie, such data gave us a baseline. It enabled us to say that *at least* this proportion of men would be liable to use violence against their partners. Various researchers have found vignettes to be a useful tool for the researching of sensitive subjects (Finch 1987; Lee 1993).

The same vignettes were also presented to 100 women respondents, who were asked if they could predict their partner's likely response in any of these 'conflict' situations. This was to provide comparative data for the male responses and to discover whether women, in relationships where violence had not occurred, were still controlled by its possibility. That the violence had not occurred could be due to avoidance of the 'conflict' situations.

Stage two

Stage two involved women respondents only. The method used to obtain information has been termed the 'piggy-back' method. Every women interviewed in the first stage of the project was handed a supplementary self-complete questionnaire on domestic violence, together with a stamped addressed envelope. The interviewer was instructed to emphasise that the information recorded would be treated with confidence and that the respondent's identity would not be revealed to anyone. The personal contact made in the formal interview situation (Stage one of this project) had previously been found to motivate the respondent to complete and return the questionnaire, thus boosting the response rate. Pilot work showed that this method generated a better and more accurate response than that of the traditional victimisation survey. This is likely to be because the method ensures the respondent's anonymity. Given the intrinsically private nature of domestic violence, it is easier for the respondent to record her experiences on paper than relate them verbally to a stranger standing on the doorstep, no matter how good the interviewer. Postal surveys also allow time for the respondent to reflect on questions which results in more considered, precise answers. This stage included questions on definitions of domestic violence, the different forms of domestic violence perpetrated by husbands and boyfriends, including ex-husbands and ex-boyfriends; their incidence and prevalence; the use of various agencies by women and their assessment of the effectiveness of various agencies.

Stage three

This final stage of the project consisted of in-depth interviews with women who had experienced domestic violence. Women who spoke to the interviewer about their experiences in Stage one of the project were asked if they would mind doing a further interview. Fifteen were interviewed again. In-depth interviews were included in response to the widespread recognition of the importance of a 'triangulation' of method (Denzin 1970; Jupp 1989). That is, the collection of both qualitative and quantitative data are essential if the experience of domestic violence is to be accurately portrayed. Qualitative data, such as that generated by in-depth interviewing, are necessary to fully interpret survey data and, in turn, quantitative data are necessary to fully interpret the typicality of case studies. The intention of this stage was to provide information on the individual impact of domestic violence, the context of the violence and contribute to the understanding of the longitudinal development of domestic violence.

Findings

How do women define domestic violence?

As previously indicated, there is a wide variation with respect to what may be defined as 'domestic violence'. Women were, therefore, asked what actions they would designate as 'violence' in a relationship between a husband and wife or boyfriend and girlfriend. The results are presented in Table 2.1.

Thus, as would be expected, 92 per cent of women consider physical violence that results in actual bodily harm to be domestic violence but mental cruelty is also seen by the vast majority of women as domestic violence (80 per cent). More women would define this as domestic violence than threats of physical violence (68 per cent). Rape too, defined on the questionnaire as 'made to have sex without giving consent', (whether or not actual physical violence is used or threatened) is seen as part of domestic violence (see Chapter 4). This indicates

Table 2.1 Women's definitions of domestic violence

	Behaviours	Agreed with statement (%)
A	Domestic violence includes mental cruelty. Mental cruelty includes verbal abuse (e.g. calling of names, being ridiculed especially in front of other people), being deprived of money, clothes, sleep, prevented from going out, etc.	80
B	Domestic violence includes being threatened with physical force or violence, even though no actual physical violence occurs.	68
C	Domestic violence includes physical violence (e.g. grabbing, pushing, shaking) that does not result in actual bodily harm.	76
D	Domestic violence includes physical violence that results in actual bodily harm (e.g. bruising, black eyes, broken bones).	92
E	Domestic violence includes being made to have sex without giving consent.	76

that most women do not support the myth that rape is only an offence if the woman is beaten; that is, if there is bruising, black eyes and so on and the man is a stranger. The survey showed a clear majority of *all* women defined these five aspects, mental cruelty, threats, physical violence without actual bodily harm, physical violence with actual bodily harm and made to have sex without consent, as constituents of domestic violence. When the data was analysed by age, class and ethnicity some differences between women in defining domestic violence did emerge (see Mooney 1993). For example, women who were 55 years and over were less likely than other age groups to define the behaviours listed as domestic violence. This variation indicates that there may have been a change in attitude over the years with respect to what constitutes domestic violence and in levels of tolerance regarding 'acceptable' behaviour within a relationship. African-Caribbean women emerged as the group most likely to define all the behaviours presented to them as domestic violence. Professional women were more likely to see mental cruelty as a constituent of domestic violence than lower-middle-class and working-class women.

The broad definition of domestic violence advocated by the majority of women reflected women's attitudes to intolerable coercion in their lives. Each aspect, of course, could occur together and compounded the problem which women faced. It would be incorrect to view these violences as a simple continuum of seriousness ranging from mental cruelty through to threats and actual bodily violence. For example, prolonged mental cruelty may have greater impact than sporadic isolated incidents of actual bodily violence. Women's prioritisation of this range of events under the rubric of 'domestic violence' suggests a demand for a wide range of agency intervention. For example, not only the police and general medical practitioners but also counsellors, social services and informal support groups. To argue that a multi-agency approach is necessary is to suggest that no one agency has a magic wand which will simply 'solve' the problem. All agencies are important and the particular configuration of agencies involved, together with the decision about which are to take a leading role, will be dependent on the problems of specific groups of women and the stage at which a violent relationship is being confronted (see Chapter 16).

Incidence, prevalence and time span

The questionnaire facilitated the separating out of the incidence and prevalence of domestic violence. Incidence refers to the number of incidents of violence occurring; prevalence to the number of individuals affected. Obviously incidence rates will be higher than prevalence rates as the same individual may have several incidents within a given time span. In terms of time, we asked both 'have ever' questions and whether the violence occurred in the last 12 months. 'Have ever' questions are important in that they estimate the percentage of individuals who have been affected at some time in their lives and it should be stressed that women's fear and concern about domestic violence will relate to such lifetime experiences. As one woman who was sexually assaulted over two decades ago said, 'I should be over it, but you never forget, just little things said or done can make you remember'. 'Have ever' questions clearly facilitate a more comprehensive examination of impact. The events in the last 12 months are vital in order to know the individuals affected in a year (prevalence per year) and the number of incidents occurring per year (incidence per year). The *latter* figures represent the yearly potential demand on the agencies concerned. The total figures represent the number of women who have revealed their experiences to us. However high they may seem, and however well the research method facilitated responses, the percentages presented here represent a bottom line. Many women were undoubtedly too fearful, embarrassed or unwilling to reveal their hidden experiences to strangers. The figures that follow refer to *all* women. If I had included only those women who were or had been in relationships at the time, that is those who are at greatest risk of domestic violence, the percentages would be considerably higher than those presented here.

The prevalence of domestic violence in a woman's lifetime

Women were presented with a range of different types of violence and asked if they had experienced any of these at some time in their lives. The results are recorded in Table 2.2.

These behaviours were defined by the majority of women as domestic violence. As can be seen from Table 2.2, violence from a partner is not a rare phenomenon. Whether it is defined as mental cruelty, threats, actual violence with injury or rape, it has occurred to at least one-quarter to a one-third of all women in their lifetime. There is a continuum in terms of frequency. Mental cruelty is

Table 2.2 The prevalence of domestic violence in a woman's lifetime by type of violence

Violent behaviours	(%)
MENTAL CRUELTY	
• Including verbal abuse (e.g. the calling of names, being ridiculed in front of other people), being deprived of money, clothes, sleep, prevented from going out, etc.	37
THREATS OF VIOLENCE OR FORCE	27
ACTUAL PHYSICAL VIOLENCE	
• Grabbed or pushed or shaken;	32
• Punched or slapped;	25
• Kicked;	14
• Head-butted;	6
• Attempted strangulation;	9
• Hit with a weapon/object.	8
INJURIES	
• Injured;	27
• Bruising or black eye;	26
• Scratches;	12
• Cuts;	11
• Bones broken.	6
RAPE[1] (def. = made to have sex without consent)	23
• Rape with threats of violence[2]	13
• Rape with physical violence.	9
COMPOSITE VIOLENCE	30

[1]As many commentators have pointed out (Clark and Lewis 1977; Hall 1985; Estrich 1987) many rapes are accompanied by non-physical forms of coercion; i.e. not by overt threats of violence or actual physical force or violence such as bruising, broken bones, etc. Social and economic forms of coercion, for example, are also likely to occur, particularly when rape takes place in the context of a relationship. Rape is a violent act in itself whether or not achieved by threats of or actual physical violence. Unfortunately, whilst being made to have sex without consent is defined in Law as 'rape', it is often only when physical forms of coercion are involved that society and particularly the Criminal Justice System is prepared to accept that a rape has taken place – and, even under these circumstances, this is not always the case – see Lees and Gregory 1993.

[2]Threats of violence and actual physical violence are not mutually exclusive, as some women will be threatened and/or have physical violence used against them in different incidents.

more common than actual physical violence and actual physical violence is more common than violence which results in an injury, but *all* are common occurrences. Even if we take one of the more extreme definitions of domestic violence where bones were broken: one in sixteen women had that experience. All of these forms of domestic violence could occur together, and could have equal and compounding impact, whether mental cruelty or broken bones. Mental cruelty was seen by many women to be particularly damaging, thus confirming the finding of Walker (1979). One woman wrote, 'in my opinion mental cruelty is equally as bad as physical violence, except the scars do not show and never heal'. Another reported, 'it is not the physical bashing so much as what you are told constantly. The belittling really wears you down. It is the mental abuse that really does the damage.'

In terms of the mode of physical violence, there is a continuum from being pushed or shaken to being hit by a weapon. But even attempted strangulation, which might be considered the more serious end of this continuum, occurred to just under one in ten women and assault with an object or a weapon to over one in twelve.

A general rate of violence was constructed from the categories 'punched or slapped, kicked, head-butted, attempted strangulation and hit with a weapon/object' combined. Excluded were mental cruelty, rape, threats of violence and 'grabbed, pushed and shaken'. 30 per cent of women had acts perpetrated against them by partners or ex-partners at some time in their lives which fell into the general rate of violence. I termed this general rate 'composite domestic violence'.[5]

In this section, it is important to comment on how widespread rape is from men against their partners. Just under one-quarter of women were raped. In the population surveyed, this occurred with threats of violence to over one in seven women and with actual physical violence to just under one in ten women.[6]

In both the supplementary questionnaires and the in-depth interviews women spoke of being bitten, burned with cigarettes, scalded, knocked unconscious and of having experienced miscarriages as a result of an assault. It was not unusual for violence to begin or escalate in pregnancy; a time when women reported feeling especially physically and emotionally vulnerable.

The prevalence of domestic violence in the last 12 months

Women were asked whether the various forms of domestic violence (mental cruelty, threats, physical violence, violence with injury and rape) occurred within the last 12 months and the number of times that these violences were inflicted.

Twelve per cent of women experienced actual physical violence, including the categories 'grabbed or pushed or shaken, punched or slapped, kicked, head-butted, attempted strangulation, hit with a weapon/object from their partners in the last 12 months, eight per cent of all women had been injured, and six per cent raped by their partner. These figures alone, over such a short period, illustrate the enormity of the problem.

Table 2.3 The prevalence of domestic violence in the last 12 months by type of violence

	All (%)	Number of times (%)			
		1–5	6–10	11–20	20+
Mental cruelty	12	5	2	1	4
Threats of violence	8	5	2	0.2	1
Physical violence	12	8	2	0.5	1
Injuries	8	6	1	0.5	0.5
Rape	6	4	1	0	0.5
Composite domestic violence	10	–	–	–	–

From the above figures we are able to ascertain the extent to which domestic violence is an infrequent occurrence or a repeated event (see Chapter 18). Distinguishing those events which occurred five times or less in the year, six to ten times and over eleven times, results in the following breakdown of figures.

As can be seen in Table 2.4, domestic violence was often repeated in all categories even over the relatively short period of time of 12 months. More than one-quarter of all injuries occurred more than five times a year.

Comparing men's and women's experiences of violence from their partners

There are many who argue that men are as much at risk as women from violence from their partners (Straus 1979; Straus and Gelles 1988; Pizzey 1998). Susanne Steinmetz (1977–8) suggested that there was a 'battered husband syndrome'. When I was attempting to gain funding from the Economic and Social Research Council, the major social science research funder in Britain, one of the referees stated, 'Why restrict your study to female victims? Far more is known about them, and we know that women hit men as often as men hit women'. In order to test this assumption, men were asked about their experiences. The survey found the risk to women from their current partners was over three times greater than that for men. Also, women were more likely to endure a wide range of violent behaviours, be injured and have a weapon used against them by their partners or ex-partners than were men. Not one man was found to have had a weapon used against him by a partner. Women were also more likely to experience multiple incidents and the impact on them was, not surprisingly, worse. The qualitative data showed that women's violence towards men was often used in self-defence. These data undermine the notion of a 'battered husband syndrome'.

The nature of the relationship

Specific details of the nature of the relationship were sought, in particular whether the woman did or did not live with the man when the last incident of violence occurred and whether it occurred before or after the relationship had broken up. From Table 2.5 onwards all the figures presented, unless otherwise stated, refer to 'composite domestic violence'.

Table 2.4 Frequency of domestic violence incidents in last 12 months by type of violence

	% of incidents 5 and less	6–10	Over 11
Mental cruelty	42	17	42
Threats of violence	61	24	15
Physical violence	70	17	13
Injuries	75	13	13
Rape	73	18	9

Table 2.5 The nature of the relationship in which domestic violence occurred

Relationship	Violence	
	at any time (%)	last 12 months (%)
Husband or live-in boyfriend	62	63
Current boyfriend (not living with)	4	11
Former husband or former live-in boyfriend	26	14
Former boyfriend they had never lived with	8	11

Table 2.5 shows that a significant proportion of incidents occurred when women were not living with or had never lived with the man, 12 per cent of lifetime incidents and 22 per cent of those in the last 12 months. The absence of domestic circumstances was not a guarantee of non-violence nor was not being in a relationship. One-quarter of violent incidents occurring in the last 12 months involved former partners. Overall 36 per cent of women experiencing domestic violence in the last 12 months were not living with their partner or were not in a relationship with him. If the man was a former husband or boyfriend, women were, in addition, asked if violence occurred whilst they were together. In six per cent of the lifetime cases, and 2 per cent of those in the last 12 months, violence occurred only after the break-up of their relationship. It is necessary for agencies to be aware that domestic violence is not always associated with living together.

Impact of the violence

The serious nature of domestic violence is illustrated by the finding that 8 per cent of women experiencing violence at some time in their lives stayed overnight in hospital as a result, 20 per cent took time off work, 46 per cent reported 'feeling depressed or losing self-confidence' and 51 per cent felt 'worried, anxious or nervous'. The qualitative data supported the degree to which the experience of domestic violence affected women emotionally and psychologically, as the following comments show:

> It affects your confidence. Once your confidence has been destroyed and if its been destroyed for a long time you do need an awful lot of confidence building. You need someone constantly rationalising the situation for you because you can't be objective and if you'd been made to feel responsible for it [the violence] all that goes on for a long, long time. I still can't speak to my ex-husband without my brain going to pieces. I can't speak to him rationally.

> It's robbed me of my happiness. I went out with my friend the other day to the seaside and had such a nice time that I kept thinking something was wrong. I couldn't remember what a nice time, or being happy, felt like.

Several women also reported having nervous breakdowns, suicidal thoughts and a few even attempted suicide. And, not surprisingly, the effects of experiencing such violence were found to be long-lasting. Women whose relationship had ended said that the violence had made them fearful of *all* men and worried about getting involved with another man in case they found themselves in a similar situation. 'I'm scared of men and it happening again.' It affected subsequent relationships, 'I feel nervous with men who come too close to me ... I just can't trust a man.' Many were scared of reprisals, 'I feel constantly nervous that he will return ... I am always looking over my shoulder', 'my husband threatened to kill me and I'm always worried he might find me'. As the relationship data reveals, these fears were based on reality given the number of women who were subjected to violence from ex-partners.

Reporting of the violence

The predominant reporting of violence is restricted to the private sphere to friends and relatives. Pahl (1985) pointed out that it is only when these informal sources of support prove inadequate that women report to official agencies. Friends were considerably more likely to be informed than relatives: 46 per cent experiencing violence in the last 12 months and 31 per cent at some point in their lives. The response women received from friends and relatives varied. Some were 'wonderful', 'very supportive', whereas others expressed disbelief, blamed the woman and even pressurised her into staying in the relationship. One woman who was hospitalised on several occasions as a result of her husband's violence was told by her family that if she brought charges against him to consider herself on her own. Another reported that her family said to her that the 'woman's place is in the home and you married him for better or worse'. There is still today, despite our divorce statistics, an emphasis placed on preserving the image of the 'happy' family such as those presented in the advertisements for 'Bisto' or soap powder, or the nuclear family idealised in present government policy.

Of the agencies, general medical practitioners and the police are the two in the front line: 22 per cent reported to GPs, 22 per cent to the police. The reporting rate to general medical practitioners is in line with the findings of the percentage of women who need medical attention and with the emphasis on keeping domestic violence private. Given the restrictions placed on doctors with regards to confidentiality, women saw their revelations as going no further than the consulting room. The finding that around one-quarter of all life-time experiences are reported to the police is high compared to previous estimates. The Women's National Commission Report (1985), for example, suggests two per cent and Walker (1979) 10 per cent, but such differences may merely reflect different definitions of what constitutes domestic violence. If the widest definition of domestic violence were used, that is including mental cruelty, threats and 'grabbed or pushed or shaken' as well as the composite definition, the figure for reporting to the police would fall to 11 per cent.

Women who went to the police prior to the changes in policy introduced in the late 1980s (for example, the setting up of domestic violence units,) were extremely critical of their response. Here are just some of their comments:

> The police were reluctant to do anything. They said because I was divorced they couldn't help.

> The police were very rude and uncooperative, in other words they didn't want to know.

> They treated it like a joke.

> They weren't very nice, in fact they were terrible. They spoke to me like I was an idiot.

Those women who sought help in the more recent period were, in contrast, generally pleased with their treatment, particularly if they had been in contact with a domestic violence unit. However, the finding that 22 per cent of those experiencing domestic violence reported their assault to the police – although high in comparative terms – still points to a hidden figure of unreported violence which is a cause of concern.

The proportion of women consulting a solicitor was high (21 per cent) and, once again, emphasises the severity of the problem whilst creating worries given current cutbacks in legal aid in Great Britain. Only a small proportion contacted a women's refuge (5 per cent) which is likely to reflect the restricted finances of women's refuges and regrettably limited services they can provide. Those women who had gone to a women's refuge were almost without exception very impressed with the response they received. They were described as 'offering valuable support', 'a safe atmosphere'. One woman stated, 'it was so good to be among women who were on my side'.

The findings from the vignettes

Male attitudes to domestic violence

In Stage one of the project, men were presented with vignettes detailing a number of stereotypical 'conflict' situations and asked whether they could see themselves as hitting their partner in any of the situations and if they had actually hit her. Thirty seven per cent of our total sample of men claimed that they would never act violently, about one-half said they could see themselves as doing so in up to two of the vignettes and 17 per cent said they would act violently on every example. The most frequently cited situation was sexual infidelity where just under one-third of all men said they would be liable to hit their partners. There was no difference between sex with a stranger or with a close friend where one in eight saw the assault as justified: these men clearly view their wives or girlfriends as their sexual property. The qualitative responses of women showed that many report their partners as irrationally sexual jealous: 'I had to give up working in the pub because he said in between pulling pints I'd go out the back to have sex with someone and go back to pulling another pint. It was so ridiculous.' Liz Kelly (1988) also commented that accusations of 'nagging' and 'arguing back' are often used by violent men to justify their behaviour. Nineteen per cent of men actually admitted to using violence against their partners at least once within the range of incidents presented to them. Seven per cent had acted violently in two or more of the situations. These results, even though they are base-line figures, support the other findings presented in this chapter. They show that domestic violence is a common occurrence.

Women's responses

One hundred women were asked if they could envisage their partner hitting them in any of the 'conflict' situations. The results were similar to those generated by the male questions: 35 per cent said their partners would not act violently in any of the situations, 18 per cent said they would on every example, 61 per cent in two or more of the vignettes. Of those women who responded to this section who had *not* reported on the supplementary questionnaires that they had been threatened with violence or experienced actual physical violence, slightly over one-half said they would expect their partner to hit them if one or more of the situations occurred. That there has been no violence of this nature may well be due to avoidance of such 'conflict' situations, indicating that the behaviour of some women in domestic relationships is controlled by the *possibility* of male violence.

Concluding comments

From these results, it is evident that the survey has uncovered high levels of domestic violence. On a methodological level, we must ask two major questions of this work. Firstly, is the area in which it took place an exceptional one? The answer to this is 'no'; the study was conducted in an urban area and it is important to emphasise that most people in Great Britain live in urban areas. Further, it is an area that is mixed both in terms of class and ethnicity. The results can, therefore, be regarded as representative of the experiences of a wide range of urban women. Secondly, why did the study generate such large figures? This is the result of the method employed: the project used well-trained, sensitive interviewers; carefully-worded questionnaires; a supplementary self-complete questionnaire and vignettes. It was found that some women who had said to the interviewer in the first stage of the project that they had not experienced domestic violence, went on to report that they had on the supplementary questionnaires.

In terms of policy, we must work to develop strategies that challenge men's use and acceptance of violence against women. Support should be built up for women experiencing domestic violence, on both an informal and formal basis. Given the number of women who told friends and family, and the mixed response they received, we must ensure through public education campaigns that *everyone* is aware of the extent of domestic violence and the problems women face. It is an urgent priority that all relevant agencies are resourced and adequately funded and that women are informed of the help that is available. This has to be dealt with on a multi-agency basis, because of both the size and the range of problems which women experience. It is important for all concerned to recognise, as McGibbon, Cooper and Kelly (1989) have pointed out, that women see themselves, the perpetrator and the violence, differently at different stages in the relationship and, therefore, their needs and concerns will change in accordance with this. To try to alleviate the extent of domestic violence, let alone make a sizeable reduction in its incidence, demands substantial political commitment at both national and local government levels. The experiences of the many women who have cooperated with this research make it imperative that more should be done. Justice demands a major social initiative.

Notes

1   The work of the Family Research Laboratory – often described as the 'family violence' approach – has been subject to detailed criticisms by feminists (see, for example, Kelly 1988; Dobash and Dobash 1992; Walklate 1992a, b; Brush 1993; Kurz 1993; Currie 1998).
2   These researchers are associated with the 'family violence' approach.
3   Once the survey area had been selected, the Post Office Address File was used as the sampling frame. From this, 50 per cent of all households were selected. At each household an alternative male/female respondent, aged 16 years or over, was identified for interview. To ensure a random selection within the household, a Kish grid was used (Kish 1965).
4   This method is distinct from the Conflict Tactic Scales used by the 'family violence' researchers which does not suggest specific scenarios (Straus 1979; Straus *et al.* 1981).
5   This is not to suggest that violence does not occur outside this composite, or is less serious. This study starts from the premise that mental cruelty, threats, sexual violence, physical violence and any other form of controlling behaviour used against a woman are all to be understood as violence. However, I found in both the quantitative and qualitative work that the composite category is a definition of violence on which virtually all women agree. With other forms of violence, there is a greater divergence of opinion. The use of a consensus definition counters the argument that violence rates are simply a reflection of definitional variations between different parts of the population (see Hough 1986; Young 1986). This composite domestic violence category is incontestably domestic violence whoever's definition one utilises.
6   Rape and sexual assault on dates were likewise found to be common experiences. Nine per cent of women reported being raped on a date at some time in their lives.

References

Bains, S. (1987) *Manchester's Crime Survey of Women for Women*, Manchester Council: Police Monitoring Unit.

Bograd, M. (1988) 'Feminist perspectives in wife abuse: an introduction', in Yllo, K. and Bograd, M. (eds) *Feminist Perspectives on Wife Abuse*, Beverley Hills: Sage.

British Medical Association (1998) *Domestic Violence: A Health Care Issue*, London: British Medical Association.

Brokowski, M., Murch, M. and Walker, V. (1983) *Marital Violence: The Community Response*, London: Tavistock.

Brush, L. (1993) 'Violent acts and injurious outcomes in married couples: methodological issues in the national survey of families and households', in Bart, P. and Moran, E. (eds) *Violence Against Women*, Beverley Hills: Sage.

Chambers, G. and Tombs, J. (1984) *The British Crime Survey: Scotland*, Edinburgh: HMSO.

Clark, L. and Lewis, D. (1977) *Rape: The Price of Coercive Sexuality*, Ontario: The Women's Press.

Clarke, A. (1992) 'Humanity or justice? Wifebeating and the law in the eighteenth and nineteenth centuries', in Smart, C. (ed.) *Regulating Womanhood: Historical Essays on Marriage, Motherhood and Sexuality*, London: Routledge.

Cobbe, F. (1904) *Life of Frances Power Cobbe, As Told by Herself*, London: Swan Sonnenschein & Co.

Crawford, A., Jones, T., Woodhouse, T. and Young, J. (1990) *The Second Islington Crime Survey*, Middlesex Polytechnic: Centre for Criminology.

Currie, D. (1998) 'Violent men or violent women? Whose definition counts?', in Kennedy Bergman, R. (ed.) *Issues in Intimate Violence*, Thousand Oaks, California: Sage.

DeKeseredy, W. and Hinch, R. (1991) *Woman Abuse: Sociological Perspectives*, Ontario: Thompson.

Denzin, N. (1970) *The Research Act*, Chicago: Aldine.

Dobash, R. E. and Dobash, R. P. (1979) *Violence Against Wives: A Case Against the Patriarchy*, New York: The Free Press.

Dobash, R. E. and Dobash, R. P. (1992) *Women, Violence and Social Change*, London: Routledge.

Doggett, M. (1992) *Marriage, Wife-Beating and the Law in Victorian England*, London: Weidenfeld Nicolson.

Edwards, S. (1989) *Policing 'Domestic' Violence*, London: Sage.

Estrich, S. (1987) *Real Rape*, London: Harvard University Press.

Finch, J. (1987) 'The vignette technique in survey research', *Sociology*, 21, 105–14.

Freeman, M. (1979) *Violence in the Home*, Farnborough: Saxon House.

Gelles, R. and Cornell, C. (1985) *Intimate Violence in Families*, Beverley Hills: Sage.

Genn, H. (1988) 'Multiple Victimisation', in Maguire, M. and Pointing, J. (eds) *Victims of Crime: A New Deal*, Milton Keynes: Open University Press.

Hall, R. (1985) *Ask Any Woman*, Report of the Women's Safety Survey conducted by Women Against Rape, Bristol: Falling Wall Press.

Hanmer, J. and Saunders, S. (1984) *Well-Founded Fear*, London: Macmillan.

Hanmer, J. and Stanko, B. (1985) 'Stripping away the rhetoric of protection: violence to women, law and the state in Britain and the USA', *International Journal of the Sociology of Law*, 13, 4; 357–74.

Hough, M. (1986) 'Victims of violent crime: findings from the first British crime survey', in Fattah, E. (ed.) *From Crime Policy to Victim Policy*, London: Macmillan.

Hough, M. and Mayhew, P. (1983) *The British Crime Survey: First Report*, London: HMSO.

Hough, M. and Mayhew, P. (1985) *Taking Account of Crime: Key Findings from the 1984 British Crime Survey*, London: HMSO.

Jones, T., MacLean, B., Young, J. (1986) *The First Islington Crime Survey*, Aldershot: Gower.

Jupp, V. (1989) *Methods of Criminological Research*, London: Unwin Hyman.

Kashani, J. and Allan, W. (1998) *The Impact of Family Violence on Children and Adolescents*, London: Sage.

Kelly, L. (1988) *Surviving Sexual Violence*, Cambridge: Polity Press.

Kinsey, R. (1985) *First Report of the Merseyside Crime Survey*, Liverpool: Merseyside County Council.

Kinsey, R. and Anderson, S. (1992) *Crime and the Quality of Life: Public Perceptions and Experiences of Crime in Scotland*, Edinburgh: Scottish Office.

Kish, L. (1965) *Survey Sampling*, New York: Wiley.

Kurz, D. (1993) 'Social science perspectives on wife abuse: current debates and future directions', in Bart, P. and Moran, E. (eds) *Violence Against Women*, USA: Sage.

Lea, J., Jones, T. and Young, J. (1986) *Saving the Inner City: Broadwater Farm*, Middlesex Polytechnic: Centre for Criminology.

Lee, R. (1993) *Doing Research on Sensitive Topics*, London: Sage.

Lees, S. and Gregory, J. (1993) *Rape and Sexual Assault: A Study of Attrition*, Islington Council: Police and Crime Prevention Unit.

London Strategic Policy Unit (1986) *Police Response to Domestic Violence, Police Monitoring and Research Unit Briefing Paper 1*, London: London Strategic Policy Unit.

McClintock, D. (1963) *Crimes of Violence*, London: Macmillan.

McGibbon, A., Cooper, L. and Kelly, L. (1989) *What Support?*, Polytechnic of North London: Child Abuse Studies Unit.

MacLean, B. (1985) 'Review of *Ask Any Woman* by Ruth Hall', *British Journal of Criminology*, 25, 390–1.

Martin, D. (1976) *Battered Wives*, San Francisco: Gide Publications.

Mayhew, P., Elliot, D. and Dowds, L. (1989) *1988 British Crime Survey*, London: HMSO.

Mayhew, P., Maung, N. A., Mirrlees-Black, C. (1993) *The 1992 British Crime Survey*, London: HMSO.

Mirrlees-Black, C., Mayhew, P. and Percy, A. (1996) *The 1996 British Crime Survey*, London: HMSO.

Mooney, J. (1993) *The Hidden Figure: Domestic Violence in North London*, Islington Council: Police and Crime Prevention Unit.

Mooney, J. (1995) *Violence, Space and Gender: the Social and Spatial Parameters of Violence Against Women and Men*, Middlesex University: Centre for Criminology.

Pahl, J. (1985) *Private Violence and Public Policy*, London: Routledge & Kegan Paul.

Painter, K., Lea, J., Woodhouse, T. and Young, J. (1989) *Hammersmith and Fulham Crime and Policing Survey*, Middlesex Polytechnic: Centre for Criminology.

Painter, K., Woodhouse, T. and Young, J. (1990) *The Ladywood Crime Survey*, Middlesex Polytechnic: Centre for Criminology.

Pizzey, E. (1998) 'Men Are Strong...', *The Observer*, 5 July: 24.

Radford, J. (1987) 'Policing Male Violence – Policing Women', in Hanmer, J. and Maynard, M. (eds) *Women, Violence and Social Control*, London: Macmillan.

Schwartz, M. (1988) 'Universal risk theories of battering', *Contemporary Crises*, 12, 4, 373–92.

Smith, L. (1989) *Domestic Violence*, London: HMSO.

Steinmetz, S. (1977–8) 'The battered husband syndrome' *Victimology*, 2, 3–4: 499–509.

Straus, M. (1979) 'Measuring intrafamily conflict and violence', *Journal of Marriage and the Family*, 41: 75–88.

Straus, M. and Gelles, R. (1986) 'Societal change in family violence from 1975 to 1985', *Journal of Marriage and the Family*, 48, 465–79.

Straus, M. and Gelles, R. (1988) 'How violent are American families? Estimates from the National Family Abuse Violence Resurvey and other studies', in Hotling, G., Finkelhor, D., Kirkpatrick, J. and Straus, M. (eds) *Family Abuse and its Consequences*, California: Sage.

Straus, M., Gelles, R. and Steinmetz, S. (1981) *Behind Closed Doors: Violence in the American Family*, New York: Anchor/Doubleday.

Tomes, N. (1978) 'A torrent of abuse: crimes of violence between working-class men and women, 1840–1875', *Journal of Social History*, 11, 238–345.

Walker, L. (1979) *The Battered Woman*, New York: Harper and Row.

Walklate, S. (1989) *Victimology*, London: Unwin Hyman.

Walklate, S. (1992a) *The Kirkby Inter-Agency Response to Domestic Violence*, University of Salford: Department of Sociology.

Walklate, S. (1992b) *Responding to Domestic Violence*, University of Salford: Department of Sociology.

Walklate, S. (1995) *Gender and Crime*, London: Prentice Hall.

Wilson, E. (1983) *What is to be Done About Violence Against Women?*, Harmondsworth: Penguin.

Women's National Commission (1985) *Violence Against Women*, London: Cabinet Office.

Worral, A. and Pease, K. (1986) 'Personal crime against women: evidence from the 1982 British Crime Survey', *Howard Journal*, 25, 2, 118–24.

Young, J. (1986) 'Risk of crime and fear of crime: a realist critique of survey-based assumptions', in Maguire, M. and Pointing, J. (eds) *Victims of Crime: A New Deal*, Milton Keynes: Open University Press.

3 Violence against black women in the home[*]

Amina Mama

Introduction: myths and truths

Discussing violence in the black community is a controversial exercise for a black woman such as myself. On the one hand, one risks being accused of fuelling damaging racist constructions of black people. On the other, one risks provoking the ire of one's peers, many of whom are defensive because they are only too well aware of the dominant society's portrayal of them. Because racists presume all blacks to be violent, black people prefer not to discuss black violence. Violence against black women is a particularly unpopular topic, unless it has been perpetrated by white racists or the police. When black men are violent towards black women, the ideologues amongst us would rather blame racism than look critically at black gender relations. Racism is the problem, according to this line of thought, and sexism is a white woman's preoccupation. Either way, myth obscures truth, clouding the distinctions between racial fiction and social fact.

That family life, black or white, merits continuous discussion cannot be denied in a society constantly bombarded with media images of ghoulish homicides. In this coverage, 'the family' is treated as a repository for all manner of social ills: each time a heinous crime is discovered, the family background of the perpetrator is subjected to extensive probing, while the mother and welfare agencies are chastised by the forces of law and order for having failed to produce a better product. Implicit in such rhetoric is an ideal family type, often alluded to but seldom defined. The tone of the dominant discourse on family life is sanctimonious, a moralistic and conservative voice propagating an atavistic, fundamentalist rhetoric which narrows the options for domestic arrangements to the couple-with-house-car-dog-and-two-point-four-children model. It is a model which precludes the vast majority of family forms prevailing, and very often thriving, in the real world. It is a discourse that conveys a racial subtext denying respectability to black families.

The black family is construed as the antithesis of the ideal family, a fictional opposite incarnating all the vices that the ideal is free of. It is an image which misrepresents the complex and varied familial forms manifested in Britain's black communities, simplifying and derogating black family life in a single stroke. All manner of non-white households are causally depicted as black families: families from India, Guyana, Jamaica, St Kitts, Ghana, Uganda, Morocco, Somalia, and other countries live in a post colonial Britain which views them as black. The racial, cultural and class variation within all these communities and the diverse family forms that do exist are obscured by a racialised discourse in which the complex realities are either homogenised or completely suppressed.

Instead of boasting a male householder, the black family is portrayed as comprising a brood of children dominated by an aggressive matriarch. Often portrayed as a violent street criminal, the black man has only a tangential and shifty relationship to the family unit. He is supposed to spend most of his time outside it, not as a breadwinner, but gambling, drug-running and growing dreadlocks, hanging out on the street corners, in clubs and in pubs in a bid to avoid the tongue-lashing of his frustrated partner. The black woman is depicted either as a young, sexually licentious, unemployed night clubber, or an overweight mammy who cooks up steaming pots of rice and peas between shifts at the factory, hospital, or office block where she works as a menial. Instead of a Bisto-ad family harmoniously sitting around a neatly laid table with 'Daddy' carving the Sunday joint, the black family is more likely to be portrayed like a scene from a slapstick comedy: the youth locked in generational conflict with their elders, the man lashing out at his nagging woman. It is the same black family which leaves the baby neglected, and the children fending for themselves in inner-city tower blocks while the black mother street walks to supplement her giro. The script on black family life ignores the vast majority of black families, and contrasts the shibboleth it creates to the white ideal family which it elevates and sanctifies. So what is the truth?

First, there cannot be one truth about the diversity of family forms in the various ethnic, national, cultural and class groups amongst those dubbed as black in contemporary Britain. Secondly, although each element of the mythical black family described above may capture something about some families, it fails to represent anything recognisably true about black families in general.

Even if one limits oneself to families of African-Caribbean derivation, the majority are not single-parent families, nor are they headed by an aggressive matriarch. Heterosexual marriage is an ideal adhered to by most black people, whatever their cultural origins. In fact, many women would rather tolerate an abusive relationship than face the stigma and hardship of living singly, or raising children without a father. More often than not, even when legal marriages have not been entered into, common-law or other long-term arrangements between men and women precede parenthood. Legal and religious marriages are the norm in the African and Asian communities, a norm adhered to more rigorously by these minorities than by white people, amongst whom common law arrangements have been in vogue since the 'swinging 1960s'. Statistics (Owen 1993) show that 31 per cent of white households contain only one adult, as compared to 28 per cent of black[1] households. Within this 28 per cent there are variations according to ethnicity, such that people of Caribbean,

African and 'black other' origin have a higher proportion of single adult households than white people (45 per cent), but people of Asian origin have lower proportions (South Asian 13 per cent, Chinese and others 29 per cent).

The stereotypical representation of black families as 'extended' is also inaccurate. It is also unclear just what is meant by 'extended family'. If one considers the presence of grandparents, then it needs to be said that white grandparents often play a significant part in the lives of children, while a great many black parents receive little help from relatives who may live in other parts of the world, or hold different views on childcare. It may be true that black single mothers are helped out by their mothers more than most white single mothers, but (to my knowledge) there is no empirical evidence that this is so. It may also be truer of families of African and Asian extraction than of families of Caribbean extraction who, for the most part, seem not to have families significantly more extended than their white counterparts. Statistics (Owen 1993) do show that more black households include three or more adults than white households: 25 per cent as compared to only 17 per cent. Once desegregated, we find that this difference is true of both African-Caribbean and Asian households, although it is more marked amongst South Asians (36 per cent) than amongst Caribbean (19 per cent), African (17 per cent) or Chinese-and-other households (20 per cent). In any case, the presence of three or more adults in a household does not mean an extended family. It could also be a result of multiple occupancy, or of children leaving home at later ages. These statistics do not therefore offer any firm support for the assumption that black people live in extended set-ups and white Britons do not. It seems a highly unlikely proposition, particularly if one is considering the second and third generation settlers, who constitute most of today's black Britons. An alternative proposition worth considering is that black people have less contact with relatives beyond the nuclear unit: after all, many have migrated away from their kin, and others have simply adopted European middle-class family forms and, therefore, defining features of black 'family life' become more unclear.

The idea of the black man as irresponsible and peripheral to his family is also true of some but not all black men, just as there must undoubtedly be white men who fit this description. Familial irresponsibility seems unlikely to be the result of an inherent or racially-linked factor. We know of black men who are doting fathers, who are supportive partners and companions to the women they live with, and of black women who are caring parents, loving partners and competent professionals. Why do these men and women not feature in the dominant discourse on black families? Proper study of black families will make nonsense of the misrepresentations discussed above. Even the specific study of female abuse does this. The research findings discussed below also force a broader rethinking of the complex relationship between the late capitalist state relations within the household, across Britain's various communities.

The domestic violence study[2]

The domestic violence study was an activist research project carried out in London, in collaboration with the women's refuge movement and community organisations, with the express purpose of empowering community efforts to address the problem of female abuse. It involved several research strategies, aimed at documenting the manifestations of abuse in the African Caribbean and Asian communities, and assessing the interventions of both statutory and voluntary organisations. Over one hundred abused women were contacted through various community organisations and networks, notably Women's Aid and the independent refuges set up for minority women, and interviewed in-depth. Members of housing, social and legal organisations were also interviewed. In addition to these interviews, consultations were held with both management and workers at 18 London refuges, and with Women's Aid Federation (WAFE) staff at the London and national offices.

Experience of abuse

Elsie, a 25-year-old woman of mixed Caribbean and European parentage who works in catering, has been subjected to violence by the father of her child for the last 18 months. Their fights, which centre around domestic roles, financial matters and sex, usually start as verbal arguments but escalate into physical abuse, with him kicking and punching her on the head, beating her with an iron bar and frequently slapping her face. She has sustained a broken nose twice, bears several unpleasant scars and has attempted suicide at least once.

Sangita, a 22-year-old East African Asian was married at the age of 19. After only three months of marriage, her shy, quiet husband metamorphosed into a suspicious and jealous assailant:

> If he didn't like anything I was doing, if he didn't like the cooking, if I made vegetables he'd just throw the pans everywhere, throw the food everywhere. If I didn't talk to his parents – his Mum – properly, or if I was talking to his sister, he didn't like that. If I went shopping without telling him, if I left the house – I was just a prisoner in my own home. I wasn't allowed to go anywhere … He used to kick me, throw things at me, he used to pull my hair to pieces. No broken bones, but I've had black eyes and I've got scars, loads of scars to prove it, because he used to have quite long nails, he'd just grab and the skin would sort of come away. When I did refuse to have sex with him, he'd say to me, 'Are you sleeping with another person?' 'You must be sleeping with other men'. And he'd sort of force himself on me.

Mabel, a 33-year old Ghanaian businesswoman, is married to a man of the same strong religious convictions as herself, with whom she has two children. She blames her envious in-laws for spoiling her relationship with her husband, whose behaviour is erratic:

One minute he's alright and then the next he's like a monster ... A very nice father. He is wonderful. He really cares for his children ... But then suddenly he's a different man.

His violence leaves her bruised, covered with bite marks, and requiring hospital treatment on at least one occasion. After his recurrent outbursts of violence, he would switch into a penitent, pleading soul:

He would break down, he would kiss my feet like Jesus did and would quote from the Bible – 'the Bible says this, the Bible says that' – but he would do it again.

Shuewi and her husband are both doctors specialising in acupuncture. Together they ran a joint practice, until she could no longer tolerate her husbands' cruelty. Keeping her virtually penniless, he left her to do all the professional and domestic work, taking all their earnings into his own bank accounts. Violent within a month of their marriage, he caused Shuewi to suffer from constant headaches and nausea, and forced her to have an abortion because he did not want children. She finally ran away after being hospitalised with seven broken ribs.

Linda is a 31-year-old Filipino with a 2-year-old son. She met her English husband in the Middle East, where she worked for a cosmetics company. After months of courtship, he returned to England, but then sent for her to join him. It was after they were married that he became violent and suspicious, verbally abusing Linda, hitting her head against the wall, kicking and punching her in the stomach. When she became pregnant she was finally driven to leave, fearing for the survival of her unborn child.

Women in the study experienced various forms of abuse at the hands of their (black or white) male partners, ranging from physically threatening behaviour to serious assaults. The descriptions of violence that black women give do not differ in kind from similar accounts given by white women, with abuse occurring under a range of social and economic conditions. However they do display much greater cultural diversity amongst the women interviewed than in any pre-existing studies. Although all are permanent residents of Britain, these women originate from 21 different Caribbean, African and Asian countries.[3] The degree and severity of violence described by women in this study probably reflects the fact that we relied largely on women's refuges for contacting most of them: this meant that most of them had been forced to leave their homes on at least one occasion prior to their interview. This study does not provide any evidence to support the commonly-held view that there is a higher incidence of abuse among black as compared to white couples. However, it does suggest that black women may be particularly reluctant to seek outside help: many endure a high level of abuse over long periods of time, rather than run the risk of homelessness and its attendant vulnerability, hardship and indignity, not to mention the bureaucratic intransigence that is revealed below.

Compounding abuse: agency responses

The debilitating effects of domestic violence on black women and their children are often compounded by the treatment that is meted out to them when they seek the assistance of statutory agencies. The experiences tell the story of what it means to be caught up in a complex and alienating web of bureaucracies. Getting in touch with one agency, for example reporting at a housing department, requires contact with others – the police, the social services, and perhaps a legal agency or a women's refuge. Communicating with the police, often an essential condition for getting rehoused, may lead to immigration harassment; contact with a refuge may result in interventions from a social services department concerned with child protection; and so on. In this way, individual women, many of whom are already suffering from trauma and depression, are passed from agency to agency over a period that can last for years. The evidence suggests that while all women experience hardship in seeking to leave abusive men, the situation is worse for black women, partly because the agencies that have moral and legal obligations to assist them are often staffed by people who hold racist views. As a result of this, many public officers arrogate to themselves a gatekeeping role, denying or delaying access to those they deem to be 'undeserving'. Prevalent images of black people as disreputable social security scroungers, or as newly-arrived immigrants, do not facilitate racial equity in service delivery, whether it be the allocation of housing or the provision of financial support (see Chapter 10). To these images we must add the moral judgements that British society makes about black women who are commonly perceived as irresponsible, and as unfit mothers, imbued with promiscuous sexuality.

'Old Bill' and the law

Special training and domestic violence units notwithstanding, the police often fail to enforce the laws against violence assault when they are called to black homes. Black women report a variety of inappropriate interventions:

> Yvonne describes the police regularly responding by arriving at the house in large numbers, not to arrest or prosecute her male partner, but to beat him up. In any case, on the one occasion when charges were pressed against him, he was released by the court, despite the protestations of the police.

> Police arrive at Patience's home in response to a call from her neighbours. On arriving, they find her in a dishevelled and battered state, whereupon the police officers joke around, chanting 'Eenie, meenie, minie, mo' before opting to arrest her instead of her husband. Taken to the police station, she is subjected to humiliating ridicule, before being kicked down the steps into the police cells where she spends the night. In the morning she is dumped on the street and left to find her way home.

Generally it seems that the police are reluctant to intervene at all, perhaps because of the prevalent view that battering women is an acceptable aspect of black culture. Misrepresentations of 'black culture' operate in ethnically-specific ways. In the case of young Asian women, refusal to respond has resulted in several deaths, but in other cases Asian women describe over-responses in which large numbers of people and social services personnel arrive to ship the victim off to the nearest refuge.

Although women are more often vulnerable to immigration investigation because of their status as wives of British citizens, at least one British-born Asian woman recounted how police intervention had been followed by the deportation of her Pakistani husband, something which she did not anticipate. In other cases, British husbands of whatever race urge the police to deport black women they no longer wish to live with, and whose immigration status rests on their marriage.

African and Caribbean women generally report that the authorities respond in ways which suggest that they are not easily perceived as victims of male violence. Perhaps because they are typecast as aggressive, they tend not to be believed when they call for help. Asian women, on the other hand, because they are viewed as passive, docile child-brides forced into arranged marriages, are more easily seen as victims, and responded to as such.

In all cases the police appear more ready to investigate immigration status than to respond to domestic violence in black communities. This practice has led to some deportations, a fact which has affected gender relations, in so far as men now threaten black women with deportation as another way of exercising coercive control over them. It has also led to a number of well-publicised anti-deportation campaigns. For example, when Women's Aid reported that Lisa Huen's 5-year-old son might be in danger, the social services department put him on the at risk register and warned Lisa that they would take him away if she kept returning to her abusive husband. However, when she did leave this man she became the subject of a deportation order, on the basis that, although her son was a British citizen, her residence in Britain was contingent on her marital status. She was faced with the prospect of returning to a country she had left many years previously, either taking her young son with her to an unknown destination, or leaving him in state custody.[4] The most helpful police responses include taking abused women to a women's refuge, escorting them home to collect a few possessions, or supporting those who do decide to press charges against the man.

Legal services do not appear to function effectively in the women's interests. Many women describe how ineffective injunctions are, on occasion endangering them further by antagonising the man, who is left at large. It is becoming harder to obtain legal aid and many women lack the necessary financial and/or emotional resources to pursue lengthy court cases which often lead to unsatisfactory results.

Housing and social services

The Social Services Department is only legally obliged to intervene in cases where there is risk to a child. Women with children are therefore the most likely to have contact with social workers. A great many black women are also obliged to undergo interviews with social services departments in the course of seeking financial assistance and housing. Housing officers may decide that a social worker's report should be included in the files, either because they want to confirm that the woman's housing need is as dire as she has said it is, or simply because they think she or her children should be seen by a social worker. The rates of contact with social workers vary between ethnic groups, with Asian women having the highest rates (50 per cent of the women interviewed had seen social workers) and Caribbean women the lowest (20 per cent had contact with social workers).

Black women's access to public housing is severely circumscribed by a range of mechanisms. The evidence indicates that housing departments allocate the worst housing to their most desperate clients, who often happen to be black women. Many are left homeless for long periods, with some of the women interviewed having spent as long as two years in overcrowded women's refuges. All the women in this study had experienced severe stress over their housing: in fact, 77 per cent of the sample were homeless at the time of interview.

Shaba, an Iranian woman, has lived with her husband and young daughter in a cramped rented room in Barnet for 12 years. They have been on the waiting list for local authority housing for the last four years. When her husband turned violent, causing her to suffer a miscarriage, a broken nose and extensive bruising, she began to plead with the housing department, to no avail. Eventually, after her husband had tried to strangle her, she picked up the child and ran for her life. Destitute, she was advised to contact Women's Aid. The Local Authority housing officer who interviewed her after this traumatic experience treated her so callously that she burst into tears in his office, after being told she should 'go back to Iran'.

Mary, a 32-year-old working mother, became single after persuading her violent husband to move out of the Hackney flat they shared with her sister during her pregnancy. His continued harassment forced her to apply for rehousing, but the Housing Department told her she would not be attended to until after the baby had been born. After the birth of her son, weekly visits to the Housing Department produced no results for a whole year. The only accomodation she was offered during this time was a flat in a remote waste area, in a block so run down that she was afraid to climb the stairs to it. It had no door, and appeared to have been burnt out by the previous occupants. Abandoning hope, she moved to Haringey, where she stayed with a younger relative, and applied for housing again. After the baby was born, she was moved into unpleasant hostel accommodation. Only when she took the case up with a local councillor and brought it before the committee was she eventually offered a decent home. The son she had been expecting when she first applied was three years old before her application came through.

Women who continue to live in violent situations give their fear of being homeless as their reason for remaining, a fear which this evidence suggests is valid. Those who leave but then return to violent men also cite the lack of housing as a main reason for giving in. Women generally depend more on public housing than men, partly because of their low earning power, something which is clearly more pronounced in the case of minority women as a result of racism on the job market. Despite the statutory obligation of local authorities to rehouse women with children and to prioritise cases where there is domestic violence, the fact that the housing stock was consistently depleted by a decade and a half of Conservative government reduced the chances of housing for all women. Moreover, in view of housing discrimination, the situation facing black and minority women can only have worsened disproportionately (see Chapter 13).

Women's refuges

The women's refuge movement has played a major role both in offering temporary accommodation to women seeking to leave violent situations, and in supporting women's applications for rehousing. The Women's Aid Federation England (WAFE) is a national network which aims to address the needs of abused women (see Chapter 12 and Appendix 1). Figures collected by WAFE at the end of the 1980's showed 6627 referrals per annum to the London Office, at a time when there were only 3400 bed-spaces in London refuges. Since that time, refuges have continued to be under-resourced as well as numerically inadequate. It also needs to be pointed out that WAFE figures do not begin to estimate the size of the problem because so many women, particularly minority women, have never heard of Women's Aid. The small number of refuges set up by black women's groups specifically to meet the needs of black women[5] have also faced difficulties with funding, and the poor quality of accommodation made available to them. Resource constraints limit both the holding capacity and the outreach and support work that the refuge movement can undertake, while the depletion of public housing has the effect of converting what was intended to be temporary accommodation into long-stay hostels.

Race, the state and gender relations

What does all this say about the relationship between men and women in late capitalist states? Having enumerated the many ways in which agency responses to black woman often exacerbate the negative consequences of violence on black women and their children, it is worth looking at the relational situations in which the women in this study experienced abuse. The purpose of doing so is twofold: one, to continue to debunk the oversimplified notions about black families that I discussed in the introduction, and two, to see if we can draw any general conclusions about those black families in which the man abuses the woman.[6]

The women participating in this study lived in a variety of relationships, which I divided into three categories for the purposes of the research:

1   women legally married (either under British law or according to their
    particular cultural traditions);
2   women cohabiting with their assailants; and
3   women in visiting relationships, in which the man often stayed with the
    woman, but did not officially reside with her.

This third category is not always clearly distinguishable from cohabitees, because unemployed women often find it necessary not to be seen to be living with a man for fear of losing their social security benefit, and so being forced into dependency on a man who may himself be jobless, particularly where he is prone to violence.

The three categories of relationship are not independent of ethnic origin: all the women of African and Asian extraction were married to the men they lived with, more than half of the women of Caribbean descent were not. However, before concluding this to be an 'ethnic characteristic' it is worth pointing out that far more of the women of Caribbean descent were born and raised in Britain, where a growing proportion of the population cohabit at some stage in their life (Barrett and MacIntosh 1982). It may also be a function of socio-economic class, the majority of the women of Caribbean descent being from working-class backgrounds.

The fact that so few of the couples in this study comprise women living with male breadwinners upon whom they are economically dependent, suggests that economic dependency is not as central to female abuse as research conducted on white communities suggests (e.g. Dobash and Dobash 1989). Only the Asian married women were commonly dependent on their husbands, and even here, a number were economically active, on occasion more so than their husbands (as in the case of Shuewi, cited above). The African women were all professional wage earners or entrepreneurs. The Caribbean women were most often under-employed or unemployed, but even fewer of them were financially supported by the men they had relationships with, regardless of marital status. This was because few of the male partners of Caribbean origin in this sample bore any economic responsibility for the women they were having relationships with, a fact which must be linked to their own marginal economic status, and the fact that many were in visiting relationships.

Housing seems to be the most pervasive problem experienced by the women in the study. Interestingly, about half of the women of Caribbean descent held council tenancies in their own name, which meant that, legally at least, their abusive partners depended on them for housing.[7] A further 29 per cent of all the women in the study held joint tenancies with their male partners, and 33 per cent lived with men (usually husbands) who held tenancy (albeit on their and the children's behalf). What this tells us is that holding the tenancy does not necessarily empower the woman to force the man to leave the home when he is abusive, even though she is legally entitled to do so.

A significant proportion of women are assaulted by ex-partners they no longer live with, who succeed in terrorising them into leaving their homes because so little protection is afforded to them by the law. Women who do not live with their assailants cannot obtain injunctions under the Domestic Violence and Matrimonial Proceedings Act.[8]

All this means that many couples live together to avoid homelessness, in what we may term 'cohabitations of convenience'. Several women describe their male partners moving in with them without there being a mutually agreed decision that they live together:

> Sarah: We were going out for about three years, but that didn't entitle him to just move in automatically as he did. But I didn't really say too much. I just sort of asked him and he said he thought that was what I wanted.

Sukie has been homeless for nearly two years as a result of violence from a man who moved into her flat after helping her to decorate it. During that time she has stayed in a number of refuges and bed and breakfast hotels with her children. She left her job too, because she feared reprisals after her husband was given a six month suspended sentence for grievous bodily harm after he had tried to strangle her to death.

In some cases, a man has more than one visiting relationship. Having no home of his own, he commutes between women, officially living with none of them. He moves on whenever a spot check from social services is anticipated, or when the woman tries to make any demands on him, or after each violent incident. In some cases both the man and the woman are rendered homeless, and spend their lives moving from one temporary abode to another, in inadequate, overcrowded and unsanitary facilities.

To be a homeless black man or woman is a dangerous situation in a country where black people are frequently subjected to race attacks and police harassment on the streets. Racist assumptions mean that black women on the streets are likely to be pulled in for prostitution, and black men arrested on suspicion of any number of unproven nefarious activities.

From this we can see how the various manifestations of class, race and gender oppression interact both to create conditions under which violence occurs, and to keep many black women living in violent situations. It is also clear that poor housing and financial stress exacerbate gender conflict, sometimes bringing about cohabitations that do not work, sometimes undermining the positive potentials of personal relationships, and always making it hard for either party to leave. Housing stress can also bring about cohabitations which are not the result of free choice, but because of poor material conditions. It also needs to be said that not all poverty-stricken men beat up their partners, since a great many black couples support each other through the stresses of life in a racist society.

There has been a tendency, particularly within black discourse, to blame female abuse by the black man on racism.[9] It therefore needs to be said that however bad racial oppression may be, racism does not take up the hand of the black man and oblige him to beat up his partner. There are many different ways of responding to oppression. Female abuse is not racially or ethnically linked, but a function of gender inequality which prevails, whether one is considering marriage, cohabitation or visiting relationships.

Notes

* This chapter is based on previously published work by the author (see Mama 1989).

1 The term used is 'ethnic minorities' comprising black (African, Caribbean and other), South Asian, Chinese and others, usage which is the same as my usage of 'black' to mean persons of Caribbean, Asian (including Chinese) and African descent.

2 The original research project was funded by the London Race and Housing Research Unit over an 18–month period, and published in collaboration with Runnymede Trust under the title *The Hidden Struggle* (Mama 1989).

3 A number were of mixed parentage, usually with one white British parent.

4 Lisa Huen became one of the few cases which was successful in appealing to the Home Office for compassion.

5 At the time of the research there were six refuges for Asian women and one for African and Caribbean women in the Greater London area.

6 Moreover, not all of them live with men of the same ethnic origin, although most of them do. A few live with abusive white men, and there are a small number of Asian-African relationships.

7 This is a result of the fact that local authorities are obliged to accommodate homeless people with children, most of whom are women.

8 This has been modified with the new Family Law Act 1996 and the Protection from Harassment Act 1997.

9 Within white society there has been a historical tendency to portray wife-beating as a 'working class thing', supplanted only by the tendency now to view it as 'a black thing', with black men incarnating phallic sexuality in the way that working class men used to. Black discourse reinforces this position when it portrays the black man as a mindless victim of his oppression. In denying the gender dynamics of woman abuse, such a discourse offers no explanation as to why black women and black men do not react to their experience of racism in the same way. What is suggested instead is a mindless hierarchy of violence in which the white man beats the black man who beats the black woman who beats her children.

References

Barrett, M. and MacIntosh, M. (1982) *The Anti-Social Family*, London: Verso and New Left Books.

Binney, V., Harkell, G. and Nixon, J. (1981) *Leaving Violent Men*, London: National Women's Aid Federation.

Bryan, B., Dadzie, S. and Scafe, S. (1985) *The Heart of the Race: Black Women's Lives in Britain*, London: Virago.

Dobash, R. E. and Dobash, R. (1989) *Violence Against Wives*, London: Open Books.

Edwards, S. (1986) *The Police Response to Domestic Violence in London*, London: Polytechnic of Central London.

Karn, V. (1983) *Race and Housing in Britain: The Role of Major Institutions*, London: Heinemann.

Lawrence, E. and Mama, A. (1988) 'The reproduction of inequality in housing', Runnymede Lecture, Runnymede Trust, London, unpublished.

Mama, A. (1989) *The Hidden Struggle: Statutory and Voluntary Sector Responses to Violence Against Black Women in the Home*, London: Race and Housing Research Unit/Runnymede Trust.

Owen, D. (1993) 'Ethnic minorities in Great Britain: housing and family characteristics', 1991 Census Statistical Paper No. 4, *Centre for Ethnic Research*, April 1993.

4 Marital rape and marital murder

Sue Lees

This chapter traces events leading up to marital rape becoming a crime. Previous to 1991, 'the marital rape exclusion' protected rape in marriage from criminal prosecution. No separate analysis of marital rape cases has been undertaken by the Home Office, so it is impossible to know how many such cases have been brought to court since then. Analysis of cases heard between 1991 and 1995 by the Court of Appeal throws some light on how the judiciary treats the more serious cases. This analysis indicates that marital rape is still not taken as seriously as rape by strangers, although research reveals that marital rape is often linked to life threatening violence, including murder. This chapter also documents the link between marital rape and wife killing and shows how the judiciary are treating marital rape and the killing of wives according to different criteria than such attacks by strangers.

Background

Marital rape is a neglected topic. An exception is a paper by Naffine (1994), an Australian sociologist, who seeks to explain why it has taken so long in all jurisdictions to abolish the rape immunity law for husbands. She argues that its abolition challenges the view of women as the possessions and passive objects of their husbands' desires. Its abolition, therefore, carries the clear implication that a woman does have the right to self determination. The lives of married women who are raped by their husbands, particularly after separation, can be in severe danger, but threats and intimidation are still not often recognised as such by the judiciary.[1]

The marital rape exemption was an extension of the historic domination and control of husbands over wives. The law gave male power over wives an institutional legitimacy, in so far as the law on sexual assault was only significant when it involved the 'property' of a man, usually a virginal daughter or a wife. The exemption had its origins in the following statement by Lord Chief Justice Matthew Hale, in 1736:

> But the husband cannot be guilty of rape committed by himself upon his lawful wife, for by their mutual matrimonial consent and contract the wife hath given up herself in this kind unto her husband which she cannot retract.[2]

Hale wrote this at a time when marriage irrevocably bound a woman to her husband as his property. During the eighteenth century, therefore, the law on rape evolved to protect the theft of female sexual property, not to protect women themselves.[3] Rape violated not her bodily integrity, but the patriarchal ownership of her sexuality. Therefore it was not possible for a man to rape his wife as she belonged to him. It was an extension of the historical domination and control of husbands over wives (see Clark 1987).

It was not until the end of the nineteenth century that it became criminal for a husband to beat his wife. A husband was supported by the law in some circumstances even if he kept his wife locked up. In a case decided in 1861 (*R v. Jackson*) the majority held that a man did not have the right to kidnap his wife when she had left him and did not want to return. However, some of the judges argued that there were circumstances where a husband might rightly keep his wife imprisoned if she had not already left him. Such circumstances included occasions when the wife intended to go on a shopping spree, where the husband feared she might spend all of 'his' money (Scutt 1993: 204).

The regulation of sexuality plays an important part in maintaining the institution of the family and in limiting women's sexual rights and autonomy. Susan Brownmiller (1976: 380), in her groundbreaking history of rape, was one of the first to point out the meaning of the marital rape exemption:

> To our Biblical forefathers any carnal knowledge outside the marriage contract was 'unlawful'. And any carnal knowledge within the marriage contract was, by definition, 'lawful'. Thus, as the law evolved, the idea that a husband could be prosecuted for raping his wife was unthinkable, for the law was conceived to protect *his* interests, not those of his wife.

The law on marital rape in the UK

Rape originated as a crime of common law. The penalty for the crime, and the fact that the crime was a felony, were referred to in a series of statutes which were consolidated first in the Offences against the Persons Acts (1861) and then in the Sexual Offences Act (1956). A statutory definition of rape was not given until section 1 (1) (a) of the Sexual Offences (Amendment) Act (1976) which expanded on the 1956 Act by providing that 'for the purposes of section 1 of the Sexual Offences Act (1956) [which relates to rape] a man commits rape if he has *unlawful* sexual intercourse with a woman who at the time of the intercourse does not consent to it'. Where used elsewhere in the 1956 Act the expression 'unlawful' sexual intercourse had been assumed to connote intercourse outside marriage, so it was generally accepted that, by using the word unlawful, Parliament intended at least in some respects to retain the marital immunity (see Law Commission 1992: 4).

Hale's declaration stood uncontested until a case in 1949, more than 200 years later. This case confirmed Hale's view, but established that there were *exceptions* to this statute law, namely where there were court orders between the couple such as decrees nisi, judicial separation or non-molestation orders. In other words, where the woman had established a status as a separate woman, a husband's indictment to rape was valid. The exception to immunity was limited to husbands living separately under court order as was shown by a case in 1955 where, although the husband and wife were living separately, and the wife had started divorce proceedings, there was no evidence 'to say that the wife's implied consent to marital intercourse had been revoked by an act of the parties or by an act of the courts'.[4] The Criminal Law Revision Committee considered the law should be changed but only in cases where the couple were not cohabiting.

In July 1990, at the trial of a man in England charged with raping his wife (R v. R) the question was raised as to whether a wife's consent to sexual intercourse could be revoked, not only by court order or mutual consent, but also by a unilateral withdrawal from cohabitation. The wife had moved out of the matrimonial home the previous October, and had gone to live with her parents. The defendant had broken into his wife's parent's house a month later and attacked her. He had ripped her clothing and put his hands around her neck and threatened to kill her. The defendant did not dispute the facts, just the legality of the charge. There was bruising on her throat, a clear sign that he had tried to throttle her by squeezing her neck with both hands. This was accepted as evidence that she had not wanted sex. This case was the first in which a husband was accused of rape where there was no legal separation or court order prohibiting him from molesting his wife.

The House of Lords precipitated a change in the law by its decision in R v. R in 1991, in which they declined to apply the generally accepted marital rape exemption.[5] Lord Lane, the Lord Chief Justice, headed the special five-judge Court of Appeal hearing and upheld the R v. R decision stating: 'This is not the creation of a new offence. It is the removal of a common law fiction which has become anachronistic and offensive.'[6]

In doing so the Court overturned 250 years of legal immunity for wife rapists, a decision that was upheld by the House of Lords on 23 October 1991. The House of Lords emphasised that Hale's statement no longer represented the law and that the time had now arrived 'when the law should declare that a rapist remains a rapist and is subject to the criminal law, irrespective of his relationship with his victim'. The abolition of the marital rape immunity was finally integrated into statute in June 1994.

The incidence of marital rape

It is difficult to assess the incidence of marital rape as not all women who are coerced into sex define it as rape. The question of how exactly rape or 'lack of consent' should be defined has preoccupied lawyers and is at the time of writing, in April 2000, under consideration by the Sex Offences Review Committee. Section 1 of the Sexual Offences Act 1956 defines rape as penetration of the vagina or the anus by the penis without the woman's consent.[7] Emission of semen is not required. Attempted rape occurs where an assault stops before actual penetration has occurred. Three issues have to be proved for rape itself. Firstly, that sexual intercourse took place, secondly, that it was without the woman's consent and thirdly, that the defendant knew that she did not consent or was reckless as to whether or not she consented. If a man believes that a woman consented to sex he cannot be guilty of rape even if his belief was unreasonable (the 'mistaken belief' defence). In deciding whether or not a man believed that a woman was consenting to sex, the jury is instructed to have regard to the presence or absence of reasonable grounds for such a belief.[8]

Painter (1991) in her study of a representative sample of 1007 women in 11 different cities in the UK, found that divorced or separated women were the most likely to be coerced into sex. One in three divorced women compared to one in seven of cohabiting women said they had been coerced and divorced or separated women were seven times more likely than married women to have had violence threatened. Of those who said they had been hit and raped, 51 per cent were divorced or separated. Painter calculated that marital rape was seven times as common as rape by a stranger. Of women raped by their husbands, 91 per cent had never reported or discussed the matter with any official agency.

Implementing the legislation

By 1999, only 6 per cent of reported rapes in England and Wales resulted in a conviction. This was a drop from 30 per cent in 1985 (Harris and Grace 1999). Although the number of rapes reported to the police over the past decade has more than doubled, the number of men convicted has remained almost exactly the same. The victim continues to be viewed in court with suspicion. Moreover, the closer the relationship between the defendant and complainant, the more difficult it is to gain a conviction (see Lees 1996, 1997; Gregory and Lees 1996, 1999). The Crown Prosecution Service (CPS) are even more inclined to drop cases where there is a marital relationship. For example, Temkin (1997) describes a case of marital rape where the defendant had admitted the assault to the police, but the CPS decided not to bring a prosecution, arguing that there was 'very little likelihood' of the man reoffending and that charges would not be in the public interest.

Generally, sentences for rape have increased. In 1986 in response to public outrage at lenient sentences imposed by a number of judges in rape cases, Lord Chief Justice Lane issued new sentencing tariffs, now referred to as the Billam Guidelines.[9] These set down guidelines for contested cases subject to various mitigating and aggravating factors. With no mitigating circumstances, five years was the starting point with 15 years for a campaign of rape. Where there were aggravating features, such as two or more rapists acting together, rape which takes place in the victim's home, rape coupled with the abuse of a position of responsibility, or rape involving abduction and confinement of the victim, the starting point was set at eight years. Various mitigating factors were also outlined: that young offenders could claim special mitigation, pleading guilty could reduce the sentence, and where the victim 'had behaved in a manner which was calculated to lead the defendant to believe that she would consent to sexual intercourse'. The guidelines do not refer to the previous sexual relationship between the victim and assailant as a mitigating factor, but do state the 'victim's previous sexual experience is irrelevant'. This, as we shall see, has not prevented the courts using the existence of a previous sexual relationship between the victim and assailant as a mitigating factor in sentencing.

The Billam Guidelines have led to some increase in length of sentences, but the effect of these changes has been exaggerated. The proportion of custodial sentences of at least five years (including life) for the substantive offence of rape rose from 42 per cent in 1985 to 79 per cent in 1987 and for attempted rape from 10 per cent to 40 per cent. Since 1987, however, the length of sentences has decreased. According to research conducted by Dr Paul Robertshaw (1994), there appear to be wide discrepancies in sentencing in different parts of the country. In some places sentences of less than three years or non-custodial sentences are far more likely to be awarded than in other areas. This is contrary to the Billam Guidelines that sentences under three years are not appropriate for rape even in cases with one or more mitigating factors.[10] The Court of Appeal regarded such low sentences to be justified only in 'wholly exceptional circumstances' (*The Times* 14 October 1993). The Home Office does not collect statistics with reference to plea, so it is not possible to know how many of those given low sentences had pleaded guilty. Robertshaw concluded that 'nothing is known of the particular combination of factors in each case, but the statistics suggest at least that in some courts the "wholly exceptional" is fairly frequent' (p. 344).[11] According to his calculations 40 per cent of sentences in 1991 were of 5 years or less. He concluded that there were grounds for a thorough monitoring and review of rape sentences and perhaps of the criteria for approving judges for this class of case.[12]

Cases involving marital rape receive significantly lower sentences than those involving rapes by strangers. A statistical comparison of sentences for different types of rape was conducted by Rumney (1999). In comparing marital rape cases that went to appeal between 1988 and 1998, he found an average level of sentencing in cases of stranger rape of 8.7 years compared to a level of 4.9 years in cases of marital rape (which included an average of 3.3 years in cases where the married couple were still cohabiting, and 6.5 years where the married couple were no longer co-habiting at the time of the rape). This judicial response, he argued, mirrored the traditional ineffectiveness of the judiciary in dealing with violence within the domestic sphere.

Research into the effects of marital rape

Research into the effects of marital rape indicates that it is just as traumatic, if not more, than rape by a stranger. Russell (1990), in her US study of a random sample of 930 women interviewed in the 1980s, where 14 per cent said they had been raped by their husbands, found that a similar proportion of women had been as upset by marital rape compared to stranger rape, but the long-term effects of marital rape were greater. 52 per cent of women raped by their husbands and 39 per cent of women raped by strangers stated that they suffered 'great' long-term effects. Russell concluded that her findings refuted the idea that 'wife rape' is less traumatic.

Painter (1991) found that marital rape was often associated with other physical violence, involving cuts, bruises, black eyes, broken bones and psychological traumas. Depression, fear, shock, nausea and headaches were prevalent. Painter concluded that not all cases were equally grave or serious, but the fact that almost half of those women raped by a husband had sought medical attention as a consequence was clear indication that rape by a husband is a serious matter. Koss and Harvey (1991: 76), American researchers, in their study of rape trauma and how it should be treated, concluded that comparisons between victims of stranger and non-stranger rape uncovered no differences in reactions or recovery. However, rapes by acquaintances were less likely to be reported.

The *Dispatches* research found that rape by someone you know is a more personal attack than rape by a stranger. It occurs in a situation previously associated with safety and privacy. It causes a woman to question her own judgement: her internal security checks have failed. Katz (1991) collected information on 87 women over 17 years of age who had been raped at least six months prior to the interview, and compared the reactions of those who had been raped by strangers with those raped by acquaintances. He concluded that stranger rapes involved more brutal physical violence but women blamed themselves less for the rape, saw themselves in a more positive light, and felt closer to recovery than did victims of an attack by an acquaintance.

Finally, in the research carried out for the Channel 4 *Dispatches* documentary, 'Getting Away with Rape' (1994) we distributed a questionnaire which was filled in by 100 women over the age of 17 who had been raped. Of the assailants, 14 were complete strangers and 86 had had some contact with the victim beforehand. This varied from minimal social contact to non-cohabiting boyfriends and ex-cohabitees or husbands, ex-lovers, or other relatives. 20 were raped by men with whom they had had previous consensual sex, 46 by general acquaintances such as work colleagues, friends' friends, people in a position of trust, and 20 by men they had met within the previous 24 hours.

The use of violence was similar and substantial in both the stranger and acquaintance groups (69.6 per cent and 63.9 per cent respectively). A higher proportion of strangers threatened to kill their victims (39 per cent against 14 per cent) and twice as many of the women raped by strangers believed their life was in danger (81.1 per cent compared to 42 per cent). Both groups, however, were likely to slap, push or handle their victims roughly, or forcibly hold them down (70–80 per cent) and more of the acquaintance group choked or strangled their victims (23 per cent as against 15 per cent). This puts women in greater danger than is often appreciated as, in England, strangulation is a common method by which men kill women they know. Injuries and physical effects suffered by the women in both groups were remarkably similar. About half of both groups suffered minor bruises, scratches and soreness (55 per cent and 46 per cent) and 27 per cent, and 28 per cent of the respective groups suffered severe bruising and 2 per cent suffered serious cuts.

The analysis of the questionnaires indicated that the effects on survivors were often dramatic and long lasting. Many changed their lifestyle, moved house through fear that the rapist might return, had time off or gave up work, broke up relationships with men and required long-term medication or coun-selling which was often not available. Many reactions are typical of what American researchers Burgess and Holmstrom (1974) named the 'rape trauma syndrome' which many rape victims suffer from to some degree. The use of such a medical term to describe reactions to rape has been criticised as it reduces the complexity of women's experiences to a set of 'individual symp-toms' which once understood can be cured by the medical profession (See Foley 1994).

Women raped by acquaintances found the experience even more difficult to come to terms with than those raped by strangers. They felt betrayed – not just by the men but by their own judgement. It also made them more fearful of men generally, since they no longer knew whom to trust. The fact that some women also blamed themselves for the rape made it harder for them to recover.

Are there distinct kinds of rapists?

Treating rapes by strangers as more serious is based on the myth that men who rape strangers are a significantly more dangerous group of rapists. However, there is no evidence that rapists can be divided into distinct groups on the basis of whether or not they rape strangers, acquaintances or wives. Homicidal rapists sometimes rape and kill both their wives and those they know less intimately. Frederick West was charged in 1994 with killing 13 women, many of whom were tortured and raped, including his own wife and daughter. John Duffy, a homicidal rapist charged with raping and killing three women in 1990, also raped his wife before they separated. Richard Baker, a serial rapist, who worked as a nightclub DJ, raped both women whom he dated and leapt on women from behind in the classic 'stranger rape' scenario (*Guardian*, May 21, 1999). We do not know how many rapists have previously raped their wives but it certainly seems likely that many have. In 1993 Heather Gordon gave evidence that her husband, who was found guilty of raping and attempting to rape two girls aged 18 and 19 in Perth, had viciously raped her some time before.[13] It is a myth that different types of men rape their wives than rape strangers.

Judges' comments

The arguments judges use for justifying myths about marital rape are worth noting. In August 1988, for example, Mr Justice Rougier sentenced a man who terrorised and raped his former lover to two years imprisonment. He justified this on the grounds that: 'I don't think it was such a shock to her as it maybe would be to other women.' The judge described the woman as 'somewhat over-emotional'. In 1990, Sir Kenneth Jupp gave a man who twice raped his ex-wife a two year suspended sentence, observing: 'This is a rare sort of rape. It is not like someone being jumped on in the street. This is within the family and does not impinge on the public' (Kennedy 1992: 121). In 1992 Mr Justice McCullough sentenced Sean Riley to three years after he had pleaded guilty to raping his wife. The judge made his views of marital rape explicit: 'If you had done this to a stranger the starting point would have been 8 years' (*Independent*, 10 April). Riley's wife had decided to leave at the time of the offence but the couple were still living together. The prosecution alleged that Riley had hit his wife and then raped her. Minutes later he had held a carving knife to her throat and raped her again. The judge did not appear to think this was life threatening and commented: 'To be raped by a stranger must be more terrifying and more long lasting in its effect.' Riley's wife Pauline was reported to have said:

> That suggests that being raped by your husband is not as awful as being raped by someone you don't know. The judge has got it wrong. Being raped by your own husband is very much worse. Here you are being violated by the man you have loved, trusted and had children with. It's unbelievably terrible and heart-breaking.
>
> (*News of the World*, 19 April 1992)

The Law Commission 1992 Report stated that 'marital rape ought to be viewed by the criminal law on the same basis as extra-marital rape' (n10 at para 3.18) since 'a number of respondents agreed that one reason why marital rape was as serious as, if not more serious than rape by a stranger was that it was an abuse of an act used to express love and an abuse of trust'. Appeal Court judges have not mentioned the possibility that marital rape may involve a breach of trust that should act as an aggravating factor in sentencing. This is in spite of breach of trust being taken into account in cases of child abuse (for example in D (1993) 14 Cr. App. R.(S.) 639). A father was convicted of rape and indecent assault on two daughters over a long period. The case was described as involving 'the gravest breach of trust imaginable' (see Rumney 1999). Even in cases of theft, breach of trust is seen as an aggravating factor, and in this respect theft is being treated more seriously than rape. For example, the Court of Appeal, in *Cox*, Lord Justice Mustill concluded: 'The rape of a former wife or mistress may have exceptional features which make it a less serious offence than otherwise it would be...'

In *R. v. Thornton*, the Court of Appeal had to decide whether to uphold a two-year sentence on a man convicted of raping a former girlfriend. Lord Chief Justice concluded:

> The way in which we view the matter is this. The mere fact that the parties have over a period of nearly two years – 20 months – been living together

and having regular sexual intercourse ... is ... a factor to which some weight can be given...

(1990, 12 Cr. App. R. (S).

Why the length of their relationship should have any relevance is not explained. The problem is that judges are equating rape with sex rather than with violence. The judiciary here are making the assumption that some kinds of rape are more akin to sex and therefore should not be subject to the same sanctions as 'real' (stranger) rape. Naffine makes the point that 'traditional legal thinking about the nature of rape and how the law should best deal with it depends on outmoded and contested images of women and their relations with men' (Naffine 1994: 741–67).

Marital rape and marital murder

At least half of all homicides are domestic. Stark and Flitcraft (1996: 130) in their literature review confirmed Lachman's 1978 conclusion that 'almost a third of all homicides take place within the immediate family, another 21 per cent in romantic triangles or lover's quarrels and 27 per cent among less intimate relatives and friends. In sum, at least half of all homicides and approximately 66 per cent of primary homicides are directly or indirectly domestic.'

In spite of this finding, Court of Appeal judges appear to fail to take into account the connection between marital rape and murder. Even when the victim has become unconscious due to strangulation, defendants are not charged with attempted murder and judges do not appear to consider that the victim's life is at risk. This is in spite of evidence that women are more likely to be killed by an ex-partner or partner than by a stranger. Giving evidence against a present or past partner is also likely to place the woman's life at risk.

Marital rape and murder are linked in a number of ways. Both tend to occur when a relationship is breaking up or shortly after the couple have separated. Ending a relationship with a violent man places a woman at particular risk for her life. Marital rape can be the final straw that leads a woman to leave a violent relationship or it can be an act of revenge on the woman for leaving. Both marital rape and murder are forms of extreme coercion fuelled by revenge at the woman daring to leave or planning to leave preceded by extreme possessiveness. Wilson *et al.* (1993) computed uxoricide rates for co-residing and estranged wives and found an increased risk immediately after separation. They found that a remarkable proportion of uxoricide victims are estranged from their killers. They draw on a number of Australian research studies: Allen (1990), for example, reported that almost half of all wives who were killed in New South Wales in the late nineteenth century were separated from their killers at the time of the murder and the proportion was even higher in the 1930s.

Ann Jones, who undertook a major American study of women who killed their partners, found that at least half of all women who leave abusers are followed and harassed or assaulted again, many of them fatally. She found that the reasons that men kill women appear to be very different from the reasons women kill men. Both cases are associated with a history of violence from the husband. In explaining why women are killed she concludes: 'it is because women leave or try to, that they are killed' (1991: 367). Women most often kill, on the other hand, when violent men simply will not quit. As one woman testified at her murder trial: 'It seemed like the more I tried to get away, the harder he beat me.' According to several studies, survivors' experiences show that up to a third of women who leave violent men suffer abuse after separation. Some of them are killed (see Radford 1993: 178).

In another US study, Angela Browne found that 90 per cent of the women subjected to violence in the family thought the abuser could or would kill them and many were convinced that they could not escape this danger by leaving. She found that some violent men searched desperately for their partners once the woman left, often spending days and nights 'stalking' her. Even if she had moved away, they frequently attempted to follow her, travelling anywhere they thought she might be. Browne concluded: 'She is theirs. She cannot leave and refuse to talk to them. They may nearly kill their mates, but they do not want to lose them' (Browne 1987: 115). Some of the women had been separated or divorced for up to two years and yet were still experiencing life threatening harassment and abuse. She concluded that many women stay in violent marriages because they believe their partner would retaliate against an attempt to leave him with further violence (see Browne 1987: 113).

Finkelhor and Yllo (1983) interviewed American women who had experienced rape by a husband or lover and concluded that wife rape is most likely to occur during or after the break up of a relationship. Diana Russell (1990) found that most of the cases that reached court involved separated couples. In only one-fifth (21 per cent) of the cases in which wife rape occurred were the couples still married.

All the cases of murder, attempted murder and manslaughter in the Crown Courts in England and Wales were monitored over a three-month period in the summer of 1995 in research undertaken for the Channel 4 documentary, 'Till death do us part'. Detailed information was collected on 113 cases. This information included the previous relationship between the killer and victim, the circumstances and details of the killing (including the weapon used, if any), whether a plea of guilty to manslaughter was accepted by the Crown Prosecution Service, defences run at sentencing hearings and trials, verdict options put to the jury at trial, outcomes and sentences. In 12 cases, verbatim transcripts of murder trials were taken. The three main findings were that domestic cases were more likely than non-domestic cases to end up with manslaughter rather than murder convictions. Pleas of manslaughter were accepted in approximately one- third of cases by the Crown Prosecution Service (CPS) so that there was no trial. The defence of 'diminished responsibility' often formed the basis for the acceptance of manslaughter pleas by the

CPS, while the defence of 'provocation' rarely did so. The severity of mental illness in cases where 'diminished responsibility' was the main defence to murder was significantly lower in domestic manslaughter cases than in non-domestic – e.g. typically depression, compared with schizophrenia in non-domestic cases. Sentences for manslaughter (60 per cent of domestic cases), whether or not the case went to trial, were substantially lower (4 years or less) than in non-domestic cases (only 12 per cent of such cases were given under 4 years). Overall 62 per cent of non-domestic cases were given life imprisonment and 40 per cent of domestic cases.

Reported wife rape and wife murder are likely to occur when the marriage is breaking down or after separation and divorce. We also know that injuries are just as serious in cases where women are attacked by their husbands, cohabitees or ex-husbands/cohabitees as where they are attacked by strangers. This association needs to be recognised and marital rape taken more seriously. We know that very few rapes are reported and that the rapes least likely to be reported are marital rapes. There are two main reasons why women do not report such attacks: they do not think they will be believed nor that they will receive support from the police and they fear retaliation from their husbands or lovers, their assailants.

Court of Appeal decisions

Court of Appeal decisions regarding marital rape since its Common Law abolition in 1991 were reviewed to investigate whether any changes had occurred. These appeal cases represent the longer sentences awarded – men receiving short prison or non-custodial sentences are unlikely to appeal in case their sentences are increased. The Criminal Justice Act 1988 Section 36, confers power on the Attorney General to refer cases to the Court of Appeal when it appears to him that a sentence imposed in the Crown Court is unduly lenient.

Of the 10 cases which reached the England and Wales Court of Appeal between 1991 and 1995, five were rejected (the sentences averaged 5.4 years) and four resulted in the reduction of the sentences which had originally averaged five years. All the cases where sentences were upheld involved aggravating features, usually the use of a weapon combined with threats to kill or injure or, in two cases, theft. In all cases the wife had either decided to separate or had already left, and there was evidence of previous violence from the husband. However in no cases were the sentences increased although the presence of such serious aggravating factors and the generally low level of sentences, indicated that the Billam Guidelines had not been followed.

In the case of R v. Guy, an estranged husband, armed with a rifle and pistol, broke into his former wife's house and threatened her shortly after their separation. He forced his penis into her mouth.[14] This was in breach of a non-molestation order she had taken out two months before in response to his violence. He pleaded guilty to rape and possessing a firearm. In upholding the sentence of 6 years the Appeal judges stated:

This was a rape of an extremely bad character. We are bound in these circumstances to put first, in order of priorities, the plight of the victim and the need for women to be protected from such behaviour, even against men to whom they have formerly been married, before other considerations.

In another case (*R* v. *Malcolm*) the husband had threatened his former partner at knife point, had stolen from her and subjected her to physical violence. His sentence of eight years was upheld.[15] The third case (*R* v. *Stephen*) involving a *cohabiting* married couple, a sentence of five years was upheld. According to the evidence, on the evening of the offence, the wife had told her husband that she was about to leave. The defendant was found guilty of rape, threatening to kill and assault occasioning actual bodily harm.[16] The fourth case (*R* v. *Henshall*) where the sentence of three years was upheld is discussed below.[17]

According to Lord Taylor, the Lord Chief Justice, upholding these sentences represented a shift in sentencing policy, in spite of the fact that they are at the lower end of the scale recommended in the Billam Guidelines. He stated:

It should not be thought that a different and lower scale of sentencing attaches automatically to rape by a husband as against that set out in *Billam*. All will depend on the circumstances of the individual case. Where the parties were cohabiting normally at the time and the husband insisted on intercourse against his wife's will, but without violence or threats, the consideration identified in *Berry*[18] and approved in *Thornton*[19] will no doubt be an important factor in reducing the level of sentencing. Where, however, the conduct is gross and does involve threats or violence, the facts of the marriage, of long cohabitation and that the defendant is no stranger will be of little significance. Clearly between these two extremes, there will be many intermediate degrees of gravity which judges will have to consider case by case.[20]

This is a strangely contradictory statement, since women are most at risk for their lives when they have decided to leave. This contrasts with the sentences given to women who have been raped by burglars and intruders. According to Billam where a man has 'broken into or otherwise gained access to a place where the victim is living the starting point in sentencing should be eight years'. However as Rumney (1999) points out, when the cases are analysed, in cases of stranger rape the average sentence is 10.7 years whereas in cases involving wives the sentence falls to 6.7 years, and in cases of relationship rape the average is only half the Billam recommended starting point at 4.1 years. Rumney concludes that 'even in cases where there are serious aggravating factors the highest sentence in any case of marital or relationship rape where the assailant has gained access to the victim's home is one of eight years and in many cases is significantly lower.'

In the fourth case reviewed here (*R* v. *Henshall*)[21] the wife attempted to withdraw the complaint but the prosecution went ahead. In spite of two guilty verdicts of rape at knife-point, Henshall was sentenced to three years. A pre-sentence report indicated that the attacks were motivated by revenge, and in view of the aggravating features – the use of a weapon, threats to kill, the fact that the man on the second occasion broke in and the protracted nature of the second incident – the sentence was not increased. In the case of *R* v. *Haywood*, a five-year sentence for rape was upheld, where the defendant had also been found guilty of stealing and dishonesty, offences which appear to be taken more seriously by the Court of Appeal.[22]

The two grounds for reducing sentences are, firstly, where the couple are living together and, secondly, where there is evidence of contact with the wife. This is usually taken to imply that the couple are considering reconciliation rather than indicating that the wife is terrified of retaliation (involving as we have seen in the Collins case, the danger of murder). In the four cases whose sentences had averaged five years, the average was reduced to 3.4 years. In the remaining case (*Hind*) a 10-year sentence was reduced to six on the grounds that the 'victim had gone a long way to forgiving the defendant' and had written to him and visited him in prison. The details were horrific. When the victim had broken off the relationship the defendant had broken into the house at midnight, tied her hands behind her, undressed her, put a pillow over her head and raped her. He had forced oral sex and put his hands round her throat and squeezed until she became unconscious.[23]

The details of the other four cases where sentences were reduced were as follows: In *R* v. *Hutchinson* a six-year sentence was reduced to five years although again, the husband had broken into the house, after an injunction had been granted to the wife who was separated. The grounds for the reduction was a report that the wife had forgiven him and had indicated in committal proceedings that she wished to withdraw the complaint.[24] Similarly, in *Maskell* the husband pleaded guilty to rape and the sentence was reduced from four to three years. The Court of Appeal stated that 'he has regular visits from his children and friends and his relationship with his wife is good'. Since they had separated some months prior to the rape as a result of the defendant's heavy drinking, this seemed to be rather unlikely and no evidence was produced in court. (At the trial, defence counsel claimed to have seen letters from her to the defendant.)[25]

In the third case of *Collier* the sentence was reduced on the grounds that the appellant had pleaded guilty and 'while this was a serious rape, a sentence of 3 years was appropriate for the offence'.[26] The Lords of Appeal stated that they had taken into consideration that the assault had been aggravated by the fact that the children had witnessed the incident, at the same time as reducing the sentence!

In the fourth case (*Brown*) the defendant was subject to an injunction, and had broken into his ex-cohabitee's house, raped and badly injured her. His six-year sentence was reduced on appeal to five years. The judge who had sentenced him described him as 'an unreconstructed chauvinist of the first order'. In reducing the sentence, the three Lord Justices argued that 'having regard to the previous sexual relationship between these parties, the absence of any injury to

Miss B and the absence of any weapon, we regard the sentence of 6 years on the rape charge as being too long'. This seems a strange argument in view of the conviction for unlawful wounding and the admission by the defence that there was no mitigation.[27] In the case of couples still cohabiting, shorter sentences appear to be the rule, with a good chance of reduction on appeal.

Why some wives resume contact

There are various reasons why women who have testified against their husbands or ex-husbands should try to retract evidence or communicate with their husbands in prison. Women who leave violent husbands are in danger for their lives – a danger which, after testifying, is intensified. Cretney and Davis' study of the significance of compellability in the prosecution of domestic assault found that women voiced their fears of retribution from their husband. One woman, when asked whether her complaint had been withdrawn because she loved her husband, replied: 'It was partly that and partly the threats he made. He was going to send people up here to sort me out and for sex and things like that. He was going to kill himself. I thought well, I don't want that to happen' (Cretney and Davis 1997: 86). Yet the threat to their lives is not taken seriously by the courts. Radford (1993) points out that legal provisions for battered women such as the Domestic Violence and Matrimonial Proceedings Act 1976 and the Domestic Proceedings and Magistrates' Courts Act 1978 are not often enforced and do not guarantee protection for wives.

Secondly, there is a strong tendency for women to minimise the threat to their lives in order to cope with fear. This is analogous to the behaviour of victims of disaster and war (see also Symonds 1979). Like battered women, victims of disasters experience reactions of shock, denial, disbelief, and fear as well as withdrawal and confusion. Such denial leads to a delay in defining the situation accurately, and leads them to respond with dazed or apathetic behaviour (Browne 1987: 123). Later reactions include suggestibility and dependence where victims may become euphoric and convince themselves that they can rebuild their lives and somehow everything will be alright and that they will wake up and find it was all a horrible dream. Research on victims of rape in particular indicates that they experience acute feelings of powerlessness, vulnerability, loss of control and self blame (see Burgess and Holmstrom 1974; Koss and Harvey 1991).

Browne (1987: 125) also draws parallels between the principles of brainwashing used on prisoners of war and experiences of women in battering relationships. Key ingredients include:

> isolation of the victim from outside contacts and sources of help, humiliation and degradation followed by acts of kindness coupled with the threat of a return to the degraded state if some type of compliance is not obtained. Over time the victims of such treatment become apathetic, sometimes react with despair, and may finally totally submit.

Such reactions, combined with the real threat that their husbands may retaliate on release, explain why wives may agree to communicate with their ex-husbands, but such explanations do not appear to be introduced in court.

Effect of the Children Act (1989)

Recent government concern to encourage contact between fathers and children of divorced or separated women puts wives of violent husbands at even greater risk. The Children Act 1989 provides greater rights for fathers and facilitates access to female ex-partners by men who have been violent towards them. According to Hester and Radford (1996) professionals working in this area of family law are not taking male violence sufficiently seriously. It is not understood that men may use the excuse of wanting contact with children to locate their wives and harm or even kill them. This occurred in Birmingham, in January 1996, when a woman living in a refuge was knifed to death by her husband in a frenzied attack. After the stabbing, their four other children, whom the father had been looking after, were all found dead in his flat (*The Times*, 22 January 1996). In another case, in June 1999, Paul Russell admitted killing his ex-wife whom he had separated from two years before. After separating she had given birth to a son, to whom initially Russell had been given access. After further violence he had been banned from her home but had managed to trace her through the courts (*Guardian*, June 10, 1999).

Conclusion

The change in judicial opinion reflected in *R* v. *R* does not appear to have infiltrated the Court of Appeal. The vestiges of patriarchal rights lead judges to take the view that marital rape is less serious than rape by a stranger or acquaintance on the grounds that a husband has certain sexual rights over his wife. Although marital rape is now recognised as a criminal offence, it is treated less seriously than rape by a stranger or acquaintance. It appears from this chapter, based only on the records of cases reaching the Court of Appeal between 1991 and 1995, that the main ground for allowing appeals is evidence that there has been some contact, however minimal, between the husband and wife. The threat of retaliation is rarely entertained as an explanation for why victims should respond to requests to communicate with their ex-husbands. The threat to women's lives is still not recognised by the courts in allowing access to children, which can be an excuse for tracing the wives. This can place both their wives and children at risk.

Notes

1 See *Guardian*, January 31, 1996, 'Mother in fear defies court order on children'.
2 In Sir Matthew Hale (1736) *History of the Pleas of the Crown*. Vol. 1 Professional Books LV111 629.
3 Under the law the wife could not own property or enter contracts as marriage created a 'unity' in which the husband was supreme and the wife invisible.

4 *R* v. *Miller* (1954) 2 All ER, 448, 449.
5 According to Jennifer Temkin, speaking on Radio 4's *Woman's Hour* in 1995, the main reason why this was not enforced was because the legal definition of cohabitation was so contentious that it would have led to cases flooding to the Court of Appeal. A change in the law was therefore rejected by a narrow majority.
6 (1991) 2 All ER B 7 al 266.
7 The Criminal Justice and Public Order Act (1994) widened the definition to include male rape (penetration of the anus).
8 S1 (2) Sexual Offences (Amendment) Act 1976.
9 *R* v. *Billam* (1986) 1 All ER 986.
10 *R* v. *Billam* 1986 82 Cr. App. R 347.
11 In some courts non-custodial sentences were still awarded, which were always probation or suspended prison sentences, never discharges or fines. Robertshaw considered 655 sentences for rape awarded by courts between 1991–2. He found that almost 70 per cent of sentences passed by courts on the western circuit (which covers Truro, Exeter, Bristol and Winchester courts) were for less than 5 years.
12 His research was not well received. One leading member of the legal profession inaccurately described his research as flawed, presumably in order to discredit it.
13 *The Sun*, April 28, 1993, 'I shopped my rapist husband'.
14 (1993) Cr. App. R. (S) 642 January 28.
15 (1994) Cr. App. R. (S.) May 26.
16 (1992) Cr. App. R. (S) July 30.
17 (1994) Cr. App. R. (S) 388 July 28.
18 (1988) 10 Cr. App. R. (S.).
19 (1990) 12 Cr. App. R. (S.).
20 W (1992) 12 Cr. App. R. (S.).
21 (1994) Cr. App. R. (S) 388 July 28.
22 (1991) Cr. App. R. (S) June 28.
23 Heard in May 1993.
24 (1993) Cr. App. R. (S) 718.
25 (1991) Cr. App. R. (S) 434.
26 (1991) Cr. App. R. (S) 33 April 23.
27 (1992) Cr. App. R. (S) November 17.

References

Allen, J. (1990) *Sex and Secrets, Crimes Involving Australian Women Since 1880*, Oxford: University Press.

Browne, A. (1987) *When Battered Women Kill*, New York: Free Press.

Brownmiller, S. (1976) *Against Our Will: Men, Women and Rape*, Harmondsworth: Penguin.

Burgess, A. and Holmstrom, L. (1974) 'Rape Trauma Syndrome', *American Journal of Psychiatry*, 131, 9.

Clark, A. (1987) *Women's Silence, Men's Violence: Sexual Assault in England 1770–1845*, London: Pandora.

Cretney, A. and Davis, G. (1997) 'The significance of compellability in the prosecution of domestic assault', *British Journal of Criminology*, Vol. 37, No. 1, Winter.

Dispatches (1994) 'Getting Away with Rape', *First Frame*, Channel 4, 6 February.

Finkelhor, D. and Yllo, K. (1983) *The Dark Side of Families*, London: Sage.

Foley, M. (1994) 'Professionalising the response to rape', in Lupton, C. and Gillespie, T. (eds) *Working with Violence*, London: Macmillan. p. 44.

Gregory, J. and Lees, S. (1996) 'Attrition in Rape and Sexual Assault Cases', *British Journal of Criminology*, Vol. 36, No 1, pp. 1–18.

Gregory, J. and Lees, S. (1999) *Policing Sexual Assault*, London: Routledge.

Hale, Matthew (1736) *History of the Pleas of the Crown*, Vol. I Professional Books LVIII 629.

Harris, J. and Grace, S. (1999) *A Question of Evidence? Investigating and Prosecuting Rape in the 1990s*, Home Office Research Study 196.

Hester, M. and Radford, J. (1996) 'Contradictions and compromises: the impact of the Children's Act', in Hester, M., Kelly, L. and Radford, J. (eds) *Women, Violence and Male Power*, Buckingham, UK: Open University Press.

Jones, A. (1991) *Women Who Kill*, London: Victor Gollancz.

Katz, B. (1991) 'The psychological impact of stranger versus nonstranger rape on victims' recovery' in Parrot, A. and Bechhofer, L. (eds) *Acquaintance Rape: The Hidden Crime*, New York: John Wiley, pp. 251–69.

Kennedy, H. (1992) *Eve was Framed: Women and British Justice*, London: Chatto and Windus.

Koss, M. and Harvey, M. (1991) *The Rape Victim: Clinical and Community Interventions*, London: Sage.

Law Commission (1992) '*Criminal Law Rape Within Marriage*', Law Commission No. 205, London: HMSO.

Lees, S. (1996) *Carnal Knowledge: Rape on Trial*, London: Hamish Hamilton.

Lees, S. (1997) *Ruling Passions: Sexual Violence, Reputation and the Law*, Buckingham, UK: Open University Press.

Naffine, N. (1994) 'Possession: erotic love in the law of rape', in *Modern Law Review*, 1994 MLR 57:1 Jan, London: Blackwell Publishers.

Painter, K. (1991) *Wife, Rape, Marriage and the Law*: University of Manchester.

Radford, L. (1993) 'Pleading for time: justice for battered women who kill', in Birch, H. (ed.) *Moving Targets*, London: Virago.

Robertshaw, P. (1994) 'Sentencing rapists: first tier courts in 1991–92', *Criminal Law Review*, pp. 343–5.

Rumney, P. (1999) 'When rape isn't rape: sentencing in cases of marital and relationship rape', *Oxford Journal Of Legal Studies, Vol 2*.

Russell, D. (1990) *Rape in Marriage*, Indianapolis: Indiana University Press.

Scutt, J. (1993) 'Women and Law', in Kramarae, C. and Spender, D. (eds) *The Knowledge of Explosion*, London: Harvester Wheatsheaf.

Smart, C. (1995) *Law, Crime and Sexuality: Essays in Feminism*, London: Routledge.

Stark, E. and Flitcraft, A. (1996) *Women at Risk*, London: Sage.

Symonds, A. (1979) 'Violence against women: The myth of masochism', *American Journal of Psychotherapy*, 33: 161–73.

Temkin, J. (1997) 'A singular victory', *Guardian*, 11.9.1997.

Wilson, M., Daly, M. and Wright, C. (1993) 'Uxoricide in Canada: demographic risk patterns', *Violence and Victims*, 8: 1, pp. 3–60.

Part II

Children's experiences of violence in the home

5 Children's and mothers' experiences of support and protection following domestic violence

Caroline McGee

Introduction

This chapter will discuss a qualitative research study that sought to elicit the views of children and their mothers about their experiences of domestic violence, and services to support and protect children in this situation. The focus throughout the study was very much on directly hearing children's views. Although children may be the focus of research, research is rarely child-focused. Mothers or other significant adults are usually asked for their views of the children's perceptions of domestic violence and its impact. Children themselves are much less frequently involved directly. In recent years in the UK there has been a growing research interest in children and domestic violence (see Chapter 6). However, very little of this research has addressed the issue of how to best support and protect children experiencing domestic violence. This study, then, was undertaken in order to address the need to hear directly from children and young people themselves and to raise awareness of how services to support and protect children and mothers who have experienced domestic violence can be improved.

This chapter will briefly describe the method used in this study before going on to briefly explore the relationship between child protection and domestic violence. Children's experiences of violence as described by the children and their mothers will be outlined and an overview of the role of social services, housing, health, education and the police as perceived by domestic violence survivors will be presented. Finally, the chapter will consider children's and mothers' views of the best way to meet their needs for support and protection.

Method

The study used an opt-in procedure for recruiting mothers and children to take part in the research. This meant that participants had to make an active decision to become involved rather than the researcher obtaining lists of names and addresses from various agencies involved with the family and then making contact. Using the opt-in approach meant that women and children were free to decide whether or not to take part in the research once they had seen publicity or received information about it. In addition, this approach did not place women and children at risk by uninvited contact which may have alerted the perpetrator to the fact that the woman and children had sought help from outside agencies.

Drawing on the author's practice knowledge, gained working with children in Local Authority care and with Women's Aid, and with reference to the available literature in this area, semi-structured interview schedules were designed for mothers and children/young people. These interview tools were designed to be suitable for three age groups of children: 5–8-year-olds, 8–11-year-olds and teenagers. Two forms were also designed to be completed by the interviewer with mothers or with older children. One collected demographic information and the other detailed allegations of child abuse or neglect. Children were not asked about specific incidences of abuse they had witnessed or experienced for two reasons. Firstly, the focus of the study was on support services for children, and secondly in a one-off interview it could be distressing for the child to concentrate on recalling numerous incidents of violence, particularly if support services are not in place to support that child.

At the end of the interview each child was asked if there was anything they wanted to add. This was important in that it allowed the child more control over the kinds of things they wanted to tell the interviewer. It also meant that the child was not left with unmet expectations about being able to express her/his view of her/his experiences. At times it was evident that when the child's mother had discussed the possibility of taking part in the research the child had decided prior to the interview which aspects of their experience they wanted to describe to the interviewer. Without the last question, children would often have been disappointed. Children frequently chose to detail particular incidences of violence in response to the last question and for these children it was important that they could take the opportunity to do that without a request or pressure from the interviewer to do so.

Fifty-four children and 47 mothers took part in the research. Mothers and children were contacted in a variety of ways using publicity mail-outs to relevant organisations, direct media publicity, and approaches from workers in statutory (social services) and voluntary groups (refuges, social care and counselling agencies).

Domestic violence as a child protection issue

Research has addressed the impact on children of witnessing violence to their mother (see Morley and Mullender 1994 and McGee 1997 for overviews, also Chapters 6 and 7). Peled and Davis (1995) report that at least 18 studies to date have measured the effects of witnessing violence on children's behavioural problems and adjustment. Some researchers have attempted to isolate the particular cause of children's behavioural and emotional difficulties (e.g. Jaffe *et al.* 1990) and conclude that the impact of witnessing the violence alone is sufficient to cause the children's disturbance (Silvern and Kaersvang 1989).

While few would disagree that witnessing the assault of their mother is a very disturbing experience, it is important to address the entirety of children's experiences and not focus on particular incidents of physical violence, which are often extreme. It is extremely important that recognition is made of the on-going controlling behaviour that children and women are subjected to as part of their everyday life. This is particularly so when children may not, in fact, witness the direct physical assaults on their mother but will be very aware of other forms of abuse. For example, a teenage girl interviewed in this study said:

> Yeah if she had visitors round he used to be really paranoid about her, about him being talked about all the time by anybody, even if she was on the phone he would think that. He even used to tape our phone calls, have a tape hidden, to see if he was being talked about by her friends, and in the end her friends, even family, stopped coming round because he was so para-noid about it.

Although the concept of the Power and Control wheel (see Appendix 2), as described and used by the Domestic Abuse Intervention Project in Duluth Minnesota (Pence 1987, see Chapter 14) is becoming ever more widely adopted in Britain as a framework for understanding domestic violence, the issues of power and control as used by the abusive man remain a difficult area for people generally to understand. This is often reflected in the attitude that if a woman is not obviously marked or bruised then 'it can't be too bad' or 'at least he doesn't hit her'. Similarly, in Britain, as in Canada and the United States (Peled 1993) children who do not display obvious physical signs of abuse are not generally prioritised by child protection agencies. Children experiencing domestic viol-ence, are exposed to a variety of abusive behaviours and it is crucial that the focus both in research and in practice does not become too narrow in favour of physical abuse, particularly extreme physical violence.

In addition to witnessing the abuse of their mother, children may be directly abused themselves. In a review of studies, Hughes (1992) found correlations of 40–60 per cent between child abuse and domestic violence. Recent UK child protection research has clearly found domestic violence to be linked with the abuse of children (e.g. Cleaver and Freeman 1995; Farmer and Owen 1995; Gibbons *et al.* 1995; Brandon and Lewis 1996). The evidence is compelling enough for us to consistently ask two questions: When there is child abuse is there also domestic violence present in this family? And when there is domestic violence are the children being abused?

Children's experiences of violence

Children interviewed in this study have described witnessing the violence by being physically present when it happened, as this six-year-old boy described:

> I remember when there was fighting. When daddy had the chair in his hand and when I run over by to the chair and my mum was sort of trying to

defend herself. That's all. And I was running around hiding over there by the big chair what was there before.

Young children particularly will try to establish a cause-effect relationship in the violence. For example, one mother reported:

Yeah when he was about five he started asking things like, 'Why did daddy hit you mummy?' ... he asked 'Why did daddy go? Why did daddy always want to hurt you, mummy?' I said I don't know, daddy has problems and he would just be very loving towards me after that. He would be very comforting and telling me how much he loves me.

Children associate physical punishment with bad behaviour and they cannot understand why their mother should be treated in this way. This may also represent children grappling with an understanding of the unequal power relationship that exists in domestic violence. In sibling or peer fights (excluding sibling abuse and bullying), there is some level of equality or mutuality which is obviously not present in domestic abuse. Thus, it is very confusing for a child to see their mother being hurt in this way. Children may not be present but witness the outcome of the violence, including damaged possessions or the effects on their mother as the following quote illustrates:

Cause like she wasn't eating because of this and I knew that if we went away things would get better. When she came back she'd put on some weight and she looked better, even though she hadn't eaten a lot.

Children commonly overhear the violence and are very afraid, highlighting the fact that children do not have to directly witness the violence to be (sometimes profoundly) disturbed by it. One 19-year-old girl discussed how powerless it made her feel to overhear the violence and not be able to protect her mother:

We used to be up in bed and we used to hear them arguing all the time, fighting and we could hear her crying. It was really horrible. . . . I tried to block it out, like I put the cover over my head, but even then I kept hearing it. There was nothing I could do about it.

Children frequently talk about their powerlessness in the situation as one of the worst aspects of their experience. There may be issues for children later about revenge fantasies but at the time of a physical attack on their mother they often try to redress their feelings of loss of control and power by wanting to stay in the room. They report feeling very much that they needed to see what was happening in order to reassure themselves that their mother was not being killed. For them, hearing the violence but not being able to see what was happening was more terrifying. This point of view contrasts with the adult view that will seek to protect children by removing them from the scene of such violence.

Research has indicated that disagreements about children may be used by the abuser to precipitate a violent row (e.g. Tang 1994). One mother interviewed discussed how the violence worsened as her son got older:

> As Paul got bigger the problems got bigger in that Paul was able then to answer his dad back and that would spark him off. And he'd smack Paul. . . . I tried to stop him but all that would happen was that then I'd get thumped.

It is not uncommon for children and young people to believe that they are to blame for the abuse of the woman, as evidenced by this young boy's interview:

> When like if we'd do something bad, like we didn't take care of our trainers or our clothes that he'd bought us, he'd take it out on her.

This belief can make children feel very guilty and sometimes has very pronounced effects on their behaviour as they try to deflect or defuse the violence by not doing anything to anger the abuser. Unfortunately they often find that there is no one standard of behaviour that guarantees safety as the rules change from day to day.

The abusive man may try to draw the child in to the abuse of the woman, often using contact visits with the child to harass the woman or to send abusive messages back to her. One mother described how her ex-partner used her son in this way:

> And he said to him, 'Your mother is sad, she's a sad, dopey, slag, whore'. I mean he's eight and he has to listen to all that sort of thing about me.

(See Hester and Radford 1996 for an overview of issues surrounding contact, also see Chapters 6 and 7).

In the present study, children have described a variety of abusive behaviours directed at themselves and, for many, this behaviour is coupled with threats:

> Well he always used to say to me that, he goes, 'It don't matter if I kill you I'd only get ten years anyway, and I'll only do half of that. That's five.' That's what he used to say, 'It's no big thing, I've been inside before.' So it's like he's not bothered about getting the consequences.

One 16-year-old described part of the emotional abuse she was subjected to by her step-father:

> Well I wanted to live with my mum ... because I wasn't happy and my mum knew that because I used to get really upset every time I had to leave her but there was nothing I could do about it. My dad kept telling me that she didn't want me to live with her and everything.

This girl had also been told by her father that her mother had left because she did not love the children any more. At the time the children did not know that their mother had, in fact, been locked out of the home and was doing all she could to have the children returned to her care.

As mentioned earlier, it is often not the specific acts of violence that stand out in children's memories but the fear, intimidation and control that were part of their everyday lives, as this 16-year-old describes:

> me and Paul [brother] had to stay in our bedrooms all the time. Paul wasn't allowed to go to the toilet. We used to get kicked outside. We was afraid to move basically in case he got violent.

A mother described how the abuser controlled the children in this way:

> he would not allow them toys, he put all their toys on top of cupboards, they weren't allowed in the sitting room when he was in there, our house was very quiet, em there was no noise from the children . . . she [daughter] never had a friend around, she never had a birthday to celebrate

It is not unusual for mothers to report that once they and the children are no longer living with the abuser that the children's behaviour becomes uncontrollable for a short while. Given the type and number of restrictions they have lived with before, it is not surprising that, once free of them, children will want to test this new-found freedom to the limit. For most children this is a temporary time of testing and we should not look to such behaviour as evidence of dysfunction but as an important part of children making sense of their experiences.

Responses to domestic violence

Women and children experiencing domestic violence will have contact with a number of agencies. However, discussion of agency responses to domestic violence tends to centre almost exclusively on those of the police, social services, housing and refuges. While these agencies may be seen to be the key players, it is a situation created more by a tradition of responding than an examination of the actual needs of women and particularly children. By focusing on those agencies that women and children may turn to in times of crises, other agencies who could offer long-term or proactive support are not drawn into the frame.

Social services

A consistent finding of research is that women are very afraid that if social workers become aware of the domestic violence they will remove the children (e.g. McWilliams and McKiernan 1993) and the present study also uncovered this fear. The threat of having the children removed may sometimes be exploited by the abusive man as another form of control over the woman:

I came home with Paul when he was a few days old, I'd been indoors half an hour when there was a row ... he threatened to call social services to say that I was an unfit mother. In fact he picked up the phone and pretended to dial the number, pretending he was speaking to somebody and was saying I was an unfit mother ... I had been a mum less than a week.

Another way this fear is exploited by the abusive man is to make an allegation of child abuse against the woman when she has ended the relationship. A mother's fears about having her children removed are rooted solely in the domestic violence, not in the mother's treatment or care of the children. Ironically the perpetrator of the domestic violence does not have this fear of social workers and often appears to be confident that he can convince social services of the mother's failing as a parent based solely on the fact that she is experiencing domestic violence:

The one thing he held on me was he was going to take my children away from me and I had this sort of ... I had a lot of fear, a lot of anxiety about a lot of things and I really felt that he would get them to believe things about me. So I felt I had to be seen to be very strong and very controlled and not ... and I thought that if they found out that I was taking anti-depressants that would be the end of it, you know? They'd think I was a dreadfully unstable mother and you know that, that they'd take them away and give them to him.

Research suggests that it is not just mothers who have this fear. A study carried out by NCH (1994) found that young people may also fear that social workers will remove them if they tell anybody about the violence at home. There are particular issues for women and children from ethnic minorities in having contact with social services especially in relation to fearing negative consequences (Clark 1994). Bernard (1997) points out that black mothers' fears of a heavy-handed response from professionals is not based on groundless paranoia, as research indicates an over-representation of black, particularly Afro-Caribbean children in the public care system.

A mother's contact with social workers will not necessarily be straightforward and the mother's views about the contact may progress through many stages, from feeling threatened initially to being relieved that the problem is being recognised, to feeling positive about the contact. Mothers interviewed in this study have emphasised that they need more information about the role of social services. They need to know how social services can help them in a supportive way, rather than fearing the policing role of the social worker. If contact or residency is being disputed, or the child is involved in an alleged child abuse investigation, mothers need to be given information about the process. This lack of information about the social work role, coupled with women's fears of losing their children, inhibits a lot of women not just from seeking help from social services but of utilising the support they are offered:

I suppose because nobody was there to tell me what the situation was, nobody was there to explain that ... how it all worked. I didn't get ... I didn't get a lot of support from my solicitor who just said, 'It's unlikely this man will get custody'. I also had nowhere to live and my solicitor at the time had said, 'Oh well it's not in your best interests if you're in the refuge, if you haven't got anywhere to live.' And even just an inkling that he might get custody was enough to make me really panic. So I felt that I couldn't be vulnerable or even that, you know, tell anybody that I felt vulnerable at all.

A mother's dissatisfaction with social workers generally takes one of two forms:

- the fear of a heavy-handed response, particularly removing the children; or
- not providing enough support.

In both cases, there was the feeling that the domestic violence was not taken into account.

On the other, hand what mothers really appreciated about social work support was that the domestic violence was taken seriously and that both the mothers' and the children's needs were addressed. One very positive example of social work was when children were actually placed in a children's home for a short period to give their step-mother some respite. The children had been prepared over a long period by the social worker for the possibility of going to stay in the children's home and were happy with the arrangement when the time came:

Yeah she [the social worker] said that we might have to go away for a while, that's what she kept saying to us but we didn't really think about it. But when it did come, it was all right, when we did have to go, it was good ... yeah, we had a lot of fun! Got pocket money, ten pounds each. It was good.

Children appreciate a social work response that emphasises empathy and allows them to work at their own pace. One teenager interviewed spoke of her social worker's sensitivity around the sexual abuse the girl had been subjected to by her father:

But like when I started seeing the social worker she wouldn't always, she wouldn't talk about that straight away, like she would talk about everything, she would ask how things are going and ask me what was happening and things. And like after a while, it all built my trust up sort of thing, so when things did come up I found that I could talk to her about them more easily.

Children also particularly value being kept informed of what is happening if they are involved in a child abuse investigation, as one teenage girl said:

Well when I was taken away from my dad, I think I should have been told by social services or the police, one of them, what was going to happen because I didn't know anything and I should have been told.

Jones (1989) and Mullender (1996) both raise concerns about social work training in relation to domestic violence, particularly around the focus on family therapy which may overlook or minimise the violence. Individual worker's attitudes and value systems are crucial (Lloyd 1995) and initial and on-going training programmes are very important in raising awareness about the issues. O'Hara (1994) has identified four key areas in the development of effective professional practice in child protection work, which involve supporting the mother, consulting the child, confronting the violent man and developing strategies to protect workers as well as children and women from violence.

Housing

Hague and Malos (1994) have addressed issues of homelessness because of domestic violence and highlighted the impact on women and children. Moving to a refuge or a new home inevitably causes upheaval and confusion for children. However, it can also be a very positive experience. A young girl who had gone with her mother to refuges on a number of occasions described how it felt for her:

> They were brilliant ... I used to really like it because I was away from there [the violence at home] and I liked having other children, there was other children in there and we'd sit and talk about it and I'd say, 'Oh my god, does your dad do that as well? Oh so did mine.'

According to Clark (1994) some housing authorities seem to believe that black women 'borrow' children to get housing. Imam (1994) points out that for Asian and other black women and children, the situation is complicated further by a limited choice of safe areas for rehousing, where they can be safe not only from the abusive man but also from racism.

In January 1997, the Housing Act 1996 came into effect. This Act gives local authorities a temporary but renewable two-year duty to house certain applicants including women and children escaping domestic violence. Another major change of the Act is to broaden the definition of homelessness for women experiencing domestic violence. Previously, housing legislation only recognised violence or the threat of violence from people living in the home whereas the new Act defines domestic violence as violence or threats of violence from a person who is associated with the person under threat. Obviously the implications of the new housing legislation coupled with the introduction of Part IV of the Family Law Act 1996, in October 1997, will soon become apparent as women and children continue to seek protection from violence.

Health

Studies have found that health professionals are more likely to have contact with women and children experiencing domestic violence than any other professional group (Casey 1989; Pahl 1995). Despite this, the evidence suggests that health service professionals very often fail to help them (McWilliams and McKiernan 1993; Pahl 1995). In addition, Hague *et al.* (1995) found that health service providers and practitioners tend to be under-represented on domestic violence fora and inter-agency initiatives.

In the current study, where women and children were not happy with the response they received from health professionals, it was usually because of a refusal to acknowledge the violence or what the woman was saying about it. One woman finally plucked up the courage to seek help when she was pregnant because she was worried about the safety of her unborn child:

> I had spoken to my GP saying, 'Look I'm in this situation, what can I do?' My doctor turned round to me and said, 'I don't want to hear this. I'm going to pretend you didn't say that.' And I thought, well what the hell do I do?

It was many years later before this woman was able to seek help again, by which point her child was experiencing behavioural difficulties due, the mother believed, solely to the domestic violence.

Other responses received from doctors clearly indicated that they felt that supporting women experiencing domestic violence was outside their role or expertise:

> I went to the GP . . . But me nerves were shattered, I mean I was under a lot of stress even then so . . . em, yeah. But no he didn't seem to be able to . . . he just said, 'Well what do you expect me to do?'

One woman who was raped by her partner was very upset by the insensitive response she received from her doctor:

> I went to see my GP to get a sick certificate, and I had to tell him what had happened and I was, I mean I know I was just shaking, I couldn't speak, I was crying and that was the stage where I was at. And I told him I'd been raped and whatever and this and I was having difficulty and I couldn't go back to work. And he said, 'What did he do that for?' And I . . . I just remember thinking, I mean I just got more appalled by it afterwards that he, 'What did he do that for?' And felt like saying, 'Well you tell me, you're a man.' How am I supposed to know? Why are you asking me, why am I responsible for what he did?

A teenager interviewed was very pleased with the support she received from her family doctor. She felt that his concern each time she visited showed that he

really cared about how she was. He also picked up on the physical manifestations of her distress because of the violence she was witnessing and experiencing
and referred her to other agencies for counselling and support but continued to
be interested in her welfare:

> Because I go to see the same doctor and every time I go it would be like oh
> how are you doing, how are things going, and like it was like he was taking
> a real interest kind of thing. So he was good.

Although all of the women in the study had contact with health visitors at
some point, the majority did not disclose the violence they were suffering. The
main reason for this was that they were scared that they would be seen as unable
to cope and therefore possibly lose their children:

> I didn't go into details because I was frightened of the consequences to be
> honest, I was really frightened of him. You know I was thinking, 'God if
> these people know, what's going to happen?' They might even think I was
> an unfit mother and they'd take them off me and I'd be watched by them. I
> was really paranoid, really badly paranoid.

Similar to the situation with social services, women report that this fear of
health visitors becoming involved in removing the children could be deliberately manipulated by the abuser to prevent the woman seeking help for the
violence:

> They're going to think I'm a terrible mother, they're going to think I can't
> cope, so what he's saying is going to come to pass. You know, they are going
> to take them away from me.

Women interviewed in this study often said that there were times when they
should have attended hospital for injuries but did not. They also reported that
when they did go the accident and emergency department staff were willing to
accept that the injuries were accidental even when conflicting statements were
being made by the woman and her partner:

> They never, never acknowledged ... I mean the hospital when, when I
> went down the stairs they asked me once I think, what happened and that
> was it. They didn't push it at all.

Given that health service workers may be the first or most accessible contact for
women and children experiencing domestic violence, it is crucial that domestic
violence is highlighted as a training issue and that procedures are developed to
respond effectively in practice. A recent study (Frost 1997) found that a lack of
initial and subsequent training for health visitors around domestic violence
increased the vulnerability of health visitors and clients.

Education

Those working in education are arguably the best placed to help children experiencing domestic violence as they not only have a lot of contact with the children but also can provide support in a familiar setting that the child can easily access. Unfortunately educators are not usually among the key players when it comes to meeting the needs of children who have experienced domestic violence. In order to help specific children who have suffered domestic violence, it is important that the issues are raised in a general way with all children as part of the curriculum. There is a massive silence in schools surrounding domestic violence generally; it is a non-issue. Children should not be expected to be able to disclose their own painful experiences when domestic violence is not acknowledged at all within the school. Mothers and young people interviewed referred to other issues such as bullying or drug abuse being discussed in schools but no mention ever being made of domestic violence:

> (They) sort of tell people, but there isn't ... there is nothing, there's no children's books on it. They don't cover it ... they cover asthma, they cover everything else but no one wants to really touch it [domestic violence], not really.

Mothers reporting a positive response from schools emphasised how the school worked with their child's behavioural or learning difficulties by understanding the domestic violence as the precipitating factor in these difficulties. Children who were happy with the response they received from their teachers talked in terms of the teacher being available to speak to the child when the child needs it and making it clear that the child can approach them at any time. What seems to be often crucial in developing this relationship is that the teacher initially approaches the child and acknowledges that there may be something wrong at home. In these instances, once the teacher has allowed the child to break the silence, the child will happily initiate discussions of their experiences and feelings at later points.

Children, even at an early age, are aware of the stigma of domestic violence, and a number of children talked about not telling anyone in school (both staff and pupils) about the domestic violence because they did not want to be stigmatised. Mothers also were fearful that their children would be stigmatised by the school if they knew:

> it's still society's assumptions about me as a woman being responsible for staying in the relationship and ultimately responsible for any abuse that was inflicted on my children. Rather than him being the person who did it all and being responsible ... they won't make any judgements about him, I can just imagine it ... or they'll be looking at my children in that way. And I think that at school 'cause as a microcosm of everything else, there will be people with those values in it. And I've had a sort of mixed response. So very few people know.

Another reason children do not tell anyone at school about the domestic violence is that they enjoy school and want to keep it separate from the bad things that are happening at home:

> You got to school, that was like my second life, that was where I was happy. So to bring it into school, to bring it into school is like you're overloading the two.

Some children talked about using the school or school work as an escape from the violence:

> But I liked being at school rather than home, most kids don't like being at school but I loved being at school just to get away from it. I wanted to be at school all the time. And I used to make myself have detention so I could stay later, so I would miss the last bus.

What is generally missing from children's accounts is evidence of an active response from teachers in terms of supporting the child. For example, it did not seem to be common practice to refer the child to another agency or offer any help on self-protection.

Police

Traditionally women have often not involved the police in domestic violence because they felt that the police would not be interested. McWilliams and McKiernan (1993) found that only 26 per cent of women who had contact with the police found them to be helpful, usually because they removed the abuser.

Involving the police is a difficult decision for women, not least because of the fear that contacting the police may make things worse by angering the abuser. Making the decision to involve the police is often accompanied by feelings that the woman cannot or will not take any more abuse:

> And when I saw the state of myself in the morning I just phoned the police. I just couldn't believe it, I mean I was just black and blue from head to foot. I thought, 'No, you're not going to do it to me anymore.' And . . . well basically, they arrested him.

Fear that the abuser will hurt the children is commonly a trigger for women involving the police:

> I didn't get the police involved up until that point but he was frightening me because if he was still going to go and do it when the babies were born I was thinking, 'Oh God you know, what am I doing?' You see on the news all the time people doing things to babies, and I was thinking, 'Oh Jesus.' And that would frighten me even more that he was going to hurt them.

One factor inhibiting women from contacting the police, and one which adds to their fear, is that they are unsure exactly what the police can do to protect them:

> As I say, I didn't realise that they sort of had the powers they had to keep him away from me.

If a woman is not confident that the police can actually keep the abuser away from her and her children, it is unlikely she will take the risk of inflaming the situation by contacting them in the first place:

> I think you think to yourself, 'What's the point of involving them?' Well I didn't even know there was a domestic violence unit, I didn't even know they existed, I didn't have a clue.

Women interviewed reported that they felt that police would not be interested and would treat the violence as 'just a domestic'. When they then received a positive response from the police, women were at times amazed at how support-ive they could be:

> I mean I didn't think the police would be interested. I've got to be honest, I was totally gobsmacked at their reaction. I couldn't believe it.

When involving the police, women want to be taken seriously and have domestic violence treated as a crime. They want to be offered protection under the law so that they and their children are not put at risk. While police ser-vices may establish procedures for dealing with domestic violence, it is still the approach of individual officers that is the most crucial aspect of the response. If an officer treats the call-out as 'just a domestic' then not only are the woman and children not going to be protected, but it is likely that they are at increased risk following the police visit. While attitudinal change may not be possible, it is possible to establish a procedure for responding to instances of domestic violence which is so comprehensive it by-passes individual's attitudes.

Children and young people have a very strong sense of fairness and can feel wronged if they do not see justice being done:

> The next thing I knew, he hadn't been arrested or anything, he was still free back up in his chalet, we were the ones who had to move because I knew mum couldn't stay there anymore. And we had nowhere to go, we ended up staying at a friend's but I don't think that was right at all, no.

Women who fear deportation will not usually involve the police, fearing that, if they do, they will be deported automatically. This fear can be manipulated by the abuser by deliberately giving the woman false information regarding her status so that she does not report him to the police. One woman interviewed described how her partner tried to use her immigration status against her when he was being arrested and this fear prevented her from making a statement against him:

> I was just scared of my status really, what would happen to me and my child. And . . . in terms of the immigration rules and the fact that we'd just got married and this started happening, you know, would they still consider this a valid marriage?

Support wanted

For themselves, mothers interviewed in this study wanted three main things:

1 Information to be freely available about sources of support for those experiencing domestic violence;
2 Counselling which is easily accessible;
3 Help for mothers in supporting the children to deal with their experiences.

Mothers worry a lot about the impact of the domestic violence on their children, particularly the possible long-term impacts, and need advice on how to deal with that:

> I'd like to know how it would affect her and what I can do. I don't even know how to talk to her about it, because I don't know whether talking to her would be the right or the wrong thing to do, because I don't want to lead her in to anything, thinking about things she hadn't thought about maybe and going too far. So I'd sort of need maybe professional help on that.

Mothers were very clear that there is nothing available to support children who witness domestic violence unless they are involved in a child protection investigation and receive social work support. Mothers all stressed that they wanted counselling for their children to help them deal with their experiences.

What support do children want?

The majority of children interviewed have said that they want to talk to other children about the domestic violence. They feel that it is easier for children to talk to other children for two main reasons: adults talk differently to children, and adults think differently to children, as this young girl explained:

> I think because adults think differently to children so it's easier for children to talk to people like friends or maybe cousins or brothers and sisters, but hard to talk to adults because their minds are different in a way.

In addition, children and young people stressed that support needs to be accessible to children, they are unable to go searching for support services:

> But there should be somebody there who they can ring, who can actually come out and see them, somebody who is connected with the police or social services, somebody who can meet them privately because otherwise they've got no one to turn to, have they?

Children also said that they wanted confidential counselling, they wanted to see work happening with violent men and they wanted domestic violence to be something that is discussed with them, particularly in schools and youth centres.

Discussion

There is a tendency for work on domestic violence to be viewed as a specialism with both individual workers and agencies often believing that it is outside the remit of their role. It is commonly believed by agencies that if they were to fully support women and children suffering domestic violence that the agency and individual workers would be overwhelmed by the increased workload. This reflects a view of responding to domestic violence as an additional or optional extra rather than an integral part of existing and future work. A failure to recognise domestic violence in the early stages of intervention may, in fact, mean that more resources are put into that family in the long-term as the core problem, i.e. the domestic violence, has not been addressed.

With the publication of the Children Act (1989) in Britain, an opportunity to establish a legislative framework for protecting children experiencing domestic violence was lost by the Act's total lack of acknowledgement of domestic violence. In 1995, *Messages From Research* (HMSO 1995) was published. This represented the result of a programme of research commissioned by the British Government into child protection. Not surprisingly (as researchers and activists have pointed out for many years) a number of these studies found domestic violence to be a major factor in child protection work (Farmer and Owen 1995; Gibbons *et al.* 1995; Brandon and Lewis 1996). The core message emerging from this body of research emphasises family support. In the case of domestic violence, family support must be taken to mean support for the mother as non-abusing parent to care for her children. In doing this it is important not to rigidly apply set procedures, e.g. placing children on the Child Protection Register for emotional abuse when they have witnessed domestic violence, without ascertaining if there are other ways of offering support. It is vital to look to the needs of the particular children and woman involved.

One of the most consistent findings from the current study is that children want to speak to other children about their experiences. Children interviewed who had experienced group work with other domestic violence survivors were very positive about the group. An evaluation of group work with child survivors of domestic violence by Peled and Edleson (1992) found positive results. In North America and Canada, there is greater recognition of children's needs for support following domestic violence (Mullender 1994) and we in Britain can easily apply these models to our own circumstances. Refuges have been providing services for children individually and in groups for many years now. Most have been able to do this only through their own strenuous fund-raising efforts as there is no centralised funding for refuges. Outside of refuges, there have been isolated efforts to provide services for children, for example *The Stop Pack* (London Borough of Islington 1995). Presently there are positive signs of a commitment from the current government to recognising domestic violence as an extremely important issue with, for example, the publication of the 1998 Department of Health funded training pack, *Making an Impact: Children and Domestic Violence*, and the recognition of domestic violence in the consultation paper, *Working Together to Safeguard Children: New Government Proposals for Inter-agency Co-operation* (DOH 1998). The existing version does not, however, acknowledge domestic violence. Children are telling us what their experiences of domestic violence are, and they are also telling us how we can best offer support. Our next challenge at an individual level is to listen to what they are saying, and at a community-wide level to establish accessible services with committed funding to support children who experience domestic violence.

References

Bernard, C. (1997) 'Black mothers' emotional and behavioural responses to the sexual abuse of their children', in Kaufman-Kantor, G. and Jasinski, J. L. (eds) *Out of the Darkness: Contemporary Perspectives on Family Violence*, Thousand Oaks: Sage.

Brandon, M. and Lewis, A. (1996) 'Significant harm and children's experiences of domestic violence', *Child and Family Social Work*, 1, 33–42.

Casey, M. (1989) *Domestic Violence Against Women: the Women's Perspective*, University College Dublin: Social Psychological Research Unit.

Clark, A. (1994) 'A needle in a haystack: finding support as a survivor of domestic violence', in Wilson, M. (ed.) *Healthy and Wise: The Essential Handbook for Black Women*, London: Virago.

Cleaver, H. and Freeman, P. (1995) *Parental Perspectives in Cases of Suspected Child Abuse*, London: HMSO.

Department of Health (1998) *Working Together to Safeguard Children: New Government Proposals for Inter-Agency Co-operation*, Consultation Paper.

Department of Health (1991) *Children Act 1989*, London: Her Majesty's Stationery Office.

Department of Health, University of Bristol, NSPCC, Barnardos (1998) *Making an Impact: Children and Domestic Violence, a Training Resource*, Barkingside: Barnardos.

The Family Law Act 1996 (Ch27, Part IV) (*Allocation of Proceedings*) *Order 1997: Family Law*, London: HMSO.

Farmer, E. and Owen, M. (1995) *Child Protection Practice: Private Risks and Public Remedies*, London: HMSO.

Frost, M. (1997) 'Health Visitor's Perception of Domestic Violence', *Health Visitor*, 70 258–9.

Gibbons, J., Conroy, S. and Bell, C. (1995) *Operating the Child Protection System*, London: HMSO.

Hague, G. and Malos, E. (1994) 'Children, domestic violence and housing: the impact of homelessness', in Mullender, A. and Morley, R. (eds) *Children Living with Domestic Violence: Putting Men's Abuse of Women on the Child Care Agenda*, London: Whiting & Birch.

Hague, G., Malos, E. and Dear, W. (1995) *Against Domestic Violence: Inter-Agency Initiatives*, Bristol: University of Bristol, School for Policy Studies.

Hester, M. and Radford, L. (1996) *Domestic Violence and Child Contact Arrangements in England and Denmark*, University of Bristol: Policy Press.

HMSO (1995) *Child Protection: Messages From Research*, London: HMSO.

The Housing Act 1996, Ch52, London: HMSO.

Hughes, H. (1992) 'Impact of spouse abuse on children of battered women', *Violence Update*, Aug. (1), 9–11.

Imam, U. F. (1994) 'Asian children and domestic violence', in Mullender, A. and Morley, R. (eds) *Children Living with Domestic Violence: Putting Men's Abuse of Women on the Child Care Agenda*, London: Whiting & Birch.

Jaffe, P. G., Wolfe, D. A. and Wilson S. K. (1990) *Children of Battered Women*, Newbury Park: Sage.

Jones, A. (1989) *Domestic Violence*, Home Office Research Study, 107, London: Her Majesty's Stationery Office.

Lloyd, S. (1995) 'Social work and domestic violence', in Kingston, P. and Penhale, B. (eds) *Family Violence and the Caring Professions*, UK: Macmillan Press.

London Borough of Islington (1995) *STOP: Schools Take on Preventing Domestic Violence*, London Borough of Islington: Women's Equality Unit.

McGee, C. (1997) 'Children's experiences of domestic violence', *Child and Family Social Work*, 2 (1), 13–23.

McWilliams, M. and McKiernan, J. (1993) *Bringing it Out in the Open: Domestic Violence in Northern Ireland*, Belfast: HMSO.

Morley, R. and Mullender, A. (1994) 'Domestic violence and children: what do we know from research?', in Mullender, A. and Morley, R. (eds) *Children Living with Domestic Violence: Putting Men's Abuse of Women on the Child Care Agenda*, London: Whiting & Birch.

Mullender, A. (1994) 'Groups for child witnesses of woman abuse: learning from North America', in Mullender, A. and Morley, R. (eds) *Children Living with Domestic Violence: Putting Men's Abuse of Women on the Child Care Agenda*, London: Whiting & Birch.

Mullender, A. (1996) *Rethinking Domestic Violence: The Social Work and Probation Response*, London: Routledge.

NCH Action for Children (1994) *The Hidden Victims: Children and Domestic Violence*, London: NCH Action for Children.

O'Hara, M. (1994) 'Child deaths in contexts of domestic violence: implications for professional practice', in Mullender, A. and Morley, R. (eds) *Children Living with Domestic Violence: Putting Men's Abuse of Women on the Child Care Agenda*, London: Whiting & Birch.

Pahl, J. (1995) 'Health professionals and violence against women', in Kingston, P. and Penhale, B. (eds) *Family Violence and the Caring Professions*, UK: Macmillan Press.

Peled, E. (1993) 'Children who witness woman battering: concerns and dilemmas in the construction of a social problem', *Children and Youth Services Review*, 15, 43–52.

Peled, E. and Davis, D. (1995) *Groupwork with Children of Battered Women: A Practi-tioner's Guide*, Thousand Oaks: Sage.

Peled, E. and Edleson, J. L. (1992) 'Multiple perspectives on group work with children of battered women', *Violence and Victims*, 7, 327–46.

Pence, E. (1987) *In Our Best Interest: A Process For Personal and Social Change*. Duluth, Minnesota: Minnesota Program Development Inc.

Silvern, L. and Kaersvang, L. (1989) The traumatized children of violent marriages, *Child Welfare League of America*, 86 (4), 421–36.

Tang, C. S. (1994) 'Prevalence of spouse abuse in Hong Kong', *Journal of Family Violence*, 9 (4), 347–56.

6 Child protection and domestic violence

Findings from a Rowntree/ NSPCC study

Marianne Hester

Introduction

This chapter provides an example of how collaboration between feminist researchers and an NSPCC team led to a positive impact on the team's work with abused children who had lived with domestic violence. It outlines how, through a process involving defining and identifying domestic violence issues, these were incorporated and integrated into the work with abused children. The project led to a greater understanding and visibility of the links between child abuse and domestic violence, and to a wider application of safety measures for both children and their mothers.

The project arose as a result of the previous work which Lorraine Radford, Chris Pearson and myself had carried out, and also from particular concerns arising from the practice regarding domestic violence of the team in question. Between 1990 and 1996 Lorraine and I[1] examined child contact arrangements in England and Denmark in circumstances of domestic violence (Hester and Radford 1996). Between 1995 and 1997, Chris Pearson and I[2] went on to look at domestic violence in relation to court welfare and mediation practice (Hester et al. 1997). Both of these pieces of research have had an impact on national policy discussions and the practice of various groups of professionals. In the child contact research, we looked in depth at women's experiences of negotiating and arranging child contact on divorce and separation, and related professional practice. A mismatch was found between the actual experiences of women and their children leaving relationships where male partners were violent, and a range of professionals' (family court welfare officers, solicitors and voluntary sector mediators) own acknowledged practice in incorporating such experience in family proceedings and mediation. The research was cited as the basis for a number of interventions and amendments during the Parliamentary passage of the Family Law Act, and in the adjournment debate on the Children Act 1989 (Hudson 1996: 1549). Since we carried out that earlier work, and partly as a result, there has been a greater focus on domestic violence by both court welfare officers and by voluntary sector mediators (see Roberts 1994: 450; Cantwell and Nunnerley 1996: 178).

The second piece of research involved a national survey of family court welfare officers and voluntary sector mediators in England and Wales (and also for mediators in Northern Ireland), with a view to ascertaining these changes in practice. We were, at the same time, invited by National Family Mediation (the main umbrella organisation for voluntary sector mediators) to take part in the development of their national guidelines and training scheme regarding domestic violence (see Hester *et al.* 1997 for details of the resultant guidelines).

Background to the NSPCC project

Prior to the development of the NSPCC project, the team in question had found, to a limited extent, that focusing on domestic violence within their work could have a directly positive effect on their on-going preventative and recovery work with children.[3] By incorporating the issue of domestic violence, they had been able to change a number of situations where there would have been a need for child protection in the longer term, to situations where abuse was prevented. In one example, through a re-focusing on domestic violence by the agencies involved, a mother who was previously perceived as obstructive to agency intervention, was provided with support for herself and for prevention of abuse to her children. However, the team were unsure how to incorporate domestic violence as a consistent issue, and were also unsure as childcare professionals how to work with issues that they had previously considered the domain of those working with adults.

It has to be recognised that in the UK (let alone elsewhere, see Stark and Flitcraft 1997) child protection work has traditionally developed along separate lines to support work with women experiencing violence from their partners. The former has been the preserve of social services and related children's organisations. Support work with women has mainly been developed by refuges, in particular Women's Aid, who, on the basis of women's experiences, have perceived domestic violence as part of the attempt by violent men to control and have power over their female partners. It is only within refuges that, through the work of children's workers, there has developed an understanding of the overlap between the abuse of women and the abuse of children (Hague *et al.* 1996; Hester *et al.* 1998, see also Chapters 5 and 7). In relation to child protection there has often been an expectation, by social services professionals in particular, that it is the role of mothers to protect their children, either by leaving or by controlling the man's violent behaviour (Humphreys 1997; Hester *et al.* 1998). At the same time, any violence and abuse women have experienced from male partners has tended to be ignored. It is mothers who have usually been constructed as the problem, rather than the violent and abusive men (Stark and Flitcraft 1988; Farmer and Owen 1995; O'Hagan and Dillenburger 1995). Yet, as the NSPCC team in the project had begun to surmise, incorporating domestic violence can be a potentially positive approach in child protection cases (and see Jaffe *et al.* 1990; Kelly 1994; Mullender and Morley 1994). Not only is the abuse of children, both directly and indirectly, likely to occur in a context of domestic violence, but the practice of childcare professionals may be more positive and effective where domestic violence is taken into account (Farmer and Owen 1995; Mullender and Morley 1994; Hester *et al.* 1998). Working to ensure the safety of mothers can be protective of children. This has also been recognised in recent Labour Government policy. As the Department of Health Circular on Part IV of the Family Law Act (1997) suggests:

> Where domestic violence may be an important element in the family, the safety of (usually) the mother is also in the child's welfare (p. 12).

At a national level, the NSPCC had also, to some extent, expressed the importance of addressing the issue of domestic violence in relation to work with children (NSPCC 'Cry for Children' campaign 1995). But they had no specific means of identifying where domestic violence was an issue for the children concerned, nor of incorporating the issue in practice.

Following discussion with the NSPCC team in question about the findings from our research, it became apparent that a joint project might prove useful. We (Chris Pearson and myself) would bring our knowledge and understanding of women's experiences of domestic violence, the mechanisms of identifying domestic violence and enabling disclosure which we had been involved in developing with other groups of professionals, and our research skills. The NSPCC would bring their wide ranging experience of working with children who had been abused.

Methodology

The project was carried out in close co-operation between ourselves and the NSPCC team, using a 'reflective practitioner' action research approach (Everitt, Hardiker, Littlewood and Mullender 1992; Shakespeare, Atkinson and French 1993), beginning in August 1996 and finishing in March 1998.[4] In order to introduce the issue of domestic violence into the work of the team, two main approaches were adopted:

1   Use of team meetings to discuss definitions of domestic violence, and to examine the incorporation of domestic violence through 're-framing' of past and current cases.
2   The development of a simple monitoring scheme for domestic violence to be applied across the team's work.

To ascertain and chart any changes concerning the practice of the team with regard to domestic violence, we adopted a multi-method approach, which included:

• interviews with individual members of the team;
• analysis of case files;

- analysis of monitoring forms;
- meetings with the team.

In addition, some observation of practice was carried out to help us understand the practice of the team in greater depth. In order to determine the impact on service users of being asked about domestic violence, the team's existing service user evaluation form (for both adults and children) was modified to include a simple question about their reactions to this.

Individual interviews with team members took place at the beginning of the project, and at two stages during the process of the research. Case files, where the cases had been closed, were examined in relation to three separate periods:

- the 12 months before the onset of the research project (period A);
- the first 12 months of the project (period B);
- and the 6–month period following on from period B (period C).

Together, periods A and B constituted the main case file research period, as they involved systematic and detailed analysis of all case files. In period C, we examined only those cases identified by the team as involving domestic violence, and a general analysis of the file data was not carried out.

During the main period of the research, the overall number of referrals to the team was 267 (131 in period A and 136 in period B). Of these, 111 cases were accepted for service by the team, 59 in period A and 52 in period B. The focus of the team's work was on children who have experienced abuse, and three-quarters of the cases accepted for service involved sexual abuse.

The detailed case file sample in this study, of 111 accepted for service cases, is similar in size to previous studies into children with child protection concerns carried out in the UK, and indeed provides a larger and wider sample than most of these.[5] Other studies have tended to focus on children with social services involvement, or on women and children in refuges. In this study there was social services involvement in relation to less than three-quarters of the children (72.9 per cent) in cases accepted for service in period A and less than half of the children (48.9 per cent) in cases accepted for service in period B. A small number of these children and their mothers were also, or had been, staying at a refuge.

The majority of the children in the cases accepted for service (where known) were girls. A range of adults was identified as subjects of the request for service, although mothers and their children predominated as services users.

Defining domestic violence

From the outset, we decided on a definition of 'domestic violence' with the team which could be used in the project. An inclusive definition of domestic violence was adopted, reflecting the experiences described by women in such situations (Dobash and Dobash 1980; Kelly 1988; Hester and Radford 1996).

Therefore, included in the definition were any controlling or undermining behaviours which were seen to result in one adult (usually male) exerting 'power and control over' another (usually female) in the context of an intimate relationship (whether this be marriage, living together or apart, etc.). An important aspect of the definition was a focus on the impact of the behaviour on each individual rather than assuming that there was some hierarchy of forms of abusive behaviour, which necessarily placed physical abuse as the most 'serious' form of domestic violence. In reality there is much overlap between different domestic violence behaviours, in particular between the undermining and controlling behaviours which an abuser may use and more directly aggressive or violent behaviours (see Kelly 1988; Hester *et al.* 1998).

The definition of domestic violence was revisited and discussed with the NSPCC team as the research progressed. It became clear that at different times team members would apply variations of the originally agreed definition. One recurring issue concerned whether or not domestic violence included violence and abuse of children, rather than exclusively violence and abuse of adults in (or previously in) an intimate relationship. There was also on-going discussion of whether violence from teenagers to their mothers, for instance, constituted 'domestic violence'. It was agreed that the working definition of 'domestic violence' should be seen as violence and abuse experienced by adults, and 'child abuse' as relating to children. However, one member of the team tended to apply a wider definition where abuse of children was also incorporated in 'domestic violence' in situations where children were deemed to have been directly affected by living in circumstances of domestic violence.

Across periods A and B, the case files revealed that similar words and phrases might be used by the team to describe domestic violence. These included specific use of the term 'domestic violence', and/or mention of physical acts of violence (such as being hit, being beaten, etc.) and/or mention of the woman being/having been in a refuge. Yet, there were differences in the relevance attached to this information. This was also apparent from the more limited analysis of case files in period C. Overall, it became clear that, over time, 'domestic violence' (however described) moved from a descriptive 'peripheral' location (to do with adults, separate from work with the child) to a more integrated 'central' location in the work carried out by the team.

Over time, explicit information increasingly became apparent in the files about the different forms of abuse women experienced from their male partners. This indicated a change with regard to the specific details likely to be defined as domestic violence or abuse, and/or deemed of relevance by workers to note down in the files. Thus in case file periods A and B, physical abuse to the woman/survivor of domestic violence was mentioned predominantly in relation to domestic violence. However, compared to period A, before the project began, there was in case file period B more than a two-fold increase in the identification of those cases where the violence also involved the sexual and/or verbal and/or psychological abuse of the woman. The existence of financial abuse was also mentioned for the first time after the project had started.

Although the numbers were small, in case file period B there were also more cases where there was mention of threats to kill. It became apparent that their involvement in the project was increasing consideration by the team of the effects of domestic violence on the women concerned. In the case files in period A, the impact of violent and abusive behaviour was described only in relation to any physical injuries caused, whereas in the period B case files there were also indications of some of the emotional impacts on women of abuse from their (usually male) partners.

Examples of narrative taken from each of the three case file periods provided further evidence of how the issue of domestic violence was moving from the periphery to becoming a more central and integrated feature of the work undertaken by the team as the project progressed. In the case files in period A, for instance, the existence of domestic violence might be acknowledged by the team, but tended not to be explored in the work undertaken with the child, as exemplified by the following extract:

> [*child, girl: 11*] expressed negative feelings towards her father and was concerned about episodes of violence in her birth family . . . I [*NSPCC worker*] am still unsure as to the nature and extent of the domestic difficulties which she [*child*] experienced in her birth family.

In this instance the child expressed anxiety in the initial NSPCC session about 'her dad hitting my mum', but this disappeared from subsequent sessions where the focus was on the issue of the sexual abuse of the child by the father. The connections, complexities and impact of the child's abusive experiences within the context of domestic violence were not addressed, and the worker did not attempt to gain details and information from the child to clarify the 'nature and extent of the domestic difficulties'. Domestic violence and the abuse of the child tended, thus, to be seen as separate issues.

During the first year of the project (period B) more examples of workers incorporating domestic violence into the work with the child were apparent. For instance:

> Mrs Green explained that when she was about 17 she had a partner who was violent towards her. Daisy [*daughter now aged 11*] was aged 2 at the time. Daisy said that she could remember instances from that time. . . . Daisy has informed Mrs Green that she has nightmares about her early years when Mrs Green had a violent partner. . . . Mrs Green and Daisy . . . talked about how a violent relationship that Mrs Green was in when Daisy was 1 or 2 years old had impacted on both of them.

Again, in this example, the presenting issue was child sexual abuse, but there was much more readiness to use the sessions to also explore past issues relating to domestic violence and to acknowledge the continuing impact of this for both mother and daughter. In this way, channels of communication were opened up between mother and daughter, and Daisy's current difficulties could be located within a wider context.

By the end of the project, in the cases in period C, acknowledgement of the inter-connectedness of domestic violence and the safety and welfare of the child became much more clearly integrated into practice. For example, in one case accepted by the team, the presenting issue for the child, as reported by the mother, was the need to explore issues relating to the domestic violence the child had witnessed (rather than child sexual or physical abuse as in earlier cases). Exploring these issues then led to the discovery of the direct physical and sexual abuse of the child by her father:

> Mrs Blue discussed that Lily [*daughter aged 11*] had witnessed the violence towards her mum. She [*Lily*] was threatened verbally and physically and was assaulted physically and verbally by her father. . . . Lily has told [*mum*] that she doesn't love her dad, but pretended to, to stop him from hurting Mrs Blue. . . . Lily has nightmares, cannot handle aggression in any form . . . cannot bear anyone to touch her.

Addressing the violence in this way, therefore, led to a greater awareness of the issues for the child in coping with the impact of both the direct abuse and the indirect abuse associated with living in the context of domestic violence. It also led to a greater awareness of the dynamics of the relationship between Lily and her mother, leading to more effective intervention with them both.

Identifying domestic violence

From our previous work, and the work of many other feminists working with and researching women's experiences of domestic violence, it is clear that women are unlikely to disclose domestic violence unless they can be assured that the reaction will be positive – that is, not woman-blaming, and not punitive as in taking children into care (Hester and Radford 1996; Hester *et al.* 1997). Good practice consists of asking all women routinely about domestic violence in every case. The very fact of asking about domestic violence conveys an important message to women and children that practitioners are aware of its existence and relevance, thus possibly facilitating disclosure (Hester *et al.* 1998).

The use of a monitoring scheme for domestic violence was thought to be a useful approach. It would allow domestic violence as an issue to be introduced into the team's work in a systematic way, thus not making any particular individual feel singled out; it could help to increase awareness in the team of what domestic violence entails; and could enable disclosure of domestic violence by children and/or their carers or referrers.

One of the problems with introducing a monitoring scheme was to ensure that it would fit with the ways in which the team worked. As most of the work of the team concerned recovery and counselling, and the use of client-led approaches, there was often an emphasis on 'listening' to clients rather than on any systematic asking of questions. Initially, we had thought that a monitoring form, with a set of questions about possible experiences related to domestic violence, could be used in conjunction with current intake and referral procedures. However, after discussion with the team and some observation of team practice, it was decided that a multi-stage monitoring approach should be adopted so that disclosure of domestic violence might occur at any stage in the practice process, and from service users or referrers. Thus, the scheme adopted involved a form to be completed at the referral stage of every case, and after every subsequent contact with service users.

The form consisted of a set of questions related to domestic violence, that is violence and abuse in the adult's relationship, and a set of questions regarding any impact on the child resulting from the domestic violence. There was also a question concerning how the worker obtained any knowledge about the domestic violence, that is from the adult client, child client or referrer. In practice, the monitoring process was used most frequently with the adults.

Throughout the project, some difficulties remained with establishing and maintaining the monitoring system. For instance there were occasions when workers felt it was especially inappropriate or unsafe to ask about domestic violence. This included instances where the family was seen together and the male partner, in particular, was present. The traditional practice of separating domestic violence and child abuse issues was also at times difficult to negotiate, in particular the question of how to ask about domestic violence without diverting the focus from what was seen as the main presenting issue, that is the direct abuse of the child. As one of the workers explained in relation to one situation:

> I think the main feeling was that it [*asking about domestic violence*] would have taken things down the wrong track. It would have gone away from the main issue that was being presented at that time.

This issue of maintaining a balanced focus on child abuse could be of particular concern when domestic violence was more difficult to establish, and led to some anxieties about keeping the centrality of child abuse at the perceived expense of discovering domestic violence issues:

> sometimes where it's [*domestic violence*] not quite as obvious as that where somebody isn't saying it so explicitly, . . . there are a lot of things to remember and, with the focus being child abuse and also what happens if I don't get the child abuse bits right, and concerns over that, that maybe at times it [*domestic violence monitoring*] has taken second place.

There was also a tendency at times for team members to see domestic violence purely as an emotional abuse for children (in the sense of living in a violent environment), and perhaps as separate from the sexual or physical abuse of children. In other words, if domestic violence was the presenting issue, emotional abuse of the children would be seen as the potential problem – rather than other, direct forms of child abuse. As one member of staff put it:

> that's been the most major thing I suppose; it's changed our remit in some way from just sexual abuse to domestic violence. It seems to be two remits now – children who've been sexually abused and children who have experienced domestic violence.

Yet, interviews with team members also indicated that use of the monitoring forms was having an impact on their general awareness of domestic violence, and that the forms were seen as enabling a focus on issues of relevance to practice:

> The very existence of the forms I think has meant that we have concentrated more on whether domestic violence is an issue.

And as another team member pointed out, the form and the research had enabled her to ask in cases where she had previously suspected domestic violence:

> there's two cases I've got that I was working with before you came, and one of them I did suspect domestic violence and I have now asked because the monitoring form has enabled me to ask.

There were also concerns about the appropriateness of using the monitoring forms with children to raise domestic violence issues. This did not necessarily 'fit' very easily with the client-led emphasis of the team, and could feel overly intrusive, especially as domestic violence was not usually the presenting issue for the child. Yet, in practice, asking children about domestic violence was positive. One 11-year-old girl who was receiving therapeutic treatment from the NSPCC in connection with physical abuse from her father, when asked about the context of domestic violence (gross physical, sexual and emotional abuse of the mother) within which she had lived, wrote that she found it both upsetting and frightening to talk about because of the potential dangers of disclosure:

> I thought if I tell someone then they go and tell someone and they will come and hurt me.

Clearly, disclosing information about the violence to her mother seemed even more dangerous than disclosing and talking about the direct abuse to herself. However, being enabled to talk about the domestic violence in a safe context, which included a safe location away from the violent man for her mother and herself, proved very positive.

Overall, the monitoring scheme was found to be useful, and had a very clear impact, with the incidence of domestic violence in cases accepted for service by the team rising from one-third to nearly two-thirds as a result of routinely asking about domestic violence in every case. While the research resulted in a small increase in referrals involving domestic violence, mostly the instances of domestic violence became more acknowledged and recognised where it had previously been hidden. With regard to disclosure, domestic violence was mostly disclosed by the abused woman, although children, referrers and others also provided evidence of domestic violence. During the period of the research, the amount of disclosure from children remained unchanged, whilst there was a marked increase in disclosure from abused women themselves and from referrers. The former can be explained by the fact that women were being asked specifically about experiences of domestic violence as a result of the monitoring process. The latter was probably due to the fact that knowledge about the project locally led to an increase in referrals concerning domestic violence.

Incorporating domestic violence

In order to explore the use of a 'domestic violence focused' framework in the team's work, some of the team meetings were used to re-examine and reframe certain cases. Previously closed cases where we as researchers had identified domestic violence, but where this had not been made apparent or explicit by the NSPCC team, or where its existence remained as a possibility in the background, were brought to the team for discussion.

This reframing exercise involved the exploration of the effect that taking domestic violence into account might have had on each individual case. In this way, domestic violence was used as one of the 'lenses' through which to look at the practice which was carried out. The use of 're-framing' to incorporate domestic violence proved a very useful mechanism for the integration of work around both child abuse and domestic violence. As one team member explained, it was these re-examinations of cases which had proved a very useful approach to examining alternative practice possibilities, and, in particular, clarified for her how the 'domestic violence lens' could enhance her work with children:

> the thing that brought it home to me was that session we had when we looked at some cases, we traced the domestic violence, we traced the problems back and it sort of really brought it home to me that there we all were, all the different agencies, running round in circles basically trying to help families, not actually considering the issue of the domestic violence and how problems that had either arisen from that or been exacerbated by that, and that in fact we probably had to go back and deal with that domestic violence issue to make any headway at all and to get people in a stable sort of settled environment, to be able to benefit from some therapy and get their lives back on course.

Discussing cases in this way emphasised to the team the need to put child protection concerns into the domestic violence framework, and to look at the impact of domestic violence on the child in a much broader context. In addition to this, looking at cases through the domestic violence 'lens' led to the reframing of some cases as involving domestic violence as well as child abuse.

For instance, in one particular case the team had investigated an allegation that the key worker of a 15-year-old girl in residential care was involved with her in a sexual relationship. This was an allegation made by the girl herself, and was subsequently retracted. The man involved was consequently suspended for abusing his position of authority. The team had identified the case as involving child sexual abuse, even though the young woman concerned considered herself in some ways to be in a relationship with this man. As the investigation by the team progressed, they learnt more details about the young woman's relationship with this man, including instances where he had put his hands around her throat in a very threatening way. On at least two occasions she reported that when he was displeased with her 'he was rough and angry . . . he pushed her, but did not hit her'. In another instance, 'he frightened her by shaking her violently'. There were also suggestions by her that he was being sexually coercive in that she described how 'he wouldn't leave her alone'.

Reframing did not alter the impropriety or nature of the man's behaviour. Reframing did, however, provide an additional way in which the team could have carried out recovery work with the young woman, and would have allowed them to work in a child/person-centred way that incorporated her own apparent perspective. Incorporating domestic violence into the picture would also have allowed information regarding refuges and other support for women experiencing domestic violence to be imparted with regard to safety planning with the young woman.

Thus, incorporating domestic violence as a possible feature in the lives of the children concerned provided a much wider view and context for understanding their presenting behaviour. It also resulted in more effective work.

Increasing visibility of domestic violence

During the period of the project, the existence of domestic violence in the lives of children who had been abused became increasingly visible. As indicated earlier, by the end of the project it was apparent that two-thirds of the cases accepted for service by the NSPCC team also involved domestic violence (virtually always violence against the mother by her male partner). It also became apparent that in the cases where domestic violence was identified, the perpetrator of the domestic violence and the abuser of the child(ren) was likely to be the same individual, usually the child's natural father. Moreover, there was much evidence of the generally abusive impact on children, both 'indirect' and 'direct', of living in circumstances of domestic violence.

Analysis of the case files indicated that of the sexual abuse cases, over half involved domestic violence. With regard to the perpetrator, in over half (53 per cent) of the child sexual abuse cases the abuser was the children's father or father figure. This rose to over two-thirds (69 per cent) in instances where domestic violence was also identified. In other words, fathers or father figures were even more likely than other men to be sexually abusive to their children where these same men were also violent and abusive to the mothers. These findings are consistent with a range of other research which has found links between child abuse and domestic violence (Goddard and Hiller 1993; Farmer and Owen 1995; Forman 1995; Brandon and Lewis 1996; Humphreys 1997).

For the team, being made aware of these patterns in the cases they dealt with was important in relation to their practice. Such evidence helped members of the team to work more realistically with children and their carers where domestic violence was also a part of their experience. Realising that for some children their abuser was also violent to the mothers, and vice versa, led to greater understanding of the abusive dynamics experienced by the children con-cerned. It also meant that, in the few instances where mothers contacted the NSPCC regarding support for their children who had lived in circumstances of domestic violence, team members became more open to the possibility that the children had been directly abused, in addition to witnessing violence to their mothers. Case files in the final period of the research indicated that, as a con-sequence, there was work with children on this wider range of abusive experi-ences.

From the case files there was also evidence of the close interaction between the man's sexual abuse of the child and the physical, emotional, and/or sexual abuse of the mother, complex dynamics of survival and protection which have been highlighted in other research (see Hester *et al.* 1998). There were instances of the male partner using threats of physical abuse and threats to kill the mother and/or the child in order to secure the child's silence about his sexual abuse of her/him. This may be seen to add an additional level of emo-tional abuse to children who in this way became responsible for their own and their mother's safety.

It is clear that cases of children witnessing domestic violence began, during the project, to be labelled as emotional abuse. Emphasising emotional abuse as a consequence of the child living with domestic violence appeared to suggest that such abuse of children was merely an unintended effect. However, the narrative from the files also indicated some instances where the emotional abuse of the child was probably a deliberate act against the children. This included one case where the children were shut in a room with their mother whilst she was being beaten by her male partner. In this same case the older boy (aged six at the time) was later blamed by the man for the injuries he had caused the mother. In another example the man was threatening suicide and cutting himself in front of his children in order to 'prove' his wish to be reconciled with his ex-wife.

Generally the findings confirm those of other studies, which have shown the range of detrimental effects on children of living with domestic violence (Jaffe *et al.* 1990; Abrahams 1994; McGee 2000). Thus several children were described as having witnessed attacks of physical violence towards their mothers. This included knife attacks, for instance a child witnessing her mother being stabbed in the head, and another seeing her father putting a knife to her mother's throat. Some children witnessed their mother being strangled whilst others were also witnesses to the after-effects of the violence in the form of their mother's black eyes and broken bones. A boy aged five, who saw his mother being strangled was said to have 'just stood there while it happened'.

Some children remembered the violence even though their mothers did not realise that they had been aware of it. One older child recounted the violence she had witnessed as a much younger child (aged two or three), and in another instance a five-year-old daughter used the first interview session with the NSPCC

> to recount unprompted memories from the past of abuse … that she observed and which … [mother] remembers but never thought [daughter] had seen.

Throughout the research period there were children who were reported as having tried various methods to try to protect their mothers. One child requested a weapon to take home with him from his session at the NSPCC so that he could kill the man who was being physically violent to his mother, and thereby protect her from any further abuse. Similarly, a son (aged 17) was described as sleeping with a baseball bat in order to protect himself and his mother in case his father came to the house, and a 12-year-old expressed a desire to kill his mother's abusive partner. In another example, a 15-year-old daughter had tried to physically intervene between her mother and her mother's partner when they were having an 'argument', which had resulted in the partner chasing the daughter and attempting to strangle her. One daughter (aged 11) described how she pleaded for her mother's safety whenever her father had a knife to her mother's throat.

There were other examples where the effect on the child appeared to be linked to their living with domestic violence. Two boys (aged eight and six) who had witnessed their mother being attacked with a knife had both subsequently 'acted out with knives'. The reaction of some children was the opposite of this 'acting out' aggression in that they became withdrawn and retreated to the safety of their room, and/or felt frightened and silenced. One young child expressed his fear that he was going to be beaten up 'like mummy', and a seven-year-old daughter was said to be fearful that their father 'could kill them all'. An 11-year-old girl was variously described as having nightmares, scared of the dark, frightened of loud noises, having temper tantrums, being 'uncontrollable' and self-harming. This behaviour was seen by the team to be the result of the child witnessing violence to her mother, coupled with experiencing physical abuse from her father. One mother had placed her children in care because she perceived this as the best means of protecting her children from further domestic violence. Another mother was 'harassed' to such an extent that she escaped from the house, but had to leave the children in the care of the father. In another case there was recognition that children were 'exhibiting major problems as a result of living with domestic violence', and that these were compounded by the fact that the violence had necessitated many changes of address and brought much uncertainty.

Echoing our earlier work (Hester and Radford 1996) it was clear that children's contact with violent fathers post-separation of the parents created ongoing abusive situations for the children (and women) concerned. Difficulties arising from children's residence or contact arrangements appeared regularly in the case files, and were especially linked to the domestic violence context. Between two-thirds and three-quarters of the cases where there were contact/residence difficulties also involved domestic violence. Cases involving domestic violence were more likely to involve problems concerning residence, and especially contact, than in the sample as a whole. As we had found previously, it was the potential or actual abuse of children during contact, the need for supervised contact, and the potential for a conflict of interests between the mother and child(ren), which were the main concerns (Hester and Radford 1996; Radford and Hester, in press). There was a clear overlap between the existence of domestic violence and the abuse of children during contact, whether physical, sexual or emotional.

Implementation

In the team's recovery work a variety of practice approaches were drawn upon, such as play therapy, drama therapy, art therapy and family therapy, with an emphasis on integration and on the process being client-led. The main focus of all the work undertaken was the abuse of the child, and this included focusing on a range of areas, such as self-esteem work, keeping safe work, looking at 'muddles', or exploring anxieties/feelings/difficulties through play and art. However, the work of the whole team was increasingly carried out within a 'systemic' framework, whatever the approach used by the individual members of staff.

There has been much discussion and feminist critique concerning the relevance of systemic or family therapy approaches in relation to child abuse and domestic violence. The classic family therapy approach has been criticised for blaming mothers for the abusive acts of fathers while negating fathers' responsibility for their abusive activity, and for the lack of recognition of power and gender in family relationships (MacLeod and Saraga 1988; 1991; Will 1989). The team did not use the 'classic' family therapy approach because of the omission of notions of power and gender, and because of the lack of a dynamic understanding of the family which results. However, they were interested in the application of what they termed a 'systemic' approach because they saw that as allowing them to examine the context for the child who had been abused – such as the individual(s) involved, and the significant relationships for the child. They were concerned that the particular focus on the child in their work was leading to a simplistic pathologising of children as victims, whereby the child was being perceived in practice as needing 'rescuing' and needing 'treatment' as if ill. Instead they were wanting to enable children to be safe through incorporating and understanding the children's contexts and relationships, and by working in conjunction with the caring adults as well as the children them-selves. Where the team was concerned, this change in approach had enabled them, and the service users, to decide when to see children individually, when to see children and their parent(s) (or other carers/adults), or perhaps to only see the parent. Previously they had always tended to see the child alone.

Based on this 'systemic' approach, the team increasingly moved towards what feminists have identified as a positive approach – supporting both mothers and their children in domestic violence cases. This placed the support and protec-tion – and therefore recovery – of the child within a context where the key carer (the mother) was also supported. As one team member explained:

> if a child has been abused, it's what happens next in terms of the help, of an acceptance from particular key carers … that will determine the outcome in terms of the child's recovery … So, therefore, if we can work with women as well as children, carers as well as children, taking account of domestic violence … of the power dynamics around, and the frequency with which men abuse women we know about just in a factual way, then I think that we can start to create with those carers safer environments for them and their children.

Conclusion

By the end of the project there was a clear change within the team, both in relation to awareness of domestic violence issues and in relation to the team's practice. Crucially, there was a change from seeing domestic violence usually as a separate issue from children and child abuse, to seeing domestic violence as a possibly central issue for children, and as a part of their abusive experiences. Thinking about both child abuse and domestic violence had allowed the team to reflect more thoroughly on their use of particular approaches, largely because many of the underlying dynamics and issues were the same or overlapped. Both domestic violence and child abuse involve one person (often the same indi-vidual) exerting power and control over another. The team felt that routinely asking about domestic violence had been very important to their practice. Overall, the project had enabled the team to incorporate domestic violence as part of the picture in working with abused children and their families, leading to much greater emphasis on safety and more effective work with both women and children.

Notes

1   In conjunction with Chris Pearson, Julie Humphries, Maja Fogh, Anne Mette Kruse, Khalida Qaiser and Kandy-Sue Woodfield. The research was carried out with the aid of grants from the Joseph Rowntree Foundation, Nuffield Foundation, British Council and the Danish Academy of Research.
2   With Lorraine Radford.

3 The nature of the NSPCC's work has changed during the past decade from an emphasis on emergency child protection work (under section 31 of the Children Act 1989) to an increasing emphasis on treatment or recovery work. This reflects the wider policy move towards 'children in need' and provision of family support which followed *Messages from Research* (DoH 1995), and also to avoid duplication of the work carried out by social services.

4 The project was carried out with funding from the Joseph Rowntree Foundation.

5 See Maynard (1985), Cleaver and Freeman (1995), Farmer and Owen (1995), Brandon and Lewis (1996), Glaser and Prior (1997), Humphreys (1997), Gibbons *et al.* (1995).

References

Abrahams, C. (1994) *The Hidden Victims – Children and Domestic Violence*, London: NCH Action for Children.

Andrews, B. and Brown, G. W. (1988) 'Marital violence in the community: a biographical approach', *British Journal of Psychiatry*, 153, 305–12.

Brandon, M. and Lewis, A. (1996) 'Significant harm and children's experiences of domestic violence', *Child and Family Social Work*, 1 (1), 33–42.

Cantwell, B. and Nunnerly, M. (1996) 'A new spotlight on family mediation', *Family Law*, 177–80.

Cleaver, H. and Freeman, P. (1995) *Parental Perspectives in Cases of Suspected Child Abuse*, London: HMSO.

Department of Health (1995) *Child Protection – Messages from Research*, London: Department of Health.

Dobash, R. E. and Dobash, R. P. (1980) *Violence Against Wives: A Case Against the Patriarchy*, Sussex: Open Books.

Everitt, A., Hardiker, P., Littlewood, J. and Mullender, A. (1992) *Applied Research for Better Practice*, London: Macmillan.

Farmer, E. and Owen, M. (1995) *Child Protection Practice: Private Risks and Public Remedies*, London: HMSO.

Farmer, E. and Pollock, S. (1998) *Substitute Care for Sexually Abused and Abusing Children*, Chichester: Wiley.

Forman, J. (1995) *Is There a Correlation Between Child Sexual Abuse and Domestic Violence? An Exploratory Study of the Links Between Child Sexual Abuse and Domestic Violence in a Sample of Intrafamilial Child Sexual Abuse Cases*, Glasgow: Women's Support Project.

Gibbons, J., Conroy, S. and Bell, C. (1995) *Operating the Child Protection System: A Study of Child Protection Practices in English Local Authorities*, London: HMSO.

Glaser, D. and Prior, V. (1997) 'Is the term child protection applicable to emotional abuse?', *Child Abuse Review*, 6, 315–29.

Goddard, C and Hiller, P. (1993) 'Child sexual abuse: assault in a violent context', *Australian Journal of Social Issues*, 28 (1), 20–33.

Hague, G., Kelly, L., Malos, E., Mullender, A. with Debbonaire, T. (1996) *Children, Domestic Violence and Refuges: A Study of Needs and Responses*, Bristol: Women's Aid Federation (England).

Hanmer, J. (1989) 'Women and policing in Britain', in Hanmer, J., Radford, J. and Stanko, E. (eds) *Women, Policing and Male Violence*, London: Routledge.

Hester, M. and Radford, L. (1996) *Domestic Violence and Child Contact Arrangements in England and Denmark*, Bristol: Policy Press.

Hester, M. and Pearson, C. (1998) *From Periphery to Centre: Domestic Violence in Work with Abused Children*, Bristol: Policy Press.

Hester, M., Pearson, C. and Harwin, N. (1998) *Making An Impact. Children and Domestic Violence. A Reader*. London: Barnardos in association with Department Of Health.

Hester, M., Pearson, C. and Radford, L. (1997) *Domestic Violence: A National Survey of Court Welfare and Voluntary Sector Mediation Practice*, Bristol: Policy Press.

Hudson, R. (1996) 'Contact and domestic violence', *NLJ Practitioner*, October, 1549.

Humphreys, C. (1997) *Case Planning Issues Where Domestic Violence Occurs in the Context of Child Protection*, Coventry: University of Warwick.

Jaffe, P., Wolfe, D. A. and Wilson, S. K. (1990) *Children of Battered Women*, California: Sage.

Kelly, L. (1988) *Surviving Sexual Violence*, Cambridge: Polity Press.

Kelly, L. (1994) 'The interconnectedness of domestic violence and child abuse: challenges for research, policy and practice', in Mullender, A. and Morley, R. (eds) *Children Living with Domestic Violence*, London: Whiting and Birch.

McGee, C. (2000) *Childhood Experiences of Domestic Violence*, London: Jessica Kingsley.

MacLeod, M. and Saraga, E. (1988) 'Challenging the orthodoxy: towards a feminist theory and practice', *Feminist Review*, 28, 16–55.

MacLeod, M, and Saraga, E. (1991) 'Clearing a path through the undergrowth: a feminist reading of recent literature on child sexual abuse', in Carter, P., Jeffs, T. and Smith, M. K. (eds) *Social Work and Social Welfare Yearbook: 3*, Buckingham: Open University Press.

Maynard, M. (1985) 'The response of social workers to domestic violence', in Pahl, J. (ed.) *Private Violence and Public Policy*, London: Routledge.

Mullender, A. and Morley, R. (eds) (1994) *Children Living with Domestic Violence: Putting Men's Abuse of Women on the Child Care Agenda*, London: Whiting and Birch.

O'Hagan, K. and Dillenburger, K. (1995) *Abuse of Women Within Childcare Work*, Buckingham: Open University Press.

Parton, C. (1990) 'Women, gender oppression and child abuse', in The Violence Against Children Study Group, *Taking Child Abuse Seriously*, London: Unwin Hyman.

Roberts, M. (1994) 'Who is in charge? Effecting a productive exchange between researchers and practitioners in the field of family mediation', *Journal of Social Welfare and Family Law*, 4, 439–54.

Shakespeare, P., Atkinson, D. and French, S. (1993) *Reflecting on Research Practice: Issues on Health and Social Welfare*, California: Sage.

Stark, E. and Flitcraft, A. H. (1988) 'Women and children at risk: a feminist perspective on child abuse', *International Journal of Health Studies*, 18 (1), 97–119.

Stark, E. and Flitcraft, A. H. (1997) *Women at Risk*, London: Sage.

Will, D. (1989) Feminism, child sexual abuse, and the [long overdue] demise of systems mysticism, *Context*, 9, 12–15.

7   Unsung innovation

The history of work with children in UK domestic violence refuges

*Gill Hague, Audrey Mullender, Liz Kelly and
Ellen Malos with Thangam Debbonaire*

Introduction

Domestic violence is now an issue of considerable social concern world-wide. Until recently, however, the effects on children of living with and experiencing domestic violence against their mothers, and the possible connections between domestic violence and child abuse, have been issues which have escaped the public gaze. Now, though, in many countries, the impact on children of domestic violence is an issue which has 'found its time'.

In the UK, Women's Aid and the refuge movement, together with other women's campaigning groups and grass-roots feminist organisations, form part of the wider movement against domestic violence internationally. The passionate vision of this movement, inspired by feminist theory, practice and imaginings, has always been of a world where domestic violence against women is a thing of the past, and women and children can live safely in their own homes (see Schechter 1982; Dobash and Dobash 1992; Hague and Malos 1998). The principal UK organisations co-ordinating the provision of refuge, advocacy and support services for abused women and their children are the four Women's Aid federations: Northern Ireland Women's Aid, Scottish Women's Aid, Welsh Women's Aid and the Women's Aid Federation of England who, together, have led the struggle against domestic violence within the country for a quarter of a century. In addition to their work with abused women, these federations have attempted over many years to advocate on behalf of children witnessing domestic violence against their mothers and to develop creative work specifically to meet their needs. However, their experience in conducting this work has, until recently, been rather that of raising a lone voice.

We report here on a cross-institutional piece of research, funded by the WAFE Charitable Trust and conducted between 1995 and 1997. The study involved researchers from the Child and Woman Abuse Studies Unit, University of North London, from the Domestic Violence Research Group, University of Bristol, and (at the time) from the Centre for Applied Social Studies, University of Durham. It was conducted in partnership with the national Women's Aid Federation of England which, together with the other federations, provides refuge accommodation for more than 60,000 women and children annually, and offers advice, information and support to many thousands more. The federation (also discussed in other chapters of this book) has led the way in England in developing work with children in refuges, and their National Children's Officer was involved in managing this project. However, refuges not affiliated to Women's Aid have also developed child work initiatives which were included in our research.

The study was designed to investigate the contribution of children's workers in domestic violence refuges to practice with abused children and the children of abused women within England specifically, and to examine the impacts on children of domestic violence. One aspect of the research was to conduct archival and historical research on the development of children's work in refuges from the 1970s onwards, and it is this aspect which we discuss here. There is almost no published material relating to this largely hidden but important piece of women and children's history. This is the first time that the telling of such a history has been attempted.

The project was carried out on a collaborative basis, and from a broadly feminist and anti-discriminatory perspective, as a contribution to feminist inquiry and research methodology. It was based on principles of:

i   working collectively and collaboratively within the research team;
ii informing all aspects of the research with feminist understandings of domestic violence;
iii linking with the refuge movement;
iv consulting widely with women, with workers and with children;
v   being accountable, as far as possible, to the Women's Aid Federation of England, to children's workers in refuges, and to women and children experiencing domestic violence;
vi working towards the empowerment of abused women and children;
vii basing the research at all times on the needs of women and children and of the refuge network; and
viii treating children in particular (as well as women in refuges and workers) with dignity and respect.

The history of work with children in UK refuges

The story of the development of work with children within domestic violence refuges in the UK is not only an unpublished one. It is also largely unwritten. This is common to much of the history of the refuge movement, both in the UK and elsewhere, as it is generally to grass-roots organising within the wider women's movement. In some ways, however, the history of work with the children of abused women has been particularly hidden, since, in the past at least, children's work in the refuge movement has tended to be given lower status than work with women, so that the struggle to get children's views and rights taken seriously has often outweighed the need to record the process. Yet, recording the development of an area of involvement such as this may be an important way of reclaiming and 'owning' it within the women's movement, as well as of documenting a creative and innovative aspect of women's and children's history for the notice of the wider world. (See also Hague *et al.* 1996, for a full account.)

Certainly, in practice if not in print, refuges have a longer and more active record of recognizing the needs of children who are living with women abuse or its aftermath than any other agency in the UK (Mullender and Morley 1994). They were also a location of some of the earliest awareness of widespread child sexual abuse, many years before its links with the abuse of women began to be noticed by the childcare 'mainstream' (Department of Health 1995). This chapter will celebrate the importance of the still developing work with children in refuges in England, both by Women's Aid groups and other women's organizations, charting its growth from offering play activities at the start, to developing specially tailored responses at the present time. It will illustrate the central location of 'child centred' work within the feminist project, contrary to the views of those who regard many activist women authors as obscuring the needs and rights of children (Featherstone and Trinder 1997). That this has been achieved against a background of chronic funding shortages is all the more remarkable.

This unending shortage of resources within the refuge movement as a whole is another reason why the record presented here is inevitably partial. And funding has been even more limited (or non-existent) for refuge-based children's work specifically, which has meant that basic documentation and the maintenance of archives have often taken low priority. Such specialised difficulties exacerbate the more general challenge of recording the full complexity and richness of any social movement over time. The history related here, then, relies on such local documentation as exists in a selection of local refuges throughout England, and on central Women's Aid records, supplemented by the memories and recollections of selected interviewees who were known to have played particularly central roles at different periods and, more widely, by telephone interviews with present children's workers in each refuge in England. It aims only to begin a process: to take a step forward, for those of us who are or have been directly involved with the women's refuge movement, towards writing our own history.

While this account is specific to England, it has resonance for refuge movements and activists against violence against women more widely. Further accounts both from the movements in other countries and from the UK Women's Aid federations apart from Women's Aid in England may, perhaps, expand this history in the future.

Early days

The emergence of refuges in Britain occurred in the early 1970s in a burst of activity under the impetus of the Women's Liberation Movement and alongside similar developments in other countries in Europe and elsewhere. As more and more refuges were established in quick succession throughout the UK, a national organisation, the National Women's Aid Federation (NWAF) was set up. Initially the federation covered all of England, Wales, Scotland and Northern Ireland, but a separate Scottish federation rapidly developed. The NWAF sub-divided into English, Welsh, and Northern Irish federations in 1978 to further encourage autonomy of organisation (see Dobash and Dobash 1992; Hague and Malos 1998). Up to that year, therefore, this chapter relates to NWAF, and, after it, to the Women's Aid Federation of England (also known until recently as WAFE).

Understanding how children's needs have been viewed, and responded to, by the refuge movement requires an awareness of the context in which domestic violence was made a public issue in the 1970s. Until the emergence of Women's Liberation (and of course, to a lesser but still significant extent now), women's place in society, as played out in social policy and service provision, was delineated almost entirely by their relationship to others: as men's wives and as children's mothers. The perception of violence towards women as a social and 'political' problem, as well as an individual one, developed out of (and fed into) the assertion by the women's movement of the rights of women whose needs and requirements could be separated from those of men and of children and regarded as important in their own right (Dobash and Dobash 1980; 1992).

Thus, highlighting the needs and experiences of children living with domestic violence was sometimes viewed as counter-productive during the early period of refuge organisation, since it could act to reinforce views which the movement was attempting to challenge. Asserting women's independent right to belief, support and protection was at that time, and rightly in our view, deemed the priority. In the context of the 2000s, the resistance that many groups encountered to this simple message can be hard to believe. All the early refuge groups had to struggle with invisibility, hostility, lack of interest or judgemental, woman-blaming attitudes on a level which is scarcely credible today (although these struggles do, of course, still occur).

During the formative years of Women's Aid in the UK, the immediate, pressing need was to provide some kind of safe place to which women and their children who were experiencing male violence could escape, a new – and, at the time, staggeringly audacious – idea with almost no historical precedents in any country (although see Pleck 1987; Gordon 1988). Groups formed themselves as collectives and worked extremely hard over long periods of time to establish each new refuge, often against the odds. Usually there was no funding available and no possibility of employing workers but, instead, there was a high level of commitment and energy. Houses operated on principles of mutual self-help between the women residents, with support from volunteers and members of the Women's Aid group (Dobash and Dobash 1992; Hague and Malos 1998).

From the beginning, however, it was clear to everyone in the refuge movement that children as well as women needed an escape from the violence, and children were almost always the majority of refuge residents. The first draft of the Aims of NWAF specified that members were to care for the needs of 'battered women and their children'. Thus, a degree of visibility was accorded to children from the outset.

Given that most of the earliest refuges in Britain grew out of the work of Women's Liberation groups, which were at the time developing ideas about alternative forms of childcare, collective responsibility for children was a fundamental principle in how groups envisaged refuges working. The ability to put this ideal into practice sometimes fell short of the imagined possibilities, but there were many discussions within and between groups about how childcare could be organised differently and innovatively. Alongside this idealism was a tendency, sometimes, to view work with children as somehow worth less than work with women, a status issue both for workers in refuges and for women and children living in them. In many senses, refuge work with women was regarded as the 'real' work and women refuge residents as more important than children. Whilst trying to 'do things differently', refuges could not help reflecting, at the same time, the wider social valuations of children and of those who work with them.

However many groups provided activities and some held special meetings for children. The early work with children took issues of anti-sexism very seriously, and these were understood as involving more than gender stereotyping. Some of this work involved the employment of consciously anti-sexist male workers to offer children the opportunity to have contact with non-violent, gentle men (a distinction seen as less problematic then than now), until the movement became women-only in the late 1970s, as a move towards autonomy and empowerment for women. It was also the case that all refuge groups had to negotiate school and nursery places for children (often with great difficulty), and to start the long process of educating teachers and school heads about the impacts of domestic violence and about safety issues, matters which had almost never been raised before – ever.

Old NWAF and WAFE surveys tell us that there were debates and tensions about issues involving children within and between groups. An important issue of contention in the 1970s was the age limit for boy residents in refuges, with different refuges adopting different limits (on complex grounds including the potentially disturbing effect of the presence of women's teenage sons on other abused women). The organisation of creches at conferences (often, at the time, run by men) was another matter for discussion. Matters such as these were debated locally, regionally and nationally, and policy continued to be made at national conferences, throughout the 1970s and 1980s. There was a brief break in this process when the national federation in England temporarily lost central government funding for co-ordination work in the early 1980s. Central funding was resumed in 1986.

The development of child work policy

In 1986, a revision of the Aims and Principles of Women's Aid led to the inclusion of a specific statement that children are independently affected by domestic violence and that refuges should provide specific support for children. In 1989, a minimal child work policy was adopted and a national worker was employed on a one-year contract to look at developing services for children. Funding for the present full-time, permanent National Children's Officer post was secured in 1990.

In 1992–3, a Children's Rights policy was developed which set minimum standards for the conditions and services which children in refuges have the right to expect, and training workshops on children's issues have been held regularly at national Women's Aid conferences for many years (including, more recently, workshops on sexual abuse for adult survivors and on child ritual abuse).

The employment of children's workers

In the early days of refuge organisation in England, most groups which had made a decision to provide services for children either employed short-term staff on the relevant government Department of Employment schemes of the period or used unpaid volunteers. The employment of specific children's workers became more common in the early 1980s. Since general refuge workers were often already employed on more secure funding, this employment situation tended to cement differential attitudes as regards the relative importance of refuge workers (who mainly work with the women) and child workers. As child workers became more established in the late 1980s, however, these attitudes diminished to some extent, and the majority of groups now employ at least one child worker and a few employ several. Many workers have remained part-time or on short-term contracts, however, and some groups are still forced to rely on volunteer children's workers, although, in recent years, they have become much more likely to provide proper volunteer training, supervision and support.

Women's Aid groups throughout the UK have principally operated as collectives throughout their history (although this has now changed in many refuges). One of the guiding principles has always been equality of pay in order to avoid the introduction of formal and informal hierarchies. Initially, this principle was not always applied to child work but, in 1991, children's workers put forward a proposal for pay parity for all workers which was then adopted as official policy (though this remains difficult to implement).

Some children's workers have obtained grant-aid funding from local authorities or from other bodies, but many have been financed by short-term BBC Children in Need Appeal funding, and more recently by National Lottery money. Thus, the problem has remained of how to keep paid children's workers in post in the long term, and has frequently entailed a worker having to fundraise for her own job. Monies for children have sometimes been forthcoming in small quantities from donations and from charities and other bodies, but these have tended to be aimed specifically at providing equipment, activities, playschemes and events. The lack of secure basic funding for the employment of children's workers has been an enduring and major difficulty.

Despite such funding problems, by the early 1990s the majority of Women's Aid groups accepted the importance of conducting children's work. However, in some groups, child work continued to be regarded as residual in that 'any one of us can work with the children if we've got the time' (study interviewee) so that whoever was available might provide activities or take the children out, with little or no acknowledgement of the skilled nature of the work. In recent years, such attitudes appear to have been on the decline. There has been an increasing recognition that children's work is skilled and complex, and that specialist, trained workers are needed, committed to advocating with and for children.

Similarly, there has been an increasing commitment over recent years to providing good play facilities and children's areas in refuges. Whereas older refuges have often had an inadequate play-room squeezed in somewhere, or no play-room at all, recent purpose-built refuges have usually included specially designed children's facilities, indoors and out, and some other refuges have added new purpose-designed extensions or conversions for children.

Training

In common with generalist refuge workers in many groups, children's workers often had no training at all in the past. They were frequently employed on the basis of their personal qualities and life experience including, perhaps, their own experiences of domestic violence. However, the need for specialist training has been increasingly recognised, and children's workers often now have qualifications. Specialised and wide-ranging in-service training courses have been provided by the Women's Aid federations (including such issues as non-violence policies and alternatives to physical punishment, child abuse and protection, the 1989 Children Act, antiracism and HIV and Aids awareness) and there is a desire to link some of these courses into the NVQ framework. Non-affiliated groups have also participated in Women's Aid training provision. While this training is designed specifically for childworkers, some refuges train all their workers in children's work as a positive example of shared responsibility.

Children's workers often engage additionally in social services or inter-agency training within their localities. In general, this increasing training commitment has been part of a move to enhance the status of child workers. On-going training has also become increasingly necessary with the development of the 'contract culture' in which some grant aid agreements have begun to include specifications about child protection issues and provision for children.

The Children's Workers Group

The nationally-based Children's Workers Group was initially established in 1989, and provides support, liaison and information to participants. Initially the group was small, partly because it could be difficult for children's workers working alone or part-time to prioritise a group meeting which was being held many miles away. Over the last few years, however, the Children's Workers Group has become well established and attended, meeting regularly on a national basis in different parts of the country. Increasingly its work has encompassed training and policy development. It has provided vital national networking and support, augmented by regular national child work mailings, and has given an opportunity for a dialogue between the Women's Aid Federation of England National Children's Officer and the women doing direct work with children in refuges. Our research team conducted consultation with the Children's Workers Group and disseminated information on research implementation and findings through both the Group and the national mailing.

Children's meetings

An innovatory aspect of children's work in refuges has been the development of specific meetings for children which have acted as a forum to allow children's voices and views to be heard. In many refuges in the UK, a system of such meetings has been in operation for many years. These meetings have varied in frequency and scope, but have normally acted as a forum for children to meet together, to support each other, to discuss issues and to air their views. In some groups, although not all, the children's meetings have been in a position to make decisions, and to influence the larger house (or women's) meetings or workers' meetings. In one refuge visited in the research, for example, the children's meeting had made decisions about smoking in the refuge. Women residents and workers had then had to abide by these new rules. In some refuge situations, child workers have advocated on behalf of the children and of the children's meeting, and in others children have been empowered to take on this role themselves, to attend residents meetings and to make proposals for change. For example, in one refuge with which we worked, children had attended house meetings to engage in serious and careful discussion and decision-making about bedtimes. Overall, the experience of children's workers has been that children's meetings can provide a supportive forum to discuss issues and problems and to build children's confidence that their opinions are important and will be listened to. As a result, women residents have, on occasion, also had to challenge their own ideas about the importance of children.

Racism, discrimination and children's work

The emergence of issues in relation to race and racism inside the refuge movement developed as a result of several factors back in the 1970s. These included the presence and voices of black women and children in refuge groups, and the differential responses which they received from housing departments, schools and also within refuges themselves. In some cases, there was also a political commitment to challenge racism inside the refuge groups of the time as well as outside.

While some refuges overlooked issues of racism and groups tended to be mainly white, the research reported here found that, contrary to statements sometimes made these days, it is not true to say in any general way that refuges and feminist services and campaigns, during the period, failed to take on issues of race, class and sexuality. How individual groups responded to these issues varied, and there is little documentation of these variations beyond limited records from NWAF conferences and meetings and from individual groups. Some of these records show that, from the earliest days, children's work in a variety of refuges incorporated early stages of anti-racism awareness.

More recently, children's workers have attempted to work out how to challenge inter-personal racism and to undertake detailed anti-racism work with children in refuges. This has involved challenging racist behaviour and stereotypes, supporting and advocating for black children, engaging in general anti-racist struggles, and building a child work practice which is committedly anti-racist. Child workers have made use of anti-racist teaching materials, toys and books, and have attempted to develop their own materials as well. For example, children in the Hammersmith refuge in London, working together as a group and in conjunction with childcare workers, have developed their own anti-racism policy and designed the accompanying anti-racist materials. This type of work has extended in many cases to other forms of oppressive discrimination as well as racism, and has attempted to take on, with varying degrees of success, disability, class and sexuality issues in relation to children.

Some general refuges which employ predominantly black staff have developed particularly sensitive and principled ways of working against racism and discrimination, taking on such issues as an integral part of the daily, routine work in a way which many other refuges have yet to do. Specialist refuges, specifically for black women and children and for women and children from minority ethnic communities, have continued to be set up, and some of these have been in a position to develop specific anti-racist child work strategies. Not all have been able to employ child workers, however, due to the under-funding of many such specialist refuges which can sometimes be even more severe than for generalist refuges (see also Mama 1996).

Recent general developments in the awareness of children's issues and domestic violence

In the last few years, there have been increases in awareness at a general level, including amongst mainstream childcare agencies, about the impact on children of living with domestic violence (see, for example, Morley and Mullender 1994; Hester *et al.* 2000). Picking up on work in Canada (Jaffe *et al.* 1990), a few British local authorities began to highlight the issue in the early 1990s. Two pioneering conferences on the subject of children and domestic violence were held in the London Boroughs of Hackney and of Hammersmith and Fulham in 1992 (Holder *et al.* 1992; London Borough of Hackney 1992), leading to a variety of other national and regional conferences and training events.

The first British book on children and domestic violence was published in 1994 (Mullender and Morley 1994). Also in 1994, the children's charity, NCH:

Action for Children, published the report of a research study which they had conducted on children and domestic violence (Abrahams 1994). The Women's Aid Federation of England itself continued to develop policy and training on children and domestic violence (see Debbonaire 1994) and participated in publishing a book rooted in children's experiences of domestic violence (Saunders 1995). Further research has recently been completed by the NSPCC (McGee 1998; see also Chapter 5) and by the present authors (with others) (Mullender et al. 2000). The latter study examines children's own views, knowledge and coping strategies in relation to domestic violence.

All of this work shows how complex the impacts on children of domestic violence are. While children may be severely traumatised, they often also demonstrate remarkable strengths and resilience and develop wide-ranging coping strategies. In this country, researchers and Women's Aid workers and activists find that there is no one 'set' of effects or responses. Children respond in a wide variety of ways which may include increased aggression, withdrawal, school problems, anxiety, grief, insomnia, loss of confidence and psychological and behavioural difficulties. These varied reactions cannot be divided straightforwardly down neat gender lines (see, for example, Kelly 1994; Saunders 1995; Hague et al. 1996; Mullender 1996). What is clear, however, is the depth of the pain and anxiety which is caused to children by domestic violence between adults, and the enduring nature of emotional effects which can extend into the long term.

Professionals who have previously ignored the impacts on children are now developing an interest, with the subject becoming a popular one for training events in many agencies, often with input from Women's Aid. New policy and practice developments, sometimes connected with inter-agency domestic violence forums, are occurring in various areas (see, for example, Hague et al. 1996a) and guidance materials, named *Making an Impact,* were prepared in 1998 for social services through the Department of Health (Hester et al. 2000). These materials, which are now being widely used, include a reader and training pack and were produced by the Domestic Violence Research Group at Bristol, the NSPCC and Barnado's, with input from Women's Aid.

While welcome, however, these developments have occurred alongside widespread cutbacks in the social and caring services which children and women experiencing domestic violence need, and increasing attacks on single parenthood as part of a 'dependency culture', despite some new programmes put in place by the Labour government.

Developments in refuge children's work

Meanwhile, within refuges there has been a continuing development of sensitive ways of working with and 'alongside' children, taking children's views and needs seriously, and attempting to enable children's voices to be heard. The value of play in terms of creative expression, its potential as a way of dealing with experiences of domestic violence and the therapeutic importance of child work in refuges have been increasingly recognised. In addition, child workers have developed innovative work practices around the empowerment of children and advocacy with and for them, as well as children's self-advocacy. One such practice is the way in which, whenever they can, child workers really listen to children in a deep way (which is hard both to describe and to achieve), and attempt actively to avoid imposing on them patronising adult attitudes or unnecessary adult power and ideas. Enabling children to take some control of their lives, to openly talk about their feelings and experiences, or to have a 'special person' to be there for them and to always take their part, are empowering concepts in themselves.

In both one-to-one and groupwork, child workers have frequently also worked in an open-ended way in order to respond to the needs of children who may choose, for example, to open up about the abuse they have experienced in less formal contexts, such as in the mini-bus or when discussing a painting. Thus, children's workers have been able to develop a flexible, child-led approach to dealing with abuse and other issues.

In our study, we found many examples of child workers using guided play to help children to come to terms with the violence they had experienced (Hague *et al.* 1996: 56). In the words of one interviewee, workers were able 'to take them just as far as they want to go and validate them', which sounds simple but, in fact, requires a skilled approach and the ability to make a range of sensitive judgements. Some workers used art and creative play. Colouring book materials on refuge life provided by the Women's Aid Federation of England were used by a variety of groups and, in some, the children had written their own documents on what new children might need to know on first arrival.

For many years there has been a tension within refuges between the provision of immediate childcare to relieve mothers (which is what many women have said that they want and need when they come into a refuge) and work with and for children which is deeper and broader, and which may include enabling women and children to further develop their relationships with each other. However, most refuges with provision for children have attempted to do both, and to supplement groupwork with longer-term preventative and developmental work together with both women and children.

In recent years, there has been an increasing focus on strategic thinking about the development of child work within refuges, both in terms of 'career development' for workers and of what child work should or could be, although often it has only been the well-resourced groups which have been in a position to implement any of this. As a result, there has been the potential for divisions to develop between minimally-funded groups and those with the resources, stability and confidence to move forward in new ways.

Workshops

Many refuge child work projects now run innovative workshops with children on specific topics such as bullying. In 1994, an evaluation of work with children in one particular refuge was undertaken by one of the authors of this chapter. The group concerned provided structured workshops with children on racism, bullying, anger, sexism and keeping safe (sexual abuse), as well as one-to-one sessions with children who wanted them. The workshops were both proactive – working on issues which the child workers thought were important for all children – and reactive – picking up on things which were happening in children's lives. An interesting finding of the evaluation was the high take up of one-to-one sessions by boys and by black or ethnic minority children. The child workers clearly encouraged and enabled boys to take part in personalised, self-reflective work, and were also committed to dealing with complicated issues about identity and ethnicity.

A comparison of what children wrote at the beginning and end of their one-to-one work (which was structured through a workbook developed by the child workers) was revealing, developing from single words to lengthy and complex responses. An observation of one of the workshops revealed both the importance of children setting their own ground rules and the sensitivity of the children to each other. The expectation and enabling of children to interact with each other and with adults in a respectful and engaged way, whilst knowing that they would be listened to, were clear in these workshops and formed a foundation for developing non-abusive relationships.

Non-violence policies

In 1990, after debate in refuges for many years, a policy of 'no violence to children' or 'no smacking' was adopted as a goal for refuges. This built on the practice which many refuges had already been using of discouraging smacking and encouraging alternative approaches to childcare difficulties. The original initiative for the adoption of this official policy on non-violence against children was put to the annual national Women's Aid conference in 1990 by Greenwich Women's Aid supported by Lewisham and Kingston Women's Aids. 'No smacking' has been promoted as a formal policy since that time and Women's Aid refuges now attempt as a matter of course to provide environments in which children are not hit while they and their mothers are resident there. Specific, often written, 'non-violence to children' practices and policies have been extensively developed within individual refuges. These initiatives have led to often sensitive and respectful attempts to build a way of implementing the policies, together with the women and children concerned, in a sympathetic and collaborative manner. Support and training from the Women's Aid federations has been of help in these attempts. In particular, courses on alternative approaches to disciplining children have been developed. Other agencies could undoubtedly learn from this work.

Child protection

After years of official indifference, the connections between domestic violence and child abuse on a general level have been increasingly recognised recently

(Kelly 1994), and there have been various developments in services as a result. (See, for example, Humphreys 1997, on child protection case planning issues in the context of domestic violence, and Hester and Pearson 1998, on some ways in which domestic violence work with abused children is moving – in the name of their publication – *From Periphery to Centre*.)

The emergence of the recognition of child abuse in general as a key issue within refuges themselves goes much further back, however. It initially occurred in the 1970s, but to a greater extent in the early 1980s, and the Women's Aid Federation of England was part of the network of feminist services and campaigns which originally brought the specific issue of child sexual abuse into the open. In fact, the involvement of refuges in sexual abuse work and in child protection pre-dated the growth, over the last 15 or so years, of vastly increased state concern for these issues in general.

Internally, refuges have now developed comprehensive child protection policies, following a Women's Aid training initiative in 1991. Developing such internal policies has been a complex and difficult process, however, since it has required groups to think about circumstances in which women's and children's interests might not be the same and at times to opt in favour of children. What emerged over time were attempts to develop specifically feminist approaches to child protection. Many groups have developed ways of thinking and talking about these issues with each other, with women residents, and with children, which have moved their refuge work forward in confident and productive ways, although supporting women and treating them with respect while dealing with their possible abuse of their children is no easy task.

In addition, the increasing interest in the impact on children of domestic violence, while welcome, has led to some examples of bureaucratic or punitive child protection responses to the mother. A common thread is that, if a woman does not leave, or if she returns to, a violent partner, this can be designated 'failure to protect', with the non-abusing parent thus being deemed responsible for exposing children to significant harm. On the other hand, the new awareness has begun to lead to more creative initiatives in child abuse work in relation to domestic violence in some areas, including the establishing of connections between Area Child Protection Committees (ACPCs) and inter-agency domestic violence forums, and the development of multi-agency or ACPC domestic violence and child protection policies guidelines (see, for example, Cleveland Area Child Protection Committee 1995; DoH 1999; also Chapter 15). The emerging philosophy that the protection of women can be the most effective form of child protection (see, for example, Kelly 1994; Morley and Mullender 1994) has begun to open up a constructive exchange between refuges, social services and children's charities.

Legislation and lobbying

Children's workers in refuges and the Women's Aid National Children's Officer have participated in lobbying work around many pieces of legislation and in the production of a whole variety of policy guidelines and briefing papers. Just a few examples of their legislative and campaigning work are included here. For example, the passage of the 1989 Children Act in England and Wales was regarded by many as a move forward in British childcare legislation. Nevertheless, the Children Act has nothing to say about domestic violence, and children's workers and the Women's Aid federations (together with researchers and other agencies) have been active in trying to address this situation. One approach put forward by Women's Aid and by some other agencies has been to define children who have experienced domestic violence as 'children in need' under Section 17 of the Act in order to access funds for preventative and support work in refuges.

As regards the private provisions of the Act, there have been some improvements in practice by court welfare officers and others. However, the granting of contact and residence orders for fathers after separation under Section 8 of the Act has remained a problem in terms of repeated abuse, and children's workers, refuge groups and the Women's Aid Federation of England have monitored incidents where further violence towards either the woman or the children has occurred, purely as a result of such orders (see also Hester and Radford 1996). A new women's campaign on the issue called The Best Interests Campaign is now in progress which is campaigning on contact arrangements for children affected by domestic violence.

Women's Aid has also campaigned around the 1991 Child Support Act (which aims to make absent fathers financially responsible for their children, particularly where the mothers and children are otherwise dependent on state benefit), and contributed to the inclusion of the clause which enables women experiencing domestic violence to be exempted.

On-going issues for children's workers

In the study, general current concerns of children's workers included the move away from collectives and the consequent shift from 'collective' to 'worker' responsibility, as well as the skew in work practices which has meant that children's workers have invariably also worked with women, whereas generalist refuge workers have not been similarly expected to work with children. The fact that differential pay and conditions have continued to apply to child work in many refuges, despite the policy of pay parity, has remained a further matter of concern. This enduring differential reflects the persistence of broader social values about the lower importance accorded to work with children. It also reflects tighter financial and organisational controls from funders which have placed limits on the possibilities of 'income sharing' and have reinforced divisions in levels of status.

The complex project of developing equalities work with children and challenging discrimination of all types have continued as a basic and integral thread running through all child work. Access to schools has continued to be an issue and has worsened in some areas in recent years with the introduction of local management of schools. One result of this has been that some schools have failed to welcome refuge children (who almost invariably stay for a short period only) in the push to improve exam result ratings. On the other hand, an encouraging sign has been the beginning of the development of preventative anti-violence work in schools. This work has been initiated through children's workers locally and Women's Aid nationally, through inter-agency projects, or through local authority staff specialising in domestic violence and in women's equality issues. Various education packs for use in schools have now been produced. Excellent examples were published, for instance, in 1995 in Islington (London Borough of Islington 1995), and in 1999 in Hackney (Morley 1999).

Overall, funding problems have remained the major difficulty in the provision of children's services. Many child work projects in refuges have been prevented from developing properly, with clear goals and forward planning, due to financial insecurity. There has also been a danger, still continuing, of losing a considerable proportion of children's workers as BBC Children In Need in England withdraws from funding salaries in the belief that these should be funded by local authorities. Many such authorities, however, have remained cash-strapped themselves so that obtaining new grant-aid has become more difficult in many areas.

Conclusion

Over recent years, the children's rights movements in various countries, and also the UN Declaration on the Rights of the Child, have drawn attention to the need to focus on children, independently of those who care for them, and to listen to what they say. For far longer than this, however, refuges have attempted to provide an arena where children's rights have been developed in a committed and principled way, in conjunction with a recognition that most children benefit from support and safety for their mothers. Overall, however, women still carry more or less total responsibility for childcare within society, and are still the targets of blame for children's behaviour or difficulties. Refuges have tried to introduce imaginative responses to these over-arching realities and to women and children's often intersecting concerns. Conversely, the evidence appears to be that some other childcare agencies have artificially split their concern for children from any very developed recognition of women's needs.

The work done with children in refuges has become one of the strongest arguments, alongside women's safety needs, for increasing refuge provision since children have received minimal, if any, support in other forms of temporary accommodation. However, child work projects within refuges have remained far more insecure than refuges themselves, and strong arguments have repeatedly needed to be made about the importance of this form of intervention with abused children and the children of abused mothers. Alongside this tiring work, children's workers have developed creative, and sometimes inspiring, ways of 'being' with children and of promoting children's interests and views.

Thus, insights from the history of how children's work in the refuge movement has developed in England may be of use in highlighting the importance of this work (both in the UK and in other countries), in exploring the difficulties and contradictions which currently beset it, and in celebrating its achievements in offering children survivors of domestic violence a positive and creative experience at a most difficult and painful time in their lives. For many years, children's workers in refuges have conducted brave, compassionate and innovative work with children, with almost no recognition, rewards or resources. We could all, perhaps, learn from their example.

References

Abrahams, C. (1994) *The Hidden Victims*, London: NCH.

Cleveland Area Child Protection Committee (1995) *Cleveland ACPC Practice Guidance. Domestic Violence: Whose problem is it?*, Middlesbrough, Cleveland: Cleveland ACPC.

Debbonaire, T. (1994) 'Work with children in women's refuges and after', in Mullender, A. and Morley, R. (eds) *Children Living with Domestic Violence*, London: Whiting and Birch, pp. 142–69.

Department of Health (1995) *Child Protection Messages from Research*, London: HMSO.

Department of Health (1999) *Working Together to Safeguard Children*, London: DoH.

Dobash, R. and Dobash, R. (1980) *Violence Against Wives*, London: Open Books.

Dobash, R. and Dobash, R. (1992) *Women, Violence and Social Change*, London: Routledge.

Featherstone, B. and Trinder, L. (1997) 'Familiar subjects? Domestic violence and child welfare', *Child and Family Social Work 2*; 147–59.

Gordon, L. (1988) *Heroes of Their Own Lives: The Politics and History of Family Violence*, London: Virago.

Gulbenkian Foundation (1995) *Children and Violence*, London: Gulbenkian Foundation.

Hague, G., Kelly, L., Malos, E. and Mullender, A. with Debbonaire, T. (1996) *Children, Domestic Violence and Refuges: A Study of Needs and Responses*, Bristol: Women's Aid Federation of England.

Hague, G. and Malos, E. (1998) *Domestic Violence: Action for Change*, Second Edition. Cheltenham: New Clarion Press.

Hague, G., Malos, E. and Dear, W. (1996a) *Multi-agency Work and Domestic Violence*, Bristol: The Policy Press.

Hester, M., Harwin. N. and Pearson, N. (2000) *Making an Impact*, Department of Health with Barnado's. Republished by: London: Jessica Kingsley.

Hester, M. and Pearson, C. (1998) *From Periphery to Centre: Domestic Violence in Work with Abused Children*, Bristol: The Policy Press.

Hester, M., Pearson, C. and Radford, L. (1997) *Domestic Violence: A National Survey of Court Welfare and Voluntary Sector Mediation Practice*, Bristol: The Policy Press.

Hester, M. and Radford, L. (1996) *Domestic Violence and Child Contact Arrangements in Britain and Denmark*, Bristol: The Policy Press.

Holder, R., Kelly, L. and Singh, T. (1992) *Suffering in Silence*, London: Hammersmith and Fulham Domestic Violence Forum.

Humphreys, C. (1997) *Case Planning Issues where Domestic Violence Occurs in the Context of Child Protection*. Coventry: University of Warwick.

Jaffe, P., Wolfe, D. and Wilson, S. (1990) *Children of Battered Women*, Newbury Park, California: Sage.

Kelly, L. (1994) 'The Interconnectedness of domestic violence and child abuse', in Mullender, A. and Morley, R. (eds) *Children Living with Domestic Violence*, London: Whiting and Birch, pp. 43–56.

London Borough of Hackney (1992) *The Links Between Domestic Violence and Child Abuse: Developing Services*, London: London Borough of Hackney.

London Borough of Islington (1995) *Stop: Striving to Prevent Domestic Violence: An Activity Pack*, London: London Borough of Islington.

Mama, A. (1996) *The Hidden Struggle: Statutory and Voluntary Sector Responses to Violence Against Black Women in the Home*, London: Whiting and Birch.

Maynard, M. (1985) 'The response of social workers to domestic violence', in Pahl, J. (ed.) *Private Violence and Public Policy*, London: Routledge, pp. 125–41.

McGee, C. (1998) *Children's and Mother's Experiences of Child Protection Following Domestic Violence*, London: NSPCC.

Morley, R. (1999) *Respect: A Resource Pack for Schools Challenging Violence and Abuse*, Hackney: Hackney Community Psychology Department; Child and Adolescent Services.

Morley, R. and Mullender, A. (1994) 'What do we know from research?', in Mullender, A. and Morley, R. (eds) *Children Living with Domestic Violence*, London: Whiting and Birch, pp. 24–42.

Mullender, A. (1996) *Rethinking Domestic Violence*, London: Routledge.

Mullender, A., Kelly, L., Hague, G., Imam, U. and Malos, E. (2000) *Children's Needs, Coping Strategies and Understandings of Woman Abuse. ESRC Report*, Warwick: University of Warwick.

Mullender, A. and Morley, R. (eds) (1994) *Children Living with Domestic Violence*, London: Whiting and Birch.

Pleck, E. (1987) *Domestic Tyranny: The Making of Social Policy Against Family Violence from Colonial Times to the Present*, Oxford: Oxford University Press.

Saunders, A. with Epstein, C., Keep, G. and Debbonaire, T. (1995) *It Hurts Me Too: Children's Experiences of Domestic Violence and Refuge Life*, Bristol: WAFE and London: NSW and ChildLine.

Schechter, S. (1982) *Women and Male Violence: The Visions and Struggles of the Battered Women's Movement*, Boston, MA: South End Press.

Part III

Women who fight back

Experiences and outcomes

8 Women, anger and domestic violence

The implications for legal defences to murder

Sue Griffiths

The debate concerning women who kill violent/abusive male partners, and the inability of existing murder defences to encompass their experiences, has been on-going for the last decade (see Chapter 9). Feminist groups such as Justice For Women, Southall Black Sisters and Rights Of Women have worked tirelessly to support individual women charged or convicted of murder whilst publicly exposing the inadequacies of the legal system and campaigning for legal changes (see Chapter 10). The success of a number of women's appeals against murder convictions (for example, Kiranjit Ahluwalia, Sara Thornton and Emma Humphreys) appears indicative of a shift in both the public's and the law's understanding of women's homicidal responses to 'domestic' violence. But is this enough? All three women were initially convicted of murder. Emma Humphreys spent ten years in prison before being released. Sara Thornton had her first application for leave to appeal rejected. As a member of Justice For Women, I believe that a new defence to murder is required: one that acknowledges women's experiences of, and responses to, domestic violence in much the same way that self-defence or provocation were constructed to reflect men's experiences of imminent attack or provocation.

In this chapter I use the defence of provocation to demonstrate the ability of the law to change understanding and interpretation whilst maintaining its founding principle, the right to angered retaliation. But applying this principle to women who kill violent male partners appears problematic. Part of the reason is that the role of anger in women's responses to domestic violence remains relatively unaddressed. My analysis of interviews with 18 women subjected to domestic violence shows anger to be an influential factor in their responses. The question is how to incorporate women's experiences into legal defences to murder? The debate over legal reform as an effective feminist strategy is outlined before I conclude the chapter by advocating the proposed new defence of self-preservation (see also Chapter 9).

The provocation defence: its historical and philosophical roots

Jeremy Horder's *Provocation and Responsibility* (1992) is unique in that it combines historical and philosophical sources with legal material to trace the aetiology of the defence of provocation. Using this material Horder traces the moral and legal development of the doctrine of provocation and in doing so explores the changes in legal understandings of anger. Despite these changes the defence of provocation has always been based on the right to angered retaliation.

Anger, Horder maintains, was initially conceptualised as a rational and reasonable emotion to be acted upon – the 'honourable men' of the sixteenth and seventeenth centuries were expected to feel anger and to challenge any affronts they encountered. The acts defined as provocative by C. J. Holt in 1707 were those that seriously threatened a 'man's honour' (Ashworth 1976). However, the yardstick for assessing the degree of retaliation proportionate to the provocation was the Aristotelian 'mean'; the 'mean' being action sufficient to return the status of the provoked person. Should retaliation be seen to be greater than this 'mean' then punishment was warranted as a way of teaching the wrongdoer that they had overstepped the mark of 'honourable' retaliation. Provocation was thus a partial defence – for whilst the defendant had been provoked their retaliation could be seen as excessive.

Horder (1992) refers to this understanding of anger as 'anger as outrage'. But, he argues, anger as outrage has been unjustifiably excluded from the modern definition of provocation. This was brought about by the increasing usage of the terminology 'loss of self-control' during the eighteenth and nineteenth centuries. During these centuries the increasing focus on the mental workings of the mind meant that anger was no longer seen as a reasoned process but rather as an overpowering passion that temporarily usurped reasoning faculties. Since then, the twentieth-century legal understanding of anger has returned to the issue of proportionality in retaliation. Whilst the modern conception of anger as loss of self-control differs from the earlier concept of anger as outrage, both legal periods involve assessing the defendant's degree of correspondence to a 'mean'. The difference being that the modern 'mean' of measurement is no longer some abstract ideal, but is embodied in 'the man on the Clapham omnibus'. Despite these changes in conceptual understandings of anger, Horder claims that:

> In practice, for hundreds of years judges have been instructing juries to consider the defence of provocation where defendants have killed out of outrage, satisfying an urgent desire for retaliation, as well as in cases where defendants lose self-control and have satisfied that desire immediately. [. . .] The doctrine of provocation has always been a condescension to fatal retaliation inflicted in outrage *or* following a loss of self-control, not a condescension to the latter alone, and the terminology of the latter has historically always included the former within its working ambit
>
> (Horder 1992: 71–2 – emphasis in original).

Anger as outrage would appear more adequately to encompass women's responses to domestic violence allowing for the concept of provocation as 'slow-burning'. Indeed, as Horder states, until the *Duffy* case (1949) resulted in the restriction of the defence of provocation to a 'sudden loss of self-control', no extension would have been necessary to incorporate the 'slow-burn' cases within the scope of the defence.

> The root of the trouble and misunderstanding has been the recent failure to recognize that the law's conception of anger has never always been loss of self-control alone, but has historically included outrage. [...] The person who boils up when her long-term violent abuser is asleep in his chair may well be acting out of provoked outrage, despite the absence of any imme- diate provocation. Such a person's anger would always historically have fallen within the scope of the defence. What is required is a reinstatement of this legal position, through substitution of references to provoked angry retaliation in place of references to provoked loss of self-control in the Homicide Act 1957, section 3
>
> (Horder 1992: 190).

Horder thus identifies the reason for the current exclusion of women's experi- ences of provocation, the mistakenly (re)defined concept of angered retaliations as being only those resulting from a sudden loss of self-control. He promptly proposes the means for rectifying this exclusion by reinstating the defence's his- torically accepted concept of anger as outrage. This would seem to resolve, in one fell swoop, feminists' criticisms of the defence. However, Horder then goes on to dismiss women's homicidal retaliations as being either acts of outrage or resultant from the loss of self-control. Horder effectively denies women's experi- ences as angered and suggests their actions are better suited to the defence of diminished responsibility.

I believe Horder denies women's responses as triggered by anger (whether as outrage or as loss of self-control) in order to further his own argument that the defence of provocation be abolished. He claims that whilst feminists' attacks on the defence have 'lacked an understanding of the historic scope of the law's conceptions of anger', they nevertheless justify the abolition of the defence. Arguably, feminists have a clear understanding of the law's conceptions of anger; an understanding based on the gendered application of the right to angered retaliation. The problem for women is that the power to define what constitutes provocation, whom it is allowed to affect, and when and how they can be expected to respond, has been largely outside women's sphere of influ- ence. Edwards (1991), Radford (1993) and Lees (1994) identified this problem when they argued that 'justifiable anger' is applied selectively.

> The right to justifiable anger is not universal in our culture – men have the right, under certain circumstances, but women have no right under any. This is reflected in the interpretation of the law and what things 'said and done' constitute provocation. But provocation is not simply about *being* provoked; it is also about the *right* to be provoked. Men have the right to react to provocation while women do not. Women's response to similar

situations is bound by gender expectations of women's appropriate response as one of patience, tolerance and acquiescence. When women try to present a defence of provocation, they rarely succeed

(Edwards 1991: 182–3 – emphasis in original).

Horder (1992) argues that 'righteous indignation' is a morally better virtue than angered retaliation. Righteous indignation is similar to anger as outrage and anger as loss of self-control in that it stems from a judgement of an act as a wrongdoing, leads to a hot-blooded response and the desire for retribution. But the desire for retribution differs; whereas angered retaliation calls for the inflicting of retaliatory suffering, righteous indignation calls for raising the provoker's awareness of the wrongdoing, whether through the involvement of others as in a public denunciation, or through the perpetrator's acknowledgement of their wrongdoing. Righteous indignation, Horder claims, is more typical of women's experiences of anger. Thus he sweepingly denies women's experiences of anger as resulting in outrage or loss of self-control and sets their anger on the morally higher ground of righteous indignation. His final recommendation is that, with righteous indignation logically bringing about the demise of the defence of provocation, the 'morality of retribution will then be left to the institutions of state punishment'.

The weakness and irony of Horder's recommendation is that women already pursue the righteous indignation approach to challenge men's violence. Women call upon the 'institutions of state punishment' every time they contact the police, apply for injunctions, or bring assault charges. It is when these institutions fail to act on women's angered sense of righteous indignation that many women find themselves having to seek retribution, or rather self-preservation, through their own actions: actions which often place them outside the remit of the existing defence of provocation. It is this gendered aspect of legal formulation and implementation that Horder fails to account for; hence the inherent weakness in his reasons for recommending the abolition of provocation.

Significant in Horder's work on provocation is the identification of shifts in discourses concerning the acceptable ways of responding to provocation, and the legal encoding of these new understandings in the defence's changing criteria. Ashworth (1976) cites the 1707 *Mawgridge* case as the common law statement in which the legal definition of what was and what was not considered provocation was specified. Ashworth notes that much significance was placed on an assault or physical threat – so much so that if an act falling within one of the five 'insufficient' categories were accompanied by an assault, 'even a trivial assault such as nose-pulling or "filliping upon the forehead"', this would justify a claim to provocation.

Despite the exclusion of words alone as a form of provocation in the 1707 *Mawgridge* case, Taylor (1986: 1695) noted that where a woman's adultery was involved then words alone were sufficient to support a claim of provocation: 'From 1871 to 1946, a line of English cases held that words alone could effectively provoke if those words confessed adultery.' The acceptance of words alone, even when concerning a wife's adultery, was quashed in common law in the

Holmes appeal of 1946. Here a man who killed his wife when she admitted to adultery during an argument was found guilty of murder. His appeals went to both the Court of Appeal and the House of Lords where Viscount Simon declared:

> In my view, however, a sudden confession of adultery without more can never constitute provocation of a sort, which might reduce murder to manslaughter. The dictum attributed to BLACKBURN, J., [1861] and in any cases which seem to accept or apply it, can no longer be regarded as good law
> (1946 All E.R. 124 at pp. 127–8).

Within 11 years this legal pronouncement was to be overturned when 'words alone' were reinstated as reason for claiming provocation in the Homicide Act 1957. Viscount Simon in the same 1946 *Holmes* case also articulated the legal acceptance of law as a reflection of changing social values and thus as a fluid rather than static enterprise:

> the application of common law principles [. . .] must to some extent be controlled by the evolution of society. For example, the instance given by BLACKSTONE'S COMMENTARIES [. . .] that if a man's nose was pulled and he thereupon struck his aggressor so as to kill him, this was only manslaughter, may very well represent the natural feeling of the past, but I should doubt very much whether such a view should necessarily be taken nowadays. The injury done to a man's sense of honour by minor physical assaults may well be differently estimated in differing ages
> (1946 All E.R. 124 at p. 128).

These pronouncements clearly demonstrate that there is the facility for change in legal understandings and definitions of provocation. However, although the acts constituting provocation and the manner of responding may have shifted to keep in line with social mores, the underlying principle of the right to angered retaliation remains intact. Yet the connection between women's anger and their responses to domestic violence is relatively unexplored.

Women and anger

Part of the reason for the lack of work making these connections is the lack of literature on women and anger in general, and women, anger and heterosexual relationships in particular.[1] What literature there is tends to focus on women and aggression (Campbell 1993; Hart 1994; Kirsta 1994). Campbell's (1993) study on aggression explores the gendered differences in cultural and social experiences and outcomes of anger. Her interchangeable usage of the terms 'anger' and 'aggression' implies an inherent relationship between emotion and actions. Campbell argues that social perceptions inform the negative view women hold concerning their own anger whilst the same source of perceptions reinforce the positive view of anger in men. For women, anger is seen as the loss of self-control whilst for men it is the means of imposing control over others. Women's anger is thus viewed as expressive and men's as instrumental.

Kirkwood's (1993) study observed that, for many of the women in her research, anger was experienced as an 'intense surge of energy' resulting in one of two outcomes: if the means of leaving abusive men were available, then anger triggered leaving; if the resources were absent, then anger became manifest in thoughts of homicide and/or suicide. Kirkwood acknowledged that many women in general have difficulty in identifying or expressing anger, and wryly pointed out:

> The fact that this anger, for many of them, was an essential tool in breaking free from abuse, and that the culture in which they live promotes the loss of this tool in women, indicates another way in which abuse and the dynamics of control are linked to and supported by the social construction of masculinity and femininity.
>
> (1993: 81).

For both Campbell (1993) and Kirsta (1994), the discussion of women and anger quickly turns to claims that women are as violent as men. Campbell cites the work of Straus *et al.* (1981) to claim:

> But of all the forms of criminal violence, it is only those committed in the privacy of the home that do not show the usual marked gender differences. What is it about cohabitation that can lead to this increase in women's *aggression*? How can we explain the fact that women, so infrequently represented among muggers and robbers, recoil far less often from assaulting the men with whom they live?
>
> (1993: 103–4 – emphasis added).

Campbell does concede that physical differences between men and women frequently result in women's injuries being more severe, and that the issue of 'spousal' violence has 'rightly' focused on the suffering of women rather than men. Kirsta (1994) goes further and entitles her book *Deadlier than the Male: Violence and Aggression in Women*. Citing various research projects Kirsta argues:

> there is growing evidence that women are as wholly capable of carrying out certain despicable outrages as are men, with the same compulsion to dominate, humiliate and terrorize others. Their propensity to give full cathartic vent to years of pent-up hatred, fury and resentment, when they choose to unleash these, can equal, if not exceed, men's
>
> (1994: 144).

The cause of women's 'pent-up hatred, fury and resentment' is left undeveloped. Instead Kirsta rapidly moves into discussing women who kill and her book remains descriptive of the violent manifestations of women's aggression rather than a serious study of the factors influencing or giving rise to such aggressive behaviours.

Campbell (1993) appears alone in attempting to draw some connections between women's anger and their killing of known abusive men. She argues that the 'cumulative rage' experienced by women be seen as the mitigating factor when women kill known abusers. But she acknowledges that this contextualising of women's use of violence is problematic for courts as it over-emphasises the individual perceptions. Instead she calls for a 'middle path' to be found:

> by requiring that the woman's actions be those that would be taken by *any reasonable woman* faced with such a situation
>
> (1993: 148 – emphasis in original).

Women's experiences of anger in general, and the role of anger in terms of women's experiences of domestic violence in particular, remain relatively unre-searched. Making the link between the founding principle of the defence of provocation, the legally accepted means by which provocation is evidenced and women's actual experiences was crucial to my research. It enabled systematic exploration of women's changing responses and the factors constraining and influencing women's response choices.

Women's experiences of domestic violence and anger

Any exploration of women who kill abusive men that isolates their experiences implies homicidal women are in some way different to the majority of women subjected to domestic violence. By examining the experiences and responses of both groups of women, we can begin to explore any similarities and/or differ-ences in their histories and experiences and so develop an understanding of why and when women kill abusive men (Browne 1989).

Comparing the experiences of women who killed with women who had not formed the starting point of my doctoral research (Griffiths 1997). I carried out in-depth interviews with 18 women who had been, or were still in, abusive het-erosexual relationships. Ten of the women (some from refuges, others from local self-support groups) never faced criminal charges for their responses to the domestic violence. Four of the remaining eight women faced a variety of assault charges and convictions, and for one woman the charges involved fraud and deception. The final four women had been convicted of murder or, for one woman, attempted murder.

Many of the women in the study found it difficult to identify their experiences as 'angered', though indications of this were contained in their stories. Fay[2] was in a refuge because her home was uninhabitable after her partner's final attack. When asked about her experience of anger, Fay explained that she kept it bottled up.

SUE: And how do you cope with that anger?
FAY: I'm one of these people really who keep things bottled up inside them so I

don't think I do cope with it, just let things build up. And then try and shove it, y'know, to back of me mind. Put up with a lot, y'know – it takes a lot before I sort of like explode.

In the analysis of the interviews it became evident that anger was experienced on two planes, as an emotion and as a trigger to action.[3] Anger, when experienced, most typically resulted in the women's own use of violence, albeit not always directed at the men. Some women put their anger towards repairing the damage that resulted from the men's assaults, or, as in the case of Jill, repairing the doors *she* had kicked in out of anger at her partner's abuse.

As an emotion, anger was described predominantly by the non-homicidal women. Their anger was triggered by the post-violence reactions of the women themselves, other people and/or institutions. Women were angry with themselves for allowing the abuse; they were angry when the legal system failed to punish the men with any degree of seriousness; and they were angry at the outcomes of the violence.

ANNE: And I was expecting having to go to court and everything. Police told me, I didn't even know that it'd been seen to. And police told me when I had them out last week, that he'd been fined £30 and he got 12 months suspended.
SUE: And that was a charge of. . .
ANNE: that was for cutting me face and breaking me nose, so. They've just got a slap on hands, didn't he?
SUE: They've just?
ANNE: He got a slap on hands that's it. If it had been a man, I think he'd have done time wouldn't he? Just 'cos I'm a woman it's that way.
SUE: How are you feeling?
ANNE: Mad about that but life's got to go on, hasn't it?

SAM: Never let, ever, ever let any man make me feel as small as what he made me feel when he did that to me.
SUE: How did he make you feel small?
SAM: 'Cos I felt as though he were in control I felt as though I weren't even in control of meself anymore, because if I fought back I came off worse so that meant he were in control – he were even in control of what I was doing, not just what he was doing – he was in control of my actions as well. And I hate that. Because I couldn't respond because if I did I came off worse so it felt as though he just had total control of everything and I couldn't cope with that.

Fewer women in the homicide group expressed anger as part of their experiences. Two women in this group, Noola and Pam, consistently denied any sense of anger either as an emotion or as a trigger to responses. This is an indication of the difference in the two women's perceptions of the violences they experienced. They regarded themselves as entirely sexually or mentally abused. Noola perceived the violence as part of life, seeing it as an extension of her childhood experiences and therefore normal.

SUE: Did you ever feel angry about it [the abuse]?
NOOLA: No. No because – perhaps angry's not the right word. No 'cos it was just a normal way of life, don't you see?

Pam, subjected to continuous mental abuse, denied ever experiencing the emotion of anger. Rather she describes the insidious nature of such abuse.

PAM: At the time – I don't think I felt angry I just felt useless that, I didn't seem to be able to do the right thing. And as I say I think the fact that you feel like that – I felt belittled, I felt – erm . . . oh I'd got no self-esteem.

The simplistic, sequential process of provocation – anger – retaliation inherent in the defence of provocation was not replicated in women's experiences. The role of anger as an influence in women's responses was complex and not always easily discernible. Often denied as an emotion or trigger to action, anger, nevertheless, appeared in many of the women's stories.

Three distinct stages of responding emerged from the interviews; first reaction, then resolution and finally resistance. This reflected the overall structure of the women's responses as a systematic movement away from the individual incidents of violence. The initial stage of reactions ceased for a number of reasons but it was mainly the men's behaviour that triggered the shift in women's responses. The men's greater strength prevented women fighting back on future occasions, whilst their use of apologies and promises that the violence would cease ensured that those women who left during this first response stage returned to their relationships. Further triggering the shift into the second response stage was the women's pragmatic realisation that their initial reactions failed to prevent the violence, coupled with a growing awareness of the impact of the violence on their perceptions of themselves and their relationships. A sense of duty to maintain the relationship was expressed by a number of married women which, coupled with shame and/or a belief that the violence was their fault and the lack of financial or family resources to facilitate leaving, all influenced the enactment of a new set of responses. These responses were aimed at deflecting or defusing the potential for men's use of violence and formed the second response stage – resolution.

This second stage contained the least potentially lethal responses for the men but the most damaging for the women. The use of tranquillisers, alcohol and/or illicit drugs as a means of blocking out the effects of the violence, and the mental strategy of 'blanking out' the abuse, were undertaken as part of the women's efforts to reduce the likelihood of the men becoming violent or abusive. It was the lack of impact of these responses of resolution on the men's continued use of violence, combined with the women's experiences of the violence as 'grinding down', their experiences of fear as an on-going aspect of their lives, and their increasing awareness of self-diminishment that were the salient factors triggering the women's shift into the final response stage, resistance.

The women's use of resistances was important on two levels: practically, for the women, they acted as a counter-balance to the self-effacing responses undertaken in the resolution stage. Theoretically, they demonstrated women's continuing agency rather than spiralling into any psychological state of learned helplessness. Resistance represented the women's determination to survive in the face of continued violence and diminishing response choices. The time distanced nature of these responses represented the constraints placed on women's response choices – distancing their responses helped to ensure that there was no immediate comeback in terms of the men's violence; distancing their responses also helped maintain the women's sense of self-worth.

These shifts in responses emerged from the women's recognition that initial directly confrontational reactions carried the likelihood of dangerous repercussions, whilst the often equally ineffectual later responses of resolution only served to further undermine women's sense of self-worth. The dual need to retain some sense of autonomy and to effectively bring about an end to the men's violence influenced the nature of the resistances women used. These responses became distanced in time, secretive and potentially or actually the most lethal of all the response stages. Lethal in that some of the resistances themselves held the potential for fatal outcomes, despite being enacted, not to kill the abusive men, but to 'hurt him as he hurt me' or 'teach him a lesson'. But lethal as well in that, having entered the third stage of resistance, more women were to 'snap' at the cumulative effects of the violence and the cumulative effects of anger.

There is no generally accepted definition of cumulative anger; however, the concept of cumulative provocation was defined by Wasik (1982: 29) as 'a course of cruel or violent conduct by the deceased, often in a domestic setting, lasting over a substantial period of time'. Taylor (1986) stated that cumulative provocation was gendered in that it was expressed by men as cumulative rage whilst cumulative terror was more typical of women. Based on this premise she argued against the idea of cumulative rage being accepted as mitigation in homicide cases as it allowed the opportunity for brooding over resentments. But Taylor's claim that cumulative rage should cease to qualify for legal mitigation denies women's experiences of such anger.

For women who used responses of resistance, anger was less obviously expressed, emerging rather as frustration at their situations and the need to employ responses that would be 'heard' by their partners. Jill and Anne (neither of whom faced criminal charges for their potentially lethal responses) implied they had reached the end of some emotional tether, and that their actions signified they had 'had enough'. Pam (convicted of murder), having denied feeling anger, clearly expressed a pent up anger in her interview. She described the events on the night of her husband's death where she appeared to have remained collected throughout his constant verbal abuse. However, when she described her emotions after the killing, cumulative anger emerged as one of her experiences.

PAM: I was in a state of shock. That's the only way I can describe it. I didn't want to admit it had happened. I didn't want, I thought if I don't admit to what's happened, to meself – then … it'll go away. If I don't look at this, it's not here, it'll go away. Erm … but we've got a body, what can we do here? I was laughing! I was relieved! I thought you bastard you've got, you've got just deserts for what – for what you've been putting me through for this past couple of years. Thought, serves you – bloody right – you know?

More typically, women's experiences of cumulative anger appeared to move women's responses out of the final resistance stage and back to the initial reactive stage, which indicates a cycle of responses. The difference being that these later retaliations were fuelled by the additional experience of cumulative anger. The circular shift in response types denoted the women's awareness that they are unable to effectively challenge or bring about a cessation of the men's violence. By examining the final incidents that triggered the use of violent retaliations, it was clear that the abuse was qualitatively different. Instead of retaliating to men's physical assaults that had grown progressively more violent and/or life threatening, women were responding to situations that carried the *potential* for a physical assault. Taken in isolation, these incidents appear to contain little or no provocation and the women's responses seem disproportionate to the violence they were subjected to.

Although women who reverted to instantaneous retaliations with weapons described their responses as 'snapping' or losing their heads, their explanations of events that led up to the incidents clearly indicated the nature of their anger as cumulative.

ELLY: [*convicted of grievous bodily harm*] … but he came towards me, and I thought I was in for a good hiding, no way! If he were going to give me another crack, no, no way. I snapped, I'd had enough. And for somebody like me to do that, some'at wrong in't there?

PAT: [*convicted of wounding with intent*] Never ever have I picked up anything you could describe as a weapon before that time, never ever.
SUE: Did you want to?
PAT: No, it never, it never crossed me mind. Even that time when he'd done that to S [son]. It never crossed me mind to go get a knife or anything like that, never. Because I don't go around with the thoughts of hurting people. I'd be frightened of hurting him, I know it sounds silly. But you know what I mean. I couldn't, I couldn't do anything like that to anybody, not to actually hurt them you see. I knew exactly what I was doing with that knife, I was warning him, I've had, I'd had enough, I can't take any more.

JOYCE: [*convicted of murder*] . . . And, it was getting more and more violent, the relationship. You know he was, got so it was, it was – it sounds silly but when somebody's prodding you or pulling your hair, constantly doing things like that to you it, it gets at you after so long. . .

The above women's experiences of cumulative anger demonstrated the cyclical pattern in women's responses. Elly and Pat had both shifted their responses from reaction to resolution to resistance yet found these tactics to be ineffectual in challenging or changing their abusive partners' behaviours. Even in a prima facie case of provocation, the evidence was dismissively referred to as minimal:

JOYCE: I mean it sounds so 'Oh he was poking me' so I stabbed him – so he's I mean prodding and – I was sat in the chair and he grabbed me wrists and pulled me and shook me, and things like that and I, I just I stood so long I tried to keep calm I did. But, when I – I was frightened and – I was getting mad, mixture of both. And I just, flipped. [. . .] It's just – you just stand so much and then you go [snaps fingers] and it's a mixture of being frightened and you can't stand any more. I mean it's the last thing I wanted that day it was a really nice day, I'd had a lovely day out with me son and that, and I had every intention of having a nice evening, couple of bottles of wine, a video or whatever – last thing on me mind was anything like that.

After Joyce's conviction for murder the judge recommended she serve a minimum of 15 years claiming, 'The provocation alleged was minimal, and rejected by the jury.' The Lord Chief Justice countered these recommendations and advised that ten years 'would be sufficient for this spontaneous stabbing during a drunken quarrel'. Even when women's responses appear to fit the criteria of the defence, they can be barred from its use. Thus women face a double bind: the enactment of resistance stage responses, by definition responses removed in time from the provoking incidents, places women outside the current interpretation of the defence of provocation. Yet when women do respond in the required 'heat-of-the-moment' style, the provoking acts are deemed minimal and women's responses are considered (legally) disproportionate. Women do experience anger – but the nature of this anger and the constraints placed on women's response choices are denied by the current criteria of the defence.

Legal reform as a feminist strategy

One intention of my research was to further the current critique of the defence of provocation with a view to re-evaluating the defence in the light of women's experiences of provocation. I did not, however, intend to propose the means whereby the defence of provocation was reformed – indeed, it is debatable whether legal reform is even a solution. Feminists seem divided as to the focus and the value of reform as a political strategy. There is a sense that, in entering into debate with the law, one is entering a world that has already established the parameters, language and even the subject matter of the debate. Klein (1981) issued a warning against legal reform in relation to violence against women as the very institution feminists seek to reform is predicated on patriarchal assumptions. Smart (1990) re-echoed this warning, arguing that feminism's strategy should focus on the power of law to define whose reality is granted legal legitimacy.[4]

Despite these warnings other feminists take the view that legal reform is a necessary means in challenging the gender-bias of law as an institution and individual legislation that affects women's lives. Littleton (1987) argued that legal reform was more positive than criticism or outright rejection of the legal system. Thornton (1991) favoured legal reform despite criticism of it being a liberal tool. Jackson (1992: 212) questioned MacKinnon's argument that law reform should be about the reconstruction of doctrine: 'It is arguable whether doctrinal change is better pursued by way of a cumulation of small substantive reforms, or through theoretical challenge.'

Legal defences to murder is one area in which the debate between piecemeal reforms and 'implementation of a feminist agenda' is taking place. This is apparent in the different proposals that emerged from the contentious issue of gender-bias in the defence of provocation in which reform, abolition and supplementation through new legislation are all advocated.

Proposals for the reformation of the defence of provocation argue that a more subjective approach to the guiding principle would allow for the consideration of the reasonableness of women's killings within a context of repeated domestic violence. Further, it is argued, the suddenness requirement of the defence should be removed and juries should consider if there has been a temporary loss of self-control rather than focusing on the suddenness of that loss. This would allow for women's situations, specifically their histories of domestic violence, to be put to a jury for consideration. Radford (1992), was unconvinced that removal of the 'suddenness' term would bring about a new understanding acknowledging the differences in women's socialisation and circumstances from men's. There is also concern that any 'relaxing' of the defence's criteria would enable more men to use the defence.

Contextualising the experiences of the individuals facing murder charges was implemented in Australia (New South Wales). In the New South Wales Crimes (Homicide) Amendment Act 1982 the suddenness requirement of the defence is premised on a concept of 'contextual suddenness'. Provocation is acceptable 'whether that conduct of the deceased occurred immediately before the act or omission causing death *or at any previous time*' (cited in Weisbrot 1982: 263 – emphasis in original). The 'reasonable person' test appears to be extended to allow for consideration of the individual defendant's situation with the qualification:

> that conduct of the deceased was such as could have *induced an ordinary person in the position of the accused* . . .
>
> (cited in Weisbrot 1982: 259 – emphasis in original).

But O'Donovan (1991) points to the potential weaknesses of these amendments.

> The Crimes (Homicide) Amendment Act 1982 allows any past conduct of the deceased towards the defendant to be the basis of provocation. The events immediately prior to the killing are de-emphasized. However, encouraging pleas of provocation in such cases may have certain drawbacks. Arguments which blame the victim may also be encouraged. Attention, which should focus on cumulative violence and the appropriate response thereto by the law, the police, the community, may shift onto the victim
>
> (O'Donovan 1991: 229).

In the reform of existing legislation, or the construction of new defences, consideration must be given not only to those most likely to benefit, but also to those against whom it may be turned. The defence of provocation could, arguably, continue to serve men better in that it continues to accept their violence against women.[5]

Because of the defence's seeming inability to encompass women's experiences of domestic violence without further endangering women's lives by extending the mitigation to abusive men, some writers have called for the abolition of the defence of provocation (Horder 1992; Lees 1994). But to abolish the defence would leave women with self-defence or diminished responsibility as the only defences remaining to a charge of murder. Self-defence, premised on consideration of the individual incident resulting in the homicide, would not provide the means for contextualising women's experiences of domestic violence. The North American work on arguing for an extension to the self-defence remit to include a more subjective consideration of women's social position and experiences has contributed to the emergence of the battered woman syndrome. This medicalised image of women is potentially better suited to a plea of diminished responsibility. And such a plea shifts the focus from the rationality of women's homicidal responses to domestic violence to consideration of a woman's mental state.

Acknowledging that abolition of the provocation defence leaves little legal room for the inclusion of women's experiences, an alternative proposal is that the mandatory life sentence be abolished with sentencing for murder convictions reflecting any mitigation the court deems suitable (Horder 1992; Lloyd 1995). There are a number of arguments against this proposal: it fails to recognise the stigmatising effect the label 'murderer' can have – a murder conviction means the defendant was found guilty of deliberately and intentionally killing. Many women who have killed freely acknowledge the killing, even feel the need to be 'punished', but do not regard themselves as 'murderers'. The label murderer carries connotations of a cold-blooded act that denies the circumstances of many such women's killings. There would be no differentiation between serial killers and women who killed as a response to repeated violence/abuse, other than the lengths of their prison sentences. Justice For

Women (McNeill undated: 45) has argued that abolition of the mandatory life sentence would leave judges to decide the extent of mitigation to be afforded in the sentence – and 'Judges are not known for being sympathetic to women'.

My research showed that whilst women's responses to domestic violence appeared to fulfil the principle on which the defence of provocation is founded – the right to angered retaliation – the constraints women experienced in terms of their response choices simultaneously distanced women from fulfilling the current criteria of the defence, namely the suddenness and reasonableness requirements. Recent successful appeals by some women suggest that the courts are beginning to redress this paradox. At the appeal of Kiranjit Ahluwalia the suddenness requirement was no longer held to be axiomatic in pleading provocation; instead theoretical recognition was given to the concept of provocation as a slow boiling up of anger.[6] Emma Humphreys' appeal allowed for the idea of cumulative provocation thus admitting that a history of violence could be taken into consideration of the reasonableness of responding rather than focusing on the final provoking act. There is, however, no guarantee that these new understandings will be consistently applied in similar cases.[7]

And what of women whose homicidal responses to domestic violence fall outside the existing defences of self-defence and provocation? Zoora Shah killed her violent partner after 12 years of being physically, sexually and economically abused by him. In 1992, fearing that his sexual abuse would now include her daughters, Zoora poisoned Azam. She was convicted of murder and given a 20-year tariff.[8] Josephine Smith was also subjected to many years of emotional, physical and sexual abuse. When she attempted to leave her husband Brian, he threatened to track her down and kill their children. Josephine shot Brian as he slept after a vicious row. She said she killed him 'to get the children away safely with no fear of him coming after me'. Josephine was convicted of murder and has been refused leave to appeal.

To overcome the limitations of reforming existing defences, a new defence of self-preservation has been proposed. Work on the new defence began in the early 1990s and was developed by a network of women and women's groups (Justice For Women, Southall Black Sisters and Rights of Women), academic researchers, legal practitioners and policy makers. The aim is to add to, rather than replace, existing defences to murder.

Self-preservation: a new defence to murder

Supplementing existing defences with the proposed new defence of self-preservation is intended to avoid the problems of reform or abolition by extending the defence options available to women.

> Because of the problems inherent in the strategy of trying to include women's experiences in laws that were written by men in response to situ-

ations in which men have found themselves, we feel that a more coherent strategy lies in the construction of a new defence constructed around the situation of women and children who have been subjected to sexual abuse/violence. We feel that this strategy is helpful in that it will add to the options open to women who find themselves in these difficult circumstances

(Radford 1992: 10–11).

This addresses my concern that fitting women's experiences into existing defence criteria contains the danger of re-presenting women's experiences in a psycho-medico model thus denying the rationality of women's actions. Central-

---

The proposed self-preservation defence

1 It shall be a defence to a charge of murder, reducing the charge to manslaughter, if:

   a the deceased person had subjected the defendant or another person, with whom the defendant was at the time of the deceased person's death in a familial relationship, to continuing sexual or physical violence; and

   b the deceased person was at the time of their death or had at any time been in a familial or intimate relationship with the defendant or with the person as described in (a) above; and

   c the defendant believed that, but for their action, the deceased person would repeat the violence as stated above, so that their life or that of the person as described in (a) above was in danger.

2 In Section 1 above:

   'Familial' means related, cohabiting or living in the same household;

   'Continuing' means any act of violence as defined below on more than one occasion;

   'Violence' means any act that would constitute an offence under the Offences Against the Person Act 1861, the Sexual Offences Act 1975 (as amended), or the Protection from Harassment Act 1997;

   'Intimate' means any sexual relationship not included in the definition of 'familial';

   'Belief' must be reasonable in the context of on-going abuse and violence.

3 It shall be for the defence to raise the issue where the circumstances are as outlined in Section 1 above, and it will then be for the prosecution to prove that Section 1 does not apply.

ising women's experiences is key to the construction of the self-preservation defence.

My research has shown that women experience domestic violence as cumulative and that their anger also takes a cumulative form. The three-stage pattern of responding demonstrates the lengths women will go to in seeking to circumvent their male partners' violence whilst working to maintain their relationships. Despite the reduction in women's response choices, they retained their agency in their refusal to be completely cowed by the violence. The fact that those women who entered the final resistance stage of responding used more potentially or actually lethal responses than at any previous response stage is indicative of their growing sense of anger: anger at a situation that is not of their making and yet one in which they continue to remain at risk of further assaults or even death.

At issue is the need to recognise women as capable of being angered and capable of acting on that anger in the face of repeated victimisation both by individual men and by a social system that fails to intervene effectively. Understanding how women respond, and the constraints placed on their response choices, is important if legal mitigation is to be sought when women kill their violent male partners. Recognition of this reality of women's experiences is important if a new defence is to truly reflect women's lived experiences. Women are not just victims of men's violence, they are also active agents who have a right to be protected from such violence and a right to respond when that violence continues and that protection fails.

Self-preservation is a partial defence that would reduce a murder charge to a conviction of manslaughter. It attempts to explicitly address the situation of women who have killed men who subjected them to continuing violence. The self-preservation proposal is drafted in 'gender neutral' language and, as such, would be available to men who find themselves in similar situations. There is an increasing body of research literature which demonstrates that it is women and children who are disproportionately victimised by domestic violence and are, therefore, the more likely to use the defence. Self-preservation thus includes children who retaliate against violent adult family members or adults protecting their children from such violence.

Central to the proposed defence is a focus on repeated sexual or physical violence from an intimate or familial member, whether the relationship is current or has ceased. To use the defence of self-preservation evidence would have to be presented about the history of violence or abuse. This could take the form of testimony from the woman herself, with or without supporting evidence. The political drive towards an ever-increasing multi-agency approach to domestic violence should increase the opportunity of providing additional evidence (see Chapter 15). Testimony from other family/household members, including children, friends and neighbours would constitute evidence, as would doctors' and police reports, legal statements, court orders or evidence from other agencies.

Self-preservation is conceptualised as being both similar to, yet distinct from self-defence. Similar in that a life-endangering situation is necessary for the defence to apply; but distinct in that the assessment of the life-endangering situation is based on the defendant's 'belief' rather than the aggressor's actions. 'Belief' being defined as that which is 'reasonable' in a context of on-going violence and abuse, so the potential for a repeated occurrence would justify such a belief. This places fear at the centre of the proposed defence. Many of the women I interviewed expressed fear at the prospect of further violence as well as being fearful during individual assaults. Joyce described the combination of both fear and anger when she stated: 'I was frightened and – I was getting mad, mixture of both.' However, not all women described fear as a trigger when their responses resulted (or could have resulted) in fatal outcomes. The over-riding impression was that women had 'had enough' and wanted to teach the abusive man a lesson, or warn him or 'hurt him as he hurt me'. For women it is also about the quality of their life being in danger. Self-preservation needs to reflect this aspect of women's experiences as well as situations where women fear for their actual lives.

As it stands, self-preservation may, inadvertently, become a new version of self-defence in cases where women kill abusive male partners. The danger being that women could face manslaughter convictions and sentences, whereas a self-defence plea would result in acquittal. Despite this concern, self-preservation marks a radical shift from 'fitting' women into existing defences to centralising their realities in a new defence. The self-preservation proposal may not solve all the legal dilemmas of women who resist male violence, but it provides the additional possibility of a defence based on what is known about many women's experiences. By focusing on the history of violence as the issue in need of legal consideration, self-preservation avoids the medicalising of women's responses and re-presents women's actions as reasonable within a context of repeated abuse and violence.

And this is perhaps the greatest strength of self-preservation. It acknowledges the responses of women that currently fall outside the scope of self-defence and provocation as rational within an intolerable situation. It also, indirectly, allows for women's experiences of cumulative anger at repeated victimisation to be admitted to the courtroom – even though the defence of provocation, based on the right to angered retaliation, would deny this same anger when experienced by women.

Notes

1   Lerner (1992) writes on this subject but her book is a self-help publication that puts the onus on women to acknowledge and constructively use their anger in the maintenance of their (heterosexual) relationships.
2   All names are fictitious except for Sam as she requested that her own name be used.
3   See Kirkwood (1993) on anger as a trigger to leaving.
4   Smart (1995: 213) claims that her arguments in *Feminism and the Power of Law* (1990) have been incorrectly interpreted as 'a call for inaction and a celebration of

theoretical *purity*'. The point she was making was that 'we might use the legal domain less for achieving law reforms than as a site on which to contest meanings about gender.'

5   I have found little research on the outcomes of the New South Wales Crimes (Homicide) Amendment Act 1982. Graycar and Morgan (1990) cite the case of a woman who killed her sleeping husband when she discovered he had been sexually abusing their daughter for many years. At her first trial the judge refused to put the issue of provocation to the jury and she was convicted of murder. At her appeal the conviction was overthrown and a retrial ordered where she was acquitted of murder even though the issue of provocation was put to the jury. Yeo (1991: 1201), on the other hand, notes that the implementation of the Act 'has not resulted in a spate of murder acquittals'.

6   'Theoretical' in that Kiranjit Ahluwalia had her murder conviction reduced to manslaughter on the grounds of diminished responsibility.

7   At the 1996 trial of Diana Butler the jury were instructed to consider only the final provoking act thus ignoring the hour-long assault which culminated in his death.

8   The 'tariff' is the minimum sentence that must be served before being considered for release on life licence. In Zoora's case she appealed against her conviction in 1998 but the appeal was dismissed. In April 2000 the Home Secretary reduced her tariff to 12 years – she now has just over three years to serve.

References

Ashworth, A. J. (1976) 'The Doctrine of Provocation', *Cambridge Law Journal*, Vol. 35, no. 2, 292–320.

Browne, A. (1989) *When Battered Women Kill*, New York: The Free Press.

Campbell, A. (1993) *Out Of Control: Men, Women and Aggression*, London: Pandora.

Edwards, S. S. M. (1991) *Policing 'Domestic Violence': Women, the Law and the State*, London: Sage.

Graycar, R. and Morgan, J. (1990) *The Hidden Gender of Law*, New South Wales, Australia: The Federation Press.

Griffiths, S. (1997) Women's Resistance to Domestic Violence and the Defence of Provocation, unpublished Ph.D. thesis, University of Bradford.

Hart, L. (1994) *Fatal Women: Lesbian Sexuality and the Mark of Aggression*, London: Routledge.

Horder, J. (1992) *Provocation and Responsibility*, Oxford: Clarendon Press.

Jackson, E. (1992) 'Catharine MacKinnon and feminist jurisprudence: a critical appraisal', *Journal of Law and Society*, Vol. 19, no. 2, 195–213.

Kirkwood, C. (1993) *Leaving Abusive Partners: From The Scars of Survival to the Wisdom for Change*, London: Sage.

Kirsta, A. (1994) *Deadlier than the Male: Violence and Aggression in Women*, London: HarperCollins.

Klein, D. (1981) 'Violence against women: some considerations regarding its causes and its elimination', *Crime and Delinquency*, Vol. 27, no. 1, 64–80.

Lees, S. (1994) 'Lawyers' work as constitutive of gender relations', in Cain, M and Harrington, C. B. (eds) *Lawyers in a Postmodern World: Translation and Transgression*, Buckingham: Open University Press, pp. 124–54.

Lerner, H. G. (1992) *The Dance of Anger: A Woman's Guide to Changing the Pattern of Intimate Relationships*, London: Pandora.

Littleton, C. A. (1987) 'In search of a feminist jurisprudence', *Harvard Women's Law Journal*, Vol. 10, 1–7.

Lloyd, A. (1995) *Doubly Deviant, Doubly Damned: Society's Treatment of Violent Women*, London: Penguin Books.

McNeill, S. (undated) 'Men getting away with murder', in *Justice For Women Information Pack* (2nd edition), London: Justice For Women, pp. 42–6.

O'Donovan, K. (1991) 'Defences for battered women who kill', *Journal of Law and Society*, Vol. 18, no. 2, 219–40.

Radford, J. (1992) 'Self preservation', *Rights Of Women Bulletin*, Summer, pp. 6–12.

Radford, L. (1993) 'Pleading for time: justice for battered women who kill', in Birch, H. (ed.) *Moving Targets: Women, Murder and Representation*, London: Virago, pp. 172–97.

Smart, C. (1990) *Feminism and the Power of Law*, London: Routledge.

Smart, C. (1995) *Law, Crime and Sexuality*, London: Sage.

Straus, M. A., Gelles, R. J. and Steinmetz, S. K. (1981) *Behind Closed Doors: Violence in the American Family*, New York: Anchor Books.

Taylor, L. J. (1986) 'Provoked reason in men and women: heat-of-passion manslaughter and imperfect self-defense', *UCLA Law Review*, Vol. 33, no. 6, 1679–735.

Thornton, M. (1991) 'Feminism and the contradictions of law reform', *International Journal of the Sociology of Law*, Vol. 19, no. 4, 453–74.

Wasik, M. (1982) 'Cumulative provocation and domestic killing', *Criminal Law Review*, 29, 29–37.

Weisbrot, D. (1982) 'Homicide law reform in New South Wales', *Criminal Law Journal*, Vol. 6, no. 5, 248–68.

Yeo, S. (1991) 'Provocation down under', *New Law Journal*, Vol. 141, 1200–1.

Cases

All E.R.   All England Law Reports.
Holmes   [1946] 2 All E.R. 124.
Duffy   [1949] 1 All E.R. 932.

9 The criminal justice response to women who kill

An interview with Helena Kennedy

Sheila Quaid and Catherine Itzin

Introduction

This chapter is based on an interview with Helena Kennedy QC by Catherine Itzin. It has been edited into the form of a narrative, covering a range of issues relating to women and the criminal justice system, and in particular explores the question of 'Why do women kill?'. In Helena Kennedy's experience of defending women, she asserts that most women kill in desperation, in self-defence or in the defence of their children. Women's experience of violence and escape from violence has received much critical comment and campaigning for law reform over the past few years and some cases such as Sara Thornton, Kiranjit Ahluwalia and Emma Humphreys have achieved a high public profile as campaigners have fought for their release from life sentences. All three women had sustained years of violence and abuse from their partners and had killed in their attempts to stop the violence.

Who women kill

Women are rarely involved in serial killing and they almost never go out and plan the anonymous killing of a victim with whom who they have no connection at all. For the most part women kill people they know and primarily these people are men. They kill within the domestic arena: they kill their husbands, their lovers, their boyfriends and sometimes they kill their children. Occasionally it might stretch beyond the domestic parameter, but the numbers are incredibly small, and when women kill it is when something is going very wrong with their domestic environment.

I've often thought it rather interesting that women don't kill indiscriminately such as poisoning beer in pubs or killing large numbers of men willy-nilly, particularly given the way women can become so damaged by what they have gone through as children at the hands of male family members. There are men who kill women who are complete strangers, coldly and systematically. However, women rarely ever do that. They actually kill their nearest and dearest, they kill their family members. For this they are regarded as monstrous, as if it were somehow worse to do it to people who are close to you, when in fact the killing of a stranger is more pathological and more bizarre. The business of actually losing control, and feeling that you can't take any more from your partner, or from your child, is far more understandable, and the psychology of that for me is much more comprehensible than going for the stranger on the High Street.

Women are still stereotyped in the caring, caretaker role and that's one of the reasons why in Victorian times it was considered one of the most heinous of crimes for women to poison the food of their men. The female poisoners somehow went down in the annals of criminology as being the most feared of offenders, because there is something perceived as particularly awful about feeding poison when you are supposed to be nurturing. Through food, one is supposed to be giving sustenance and love to those for whom you care. So there is something particularly offensive about the idea that the woman who is sup-posed to be the caretaker of the hearth, the home, and the children, the lover and the husband, should in some way provide the opposite of nurturance. It goes against the grain, because of the profoundly accepted notion that women have a nurturing role, and that to subvert that role is somehow offending against more than the criminal law. It is also offending against nature and some moral order, and the fear is that the female offender undermines the very fabric of society.

Most of us have experienced dealing with a crying child, but something usually stops us from actually shaking it so that its brain becomes damaged, or from actually hurling it against the wall, or, with a partner, actually taking the knife out of the drawer. But there are sometimes situations in which that line is crossed because circumstances come together which are so traumatising that no more can be taken. I don't think this points to the inadequacy, or indeed even the monstrosity of women. It's usually the culmination of a whole series of cir-cumstances. Very often, it's also about a sense of powerlessness, a sense of having no control over the circumstances that someone has found themselves in.

For most of the women I have represented who have killed their partners, they became unable to take either any more physical abuse or any more psycho-logical abuse. A point of no return is reached where they know that their own physical integrity is actually at risk, and that they are not going to survive. Often they've used very complicated mechanisms for survival, and then, sadly and ironically when they come into court to do the trial, the very mechanisms the women have used to survive are turned around and used against them. For example, I experience an enormous sense of irritation and frustration in cases when, time after time, I hear prosecuting counsel say to my client, 'If you were so badly beaten you would have left. You're exaggerating this account now in order to discredit your husband to get sympathy from the jury and you're a liar, a calculating liar.'

Of course, we know that the measure applied by men at the Bar is based on the assumption that if it were so terrible the woman would have left. This is the eternal question that comes up in the history of cases where women have been battered, and it does not take account of the reality of the lives of those women. For many different and complicated reasons, women try to sustain relationships. They try to keep it going, they do hang on in there and they do so because on the practical level few alternatives are available to them, of where to go with young children.

Living with violence

Women who sustain physical and psychological abuse usually have numerous strategies for dealing with the stress and the demands made on them. The contradictory nature of women's lives, and of the legal framework dealing with domestic violence, contribute to a situation where women have few possibilities for escape. Once your autonomy is being eroded continually with physical and psychological abuse, your ability to start taking decisive action is undermined. Those kind of controlling men are not going to let you walk away very easily and women know that.

Lawyers and judges are often genuinely puzzled by women's response to violence. It is necessary to get across the social demands women feel and their belief that the violence is their failure. The business needs to be understood of not telling the world because of your shame and your sense of not living up to the ideal of a perfect wife and mother whose husband would be satisfied with her. The idea that somehow if I were a better wife he wouldn't be hitting me; if I met the high standards that he's setting, then he wouldn't be feeling so angry, he would not come in making impossible demands. I'm obviously not good enough in bed, as a housewife, as a mother. Women end up blaming themselves and they don't want the world to know. They also minimise their own physical symptoms again because the sense of failure is so strong. Women will not visit the doctor, will not confide in their sister, or their mother, will not talk to friends and will actually hide or give false accounts of how they came by their injuries.

Interpretations in court

When the account of violence is challenged in the court room, prosecutors say 'Here is the medical record and it says here you had an injury to your ankle but you fell down your back stairs as you were going to hang the washing out.' She says, 'Well that is just what I told the doctor.' The prosecution will then argue the truth of the record, and that she's now making up the story to discredit her husband's character. At every turn these strategies for survival are hoisted up and used against women in court. It is very frustrating for those of us who are doing these cases. We are on a learning curve ourselves about domestic violence, but we are still amazed by the ignorance of colleagues about the issue.

A major problem is in trying to use the defence of provocation for women who kill their partners. At the moment we are slowly beginning to shift the ground, and are creating a climate in which there is more listening being done.

One of the ways I have sought to do this is by challenging the stereotypes and misperceptions. For example, when using the defence of provocation, there is a 'reasonable man' test. The measure is this: Stage 1, in the face of provocation did the accused have a *sudden* and *temporary loss of self control?* and Stage 2, would a reasonable man in those circumstances have lost self control?

The general public doesn't know, and even those campaigning on this issue don't realise, that there are two stages in the provocation argument. One is the subjective test, the second is the objective test. The reasonable man test asks, 'Would a reasonable person have responded in this way?' The rational prosecutor would say to the rational juryman, 'If someone was doing this to you, you would get your coat and hat on and you would be out the front door.' To wait and retaliate seems like an act of revenge. Unless the person on the jury knows and understands the complexities and effects of domestic violence, then the defence of *provocation* is never going to work properly for women.

Our argument now is that when it comes to the objective test, the jury have to consider the enduring characteristics of the person in the dock. In cases of women killing violent partners, the enduring characteristics of the woman who sustains battering should be taken into account: to consider what the whole history of battering can do to somebody. The jury must be entitled to know that. On this basis we argue for the calling of expert witnesses in court to talk about the effects of long-term abuse in general, and the particular effects upon the woman on trial. I have found that this approach raises some awareness. Not only does it have an impact on the cases of my individual women clients, but it is actually educating those who are involved in the process, because judges are hearing experts in the field talking about domestic violence in a way that they have never heard discussed before.

Let me explain the legal antecedents for this. The case of *Regina* v. *Camplin* decided that the test of the reasonable man could affect injustice if very particular aspects of a defendant were ignored, e.g. age or race or gender. In the 1960s there was concern about race: that it was unfair to ask an all-white jury whether a reasonable man would have been so affected, if the man in the dock was a black man, and the provocation he was subjected to was racism. What is provocative to a young black man may be very different because taunts about race relate so profoundly to his particular being. The court decided in the case of *Camplin* that a jury must attribute to the reasonable man the enduring characteristics of the person in the dock.

A line of cases has now developed, including some which allow battered women to invoke their experience of battering as an enduring characteristic. The question as to whether there are particular features that lead women to kill is difficult. It is hard to say, as cases are so different. What is much more constant is the similarity of the behaviour of the men. I hear stories about men who are extremely possessive, who imagine that their partners are interested in other men, or who imagine all kinds of slights and all kinds of ways in which their women, even by a look or a glance, are being unfaithful to them. They are usually profoundly insecure themselves, but can appear to the world as charming and attentive partners. Repeatedly, I hear about obsessional behaviour in relation to cleanliness and standards of behaviour, expectations of how proper women are supposed to behave, not just in terms of how they must look after the household, but how they are supposed to behave and look after their children. I am told of men who tour the house, running their fingers along the furniture to see that their house is kept spotlessly clean, that their children are turned out in pristine condition. If the women dress themselves up, they are whores and tarts, and if they don't, they are slags and unattractive. So they can never win.

The abuse can be very different, though. On the one hand, I have represented Pamela Sainsbury whose husband used to treat her like a dog. He used to put a dog chain around her neck and used to make her eat from a bowl on the floor. He beat hell out of her, humiliated and degraded her most of the time. Her life was wretched and in the end she garrotted him. She put a rope around his neck when he was asleep in bed, looped it around his head, went to the other end of the room and pulled. On the other hand, June Scotland's husband had hardly ever raised his hand to her, but he was a tyrant who persecuted her mentally. She lived in terror of him until she discovered that he had been sexually abusing her daughter and could take no more. This case was the basis of the *Brookside* story of a battering, abusive man who was killed and buried under a patio. The time comes when a woman somehow knows she has reached the point of no return. The point where all her usual strategies for coping will not sustain her, where she cannot be confident she is going to make it, she feels that she will end up dead or have a breakdown, she is not going to be able to carry on. Often in these situations, there is a real terror of what that would mean for her children, that she is the one who has to care for them.

Abusive relationships destroy a woman's self worth so that she ends up believing it is her own fault and she deserves no better. The abuser becomes all-powerful in the eyes of the abused. Even when women kill their husbands they can't believe he is dead. It's totally irrational, but they come running down stairs and get into the car and they think he is going to come down after them. Even if they have taken a 12 bore shotgun to him, they still think he is omnipotent. In the case of Pamela Sainsbury she ended up cutting her husband up to get rid of him. She still thought it was all a bad dream and that he was going to come and get her. This is about being so controlled by someone, that you cannot imagine that you might have taken some action to reverse that.

The concept of the 'battered woman syndrome' has come to be used to explain what happens to women in these circumstances. The best description is contained within a Canadian case, called *Regina* v. *Lavallee*. In the *Lavallee* case, judgment was given by Madame Bertha Wilson, a wonderful Scottish woman judge on the supreme court of Canada. Until recently three out of nine on the court were women, and they say that in fact now, the women don't have to protect women's rights, the men are as active as any of the women in that court. I think it's because the discourse of that court has been changed by the presence of women.

The judgment in the *Lavallee* case offers a fine presentation of what domestic violence is all about, and how it affects the person living with it. The judgment explains that it is about an abuse of power and the exercise of control. The syndrome is a sub-category of post-traumatic stress disorder and involves a constellation of symptoms engendered in abused women, including depression, feelings of hopelessness, learned helplessness, heightened arousal in relation to anticipated violence, belief in the omnipotence of the abuser.

In *Lavallee*, the accused had shot her husband as he was walking out of the room with his back to her. The prosecution maintained that it was a clear act of vengeance. The pathologist's report made it very clear that this was a man who was certainly not attacking her at the time. He was in retreat when she fired at him. She did not give evidence at the trial, but a psychiatrist testified that she was suffering from 'battered woman syndrome'. There was also evidence that she had sought injunctions against him and was in terror of him. Although he was not coming at her at the time of killing she felt unable to take any more. Knowing that he was in retreat at that moment did not mean he would not be coming back for more. She felt unable to leave him, believing he would find her, wherever she went. They allowed the expert witness to explain what long-term abuse can do to women and how, in the face of the violence, the woman knows that although Round 1 is finished, Round 2 will be starting soon.

The 'battered woman syndrome' is now used here in Britain. I am conscious of its weaknesses, but I also think it has helped me secure the acquittal of many women who might previously have been convicted of murder. Instead they have been found guilty of manslaughter and sentenced with compassion. It has also been a powerful tool in educating judges, lawyers and juries about domestic violence. But it does have shortcomings.

The risk is that women who do not have the 'full syndrome' are assumed not to be really battered. It is also not popular with very orthodox psychiatrists who readily come to court to be dismissive of its validity. Many feminists also feel it pathologises women who are actually responding perfectly rationally to life threatening behaviour. In other aspects of their lives, battered women can be effective and not helpless. They can be perfectly good mothers and hold down responsible jobs. The temptation is for the court to stereotype victims of abuse as passive, meek women when often battered women are feisty, capable women ground down by their experiences. However, good experts are able to meet such challenges and can give a real authority and weight to the reality of battered women's lives.

One of the positive outcomes for women living in violent situations is the increased awareness of the effects of violence. What's become very clear is that many of the actions taken by my clients are rational, normal responses, which are seen as normal in the face of abnormal behaviour directed at the recipient of abuse. If somebody is actually continuing to abuse you over and over again, to eventually say 'no more' is not abnormal behaviour. One has to challenge the idea that there is something not quite right or inherently susceptible in women who get into these relationships. The reality is that all manner of women can end up in situations where they are being abused. It may be right that women who have low self-esteem may be sought out by men who are violent, but it is by no means always the case. I have represented strong, interesting women who have slowly had their self-esteem eroded by abusive men.

One of the problems in all this is that it is undoubtedly true that 'cycles' do exist, and when I go into Holloway Prison to talk with women there, it is becoming clear that the majority of women who are incarcerated in prisons for killing their husbands, end up being in abusive relationships because of the damage of abuse they have previously experienced. This can mean that women's own value of themselves becomes such that they will settle for relationships in which they are badly treated very often thereafter. Retrieving that, helping people to get whole again often involves work, and few women are given that opportunity. So that 'cycle' is there. However, it has led many people who are involved in psychiatry and psychology to somehow imagine that those who are treated badly by men must themselves have some kind of propensity in that direction. These assumptions feed into the idea that women who are battered are women who ask for it. Alternatively, it can feed the idea that some women, because of ill treatment in the past, actually expect it and therefore set up that dynamic in whatever relationship they have. These assumptions exist in the field of psychiatry and certainly run around courtrooms. However, it is the case that they themselves have been previously abused, perhaps in the home as a child. This is very often the case, but not always. I have concerns about rejecting the theory of 'cycles' because there are clear connections between the effects of abuse and further abuse. There is a tendency among feminism to reject the idea of 'cycles' of abuse, which is understandable if the inevitable conclusion is that there is a trap in which women are continually victimised. It seems to me that we have to accept certain patterns.

At the beginning of the second wave of feminism, women of our age didn't want to take any hostages, because we knew that we would be penalised. If we wanted to work and have a family, you could never be allowed to say it was hard. If you did, the response could often be 'Well get back to the kitchen'. We had to go into denial about a lot of things then, but we cannot carry on doing that about some issues. For example, saying that every woman who alleges rape is telling the truth about it. The majority of women who allege rape are telling the truth, but some are not. I have represented women who have made stories up. They are few and far between, but they do exist. That is why you have to have serious protection for the men who end up on trial.

As advocates of change, we have to be careful not to distort the truth, yet still tell the very serious tale about how women have been treated and about how institutions deal with women. For example, I feel that if we do not tell the truth about the cycle of abuse patterns that do exist, we have great difficulty in getting the state to take this on, and to put some serious money behind it. There is so much talk about 'law and order', but the Home Secretary needs to see that the seeds of violence are often sown within the home, within the domestic environment and that if you deal with domestic violence you will deal with all manner of other crimes too. Not only do you confront the fact of what is happening to women and children, but you also confront other ways in which men start acting out their violence in the public domain as well.

If you talk to men in Brixton prison, you'd find that they have often been brought up in homes that were violent. So if they want talk about law and order, let's talk about domestic violence. It is at the heart of all this, and if we don't tell the truth about how damage is passed on, then I think we're not doing a service to women either. There are many stories in this, and the more I am in court, the more I hear, but it is very difficult to draw out simplistic theories. Every woman's story is unique, but there will always be features and aspects that are very similar too. Actually the women I represent are the most incredibly extraordinary women. Most of them can be seen as heroic in some way rather than victims. Most of them hold things together, and want to hold the family together. If you think about it, women down the ages have done that and it's not to be discredited. It is actually a story of quite heroic proportions.

Legislation and policy implications

The more you attach stigma to the idea of women going it alone with their children, the more you are imprisoning those women in abusive relationships. If bringing children up on your own or deciding to get away from a violent partner is frowned upon, you're a second class citizen. Such moralising will mean that fewer women will take the step. We just cannot let them get away with idealising the family in a way that is dishonest.

I think to really confront family violence is quite difficult because of denial that violence is perpetrated in all social groups and in very different ways. Middle-class men may be abusive in more subtle ways than others. Another problem is that men have more difficulty talking about violence, and women are more prepared to actually give voice to their pain. Once you can get past the initial resistance, some men will talk about it, will actually be able to speak the unspeakable about their abuse as children, or living in a household where their mother was battered, but there is far more denial by men.

I have just been chairing a commission for the Howard League for Penal Reform into young offender institutions. Bullying is a serious problem in them. When talking to some of the boys, I see there is so much bravado, machismo and all that awful male stuff which is the bread and butter of everyday life in these places, and violence feeds off it. The whole regime from the officers to the boys is based on machismo notions of power and authority. There is a pecking order and all the men fall into line underneath the screws: older boys bully the younger ones and so on. When a kid comes in, his trainers are often forcibly removed from him by other boys and he loses everything he owns from his tobacco allowance to his phone card. It's *Lord of the Flies*.

The problem is that it is an environment in which the prison officers deal with the bullies by bullying them. Occasionally you would get a boy talking and get beyond the formalities and the boorish front. Then the story would emerge of how awful it was at home, and how his mother is getting bashed. These young men often end up replicating these patterns, because when they deal with stress and problems in their own relationships they will handle them in much the same way they have seen it handled in their own families. They will also deal with their frustrations and anxieties in the outer world in the same way. We have got absolutely nowhere in beginning to confront these notions of masculinity.

Acknowledging the effects of violence and abuse in the home and domestic violence is actually a key to unravelling a whole range of social violence, not just a women's issue. It is critical that we persuade Government of the bigger picture. In Canada they have made a commitment to deal with domestic violence and put it at the heart of legal and social policy: from the same standpoint that the Zero Tolerance Campaign started in Edinburgh. The Zero Tolerance work is particularly effective. It does not involve vast sums of money, but it means a real commitment to public education on domestic violence. It promotes the view that it should be outlawed and is unacceptable, and that this message has to filter through everywhere.

I am married to a surgeon, a head and neck surgeon. He deals with congenital deformity or cancer of the face, or trauma, and every so often he will have a woman who comes to him whose face is smashed. Her orbital floor has been cracked like an egg, her jaw or her cheekbone will have been smashed up. Until he learned about domestic violence through my work, he rarely investigated the possibility that the woman was being battered. It was not part of his training. He will now actually write in his notes: 'She says she fell against the fridge, looks more like a blow to me, seems anxious when talking about it?'. He has heard me talk so often about the problems of doctors just writing notes on the basis of what they are told, even when they have suspicions. He now makes a point of saying: 'You don't deserve this, you are too good for this, you have got to realise that you don't have to take this.' To have that sort of affirmation from a male professional person can make some people feel better. The possibility of one word to help someone make a resolve is so crucial, and I think we have to find ways to do this. Health carers have to learn about domestic violence and have protocols for dealing with it. We have to make sure that on every front we educate people as we are doing with child sexual abuse.

One very clear area where there would be an impact, for example, could be the acknowledgement of domestic violence in GP surgeries. Making links in a social way between different types of abuse is very important because there are links. If men physically abuse, the chances are that they also sexually abuse, are more likely to demand sex from an unwilling partner, and likely to rape their partners. There is also a link between abuse of women, and abuse of children, both physical and sexual. It is important to recognise these links, because too often one hears judges say that 'Just because he hits his wife does not mean that he hits his children and of course he does not mean it.' It is equally important to challenge some of the more incredible explanations such as 'I only hit the wife because she deserves it and she's an adult, but I wouldn't do it to the children.' In actual fact, what we are beginning to see is that once those inhibitions and barriers are gone, then people tend to abuse in other directions as well. I do not want to overstate this but we should be vigilant. The main point here is to recognise that this is a possibility. As soon as a social worker knows that a woman is being battered, then there should be questions in their mind about what is happening with the child in the family: they should be very concerned. It is not an automatic thing, but it certainly should be raising questions. In the same way it should be happening for lawyers in those kinds of cases.

With regard to social policy areas, I believe that we have had a breakthrough with the Children Act which says that in family courts children's voices have to be heard. The welfare of the child should be paramount in the considerations of the courts over access, custody and so on. Whether or not they are taken away from their parents, the children should be listened to. The child-centred approach has not penetrated the criminal courts, and if you are about to imprison a primary carer of children, which is invariably a woman, then I think the court should have a report about the welfare of the children, the impact on the children and how the separation will affect them. I know it is important to neutralise the language around this and not to assume that the primary carer will be a woman. But the fact remains that in most situations the one with the primary responsibility for children is women. Why do we have judges sending women off to prison, when one is actually passing on the terrible effects of incarceration to the children in cases of minor crime like shoplifting? I see the awful effects of mothers' imprisonment on children and it is terrible. It should only be in the most extreme circumstances that we should be doing that. Judges do it far too regularly, and I think there should be a law which requires a report on the children.

It is important to draw attention to the role of women in specifically gendered terms, because the criminal law was never framed with women in mind. Before we examine the law's failure to women, we have to look at where the law comes from. The law is built upon case after case after case, on judgments made in higher courts where women were not present either as lawyers or judges until comparatively recently. The commentators on law, scholars who write about legal developments, have not been women. It is very recent that we have had women academics looking at the law with women's lives in mind. It is not surprising, therefore, that women's experience is not there in any of these tests that we have referred to: for example, the 'reasonable man' test in the defence of provocation. The legal norm was male. The potential criminal was a man in even-handed combat with another man, and so the tests and rules have failed women. I do not think the legal norm can be made gender neutral. I have come to believe that neutrality is a fiction.

Gender neutrality is unachievable because it does not exist. The process of gendering involves asking the question: what are the gender implications and are there any differences for men and women? I think the answer is to argue for context, placing the accused in their real social context and acknowledging, for example, the ways in which women have suffered discrimination and paternalism.

In Canada, the Charter of Rights made an enormous difference for women, and I think we could have those sorts of changes here with our Human Rights Act even though it is a more restricted piece of legislation. If you look at what has happened in Canada, and in other common law jurisdictions, they are starting to talk about not just women's rights but ameliorative rights. I was trying to explain to someone recently, it is not enough to talk simply in terms of rights, without taking account of previous disadvantage and the history of disadvantage. If the next step after the Human Rights Act were to be the creation of a Bill of Rights including gender equality, we could draft it so that it becomes a corrective to past laws. This is what I am seeking to do in these cases where expert testimony is required to give visibility to women's experience. There is a disagreement between feminists on this question. Some argue against this approach, and question why we need experts to construct women into somebody they are not. My argument rests on the fact that until we are really equal we need some mechanism to bring specialised knowledge into the court which brings women up to the same level. We cannot talk about the 'reasonable man' or the 'reasonable person' without somehow making up for the past disadvantage.

There is recent work on domestic violence from the Law Commission with suggestions about giving greater powers to the magistrates courts, about making sure that local authorities act upon that, so it is easier for women to retain tenancies. Cutting across professional lines is important, where police, courts and social services work towards a consensus approach on how to deal with abusive men and what you do in those circumstances: everybody working together in the way they work on childcare together. It is also important to draw attention to the need for good judicial training. There is a great deal of resistance. We have certainly made some headway, however, on the issues of 'race' and there are now seminars and training programmes on 'race'. The same is beginning to happen on gender issues.

I think we should be amending the defence of *provocation* as a priority. They have done this in New South Wales and I would like us to monitor how that is working. The Law Commission could easily do that, and evaluate its success there. The main point is to remove the word 'sudden' from the phrase 'sudden and temporary loss of self control'. There is a fear amongst many campaigners that this removal would be used to the advantage of many defendants, not just women who had sustained violence and abuse. It is not an unreasonable fear to think that the plethora of men who kill women and others could easily use this change to their advantage. It could be used by professional criminals. This is one of the major problems with changing the law. It is not as straightforward as we all might wish. You have to be really quite careful about changing the law, and that's precisely why we should monitor what is happening in New South Wales to see whether it is working for women and also whether it is working to the advantage of some, in a way we would find unsatisfactory.

Amending the defence of provocation

The issue is the role of the criminal justice system in restricting the number of possible options for escape for women who have sustained years of violence and abuse. Women's relationship to the legal framework for defence is different to that of men as a result of societal and patriarchal attitudes towards women who kill. The question here is: how do we reform or change the law to take account of women's experiences?

In cases of domestic homicide the legal defences that can be offered in an attempt to reduce sentences can include: provocation, self-defence and diminished responsibility. The 'rules' of self-defence are narrowly defined and women's experiences of violence do not fit neatly with the prescribed definition. Diminished responsibility reduces murder to manslaughter. It is defined as 'suffering from such abnormality of the mind as substantially impaired his responsibility for his acts or omissions in doing or being party to the killing'. The 1957 Homicide Act created the special defence where the offender's criminal responsibility was diminished because of impairment (Kennedy 1992: 103).

Where self-defence does not succeed as a plea, *provocation* can be raised. This also reduces the charge from murder to manslaughter. At the moment, the judge can decide whether or not domestic violence can be put in front of the jury. *Provocation* requires the response to be in the 'heat of the moment'; for the defence of *provocation* to be successfully used in reducing the sentence from murder to manslaughter: 'the victims' words or conduct have to render the defendant so subject to passion as to make him for the moment not master of his mind.'[1]

The issue of domestic violence as evidence of provocation is made invisible so often in the cases of women defendants as 'the immediacy principle makes no sense when the provocation takes the form of long-term abuse'. In the field of domestic homicide the relationship between the law and psychiatry is under new scrutiny as a result of the debate about the role of the expert witness. I have observed that, in the USA and Canada, some women have gone free after expert witnesses have testified to the effects of the 'battered woman syndrome'. The role of the expert witness and the admission of evidence such as a 'syndrome' have clearly altered the outcomes of some appeals. The influence of such changes is such that three women in Britain – Kiranjit Alhuwalia, Emma Humphreys and Sara Thornton, have been released following appeals on the grounds of diminished responsibility with the use of the 'battered woman syndrome' as evidence.

I have observed that the use of the expert witness and psychiatric evidence is problematic in the long term. On the issue of provocation, women will continue to have a weak defence unless the defendant is constructed as a woman who acted rationally in the face of the irrational levels of violence in her life rather than a woman with a 'disordered' mind. This is because the 'rules' of provocation restrict the admissibility of psychological evidence, because the defence relates to the actions of a reasonable woman and not to a 'disordered' one. In addition, the rules limit the defence to killings done almost immediately after the last provocation.

The rules of law surrounding domestic homicide assume men as the norm. Minor amendments to the definitions can be seen as part of a process of change in favour of women, but to reach a point of equity for men and women in the criminal justice system, much has to change first. As a woman who defends women, my observations are focused on two issues: challenging the unfairness of the sentencing patterns and reframing parts of the law to take account of domestic violence and its effects. In order for women and men to be treated in a more equal way by the courts, some would argue for the law to be rewritten around women's experiences. One suggestion is to construct a new defence of self preservation (Radford 1992; see also Chapter 8).

The dilemmas in changing the law are numerous. The unified framework of the law is the main problem for the redefinition of rules around women's experiences. In other words, if you change the law for women, it is changed for men, hence the possibility of new laws being used in ways that women would see as unsatisfactory. This is always a possibility in a system that is written in a gender neutral framework. In the shorter term, this could challenge the unfairness of the sentences for women. The rewriting of law on the basis of women's experience of violence could offer more possibilities for women's defence than the present rules governing the defence of provocation.

The future

The gender bias in the legal system is illustrated in a number of ways: the different sentencing patterns for women and men; the different experience in court, but also in the gender breakdown of victims of domestic homicide. Edwards (1989), in an examination of statistics of domestic homicide for England and Wales, illustrated a pattern of a much higher proportion of female victims in relation to male victims being killed by their spouse or co-habitee. Figures provided by the Home Office confirm that 'women are most vulnerable from spousal homicide (which accounted for around 40 per cent of all female homicide victims in 1982, 1983, 1984, 1985 and 1986...)' (Edwards 1989: 125).[2]

Such patterns raise fundamental questions about the gendered structure of the criminal justice system and women's relationship to it. The reasons for this are on different levels: the rules work against women, they are 'malestream' in their design and content, the differential treatment of women in the courts is due to deeply held patriarchal attitudes towards women. The way in which women who retaliate against violence are constructed as cold, greedy and malicious represents a deeper concern. That is to say, that women who retaliate are considered deeply threatening to society and to men in families in particular. For women seeking a 'fair' sentence and for women campaigning for change on this, there is rarely only one issue. There is an urgent need for an integrated approach to change. Without campaigning and reform the violence experienced by women in the cases referred to becomes invisible in the criminal justice system. Greater recognition of the reality of living with violence could be brought about by rewriting the law around women's lives. In addition the integrated approach would need to include gender awareness training for the judiciary. Training, positive action in facilitating access into the legal profession, to encourage the entry of more women, and an inter-agency based practice in responding to and dealing with abusive men are all measures which could be introduced. All of these would represent the possibility of a fairer legal system for women.

Notes

1   Kennedy, H. (1992) *Eve Was Framed*.
2   Between 1987 and 1996 an average of 8 per cent of all men killed were killed by a current or former spouse, cohabitant, or lover, and for the same years an average of 43 per cent of all women killed, were killed by the same current or former spouse, cohabitant or lover (*Criminal Statistics for England and Wales* 1996).

References

Criminal Statistics England and Wales 1996. (1997) CM 3764, London: Home Office.
Edwards, S. M. (1989) *Policing 'Domestic' Violence*, London: Sage.
Kennedy, H. (1992) *Eve Was Framed*, London: Chatto & Windus.
Radford, J. (1992) 'Self preservation', *Rights of Women Bulletin*, Summer.

10 Southall Black Sisters

Domestic violence campaigns and alliances across the divisions of race, gender and class

Pragna Patel

The time has come the walrus said to talk of many things...
(*Alice Through the Looking Glass*, Lewis Carroll)

I was born in Kenya and came to Britain at the age of four. I have known no other landscape, but I have never felt that I belonged here. With no other choice but to make my life here, I grew into a politics of resistance; against the racism that I experienced outside my home because I was the wrong colour, and against the injustices I experienced because I was the wrong gender. In this way I fashioned for myself a strong political identity, in struggle with other black men and women. Despite hovering on the margins of British society, this identity is a source of tremendous power and strength, and even, dare I say it, moral righteousness.

It was precisely this sense of belonging, this black identity, which fell apart in December 1992. When militant right-wing Hindu nationalists destroyed the sixteenth-century Babri-Masjid mosque in India, I was forced to confront the elements of the 'Hindu' identity within me which I had supposed had all but withered away. By virtue of being a member of that Diaspora of the Indian-Hindu origin, I was, whether I liked it or not, also part of a Hindu collectivity. This collectivity contained elements which, as part of a majority in India, were embarking in the name of god and religion on a course of annihilation of minorities and dissenters, and attacking the very foundations of democracy in that country. Yet this very same collectivity, as a minority elsewhere in the world, knows what it is like to experience discrimination and hatred. These painful contradictions compelled me critically to re-examine my own Hindu background in order to be able to both understand and, crucially, to oppose those who, in the name of Hinduism, were acting in a way which was deeply inhuman and shameful to witness.

The recognition that I may belong at one and the same time to an oppressed minority and to an oppressive majority, with all the contradictions that entails, has found an echo in my experiences in Britain. Many of the struggles we have waged as black people here have rested, sometimes uncritically, upon a white majority/black minority dichotomy. This has been useful in creating the sense of solidarity necessary to mobilise against racist attacks from the state and thugs on our streets, uninformed or otherwise; but in asserting a singular and absolute identity – as 'victims' of racism – we have evaded the need to look critically at the inner dynamics of our communities. This has resulted in a tendency to deny uncomfortable realities and has tended to give us a partial and distorted view of ourselves and the world around us. This tendency has been particularly difficult for black women to deal with, as our struggles often arise out of our experiences *within* our communities, and in fighting to force these onto the wider political agenda we have also often had to fight against the imposition of a singular identity either on ourselves or on our communities.

What follows is an attempt to locate these struggles by retracing some of the campaigns of Southall Black Sisters (SBS) and our sister organisation, including Brent Asian Women's Refuge. Early SBS involved Asian and Afro-Caribbean women and started life as a campaigning group at a time of intense anti-racist activity and growing black political consciousness amongst Asians. The group was aware that forging a progressive black identity meant confronting simultaneously, racism and patriarchal oppression encountered both within the community and in wider society. This politics was reflected in the wide range of campaigns that SBS undertook, including protests against virginity tests carried out on Asian women arriving in this country in the late 1970s, involvement in anti-racist campaigns such as the 1979 mobilisations against the provocative presence and demonstrations of the National Front in Southall and support for Asian women on strike for union rights and better pay/conditions at a local factory (SBS 1990).

In 1982/3, SBS was awarded a grant from the then Greater London Council to set up a black women's centre. Our aims therefore extended to provide, for the first time, a comprehensive front line advisory service to black women whose needs were overlooked by statutory agencies, voluntary groups and even organisations established by the progressive anti-racist left in Southall. But in all the 18 years that we have been in existence we have tried to maintain a campaigning edge to our work. We have been conscious that casework and services, however necessary, cannot empower women, conducted as they are within the parameters of various structures of power which are assumed rather than transformed. Campaigning is therefore an essential component of our work.

Initially SBS faced much hostility and opposition, emanating not only from the conservative and traditional forces within Southall, but also from the left-wing progressive men with whom many in SBS had fought side-by-side in the major anti-racist struggles in the 1970s and 1980s. The founding members of SBS were, in fact, politicised by the anti-racist struggles, but the limitations of that movement, especially its refusal to recognise gender oppression, meant that they were compelled to strike out for autonomy. SBS, together with other black women's groups around the country, had begun to challenge the dominant thinking within the anti-racist movement that the struggle for black liberation in this country was only about the struggle for racial equality.

Our struggles have, out of necessity, arisen from the routine experiences of the many Asian, African-Caribbean and other women who come to our centre with stories of violence, persecution, imprisonment, poverty and homelessness experienced at the hands of their husbands, families and/or state (see Chapter 1). In attempting to meet the challenges they pose in their demands for justice for themselves and for women generally, we have had to organise autonomously. But we have always endeavoured to situate our practice within wider anti-racist and socialist movements, involving alliances and coalitions within and across majority and minority divides. This has not always been easy, but it is the only way we know in which a new and empowering politics can be forged.

By organising in women's groups and refuges, many of us have fought for autonomous spaces and the right for our own voices to be heard in order to break free from the patriarchal stranglehold of the family. In the process we have also had to challenge the attitudes of the wider society, as well as the theory and practice of social policy and legislation which seeks to restrict our freedom to make informed choices about our lives. Our organisations and our practice are critical in unmasking the failures not only of our communities, the state and wider society, but perhaps more tellingly, of so called anti-racist and multi-cultural politics.

Throughout our campaigns on domestic violence, whilst countering racist stereotypes about the 'problematic' nature of South Asian families, SBS has sought to highlight not only the familiar legal and economic obstacles faced by all women struggling to live free of abuse, but also the particular plight of Asian women: language barriers, racism and the specific role of culture and religion which can be used to sanction their subordinate role and to circumscribe their responses. Culture and religion in all societies act to confer legitimacy upon gender inequalities, but these cultural constraints affect some women more than others in communities where 'culture' carries the burden of protecting minority identities in the face of external hostility.

It has been very difficult for Asian women to challenge cultural and traditional practices. Indeed what are often taken to be cultural or religious practices (the two are often so intertwined that it becomes difficult to disentangle), can also be inventions of 'traditions' unknown in the countries of origin, by minority communities desperate to seek solace and protection in the face of racist denigration and attacks. In practice, cultural and religious identity becomes non-negotiable as the more conservative interpretations given by male religious leaders which refer to the 'authenticity' of cultural religious identity become the dominant interpretations. The consequence for women who have the least power within the institution of the family and religion is that they are held responsible for the preservation of identity and blamed for any break up in the cultural fabric of the community. Indeed, the control of women is the main mechanism by which the boundaries of community are policed.

It is in this context that we have to formulate demands and strategies which recognise the plurality of our experiences, without suppressing anything for the sake of political expediency. Alliances have been crucial in this, not only in gaining wider support, but also in breaking down mutual suspicion and stereotypes between majority and minority communities, and to ensure that some rights are not gained at the expense of others.

We began our protests in the early 1980s over the murder of Mrs Dhillon and her three daughters by her husband who burned them to death. In 1984 we took to the streets in response to the death of Krishna Sharma, who committed suicide as a result of her husband's assaults. Organising with other women in very public ways, through demonstration and pickets, we broke the silence of the community. Until that point there had been not a single voice of protest from either progressive or conservative elements within the community. The women who led the demonstrations had themselves fled their own families in Southall, but returned to join us with scarves wrapped around their faces so they might escape recognition. We demanded and won the support of many white women in the wider feminist movement, although initially they were hesitant in offering support for fear of being labelled 'racist'. One of our slogans, 'self-defence is no offence', was appropriated from the anti-racist street fighting traditions, but ironically it has now become the much quoted slogan of the wider women's movement against male violence in Britain. The form of our protests drew directly from the varied and positive feminist traditions of the Indian sub-continent. We picketed directly outside Krishna Sharma's house, turning accepted notions of honour and shame on their heads. It is the perpetrators of violence, we shouted, who should be shamed and disrobed of their honour by the rest of the community, not the women who are forced to submit. Another slogan – 'black women's tradition, struggle not submission' – was first coined on this demonstration, and that, too, has been adapted to become the rallying cry of feminists against male violence in this country.

The lessons of those early years have ensured that we have understood the importance of campaigns and direct action as an essential means of articulating the needs of the women who turn to us daily. From the murder of Balwant Kaur by her husband at the Brent refuge in 1985, to the life imprisonment of Kiranjit Ahluwalia for killing her violent husband in 1989, our response has been driven by a recognition that those tragedies reflected, albeit in extreme forms, the day-to-day experiences of many Asian women facing violence in the home.

The Kiranjit Ahluwalia campaign

The campaign to free Kiranjit Ahluwalia, following her conviction for murder in December 1989, illustrated the need for, and the potential impact of, alliances as a form of political action. We had to raise the specificity of her experiences as an Asian woman, drawing on her own depiction of her life, but we also had to draw out the connections with the experiences of other women in order to make demands relevant to all women in this society. Black and white, young and old, activists and non-activists, we found ourselves in one of the most empowering mobilisations of women against injustices seen for a long time. The women who use our centre and refuge wept and laughed with joy at

Kiranjit's eventual release. Many from across the religious caste and class divisions claimed her personal triumph as their own personal and collective victory.

In July 1991, Sara Thornton lost her appeal to overturn her murder conviction because the legal system was not then ready to accept a feminist critique of the homicide laws. Her hunger strike and the consequent publicity, against the background of the case of Joseph McGrail who was freed after kicking his alcoholic wife to death, struck a chord with the public which was to change the course of the Kiranjit Ahluwalia campaign. In the face of government intransigence, there was growing support for our critique of the legal system's untenable position on 'battered women'. Every day yielded more voices of support, ranging from almost all sections of the media, lawyers, civil servants, Members of Parliament across the political divides, academics, activists and the general public. On our part, we were able to mobilise women in SBS and at the refuge; women who had experienced violence and who understood Kiranjit's tragic act.

Our main allies were radical feminists, with their long and rich history in campaigning around violence against women, and Asian women, particularly those working in refuges and women's centres. The unity we forged had two main aims: to ensure an early release for battered women who kill their tormentors and who are unjustly incarcerated, and to demand a reform of the homicide legislation responsible for their imprisonment. There were many points of contention within the alliance as to the nature of the demands we ought to make of the state. Should we agitate for a reform of the existing laws as a tactical demand, or should we campaign for entirely new homicide laws that more accurately reflect women's daily experience of violence? Should we aim for new laws which were specific to women, or should they subsume areas such as racial violence and harassment? These tensions were never entirely resolved, nor could they have been, but despite divergent and sometimes irreconcilable views, we have been able to sustain the alliance.

Recently our campaign for the reform of homicide legislation, and more generally for changes in the criminal justice system, have led us into a new temporary alliance with more long established women's organisations with a far from radical image, such as the Townswomen's Guild and the Women's Institute. Although we have only been able to come together on the narrow issue of changing the law of provocation, it is nevertheless, a tactically important alliance of wider political significance. Conservative and Liberal women from these groups have joined us in mutual recognition of the fact that the law fails women. The outcome in this instance is less important than the process by which consciousness around domestic violence can continue to grow. The established women's groups are extremely nervous about the radical elements within the alliance, but they are still soldiering on with us to organise a mass lobby at the House of Parliament, and a letter writing campaign to the Home Secretary. The alliance has already led to the right-wing former Home Secretary, Michael Howard, developing a defensive posture when responding to letters by members of the Women's Institute and the Townswomen's Guild. A few years ago we would not have dared participate in such a forum, fearing that our politics or terms of reference might be compromised by such co-operation. We are now much more confident about the nature and boundaries of our participation in political alliances with other women's groups.

Since the Kiranjit Ahluwalia campaign we have witnessed a resurgence in campaigns around violence against women in the South Asian and other minority communities, often in consultation with one another. These campaigns seek to redefine the relationship of women to the criminal justice system and to change the language of the wider movements. So the term 'miscarriage of justice', which initially meant the wrongful conviction and punishment of those who are innocent, has been extended to include those who are routinely failed by the criminal justice system in other ways, through the failure of the police and the prosecuting authorities to protect women from abusive partners, to the transgressions of women which the law is unable to comprehend in its wider context. Internationally, too, the debates around domestic violence and other forms of male violence are defining women's rights as human rights, and issues like rape as crimes against humanity. These developments open up the potential for creating women's alliances which transcend artificial national boundaries.

By virtue of campaigns like ours, the law has been forced to take into account the social conditions and pressures which push women into contact or conflict with the criminal justice system. The years of hard campaigning by feminists against male violence are beginning to bear some fruit within the legal system, although contradictions remain. Gains in some areas of the law are offset by losses in others, and there is no room for complacency. In the Kiranjit Ahluwalia case, the legal definition of provocation has shifted to reflect the inability of some women to retaliate immediately after an assault or threat, and expert evidence to show the psychological impact of cumulative provocation was admitted for the first time. However, the attempt to fit complex realities into neat legal definitions can construct women in ways which deny their anger and agency, rendering them less threatening to the status quo. Thus has the 'battered women syndrome' been used to explain women's inaction in the face of repeated violence, but in the process the experience of women is medicalised and relegated to the realms of mental disorder. In other words, women are not 'permitted' to be angry or to locate their actions in a socio-economic context or in the failures of the institution of the family.

As feminists we have to be careful about the uncritical acceptance of superficially attractive solutions offered by the state in response to our campaigns and demands. For example, recent shifts in police attitudes and practices on domestic violence may appear to have 'solved' the problem of previous police indifference. The domestic violence units and multi-agency forums which are the practical outcome of these shifts in police strategy have done nothing to bring the issue of police accountability any closer to being addressed. In our experience the police continue to fail women in their responses to women's call for help, and this has not inspired any confidence that the police are now 'on our side'.

Similarly, as feminists we have to be careful not to separate ourselves off from other human and civil rights demands that, at first sight, may not appear to be a feminist concern. For instance, the abolition of the right to silence will have a profound effect on the rights of many, including blacks, lesbians and gays, new age travellers and women. Kiranjit Ahluwalia exercised her right to silence at her original criminal trial, but had she been forced into the witness box in the vulnerable, confused and frightened state she was then in, the outcome of her appeal might have been very different. As Anne Jones remarked in her powerful book on women who kill, the legal system is not like an onion which, if peeled, might reveal an egalitarian core (Jones 1991). The institutions of the state represent and articulate vested interests, constantly shifting ground, the better to maintain the status quo. Any gains we make can be reversed or diluted in the face of power and privilege (see also Chapters 4, 8, and 9).

The state and the family

For us, the state has never been an abstract concept. It has a real existence which defines our roles and position in society, it negotiates our existence as women within our families. Our understanding of the family as an institution governing our relationship with the outside world is therefore vital. It has been reshaped by the women who come to us questioning their roles and their lack of rights within and outside the family. Their experiences of domestic violence, sexual abuse, forced arranged marriages and racism are reflected in their demands to assert their rights as individuals. Yet within dominant anti-racist discourse, the black family is often constructed solely as a 'haven', a bulwark against the worst excesses of state harassment and racism. Whilst not denying that the family can perform this role, the construction of the homogenous Asian families hides other realities, power relations and power struggles between different caste, class and ethnic groups, and especially between men and women.

There are different ways in which the state constructs families, whether in the majority or minority community. The law and social policy take as 'natural' or given certain power relations between different groups and between men and women. These power relations reproduce and perpetuate inequalities between different sections of society. One good example is the construction of minority families in current immigration law which operates largely to limit immigration from 'third world' countries, and to restrict freedom of movement and speech, by curtailing rights of appeal against unfair and blatantly discriminatory decisions.

Anti-racist politics has effectively illuminated the racist assumptions which lie behind the immigration laws. Black families are routinely denied the right to privacy and unity in contravention of internationally recognised definitions of human rights. Intimate and intrusive questioning is commonplace in immigration cases, and the relations between partners and their dependants is probed for the slightest hint of inconsistency. In these ways black families are denied the rights taken for granted by families in the majority community. Anti-racism, however, pays little attention to the complex interplay between racist laws and patriarchal control which acts to place women in the most vulnerable position in the operation of immigration law.

It has been left to women to highlight the manner in which immigration law can, in combination with the institution of the family, construct women as an appendage to her husband, economically and socially dependent upon him, and a potential prisoner of violence and abuse within the home. When a woman has come from abroad to marry here, should she leave her husband and/or the marriage breaks down within a year, her immigration status is rendered illegitimate (this is known as the 'one year rule'). In the absence of an immigration status in her own right, a woman's option to leave a violent or abusive home becomes virtually non-existent. In such a situation, if a woman does leave her husband, not only is she ineligible for any form of state assistance in the form of housing or welfare benefits, which are a prerequisite for giving women a real choice about leaving a violent home, but she also risks deportation. As there is no right of appeal in such cases, her fate is then entirely dependent upon political decisions taken by the Home Office. The arbitrary and discriminatory nature of such decisions, underpinned by notions of third world peoples as 'aliens' or 'undesirables' means that the majority of women in such cases are forcibly deported to countries where their futures may be at risk. Persecution based on gender is not recognised as grounds for asylum, as it is in many other western countries (SBS 1993).

In this way, as in many others, we see the state applying double standards to the treatment of families from different communities. The premise of social services intervention, for example, is to preserve the unity of the family as far as possible, whilst intervention by the police and immigration services has the consequence of dividing and separating many black families. Women in the majority community have, through their own actions, managed to extend their choices to enable women to leave unhappy marriages, but for women from minority communities, particularly those with immigration difficulties, that choice is absent. Our demand is for the right of black and minority families to live undivided when they choose, but for women to have a real option of leaving an unhappy marriage without the state and the community colluding to deny that choice. If all women are to be empowered, it is essential to understand how the intersection of race, class and gender has the effect of locking different groups of men and women into varying subordinate and dominant positions within the family, community and the wider society. It is at the point of these intersections that women's access to power and resources is differentially structured, as is their level of participation in decision making within the family and the community.

The family has always been an important battleground for resistance. In a contribution written for a public meeting organised in 1990 to launch her campaign, Kiranjit Ahluwalia delivered a devastating critique of her circumstances, unpicking the intertwining threads of religion, culture and tradition to show

how her family life had become a prison. She argues, as do many of the women who come to see us, that she tried to be a 'good' wife and mother, to live by the rules of her religion and culture.

> My culture is like my blood – coursing through every vein of my body. It is the culture into which I was born and where I grew up which sees the woman as the honour of the house. In order to uphold this false honour and glory, she is taught to endure many kinds of oppression and pain, in silence. In addition religion also teaches her that her husband is her God and fulfilling his every desire is her religious duty. A woman who does not follow this part in our society has no respect or place in it. She suffers from all kinds of slanders against her character. She has to face all sorts of attacks and much hurt entirely alone. She is responsible not only for her husband but also for his entire family's happiness. . . . This is the essence of my culture, society and religion. Where a woman is a toy, a plaything – she can be stuck together at will, broken at will. . . . Today I have come out of my jail of my husband and entered the jail of the law.

The challenge to religion and culture is not easy. Women like Kiranjit Ahluwalia are unable to define culture and religion in ways that are personal and give meaning to their experiences. The choice for many women who dare to break out of the very narrow confines of the roles prescribed by religion and culture is stark; either they remain within the parameters of permissible behaviour, or they transgress and risk becoming pariahs within their own community. Many women cannot even conceive of a life of isolation and loneliness, preferring instead to risk their health, sanity and even their lives. Suicide rates among Asian women between the ages of 16 and 35 in Britain are up to three times the national average. Others, like Kiranjit Ahluwalia, refuse to internalise their anger and rage, and transgress into the unchartered 'male' territory of outward expression through homicide, and by doing so they defy social constructs of women as nurturers and carers.

Multi-culturalism and religious fundamentalism

Religion and culture is the terrain on which the politics of multi-culturalism and variants of anti-racism are built, often amounting to nothing more than the ossification of minority cultures and religions in social policies towards minority communities.

Multi-culturalism first gained currency within the field of education as a 'progressive' and 'enlightened' approach to race relations. The emphasis lay on recognition and tolerance of ethnic and cultural diversity. It was thus a direct counter perspective to previous models on the management of race relations, most notably the 'assimilation' model which emphasised assimilation of ethnic diversity within the dominant culture, widely perceived to be racist since its effect was to seek to erase all (minority) cultural differences and assert the primacy of the dominant culture. Whilst the multi-cultural project was 'progressive' in so far as it preached tolerance of minorities, it has become a substitute for challenging much of the structural basis of racism within society, mainly because of its underlying assumption that racism will disappear if the majority white community learns to respect the different (cultural/religious) lifestyles of minorities in this country.

The collapse of culture into religion and the tendency to homogenise minority cultures has been an attendant consequence of the multi-culturalist project. Within the multi-cultural discourse, minority communities are constructed as homogenous and static entities. There is no recognition of internal divisions along gender, class and caste lines and attendant relations of power. Such constructions of homogeneity have, of course, been the outcome of political relationships between the state and minority leaders. It needs to be understood that multi-culturalism has its roots in past British colonial practices in such countries as India, where British rule depended on the appeasement of the 'natives' and containment of social disorder. This was done by appointing a layer of 'community representatives' from the various social groupings who could maintain wider social consensus in exchange for cultural autonomy and power within their community (Sahgal 1992).

In Britain, multi-culturalism allows the state to mediate between itself and minority communities, using so-called 'community leaders' as power brokers and middle-men. Needless to say, such leaders are male, from religious, business and other socially conservative backgrounds who, historically, have had little or no interest in promoting an agenda for social justice and equality, least of all the rights of Asian women (Ali 1992). In return for information and votes, the state concedes some measure of autonomy to the 'community leaders' to govern their communities. In reality, this means control over family – women and children. Together the state and community leaders define the needs of minority communities, to limit their influence and to separate off the more radical elements by labelling them as extremists.

Where women and young children are concerned, the problem is that the state in its various guises, such as social services, the police or educationalists, in deference to multi-cultural theories and practices, seek to rely on community leaders to 'discover' the needs of the 'community' and to restore public order when the status quo of state and community relations is threatened (for example, where rioting or confrontation breaks out in response to police harassment and assaults). The voices of the most vulnerable – women and children, the youth, etc. – are drowned in the alliances that are formed to accommodate the interest of the state and community leaders.

In the name of tolerance of 'cultural differences', the rights of women are dismissed, and many Asian women seeking support to escape from violence or forced arranged marriages are often told by state agencies that seeking alternatives, for example asserting their legal rights, is not an acceptable method of resolving conflict within their families and communities. In 1991 an Asian man was charged with grievously assaulting his wife, an assault which nearly killed her. He was given a very lenient (non-custodial) sentence by the judge on the grounds that he was an 'immigrant'. On passing sentence the judge commented that had he been white, he would have dealt with him more severely. The judge's remarks and actions are shot through with multi-culturalist perceptions. He acknowledged the criminal offence that had been committed, but offered effectively to 'tolerate' it as it occurred in a different cultural context. Such views not only help to shape notions of Asian cultures as backward, monolithic and static, with no internal contesting struggles, they also help to reinforce patriarchal control of women in Asian communities. The tendency of the multi-cultural project to homogenise minority cultures has served to accommo-date demands made by religious fundamentalist leaders who have been able to launch their political campaigns for resources, power and status based solely on recognition of religious identities. In order to control and gain access to the levers of power, fundamentalist leaders claim to represent the 'authentic' voice of the communities, be they Muslim, Hindu or Sikh. They represent the new religious communities as homogenous and deny internal differences or the exist-ence of on-going challenges to the interpretation of religious practice and iden-tity.

Multi-culturalism has neatly provided the ideological framework for funda-mentalist and conservative leaders within the Asian communities to emphasise the primacy of religious identities and to make demands of the state based on such newly founded identities. Religious fundamentalist movements world-wide have gained ascendancy. They have either gained state power or become significant voices of opposition to the state within their own countries. Whilst having their own historical and cultural specificity, all fundamentalist move-ments share two major objectives: recognition as distinctive movements (to legitimise the claim for access to resources) and the reclamation of traditional (family) values, with particular emphasis on control over the sexuality and fer-tility of women.[1] In this country the rise of religious fundamentalism is in part a response to the upsurge in European nationalism and racism, and the failure of progressive left politics, coupled with the fallout from the Rushdie affair[2] and the Gulf War. These developments have contributed greatly to the current state of race and gender politics. Unlike multi-culturalism, religious fundamentalism privileges religion as the main mark of identity, and constructs itself in total opposition to secularism. It seeks to reaffirm and harness religious identity in the quest for power and resources at the local and national level.

The resurgence of religious fundamentalism feeds off parallel developments within the majority community. The reassertion of Christianity as the main sig-nifier of 'British' identity in schools, or the 'Back to Basics'[3] campaign, under-lined by a Christian morality aimed at preserving the sanctity of the nuclear and heterosexual family unit, are developments that have fuelled reactionary demands for formal recognition of minority religious lifestyles.

The received wisdom in the formulation and implementation of social policy is that minority communities are identified according to their religious back-grounds. Other social divisions of class, caste and gender are ignored behind such monolithic characterisation. Increasingly references are made not to Asian culture, but to Sikh, Muslim or Hindu culture. Such multi-cultural norms are also permeating popular perceptions of Asian communities.

Women's minds and bodies are the battleground for the preservation of the 'purity' of religious and communal identities. So the role of women as signifiers and transmitters of identity within the family becomes crucial. There is a growing phenomenon of organised gangs and networks of Asian men who hunt down runaway Asian girls and women who are perceived to have transgressed the mores of their culture and religion, and to have defiled their honour and identity. The family has therefore become a site of struggle for feminists and fundamentalists alike.

In Huddersfield in 1992 we saw the emergence of the so-called 'bounty hunter'. This man had set himself up as a custodian of the morality of the local Asian communities. Offering his services to local Asian families, he claimed to be able to locate and return to their families young women and girls who had chosen to leave to make their own lives elsewhere. Some of these women had left to escape from violence, abuse, restrictions on their freedom of movement, and forced arranged marriages. Many of the women possessed court orders to restrain their husbands and families from pursuing them. When challenged about his activities, the former taxi driver maintained that he was simply responding to a need expressed by the 'community' to maintain the sacrosanct nature of the Asian family. Like many others within the community, he was personally angry at the idea that Asian women could protest and demand assistance from the state in response to domestic violence and other abuses. So with the blessing of the 'community' he engaged in what were clearly illegal activities, utilising a network of informers within the Labour-controlled local authority, social welfare systems and Asian mini-cab and business services to trace the whereabouts of 'missing' women. He even boasted that he knew the secret addresses of every women's refuge and hostel in the north of England. In such circumstances success in 'reuniting' families may rest upon threats of violence and harassment.

The response of society at large to this 'bounty hunter' was salutary for its indifference to his victims. Like the documentary which brought him to wider public attention, the rest of the media, including the 'quality' newspapers, referred to him as a 'mediator' who was 'salvaging' Asian marriages from the crisis of modernity.

We refused to turn the clocks back. In December 1992 SBS, Women Against Fundamentalism (WAF), other Asian women from around the country, and some white women who had worked with us on the Kiranjit Ahluwalia campaign, joined women in Huddersfield for a loud and visible demonstration. Armed with anger and songs set to the seasonal tunes of Christmas carols, we marched around the city centre to the bemusement of Christmas shoppers. The 'anti-racist' director of the Channel Four documentary turned up at the demonstration to lend his support to the 'beleaguered' and 'misunderstood' bounty hunter. He suggested that the underlying theme of his film was to explore the question of 'whether Asian women take freedom if given the opportunity'. His film, he claimed, suggested that they did not want freedom, as they eventually returned home. What was missing from his simple argument was any under-standing of the oppressive context in which Asian women can make 'choices' about freedom. We demanded instead the right for women to speak for them-selves and to tell their own stories; we would not be forced into our homes again. Instead we sang out:

> Jingle bells, jingle bells, jingle all the way;
> We have come to Huddersfield to chase the thugs away!
> We are not afraid, we will not retreat, we will struggle for our rights in victory and defeat;
> This is our tradition, struggle not submission, courage is our faith, and dissent is our religion.

The following year in Bradford, a committee consisting of conservative and reli-gious men was formed to ensure that Bradford police and social agencies refer to them for guidance regarding every single case of a runaway Asian woman.

The task of confronting these fundamentalist and other reactionary develop-ments within our communities has largely been left to women. The failure of progressive forces to deal with the reactionary forces is largely to do with fear of fuelling what has been termed the 'new racism' – that of the persecution of Muslims within the west. Of course it is true that Islam has been constructed as the new 'enemy' within the west, especially in the wake of the collapse of the Cold War. Nevertheless, any resistance to racism based around religious iden-tity is profoundly problematic, not least because, by its very nature, it creates an exclusive identity which makes alliances with other racial and ethnic groups facing racial oppression impossible, as well as for its dangerous implications for women's autonomy. Many of the left, however, have been unable to respond to the threat posed by religious fundamentalism. This is largely because, histori-cally, black struggle has been constructed as that against racism alone, and black resistance has been founded on the perpetuation of the myth of a homo-genous minority community drawing on its cultural and religious resources with which to fight racism.[4] There is no corresponding recognition that culture and religion also perpetuate class, caste and gender inequality within minority communities.

Given the failure and fragmentation of left politics in this country, and in the absence of a coherent socialist movement, alliances and coalitions are perhaps one of the few means we have available to us to enable us to move forward. Alliances are not easy to build, not least because of the contradictions involved in confronting gender, race and fundamentalist politics. But Women Against Fundamentalism (WAF)[5] provides one positive model showing how coalition politics can be built. WAF was a heterogeneous group, consisting of women from a variety of ethnic and religious backgrounds, such as Irish, Jewish, Asian and English. The agenda of WAF is to resist fundamentalism and its impact on women world-wide and to resist racism. We have been able to come together to share the commonality of our experiences as women, but our starting point is to oppose the rise of fundamentalism in all religions.

In the British context it is not possible to confront Jewish, Islamic or Hindu fundamentalism without simultaneously engaging in a critique of the British state: state racism (especially the operation of immigration laws), the privileging of Christianity, which has compounded the rise of fundamentalism within minority communities, and the failures of the multi-cultural project in addressing racism and women's oppression are central to our analysis of fundamentalism and indeed secularism. Whilst struggles particular to women from a minority community are led by women within that community, support is available from women from different ethnic backgrounds within WAF. In this way we place emphasis on recognising the different structural locations that we occupy. The differences in our locations are not allowed to deflect from the need for a common agenda on equality. Instead we are able to articulate a common programme of joint political action based upon our analysis of racism and fundamentalism and so avoid the paralysing effects that identity politics and multi-culturalism has had on an alliance building. Nira Yuval Davis sums up how coalition politics can work: 'We should see feminist politics as a form of coalition politics in which differences among women would be recognised and given a voice, without fixating the boundaries of this coalition in terms of "who" we are but in terms of what we want to achieve' (Yuval Davis 1994).

In the wake of the destruction of the Babri-Masjid and the burning of Hindu temples in this country, SBS and Brent Refuge became centrally involved in a loose coalition of predominantly Asian men and women from a range of campaigning backgrounds – anti-racist, feminist, anti-caste (Ambedkarite), activist, academic, secularist and humanist. We came together to form an anti-communal organisation – The Alliance Against Communalism and for Democracy in South Asia.

The word 'communalism' is specific to the Indian sub-continent. The modern history of India is, in part, a history of the rise of communalist forces. Communalism refers to the construction of a community solely around religious identity and religious conflict. Communal politics is the politics of such a religious community posing as a monolithic bloc in opposition to those who do not belong and are therefore constructed as the 'other'. Like multi-culturalism, communalism in India has homogenising tendencies denying internal variations in religious practices across regions and castes. Precisely because Hindus are in the majority in India, Hindu communalism has become a complex but dangerous phenomenon, propagating a politics of hate and domination of Muslims who represent a significant minority. Hindu communalism today cannot be understood in broad generalisations, but it involves in essence a number of Hindu right-wing and fundamentalist political parties and organisations who have drawn on (historically mythical) grievances between Hindus and Muslims to gain access to power at all institutional levels, especially in the media. In the last decade or so, with the collusion and support of certain sections of the

Indian state, Hindu communalism has been on the offensive as a nationalist movement attempting to forge India as a 'Hindu' nation.[6]

The main task of the Alliance was to support anti-communalist forces in India who were facing an uphill struggle in turning the tide of sweeping Hindu nationalism, and to prevent communalism from breaking out in our communities in Britain. For many of us, this was not only a way in which we could voice our horror and opposition to developments in India; it was also an opportunity for feminists active in the fight against religious fundamentalism to seek support from other constituencies in resisting movements which placed the control of women as central to their agenda. The Alliance was effective in unsettling the confidence of those who were galvanising financial and other support for communalist forces in India, as they liked to pretend that their support from Hindus was absolute. Our campaigning was nevertheless difficult. We found that, in the larger Hindu communities of London, Leicester and elsewhere, there was widespread across-class support for the main right-wing Hindu groupings such as the Vishwa Hindu Parishad (VHP), the Bharatiya Janata Party (BJP) and the Bombay-based Shiv Sena. The response to us at many meetings and social gatherings was to adopt aggressive and disruptive tactics in an effort to suppress us. The vociferous presence of women was felt to be particularly provocative, and they labelled us as Muslim-loving prostitutes, outcasts, women in the pay of Muslim fundamentalists or the Congress Party of India.

Within the Alliance, despite its name, many of the left, anti-racist activists could not come to a decision to oppose all religious fundamentalist movements operating here and in the Indian sub-continent. Whilst willing to compare the rise of the BJP to the rise of the British National Party (BNP), to some extent a valid comparison, they failed to go further and look critically at all our communities from within. The demonisation of Islam by the west has led to a marked reluctance by progressive and left forces to confront Islamic fundamentalism here, for fear of alienating Muslims and weakening unity against racism and class exploitation. A good example of this reluctance is shown in the way many anti-racist activists have argued that, in the current wave of anti-Muslim racism, all blacks should regard themselves as Muslims. Even as a political stance expressing solidarity, this is an extremely problematic position for women in our struggle for personal freedom and alliances with progressive social forces.

As feminists and anti-fundamentalists, we were determined to maintain the unity of the Alliance, but its failure to make women's rights a central component of the wider struggle has enormous implications for its future development. The abandonment of the women's question for short-term political gain, or making alliances with right-wing movements, offers us nothing. We must oppose all religious fundamentalism and recognise that the strength of Asian women's struggle has been in its ability to mobilise across religious, caste and class divisions. To go further, in the feminist, secular political spaces we have created lies hope for the defeat of religious fundamentalism. This is an insight which, unfortunately, has not been appreciated by our male allies in left and anti-racist movements.

Conclusion

With the collapse of the Babri-Masjid in India, I found that a wall surrounding some of my own guarded orthodoxies had crumbled. At the conclusion of a highly successful public meeting organised by some of us in the Alliance Against Communalism in the Hindu stronghold of Wembley in Brent in 1993, a friend and colleague of Muslim origin broke down and wept. Many of those who had attended the meeting had been mobilised by local and national Hindu organisations, and their virulent anti-Muslim sentiments and abuse, devoid of any rationality, had left my friend feeling as if she had been stripped of her own humanity. I understood then the full significance of the struggles we have been engaged in, and we pledged together to fight for the right to occupy and defend the secular space we had created for ourselves as feminists, even if we needed to rethink what to put in that space.

The third wave[7] of feminism has a lot to contend with. The rise of new forms of racism, fascism, nationalism and religious fundamentalism world-wide demands from us a new and visionary politics. We must avoid the pitfalls of identity politics of the 1970s and 1980s which made it so difficult to share experiences, and we must move beyond the limitations of anti-racism and multi-culturalism which equally limit our perspectives and our ability to act. We must reject the vicious and blinkered vision of nationalism and fundament-alism. Our task is to find new ways of resisting, and new ways of truly demo-cratic thinking which give us the optimism to go beyond all of these failed forms of politics. Our alliances must cross our different identities, and help us to re-conceptualise notions of democracy, human rights and citizenship. Whatever the dividing lines drawn by priests, mullahs, gurus and politicians, we will then be able to reach out to each other, to support one another in our transgressions and defiance. Above all, we must leave room for doubt and uncertainty in our own orthodoxies. The time has come, in the words of the Walrus in Lewis Caroll's poem, to talk of many things.

Addendum

This article has been reprinted from Heidi Safia Mirza (ed.) (1997) *Black British Feminism: A Reader*, London: Routledge. Since its publication, there have been some amendments – but these have been largely confined to the need for clarifi-cation, since the original article, written in 1994, was intended for a different project. Many events at the local and national level have taken place in this country but I have not sought to update the piece. To do so would require re-writing much of the article, and I would be unable to resist the temptation to make improvements!

Debates on racism and anti-racism are now completely overshadowed by the seminal case of Stephen Lawrence. The case concerned the racist killing of a black (African-Caribbean) teenager in 1993 and the failure of the police to investigate the killing as a racist murder. Police indifference and incompetence meant that the white assailants of Stephen Lawrence escaped a criminal trial. The Lawrence family launched an extraordinary campaign to force British society to acknowledge the existence of institutional racism and lack of accountability within the police and other institutions. Their campaign has given rise to a series of recommendations (The MacPherson Report 1999) to combat racism. Many of these recommendations have an important bearing on the work of SBS in respect to the response of the police, the criminal justice system and the social welfare services to issues such as domestic violence, rape and forced marriages in our communities. But much of our work highlights the need to move beyond narrow concepts of race and anti-racism to include an understanding of the interplay of race, gender and class. In our view this is crucial if we are to avoid losing the opportunity created by the Stephen Lawrence case to challenge racism and check institutional power without repeating the mistakes of the earlier anti-racist movement.

Following a hard-fought campaign by SBS, the Labour government announced a concession – a modification to the 'one year rule' – in the Immigration and Asylum Act 1999. The concession is an acknowledgement that women who are subject to domestic violence and have an insecure immigration status can be trapped in the violent relationship by the operation of the one year rule. The concession states that a person who has been granted a 12–month stay on the basis of marriage and who becomes a victim of domestic violence, may be granted indefinite leave to remain, provided she has evidence of the violence. Victories are never straightforward. The sting in the tail of this victory lies in the fact that a high standard of proof is required to show domestic violence if a woman is to make a case for remaining in this country following the breakdown of her marriage. At present the only evidence that the Home Office deems acceptable is a criminal conviction, a civil court order or a police caution. Medical evidence is not acceptable. The intention of the Government is clear – to maintain a tough stance on immigration even if it is discriminatory towards minority women. However, SBS is determined to continue its campaign to monitor the effectiveness of the concession and to challenge the Government for adopting a lower standard of protection to minority women who experience domestic violence when compared to the standard of protection afforded to women in the majority community.

In 1999, gender related persecution was recognised for the first time in this country in the landmark cases of *Shah and Islam*. This important decision recognised that women fleeing domestic violence in countries where they encounter widespread institutional discrimination and are unprotected by the state can qualify as refugees. It must be emphasised that this decision has occurred in the context of intense campaigning by black and white women in this country and abroad, to inject a gendered perspective to asylum law. The *Shah and Islam* decision is a far-reaching one. It not only recognises gender related persecution from non-governmental agencies, but also allows for other groups such as gays and lesbians in circumstances where they face persecution to qualify for refugee status. We must safeguard this decision at all costs.

My thanks are due to the editors and Hannana Siddiqui for their comments to the amendments.

Notes

1   See Yuval Davies and Sahgal (1992) for an account of the rise and content of religious fundamentalist movements world-wide and their effects on women.
2   In February 1989, Salman Rushdie unleashed a storm of protest within Muslim communities here and abroad with his controversial book *The Satanic Verses*. Many orthodox and fundamentalist Muslim leaders instigated a number of anti-Salman Rushdie campaigns in this country. They charged him with blasphemy and many supported the fatwa issued by the Iranian State which called for his death. The real agenda of community leaders in this country however, is to increase their power base in their communities by constructing a strict Muslim identity which rests primarily on the imposition of traditional roles on women and control of their sexuality.
3   The 'Back to Basics' campaign was the feeble but cynical attempt by John Major and his colleagues in the Tory party, when in power in 1994 onwards, to reassert traditional family values in an effort to garner votes. The policy was a resounding failure. Some Tories in Parliament were themselves unable to live up to the image of good Christian family men in their own private lives.
4   Sivanandan amongst other commentators, in works such as *A Different Hunger: Writings on Black Resistance* (1982), have helped to shape the myth of the homogenous black community in perpetual resistance against racism in Britain.
5   Women Against Fundamentalism ceased to function as an active organisation in 1997. But an information sharing network encouraging electronic activism exists! Contact SBS for more information about the network.
6   For an excellent analysis of the rise of modern Hindu communalism, the Hindu right and its imperatives and aims, see Basu *et al.* (1993).
7   Third Wave Feminism is a term coined by among others, Yasmin Ali, who was one of the initiators of an incomplete project in 1993/4 to bring together writing on the post-1970 phase of feminist thinking and activism in this country. This piece was originally requested for that project.

References

Ali, Y. (1992) 'Muslim women and the politics of ethnicity and culture in Northern England', in Sahgal, G. and Yuval Davies, N. (eds) *Refusing Holy Orders*, London: Virago Press.
Basu, T., Data, P., Sarka, S., Sarka, T. and Sen, S. (1993) *Khaki Shorts and Saffron Flags*, New Delhi: Orient Longman Ltd.
Jones, A. (1991) *Women Who Kill*, London: Gollancz.
Sahgal, G. (1992) 'Secular spaces: the experience of Asian women organising', in Sahgal, G. and Yuval Davies, N. (eds) *Refusing Holy Orders*, London: Virago Press.
Sivanandan, A. (1982) *A Different Hunger: Writings on Black Resistance*, London: Pluto Press.
Southall Black Sisters (1990) *Against the Grain*, London: SBS publication.
Southall Black Sisters (1993) 'Memorandum by Southall Black Sisters: Domestic Violence and Immigration Law', Appendix 9, in Home Affairs Committee (1993) *Domestic Violence, Vol. 11*, Yuval *Memoranda of Evidence, Minutes of Evidence and Appendices*, London: HMSO.
Yuval Davies, N. (1994) 'Women, Ethnicity and Empowerment', in *Feminism and Psychology*, 4, 1, 179–97.
Yuval Davies, N. and Sahgal, G. (eds) (1992) *Refusing Holy Orders*, London: Virago Press.

Part IV

Influencing state policies on violence against women from known men

11 The politics and policies of responding to violence against women

R. Emerson Dobash and Russell P. Dobash

Innovation and social change

During the last quarter of the twentieth century, male violence and the physical abuse of women in the home were recognised throughout the world as problems of importance and placed on the agendas of social and political change. Women's groups brought the problem onto a world stage and sought social and political changes and interventions in order to provide relief to women who were abused. At the beginning, prevailing perceptions of the problem and possible solutions constituted formidable obstacles (c.f., Fairbairn 1975). The myth of family unity and bliss exploded as the issue was made public and the unacceptable face of the private world of conflict, power and violence was exposed to scrutiny. Thereafter, the issue could never again be ignored or denied. Instead, it had to be acknowledged and solutions had to be sought.

The context in which activists negotiated with representatives of agencies of the state was affected by the remit and resources of these agencies, their ideologies and priorities, their power, and the willingness to enter into negotiations intended by activists to modify or completely transform the usual policies and practices of such agencies. While, in theory, any and all changes may seem possible, reality is often much more restricting and complex. This is a critical point when reflecting on progress made as it brings an element of realism to what has been achieved and provides some insight into the degree of difficulty involved at the time.

Discovery

Perhaps the most important first step in the process of social change is the very act of creating new visions and thinking new thoughts. Once a new idea has become established, it is difficult to imagine how it was ever otherwise. But at the moment of launching a new idea, it is difficult to imagine how it could ever be. Thus, it is important to acknowledge that while it may now be generally agreed that it is unacceptable for a man to use physical or sexual violence against his female partner, this is, in fact, an extraordinary departure from thinking of the recent past. This is a change of great magnitude. Once the unthinkable has been thought, it must then be articulated in public settings in order to begin the process of transforming the vision of others and of overcoming their resistance to the new idea. Next comes action. Such action will, of necessity, involve negotiations and struggles with others who have a different world in mind, often the retention of the one they already know. Developing a new vision and acting to achieve it is the core of social movements. Forming a vision which truly represents an alternative to the status quo is the core of social change. And struggling for changes that transform the lives of all women is the concrete, constructive core of feminism. All three came together in the movement for abused women which emerged in Britain and the USA in the 1970s, and began what was to become a global issue by the turn of the century (Dobash and Dobash 1992; 1997; see Chapters 1 and 10).

There was a change in the discourse about violence against women. Silence, and a general lack of public discussion gave way to public statements of disapproval made throughout the world and echoed in the media, government and in everyday conversation. What was once secret and unshareable became a topic of public discussion and concern. The new discourse constructed a vision of intolerance, albeit often limited and conditional, rather than the previous tolerance of male violence. It departed from previous notions of women by asserting that they were to be valued in their own right rather than simply as wives or mothers tending to the needs of others. Left behind was the image of a 'good wife' as one who remained 'loyal' to her husband by maintaining silence about his abuses of her body. It posed a challenge to those men who used violence and to those who tolerated its continuation uncensored and unchecked.

Traditional forms of male domination and female subordination had some powerful supporters and support systems. Institutional tolerance and indifference were rife. This legacy was challenged within social, medical and legal institutions through confrontations and negotiations with institutions of the state, as activists sought to provide support and assistance for abused women and to address the continuing problem of male violence (Dobash and Dobash 1992; Henderson and Mackay 1990). By entering into negotiations with agencies of the state, a fundamental statement was being made: the state itself could and should be a part of the solution to the problem of men's violence in the home. This also indicated that the policies and practices of the past had been a part of the problem and were in need of transformation in order to seek an effective solution. At a general level, the very fact that social movements and agencies of the state enter into dialogue about a social problem and into negotiations concerning its solution is itself a process that helps democratise the state as the governed enter into the process of government by participating in the process of legislative and policy formation (Held 1984). Simultaneously, the state becomes more democratic and more accessible to civil society as it broadens its base of participation in the process of forming policy. Some proposals for radical change are sponsored by agencies of the state while others do not fair so well or have unanticipated outcomes. In this case, the national and global process has been one in which the concerns of women became established as a legitimate part of the concerns of governments, albeit not to the degree sought by groups of activists involved in the process.

Interventionist and welfare states provide greater opportunities for reformers attempting to effect changes within the institutions of the state. The goal may be to introduce state involvement where once there was none, or to alter existing policies, practices and legislation relating to particular groups or social issues. It is critical that the battered women's movements in Britain and the USA began in the 1970s when governments were generally more interventionist and welfare oriented. The 1980s saw the Thatcher and Reagan eras and movement away from community welfare to neo-liberal policies focused on limiting or eliminating state involvement in many facets of social life. Even with the subsequent governments of Clinton and Blair, the refuge movements in both countries had to negotiate in a context much altered from the world in which the refuge movement began. Of course governments are not monolithic in approach and much of previous activity continues relatively unaltered despite the party in power. However, securing resources and negotiating for changes in legislation and policies for a particular issue may be more or less difficult when governments of particular persuasions are in power.

The last quarter of the twentieth century experienced radically different social and political contexts in which the problem of woman abuse emerged and through which it has passed. The first few years of the new millennium bring a new mixture of challenges and possibilities. Knowledge of some of the main continuities and changes of the recent past may provide useful insights into prospects for change in the not-too-distant future. With this in mind, we examine some of the main developments around the issue of woman abuse in Britain and the USA from its emergence as a public issue in the 1970s to its location as a global issue within three decades.

The problem is violence against women: past and present

Historical and anthropological evidence shows that women are the most usual victims of violence in the home (Dobash and Dobash 1979; 1984; Daly and Wilson 1988; Gordon 1988; Pleck 1988; Counts *et al.* 1992; Cook and Bessant 1997: 1–18). Within marriage and the family, the use of physical force and violence has traditionally been a prerogative of men who were given authority over and granted the right to control all members of the household (women, children and servants) by a variety of means including the use of force and violence. Through religious beliefs and legal prescriptions this was supported well into the nineteenth century and men were punished only when their violence was excessive, a flagrant outrage and/or a public nuisance (Dobash and Dobash 1981: 563–81; 1992: 267; 2001; Schneider 2001).

While women were sometimes violent to their husbands, this was not a common practice, nor was it supported or tolerated in these patriarchal societies. Instead, community rituals such as charivari and misrules were used to shame and punish a violent wife. There were also rituals and physical punishments to censure wives for nagging and thus upsetting the 'natural' patriarchal order. From late medieval times to well into the nineteenth century, the 'nagging' or 'disobedient' wife could be subjected to punishments such as the ducking stool or branks bridle which were meant to restore domestic order and the authority of the husband. Men who were 'hen pecked' or cuckolded, i.e., not in control of their wives, could be subjected to ritu-alised and symbolic ceremonies such as 'rough music' and the cuckold's court, usually frivolous and mocking affairs, meant to ridicule a man for not main-taining control over his wife and thus to correct such *monstrous* and *unusual* inversions of the patriarchal order (Davis 1971; Thompson 1972; Shorter 1975; Dobash and Dobash 1977–8; 1979: 31–74; 1981; 1992: 267–90; Dobash *et al.* 1986).

Today, evidence from police and court records, national crime surveys and victims surveys continue to confirm the asymmetrical pattern of domestic viol-ence (Dobash, Dobash, Daly and Wilson 1992; see also Chapter 2) although in some circles this remains controversial. Violence experienced by women is most likely to occur in intimate relationships and to be inflicted by husbands, part-ners and lovers. Whether sexual or physical assault, women are most at risk from the men they know rather than from strangers, and there is almost no risk of violence to women from other women (Greenfeld *et al.* 1998). The onset of systematic and severe violence against a woman is primarily associated with entering an intimate relationship with a man. The familiar stories of abused women fill out the statistics with human dimensions and make the social facts comprehensible.

Based on our studies of male abusers and abused women, we have identified a 'constellation of violence' composed of three elements: the violence, the injuries and controlling and intimidating behaviour. Measured by three scales, the Violence Assessment Index (VAI), The Injury Assessment Index (IAI) and the Controlling Behaviour Index (CBI), this forms an overall 'constellation of violence' (see Dobash *et al.* 1995: 358–89; Dobash and Dobash 1999: 155–64; Dobash *et al.* 2000: 11–31, 71–88).

It is essential that the violence is placed within the context in which it occurs and that it is examined from both the perspective of women who are abused and from the men who perpetrate the abuse. In *Violence Against Wives* (1979), we first articulated the importance of placing violence within the context in which it occurs, and have since continued to develop the 'context specific approach' (1983: 261–76; 1999) and to use it in subsequent studies of violence. Knowledge about the *context of violence* provides insight into its nature, consequences and rationales for its use that would not be possible without locating the event within this wider nexus of personal and social factors.

Women's accounts reveal the nature of men's violence, the sources of conflict leading to attacks, their own emotions and reactions and the responses of social and legal institutions (see Chapters 1 and 3). Less familiar but equally import-ant to understand are the accounts of men who usually minimise their violence, deny responsibility for their own actions and blame others for what they do. As men are the primary perpetrators of this violence and the ones who must change if *their* violence is to be eliminated, we include some comments from men who have used violence against a woman partner along with voices of women who have been victimised. All the men cited below were part of our Violent Men Study, the findings of which are reported at length in *Changing Violent Men* (Dobash *et al.* 2000).

Men say:

> We had an argument and I grabbed her by the hair and I hit her and pushed her and that was it. *She hit me over the head with her shoe.* Then somebody phoned the police
>
> (Dobash *et al.* 2000: 14).

> I didn't come in till about half past twelve [midnight], and I was really bad drunk. I don't remember whether she was in her bed or up the stairs, but I tried to have sex with her, pushed myself a lot ... but she wasn't wanting it and I just started hitting her... – head-butting – injuries: broken nose and two black eyes
>
> (Dobash *et al.* 2000: 15).

> I slapped her and I did toss the table at her, but then all I was trying to do was get her out of the room ... It was just a slap. I didn't say, 'Right, I'm going to hit you.' *She scratched me* and it was almost instantaneous. She had a bash on her head where *the table had bashed her head* that was all, and a bit of a sore face, but there was no black eye or anything. I had slapped her but nothing – not really badly
>
> (Dobash *et al.* 2000: 15).

> I was wanting to show her [by using violence] who was the boss
>
> (Dobash *et al.* 2000: 27).

Throughout these comments, we have drawn attention to the 'violence' perpetrated by women in the context of attacks upon them by the men in the study, as this provides some insight into the nature of women's violence to male partners and the context of male abuse in which it is most likely to occur (see Chapter 8). It is also interesting to note how men remove themselves from responsibility even to the extent of noting how 'the table had bashed her head'. Such attributions of responsibility for violence and for injuries are common in the comments of men speaking about their violence.

Women from various countries and different studies provide still further insights into the nature of the violence and their own estimation of potential damage, danger and lethality:

> He tried to strangle me last night. I was terrified. I did manage to get out of the house but I had to go back the next morning. You see it was Easter

weekend and my two children were afraid the Easter Bunny wouldn't come if mummy and daddy were fighting

(Kincaid 1982: 23).

He once used a stick, he hit me once with a big fibreglass fishing pole, six foot long. And he just went whoosh, he gave me such a wallop with that. I had a mark . . . right down my back. I thought my back had broke

(Dobash and Dobash 1984: 275).

Injuries range from cuts and bruises to broken bones, miscarriages and permanent damage. Women from different countries recount similar incidents and a wide range of injuries:

My father told me, 'When a man hits you with his fist, make no mistake about it: he is trying to hurt you. It don't take that much to control a woman. You can take her, sit her in a chair, walk out of the room, you can go for a walk. Just walk away if it gets too much'

(Klein *et al.* 1997: 44).

Punching, I had my nose broken, ribs broken, two black eyes – he dragged me out of bed by the hair and pulled me along the ground. He smashed the door of my parent's house down when I was there

(Evason 1982: 28).

I had treatment for a fractured skull and I lost a child in a miscarriage due to violence

(Evason 1982: 30).

Repeated violence has an effect on emotional well-being as well as upon physical health. One man comments:

Terrified. *Even though she was trying to fight back* I knew she was terrified just by looking at her. Just the look on her face, I knew she was scared

(Dobash *et al.* 2000: 22).

Women concur:

It feels as though it has made me more insecure

(Dobash *et al.* 2000: 22).

I was always terrified. My nerves were getting the better of me. . . . He knew this and I think he loved this

(Dobash and Dobash 1979: 111).

The fear of not knowing what he would do – I feared for my life

(Casey 1987–8: 26).

The sources of conflict leading to violent events reveal a great deal about the nature of relationships between men and women, men's expectations of women partners, the prerogatives and power of a 'husband', and cultural beliefs that support individual attitudes about marital inequality.

Men comment:

> *What kinds of things do you have disagreements about usually?* Money, housework, my dinner not being made
>
> (Dobash *et al.* 2000: 26).

> *[How did she provoke you?]* I come home from my work and she's never vacuumed or dusted the place
>
> (Dobash and Dobash 1999: 146).

Women add:

> I could not stand another day of him saying, 'Have you done the vacuuming, have you dusted?
>
> (Lees 1997: 170).

> I had a poker thrown at me – just because his tea was too weak – he just takes it for granted, if you're married you'll have to accept it. It's part of being a wife
>
> (Pahl 1985: 77).

> And then he had his belt and I was whipped over the shoulders, everywhere, on my face and everything. And this was to teach me not to argue with him
>
> (Dobash and Dobash 1979: 108).

> He would stay out all night and become violent when questioned
>
> (Dobash and Dobash 1979: 108).

The four main sources of conflict leading to violent attacks are men's possessiveness and jealousy, men's expectations concerning women's domestic work, men's sense of the right to punish 'their' women for perceived wrong-doing, and the importance to men of maintaining and/or exercising their position of authority (Dobash and Dobash 1979: 98–106; Edelson and Eisikovits 1986: 229–47; Morran and Wilson 1994; 1997; Pence and Paymar 1993).

Many women remain silent, sometimes for years, because of a sense of shame and/or fear of reprisal. For example, the US National Crime Survey of Domestic Violence cases from 1978 to 1982 found that 48 per cent of such cases were not reported to the police because it was viewed as a private matter or because of fear of reprisal (Langan and Innes 1986: 1). With increasing public awareness of the problem and interventions orientated to its elimination, fewer feel the need to remain silent in order to remain respectable.

When women hit back

For the most part, women believe that attempts at self protection or retaliation will only increase the severity of an attack. Most women try to avert men's violence by pleading, cajoling, diverting attention and/or attempting to escape. Although most women do not respond to men's violence with counter violence, sometimes it does occur. When women do respond to men's violence with counter violence, it is may be in self-defence in anger and/or in retaliation (Dobash and Dobash 1979; 1984; Bowker 1983; Saunders 1986; 1988: 47–60; Dobash *et al.* 1992, see also Chapter 8). Concurring with earlier research, Saunders' study of a group of physically abused women in the United States shows that their violence is typically associated with self-defence, involves a narrow range of acts and is not usually intended to inflict injury (Saunders 1988).

The predominant pattern of violence between spouses is one of male violence directed at a female partner. Women do not usually use violence against men but when they do, it is most often in a context in which they have previously been assaulted by the man, are trying to defend themselves or are attempting to stop an attack. While one measurement tool purports to reveal even more violent women than men, all others including police reports, homicide statistics and national victim surveys reveal an asymmetrical pattern with men the usual perpetrators of violence against women and not the obverse (Dobash and Dobash 1992: 272).

Homicides in the home, when men and women kill

When men kill

The world-wide pattern of homicide is one in which men are overwhelmingly the killers, usually of other men and sometimes of women and children. By comparison, women do not usually kill others and it is rare for a woman to be killed by a woman. Without a doubt, there is overwhelming sexual asymmetry in the act of homicide across the population. Except for the USA, with its changing patterns, the world-wide pattern of domestic homicides is also one in which men are primarily the killers of wives, fiancees and intimate partners (Daly and Wilson 1988; Dobash *et al.* 1992). Until the 1990s, the USA provided an unusual exception to the world-wide pattern of intimate homicides, but 'intimates committed fewer murders in 1995–6 than in any other year since 1976 … and for persons murdered by intimates, the number of male victims fell an average of 5 per cent per year and the number of female victims went down an average of 1 per cent' (Greenfeld *et al.* 1998: 1). In England and Wales, women are four to nine times more likely than men to be killed by spouses, ex-spouses, cohabitees and ex-cohabitees (Edwards 1989: 124; Dobash *et al.* 1992; Daly and Wilson 1988; Dobash and Dobash 1992: 273). In 1997, figures for homicides between spouses/lovers in England and Wales indicate that 85 per cent of the victims were female while 15 per cent were male (Home Office 1998: 70).

One of the most important single findings from an earlier Canadian study of convicted men and women is that spousal homicide 'is rarely a sudden explosion in a blissful marriage' but is based on the immediate situation and a history of quarrels, usually about sexual jealousy and possessiveness (Chimbos 1978: 67). It is the 'endpoint' in a series of conflicts: 70 per cent reported prior assaults and 32 per cent of the killings resulted from a beating, always by men, 'who can use their body and strength as tools for killing' (Chimbos 1978: 47, 61). In their comprehensive examination of homicide in many countries, Daly and Wilson conclude:

> In every society for which we have been able to find a sample of spousal homicides, the story is basically the same: Most cases arise out of the husband's jealous, proprietary, violent responses to his wife's (real or imagined) infidelity or desertion ... Men ... strive to control women, albeit with variable success; women struggle to resist coercion and to maintain their choices. There is brinkmanship and risk of disaster in any such contest, and homicides by spouses of either sex may be considered the slips in this dangerous game
>
> (Daly and Wilson 1988: 201–5).

Men who go on to kill partners after years of abusing them often refuse to 'let them go' once the woman decides to leave:

> She had been rehoused [after a stay in a refuge]..., but her husband had traced her to her new address. By this stage, [she] was convinced that the end was near. Her solicitor had achieved everything possible on her behalf, [an exclusion order and an interdict (injunction)] but the danger had not lessened. [He] stabbed [her] to death in front of their six-year-old daughter...
>
> (Cuthbertson and Irving 1983: 148).

Stories of death are more sensational and therefore more likely to be reported in the press, but they often reflect the final event following a history of male violence not deemed sufficiently important or dramatic to appear in print or in police statistics. The ultimate victim of domestic homicide may, of course, be either the woman or the man. When the woman dies, it is usually the final and most extreme form of violence at the hands of her male partner. When the man dies, it is rarely the final act in a relationship in which she has repeatedly beaten him. Instead, it is often an act of self-defence or a reaction to a history of the man's repeated attacks (Jones 1980; Browne 1987; Daly and Wilson 1988). In one American study of women who commit spousal homicide, it was found that 73 per cent of the women who killed reported that they had previously been beaten by their partner (Bernard, Vera, Vera and Newman 1982 cited in Browne 1987: 143), while another study found that 93 per cent had reported previous assaults (Totman 1978). Others have referred to this as the 'female use of lethal counter force' (Zimring *et al.* 1983: 910–30). No matter who is killed, the antecedent is often a history of repeated male violence, not of repeated female violence. This common pattern has been known in the United States since the 1950s (Wolfgang 1958). Although often ignored, the pattern is all too familiar in every country where relevant statistics are collected.

When women kill

Despite the asymmetrical pattern of domestic homicide, some women do employ lethal violence against male partners (Jones 1980; see Chapters 8 and 10; Browne 1987; Daly and Wilson 1988), and evidence indicates that the patterns and reasons are markedly different for women than for men. While men often kill women because of jealousy and possessiveness, women do not usually do so despite men's more adulterous behaviour. Men commit familicides (killing their partner and children), women rarely do. Men kill women as part of planned murder-suicides; women rarely do. Men hunt down and kill ex-partners, sometimes after years of pursuit; women rarely do. These are the acts of men, rarely those of women. However, when women do kill, the victim is usually an intimate partner. While some of these acts resemble those committed by men, most do not and many are characterised by the man's physical abuse of the woman prior to the event in which she kills him. Women usually kill men in acts of self-preservation when their situation has reached a desperate state, when they believe they are likely to be killed and while defending themselves (Jones 1980; Boudouris 1983: 667–76; Wilbanks 1983: 9–14; Daly and Wilson 1988). Some abused women think about escaping violence by killing their male abuser or themselves; some, but relatively few, actually do so:

> And we had this great big carving knife downstairs and I used to go upstairs and stand there with it and think 'If I stick it in him – will I get done for murder?' And sometimes if he threw me out I used to go and get three or four bottles of aspirins and go into a cafe and think 'Get myself a couple of cups of tea – take all these and the problem's solved – all this will be finished with'. But there was always [my son] to consider, I used to think if I leave [my son] with him what's he going to grow up like – twisted – like his dad
> (Homer, Leonard and Taylor 1984: 4).

> I could write a book about my fifteen years of anguish because you see I killed my husband, not deliberately, it was an accident, but as the doctors said it was like the straw on the camel's back. I snapped. I took it until I could take no more and for that I got three years imprisonment
> (Pers. com. 1988).

In every country where the issue of battering has now been recognised there are well-known cases of women in prison who have killed their male partner after years of his violent abuse. Some become *causes célèbres* and a few have been released. Most remain unknown and serve out sentences because they were first abused by their male partner and then failed by a society unwilling or unable to provide the necessary means of protection or escape (Browne 1987; Jones 1980; Daly and Wilson 1988; *The Guardian*, 8 July, 1995: 1, 6). In her historical and contemporary study of *Women Who Kill*, Ann Jones cites numerous cases. For example:

> [She] shot her husband four times as he slept, but only after she and her eleven children had endured years of battering, and only after she had been denied the help of local law-enforcement personnel several times.... [The judge] described [her] as a woman 'pushed to the wall'
>
> (Jones 1980: 290).

Many case records show men following, harassing and beating their woman partner for years before they are themselves killed by the woman who had for so long been their victim. For Jones, it is misdirected to ask 'why women stay' and more telling to address 'Why don't men let them go?' (Jones 1980: 299). Angela Browne's (1987) study of battered women who kill is filled with similar accounts of American women who were repeatedly beaten, abused, raped and terrorised before they killed their abuser. In Britain, Helena Kennedy (1994) used the experience of a long and distinguished career in legal practice to highlight the plight of women who first face a life of violent abuse and then face a legal system insufficiently able to deal with such cases in ways that reflect the reality of lives marked by years of repeated abuse (see Chapter 9). Instead of reflecting a context of repeat victimisation that often characterises the lives of women who kill, the legal system is geared to dealing with a context in which a single incident of violence occurs such as those that often characterise violence between men that ends in a homicide.

With expanding awareness of the problem, thousands of accounts from across the world can be added to the voices above. The patterns are strikingly similar across countries despite important and distinct cultural differences. Women, unlike men, rarely kill in the context of their own on-going, coercive, hostile aggression. When women kill men, it is usually within a context of men's aggressive and violent behaviour toward them. Thus, it would follow that a reduction in men's violence against women in the home would be expected to lead to a reduction in the number of women pressed to the point where they commit homicide (Dobash and Dobash 1992: 5–9). While this would not completely solve the problem of women who kill, it might be expected to be a major contributor to its reduction. Indeed, some have speculated that support for abused women and effective interventions for abusers may be important factors in contributing to the reduction in intimate homicides in the USA from 1976–99 (Browne, Williams and Dutton 1999). It may be worth noting that this period of decline in intimate homicides corresponds with the beginning of the battered women's movement, the provision of shelters for escape from abuse and efforts to change the responses of the justice system to this problem. Other factors are no doubt relevant, but this combination of changes may be of importance in understanding elements of this changing pattern of homicides between intimates in the United States.

A world-wide response

In response to domestic violence with its potential for domestic homicide, refuges and shelters have now been established throughout most of the world by activists who have provided an immediate, pragmatic response to the problem of male violence. Often against great odds and resourced primarily by women volunteers, refuges and shelters have opened in country after country since the early 1970s and now constitute a watershed in the traditional response to this social problem. It has become commonplace to hear women from all over the world speak of the importance of the shelters as places of escape from violence, of mutual support and solidarity, of an end to isolation, and of support for self reliance rather than continued dependence (Welsh Women's Aid 1988: 108–14). While examples still abound of old ways, previous beliefs and institutional responses and policies that offer little prospect of change, at the same time innovations break with this legacy and provide examples of positive action in the present and prospects of still further change in the future. Negotiations for change continue within the wider context of women's secondary economic, political and social positions and advances for women require changes in traditional philosophies, priorities and practices. With respect to the issue of violence against women, it has been necessary to address the definition of the problem and its consequences, of effective solutions to be pursued and of who or what must change. All of these have been controversial, and progress has been uneven within the political and policy-making worlds.

The efforts of activists reflect three main goals (assisting victims, challenging male violence and changing women's position in society). Of these, the provision of assistance for the victims of violence is the most universally endorsed, stands as the symbol of the movement with which it is most clearly identified and has provided the impetus for local development and world-wide expansion. For the most part, this has been embodied in the provision of refuges and shelters. While extensive efforts have also been directed at attempting to obtain protection for abused women through the justice system, such efforts generally remain secondary to those of providing direct support to abused women and their children. Efforts to challenge men's violence through arrest, abuser programmes or other means remain controversial and are discussed elsewhere in this volume. Overall, efforts to change the general position of women in society and to provide direct assistance to the victims of violence constitute the main hallmarks of activists in this arena.

Refuges and housing

The refuge or shelter has stood at the heart of the battered-women's movement since they first appeared in the 1970s. Shelters have been important for a variety of reasons. For abused women, the refuge has served as a place to escape to even if only temporarily, a place of safety and a place to make decisions about what to do next. Contact with other women helped overcome isolation and the feeling of being the only one with a violent partner. For activists, it provided a physical location from which to organise and served as a base for practical and political thought and action. Refuges vividly illustrate women's continued dependence within marriage and women's economic disadvantage whereby they must rely on a man, even a violent one, for one of the most basic necessities of life, a place to live. It raises most powerfully the issue of women's autonomy by clearly illustrating their dependence upon others (husband, family, the state or charity) for the material basis of daily existence. World-wide, the refuge provided a fundamental means by which feminist politics was developed, sustained and rekindled within the context of the problem itself and in close contact with the daily lives of its sufferers. The refuge provided an almost unique opportunity for creating a change for women not only to assist those who had been abused but also to stretch into the arenas of social and institutional change. The provision of a physical space so thoroughly enmeshed in the problem itself and in the lives of the women and refuge workers is fairly unique for a social movement, and it is doubtful that a movement, rather than just a provision of service, could have been developed or sustained without it (Dobash and Dobash 1992: 60). Refuges first opened in Britain in the early 1970s, followed by a rapid expansion and then a relatively steady state with some closures largely reflecting government cuts (Binney *et al.* 1985; Hague and Malos 1993; for the USA, see Schechter 1982; Ferraro 1989: 161). Currently, the pattern is mixed, showing slow growth, stability and threats to all forms of social services in both Britain and the USA (Dobash and Dobash 1992: 60–98).

A permanent home

The refuge provides temporary accommodation and can be both personally supportive and a transformative experience. It is not, however, a permanent home, and this can be one of the most crucial struggles for freedom from violence faced by women (see Chapter 13). Housing is a basic material necessity of life and if a violence-free home cannot be found, a woman cannot be free from violence. Since many women are still largely dependent upon men for this necessity, they face the bleak prospect of a life of violence or one of homelessness. It is not difficult to see why the decision to stay or leave is a very difficult one in which the best route is not clear. Without a change in women's prospects of obtaining decent housing for themselves, those who leave home because of violence must usually become dependent upon another provider (a new partner, relatives, or the state) if they are to have a home free from violence. This is tremendously difficult to organise and usually involves a drop in the standard of living, particularly for women reduced solely to the earning power of a woman's wage or of state benefits.

The importance of housing cannot be overestimated. Along with economic independence and viability, it ranks as one of the crucial factors affecting women's ability to find viable alternatives to a violent relationship. Women must have a place to live and they cannot escape violence as long as their home is occupied by a man willing to use violence or intimidation against them. As far as housing is concerned, a woman who is abused can only become free of violence under four conditions:

1   her male partner ceases his violence and lives peacefully;
2   the woman escapes to a refuge where she can live free of violence, albeit only temporarily;
3   the man is successfully evicted from the matrimonial home, remains away and does not harass her, or;
4   the woman is safely rehoused in another home and is not pursued or harassed in her new location.

The refuge is essential, but only provides temporary accommodation. To date, the overwhelming majority of men have not given up violence or managed to live without further harassment or intimidation of their female partner. This leaves eviction of the man or rehousing the woman.

Britain has been more active and innovative than North America concerning permanent housing for abused women, using legislation, public housing policy and second stage housing. Legislation was passed early in the life of the movement beginning with The Domestic Violence and Matrimonial Court Act, 1976 and The Housing (Homeless Persons) Act, 1977. For the most part, this and subsequent legislation embodied different remedies: rehousing the abused woman; eviction of the violent man; and/or arrest for breach of injunction. In the USA, there is no comparable provision for housing although the importance of permanent, affordable housing for women is recognised (US Commission on Civil Rights 1982). Despite inadequacies of housing for abused women in Britain, it has long been a part of state provision for a large sector of the community not just those in need. By contrast, public housing in the USA has generally been of an inferior standard and available only to the poorest citizens. Increasingly, this is becoming the pattern in Britain with changing policies affecting the provision of housing and responses to homelessness that reduce the number of affordable houses available for permanent accommodation (Hague and Malos 1993).

Overall, temporary refuge and permanent housing have been crucial parts of the movement to effect change in the lives of women who have been abused. They have served as vital material resources for women at a time of crisis. They have provided physical locations for mutual contact between women living and working in their temporary home rather than contact with 'clients' in the business office of therapists and counsellors. They have also provided sources of inspiration and visions about the problem that extended beyond an individual service to wider issues of changing women's social, economic and political status. They have served as living laboratories of social change. Housing represents more than simply a roof over the heads of women who have been abused. It points unequivocally to one of the fundamental indicators of women's status which leaves them dependent upon men for the material conditions necessary for life, often leaving them to choose between the unacceptable alternatives of homelessness or a life subjected to violence. In all these ways, housing provides one of the vital keys in the wider context of change for abused women and their children.

The limits of social change

Since the early 1970s, campaigns to change public policy, law, law enforcement, social services and administrative practice have taken a variety of forms and met with varying degrees of success. All such negotiations take place within the framework of the modern state which governs the affairs of western industrial societies. Without some notion of the nature of the state and what is and is not possible in negotiations with its various agencies, it is possible for negotiating parties and/or external evaluators to have very misleading ideas about the nature of such encounters and what can be achieved. While in theory virtually anything may seem possible, in reality only certain types of outcome are likely. From the outset, there are real constraints on the limits of what can be achieved even with the best efforts of all concerned. An example of a naive evaluation of activists' efforts to achieve change was made by Tierney in 1982 when she declared that, after a decade of work, the battered women's movement had not been a success because it had not completely eliminated male violence. Even with lesser ambitions, very real hurdles to change are imposed by institutional priorities and constraints, and knowledge of these very real odds assist in evaluating more sensitively and accurately those changes that have been achieved, and in considering future developments.

References

Bernard, V. and Newman, V. (1982) cited in Browne, A. (1987) *When Battered Women Kill*, New York: The Free Press.

Binney, V., Harkell, G. and Nixon, J. (1985) 'Refuges and housing for battered women', in Pahl, J. (ed.) *Private Violence and Public Policy: The Needs of Battered Women and the Responses of the Public Services*, London: Routledge, pp. 166–80.

Boudouris, J. (1983) 'Homicide and the family', *Journal of Marriage and the Family*, 33, 4: 667–76.

Bowker, L. H. (1983) *Beating Wife Beating*, Lexington, MA: Lexington.

Browne, A. (1987) *When Battered Women Kill*, New York: The Free Press.

Browne, A., Williams, K. R. and Dutton, D. G. (1999) 'Homicide between intimate partners: A 20 year review', in M. D. Smith and M. A. Zahn (eds) *Homicide: A Sourcebook of Social Research*, Thousand Oaks: Sage, pp. 149–64.

Casey, M. (1987–8) *Domestic Violence Against Women: The Women's Perspective*, Federation of Women's Refuges and Social and Organisational Psychology Research Unit, UCD, Dublin, Ireland.

Chimbos, P. (1978) *Marital Violence: A Study of Interspouse Homicide*, San Francisco: R&E Research Associates, San Francisco, CA, USA.

Cook, S. and Bessant, J. (1997) 'Australian history, policy, and denial – violence against women', in Cook, S. and Bessant, J. (eds) *Women's Encounters with Violence: Australian Experiences*, Thousand Oaks: Sage, pp. 1–18.

Counts, D. A., Brown, J. K. and Campbell, J. C. (eds) (1992) *Sanctions and Sanctuary: Cultural Perspectives on the Beating of Wives*, Oxford: Westview Press.

Cuthbertson, N. and Irving, L. (1983) 'Death of a battered woman: an examination of the circumstances surrounding the killing of Mary Khelifati by her estranged husband', *Scottish Legal Action Group*, p. 148.

Daly, M. and Wilson, M. (1988a) *Homicide*, New York: Aldine De Gruyte.

Daly, M. and Wilson, M. (1988b) 'Evolutionary social psychology and family homicide', *Science*, 242: 519–524.

Davis, N. Z. (1971) 'The reasons of misrule: youth groups and charivaris in sixteenth-century France', *Past and Present*, 51: 51–77.

Dobash, R. E. and Dobash, R. P. (1977–8) 'Wives: The "appropriate" victims of marital violence', *Victimology*, 2, 3–4: 426–42.

Dobash, R. E. and Dobash, R. P. (1979) *Violence Against Wives*, New York: The Free Press; London: Paramount Publishing/Simon & Schuster.

Dobash, R. E. and Dobash, R. P. (1984) 'The nature and antecedents of violent events', *The British Journal of Criminology*, 24, 3: 269–88.

Dobash, R. E. and Dobash, R. P. (1992) *Women, Violence and Social Change*, London and New York: Routledge.

Dobash, R. E., Dobash, R. P. (eds) (1999) *Rethinking Violence Against Women*, Thousand Oaks: Sage.

Dobash, R. E. and Dobash, R. P. (1999) 'Violent men and violent contexts', in Dobash, R. E. and Dobash, R. P. (eds) *Rethinking Violence Against Women*, Thousand Oaks: Sage.

Dobash, R. E., Dobash, R. P., Cavanagh, C. and Wilson, M. (1977–8) 'Wifebeating: the victims speak', *Victimology*, 2, 3–4: 608–22.

Dobash, R. P. and Dobash, R. E. (1981) 'Community response to violence against wives: charivari, abstract justice and patriarchy', *Social Problems*, 28, 5: 563–81.

Dobash, R. P. and Dobash, R. E. (1983) 'The context specific approach', in Finkelhor, D., Gelles, R., Hotaling, G. and Straus, M. (eds) *The Dark Side of Families: Current Family Violence Research*, Beverly Hills: Sage, pp. 261–76.

Dobash, R. P. and Dobash, R. E. (2001) 'The law and violence against women in the family', in Eekelaar, J. and Katz, S. (eds) *Cross Currents: Family Law in England and the United States Since 1945*, Oxford: Oxford University Press.

Dobash, R. P, Dobash, R. E., Cavanagh, K. and Lewis, R. (1995) 'Evaluating criminal justice programmes for violent men', in Dobash, R. E., Dobash, R. P. and Noaks, L. (eds) *Gender and Crime*, Cardiff: University of Wales Press, pp. 358–89.

Dobash, R. P., Dobash, R. E., Cavanagh, K. and Lewis, R. (2000) *Changing Violent Men*, Thousand Oaks: Sage.

Dobash, R. P., Dobash, R. E., Daly, M. and Wilson, M. (1992) 'The myth of the sexual symmetry in marital violence', *Social Problems*, 39, 1: 402–32.

Dobash, R. P., Dobash, R. E. and Gutteridge, S. (1986) *The Imprisonment of Women*, Oxford: Basil Blackwell.

Edelson, J. and Eisikovits, Z. (1986) 'Men who batter women: a critical review of the evidence', *Journal of Family Issues*, 6, 2: 229–47.

Edwards, S. S. M. (1989) *Policing Domestic Violence*, London: Sage.

Evason, E. (1982) *Hidden Violence: A Study of Battered Women in Northern Ireland*, Belfast: Farset Co-operative Press.

Fairbairn, N. (1975) 'MP attacks aid for battered wives', *Glasgow Herald*, 22 September.

Ferraro, K. J. (1989) 'The legal response in the United States', in Hanmer, J., Radford, J. and Stanko, E. (eds) *Women, Policing and Male Violence*, London: Routledge.

Gordon, L. (1988) *Heroes of Their Own Lives*, New York: Viking.

Greenfeld, L. A., Rank, M., Craven, D., Klaus, P., Perkins, C., Ringel, C., Warchol, G., Maston, C. and Fox, J. (1998) *Violence by Intimates: Analysis of Data on Crimes by Current or Former Spouses, Boyfriends, and Girlfriends*, Washington DC: US Dept. of Justice, Office of Justice Programs, Bureau of Justice Statistics.

Hague, G. and Malos, E. (1993) *Domestic Violence: Action for Change*, Cheltenham, England: New Clarion Press.

Held, D. (1984) 'Beyond liberalism and Marxism?', in McLennan, G., Held, D. and Hall, S. (eds) *The Idea of the Modern State*, Milton Keynes: Open University Press, pp. 223–40.

Henderson, S. and Mackay, A. (eds) (1990) *Grit and Diamonds: Women in Scotland Making History, 1980–1990*, Edinburgh: Stramullion Ltd and The Cauldron Collective.

Home Office (1998) *Criminal Statistics, England and Wales, 1997*, London: HMSO.

Homer, M., Leonard, P. and Taylor, P. (1984) *Private Violence: Public Shame: A Report on the Circumstances of Women Leaving Domestic Violence in Cleveland*, Middlesbrough: Cleveland Refuge and Aid for Women and Children (CRAWC), Middlesbrough, England.

Jones, A. (1980) *Women Who Kill*, New York: Fawcett Columbine.

Kennedy, H. (1994) *Eve Was Framed*, London, Chatto Windus.

Kincaid, P. (1982) *The Omitted Reality*, Ontario, Canada: Learnxs Press.

Klein, E., Campbell, J., Solar, E. and Ghez, M. (1997) *Ending Domestic Violence: Changing Public Perceptions/Halting the Epidemic*, Thousand Oaks: Sage.

Langan, P. and Innes, C. (1986) 'Preventing domestic violence against women', *US Dept. of Justice, Bureau of Justice Statistics*, Special Report, Washington DC, USA.

Lees, S. (1997) *Ruling Passions: Sexual Violence, Reputation and the Law*, Buckingham, UK: Open University Press.

Morran, D. and Wilson, M. (1994) 'Confronting domestic violence: an innovative criminal justice response', in Duff, A., Marshall, S., Dobash, R. E. and Dobash, R. P. (eds) *Penal Theory and Practice: Tradition and Innovation in Criminal Justice*, Manchester: Manchester University Press, pp. 216–27.

Morran, D. and Wilson, M. (1997) *Men Who are Violent to Women*, Lyme Regis: Russell House Publishing.

Pahl, J. (ed.) (1985) *Private Violence and Public Policy: The Needs of Battered Women and the Response of the Public Services*, London: Routledge.

Pence, E. and Paymar, M. (1993) *Education Groups for Men Who Batter: the Duluth Model*, New York: Springer Publishing.

Pleck, E. (1988) *Domestic Tyranny*, New York: Cambridge University Press.

Saunders, D. G. (1986) 'When battered women use violence: husband-abuse or self-defense?', *Violence and Victims*, Vol. 1, 47–60.

Saunders, D. G. (1988) 'Wife abuse, husband abuse, or mutual combat?', in Yllo, K. and Bograd, M. (eds) *Feminist Perspectives on Wife Abuse*, Newbury Park, CA: Sage.

Schechter, S. (1982) *Women and Male Violence: The Visions and Struggles of the Battered Women's Movement*, Boston: South End Press.

Schneider, E. (2001), 'The law and violence against women in the family', in Eekelaar, J. and Katz, S. (eds) *Cross Currents: Family Law in England and the United States Since 1945*, Oxford: Oxford University Press.

Shorter, E. (1975) *The Making of the Modern Family*, New York: Basic Books.

Stanko, E. A. (1987) 'Typical violence, normal precaution: men, women and interpersonal violence in the US, England, Wales and Scotland', in Hanmer, J. and Maynard, M. (eds) *Women, Violence and Social Control*, London: Macmillan.

Thompson, E. P. (1972) 'Rough music: *'le charivari anglais'* (trans. M. Malkowski) *Annales (Economic, Societies, Civilization)* 27, 2: 285–312.

Tierney, K. (1982) 'The battered women movement and the creation of the wife beating problem', *Social Problems*, 29: 3.

Totman J. (1978) *The Murderesses: A Psychosocial Study of Criminal Homicide*, San Francisco: R & E Associates.

US Commission on Civil Rights (1982) *The Federal Response to Domestic Violence*, Washington DC.

Wilbanks, W. (1983) 'The female homicide offender in Dade County, Florida', *Criminal Justice Review*, 8, 2: 9–14.

Wolfgang, M. (1958) *Patterns in Criminal Homicide*, New York: Wiley.

Welsh Women's Aid (1988) 'Housing', in *Tenth Annual Report*, Welsh Women's Aid, Cardiff, Wales 3: 8–9.

Zimring, F. E., Mukherjee, S. K. and Van Winkle, B. (1983) 'Intimate violence: a study of intersexual homicide in Chicago', *University of Chicago Law Review*, 50, 2: 910–30.

12 Domestic violence and social policy

Perspectives from Women's Aid

Nicola Harwin and Jackie Barron

Introduction

For nearly 30 years, Women's Aid services across the UK have provided both practical and emotional support to women and children experiencing violence and other abuse from those with whom they are living. Women's Aid grew out of the women's liberation movement of the late 1960s and early 1970s: the 'great mobilisation of women' described by Rebecca and Russell Dobash (1992). The first Women's Aid groups were set up in response to women's desperate need for a place to stay with their children, where their violent partners could not find them. In the early years, there were very few options available. Protection under civil or family law was almost impossible to get (except in the context of divorce); domestic violence was not accepted as a reason for homelessness; the police dismissed 'domestics' as a trivial and time-wasting use of their resources; and the response of most agencies was 'go back home and make it up'.

It is largely in response to this feminist direct action and associated campaigning that the legislation and other agencies' practices have gradually changed. The Domestic Violence Act in 1976 allowed a married or cohabiting woman to obtain a court order aimed at preventing further violence and excluding her violent partner from the shared home, and in certain circumstances, a power of arrest could be attached. A year later, domestic violence was specifically included in the homelessness legislation: women and children who were experiencing abuse were classed as 'in priority need' and the local authority had a duty to provide alternative accommodation. Police policies and practises were slower to change, the first major breakthrough being a Home Office Circular in 1990, which emphasised the importance of ensuring the safety of those experiencing abuse, and recommended arrest in appropriate circumstances.

In the last 10 years, the issue of domestic violence has become increasingly prominent. It is no longer of concern only to women's groups and voluntary organisations, but, largely as a result of their activism, it is also discussed by politicians and legislators, and in the media. The questions raised by, for example, the Law Commission, the Home Office, the Home Affairs Select Committee, and the Inter-agency Working Party are very similar: how to increase the effectiveness of civil protection; how should the police best respond to domestic assault? And how to overcome some of the difficulties in the prosecution process (Law Commission 1989; 1992; Smith 1989; Victim Support 1992; Home Affairs Committee 1993). There is also now considerable agreement as to the answers. After nearly three decades of campaigning, many in the Women's Aid movement are perhaps entitled to feel a certain sense of satisfaction. This is, however, tempered by an awareness that – despite heartening signs of welcome change – the dominant ideology still structures the debate in ways that are not always favourable to women.

In this chapter, we will firstly summarise the role of Women's Aid in addressing the problem of domestic violence. Secondly, we will focus on the implications for abused women and children of recent social policy initiatives (see also Chapters 5, 6 and 7). Finally we will suggest some directions for the future.

The role of Women's Aid

The Women's Aid national network of services is based on a common approach: to believe women and children's experiences of abuse, and make their safety a priority; to support and empower women to take control of their own lives; to recognise and care for the needs of children affected by domestic violence. The guiding principle behind Women's Aid's advocacy role and services was the understanding of the central importance of the survivor's perspective: that there is no 'them' and 'us' and that women can work together for change (accounts of the development of the Women's Aid movement are given in Hague and Malos 1993 and Dobash and Dobash 1992).

Domestic violence is recognised as part of a social and structural context of unequal power relationships between women and men. Domestic violence is not a 'one-off event' or 'incident' but part of an on-going pattern of controlling behaviour. Often very subtle signals can be extremely threatening: violence does not have to be overt to achieve its ends.

From this perspective, the principle of a women-only group – women helping women – can itself help to empower women who have been on the receiving end of male dominance and abuse. Women who have come to the point of approaching someone for help need above all to be listened to and have their experiences and feelings taken seriously. Women and children entering a refuge receive support not only from staff and volunteers but from other women residents. This gives them time and space to reflect on their own needs, and helps to overcome their isolation and the sense of shame which many women feel at being abused by a partner, ex-partner or other family member. In time, it may enable them to move on to a life free from violence. The proven effectiveness of this form of peer group support has also informed newer developments in Women's Aid outreach work within the community.

The Women's Aid network offers support and safety to over 150,000 women and children each year, some of whom may need to move out of their local area to another part of the country where they may not easily be found by their partners. Refuge addresses and telephone numbers are normally confidential and are not given out to partners in any circumstances. In 1999, a combination of local service development (including an increase in public contact numbers for refuge projects) and improved agency responses created a context where, for the first time, Women's Aid (England) was able to launch a public UK-wide Directory of Refuges and Helplines, *The Gold Book*, also available on the Women's Aid website, to increase access to refuge services. Direct access to local services is also facilitated by the Women's Aid National Domestic Violence Helpline which offers information, advice and refuge space direct to women who are experiencing abuse and to agencies working on their behalf.

Local refuge services provide for more than a safe space to stay (vital though that is). The support and information offered, both to residents and to other women seeking help in the area, is invaluable. Women's Aid provides detailed and accurate information about legal and housing options, welfare rights and any other services that may be available to enable women and children, in time, to move on to an abuse-free life outside the refuge. Women can be referred, as appropriate, to other professionals, such as solicitors; and local projects provide advocacy and support in dealing with a wide range of other agencies.

Specialist services and support are also given to children, and most projects try to provide outreach support to non-resident women, and resettlement support for women and children who have left the refuge; and, within the wider community, the projects aim to provide public education, campaigning and inter-agency liaison. This latter role has developed significantly in recent years with the growth of multi-agency responses to domestic violence, and has created both opportunities for enhanced service development as well as policy and resource challenges (for more detailed exploration of these issues, see Harwin, Hague and Malos 1999).

This range of services, and in particular the balance between direct services to women and children and education, campaigning and multi-agency work, is often maintained with difficulty, however, because of limited resources. An independent study into refuge services concluded that funding was grossly inadequate, inconsistent and insecure despite over 20 years of development (Ball 1994). Many projects had insufficient funding to provide all the key services identified in the report as desirable or necessary. Despite this, local Women's Aid groups have always provided support for women who may not need or want to use refuges, and new initiatives are developing all the time. Recent research conducted in 1999 by Women's Aid for the Department of the Environment has shown that recognition of the need for outreach services, particularly for women in rural areas, and from minority ethnic communities, has led to an increase in formalised outreach services at local level.

The funding of refuge, outreach and children's services is complicated and patchy across the UK, with up to 25 different funding streams. In England, just under a half of the refuge spaces recommended by the Government Select Committee on Violence in Marriage, 25 years ago are now in place (WAFE survey 1998). Existing refuges are located very unevenly throughout the country and are virtually non-existent in rural areas. There are also notable gaps in provision: despite some development in recent years, there is a particular need for more specialist services, including refuges, for women from minority ethnic groups (Mama 1989), for lesbians (Taylor and Chandler 1995) and more targeted resources for higher level support needs, e.g. for disability or mental health support.

Funding is currently under review as part of a complete overhaul of the funding of the supported housing sector. *Supporting People*, a government consultation document, sets out major changes that will affect the future of refuge services for the next 20 years: there will be greater opportunities for funding of support and outreach services, but equally, as projects will lose all their existing funds and have to compete for funds from a new single funding stream, there is the risk for some of losing what little they have.

As well as the provision of accommodation and support, Women's Aid has a key role as an independent advocate for abused women and children. Despite improvements in the last few years, many agencies that 'gatekeep' vital services or protection still do not have specific policies or protocols on how to respond to domestic violence, in particular key primary contact points in health and social services. Active intervention is often only aimed at the welfare of the children involved. This can serve to reinforce men's threats and women's fears that women will lose their children. There is still an emphasis on keeping families together, and there is little in-service training, or awareness raising. Women are often blamed or men's behaviour condoned or excused.

This situation has now begun to change: for example, the Department of Health is now taking a more active role in promoting good practice within social work and health care services; professional health bodies are developing good practice protocols and training. Nevertheless, effective implementation of this national and local guidance is contingent on the option of referring to Women's Aid or other local specialist services for refuge or expert advice and support.

Work with children in Women's Aid

When children come into a refuge or into temporary accommodation with their mothers, they will have left behind their home and many of their possessions. They may have to change schools, and they may lose friends whom they will never see again. Many children in such situations may themselves have been abused; some may have been forced to watch or take part in the abuse of their mothers; some will have tried to intervene to stop the violence; most will also have suffered indirectly from the abuse their mothers have experienced.

Children who survive domestic violence may experience a number of difficulties, including stress-related illnesses, confused and torn loyalties, lack of trust, unnaturally 'good' behaviour, isolation, shame, anger, lack of confidence, an acceptance of the abuse as 'normal', and so on. Most of these effects can, with time, be alleviated or reversed if adequate resources and support were available. Research shows that wherever child-centred activities have been provided in refuges, the results have been very positive (Ball 1990). First-hand accounts of children living in refuges demonstrate the need for further development of specialised support services for children affected by domestic violence, both in and outside refuges (Saunders *et al.* 1995).

About three-quarters of refuges in England now have at least one specialist children's worker, who tries to provide for the children's needs and who will liaise with local schools, nurseries, playgroups, health visitors and social services on behalf of the mothers (Debbonaire 1994). The recent Women's Aid survey for the Department of Environment of local refuge services showed the enormous range of services, from one-to-one counselling to activities outside the refuge, being provided for children.

There are strong links between domestic violence and child abuse. Research has shown that between 45 per cent and 70 per cent of children whose mothers are abused are themselves being directly abused, usually by the same man (Stark and Flitcraft 1988; Kelly 1994; Mullender and Morley 1994). Domestic violence is now in itself beginning to be defined as a form of child abuse. As Liz Kelly emphasises, however, (*ibid.*) it is important to recognise the complexities of both child abuse and domestic violence. Women who are subject to continuing abuse may – despite their best efforts – be less able to care for or protect their children than would otherwise be the case. However, the common professional social work practice of holding the woman responsible for any inadequate care, and even for the abuse itself, is oppressive and counter-productive (Stark and Flitcraft 1988; Humphries 1999). Care must be taken, however, that the recognition of the inter-connections between domestic violence and child abuse does not lead to punitive policies and practice. Recognition of this approach is now made within the revised Department of Health guidance, *Working Together to Safeguard Children*. To quote Mullender and Morley (1994): 'positive support for mothers subject to abuse is typically the most positive response for children' (p. 2). Women's Aid's National Child Protection Policy gives clear guidance about the management of child protection issues within refuge-based service provision.

Underlying all work with children in and after their stay in refuges is a recognition of the need for prevention. Refuge workers seek not only to promote non-violent relationships and to support women and their children in developing non-abusive strategies for managing family life, but also to challenge traditional sex-role stereotyping and support positive images of equality between men and women as part of a general prevention programme.

Recent social policy initiatives

From the early 1970s, Women's Aid has had a key role as a campaigning organisation working to end domestic violence by lobbying for legislative and social policy change. Renewed public interest in domestic violence began again in the late 1980s, with a number of local initiatives. These include: the setting up of local authority women's units; the development of domestic violence policies by some police forces, then accelerated by the Home Office Circular in 1990; the publication of the Law Commission White Paper in 1992 (following the 1989 Working Paper); and the setting up of an Inter-Agency Working Party by Victim Support, in partnership with Women's Aid. Partly in response to these latter two initiatives, the Home Affairs Select Committee held an Inquiry into domestic violence. The Government response to the Select Committee Report was published in June 1993, and was followed by the setting up by the Government of a Ministerial Sub-group on domestic violence.

After considerable delays and difficulties, the Law Commission recommendations were largely incorporated within Part IV of the 1996 Family Law Act (Bird 1996). Since the Labour Government has come to power, with a clear commitment to tackle domestic violence, and violence against women generally, the development of social policy in this area has accelerated.

Taking action under the criminal law: police and the prosecution process

The police are a key 24-hour agency for women experiencing domestic violence. They are often the first port of call for women in emergency situations; yet their response has often been extremely unsatisfactory (see for example, Dobash and Dobash 1980; Hanmer and Saunders 1984; Edwards 1989; Bourlet 1990). It is only in the last few years that real change has begun to occur.

Nevertheless improved police response has not yet been followed through into effective prosecution of domestic assault. A study undertaken by Cretney and Davis, based on a study of Avon and Somerset police, found that domestic violence cases constituted more than 40 per cent of all assault cases passed to the CPS (Cretney and Davis 1996; 1997). There was, however, still a significant attrition rate, usually following the withdrawal of the complainant (often the sole witness), and a greater likelihood of a reduced charge in those cases of domestic assault that proceeded to court. This research confirmed that very little support is given to women complainants and raised the question of whether more support might make it easier for women to appear as witnesses against their ex-partners. Measures now being enacted following the recommendations of a Home Office Working Party on Vulnerable and Intimidated Witnesses may make it easier for abused women in the future. Changes in 'charging standards' have also resulted in lower charges, cases going to magistrates courts with weaker sentencing outcomes, and women and children being put at even greater risk.

Notwithstanding these reservations, there are many welcome indications that the police, the CPS and society as a whole may at last be taking domestic violence seriously. Certainly the immediate arrest and removal of the assailant will often be helpful in providing a woman and her children with much needed safety and time to consider what they should do. Proceeding with prosecution may not, however, always be in their best interests. The difficulties have been stated many times before: women are understandably extremely reluctant to give evidence against someone whom they loved and with whom they shared a home, and who may be the father of their children; there may be little or no benefit for them – and they will almost certainly be left without adequate protection and in increased danger of reprisals from a vengeful partner or ex-partner. Since the Police and Criminal Evidence Act 1984, the courts have been empowered to compel a witness to give evidence against her or his spouse (though the research by Cretney and Davis (1996) found that these provisions were almost never used); and a woman who refuses to give evidence in these circumstances will be in contempt of court. In extreme instances, she could be sent to prison, while all charges against her assailant are necessarily dropped.

While there may be a few instances in which compelling a woman to give evidence against an abusive partner or ex-partner may ultimately operate in her interests (or those of her children), none the less there is some concern that women may be inappropriately compelled to support a prosecution which damages or endangers her life. Nevertheless many now believe recourse to the criminal law and the protection of the police and courts could provide more effective protection and redress than at present. New developments in the United States (for example Duluth and San Diego) have shown how a focus on victim safety and offender accountability within a multi-agency response can significantly improve protection from domestic violence, including significant reduction of domestic violence homicides. Specific improvements in parts of the US, which could be introduced into the United Kingdom, include: routine recording of 911 (emergency) calls; routine collection of photographic evidence at the crime scene (including of the destruction of furniture, etc.); and routine recording and use of further evidence by all officers involved in the process – including, for example, threats to the victim made by the offender when in custody. In San Diego, evidential collection is so advanced that prosecutions now take place without the victim having to attend court.

Many UK activists now believe that if domestic violence was taken more seriously, more pro-active initiatives could be introduced here, were the state to take some of the responsibility for prosecution away from the abused woman herself. However any such developments must be coupled with integrated measures under civil law to ensure protection: better access to emergency protection orders, third party non-molestation or occupation orders that police could take out simultaneously, immediate suspension of contact with children until a further hearing, as well as immediate access to specialist advocacy, refuge and support services for women and children.

One fundamental problem is that domestic violence cannot, by its nature, be dealt with effectively under the criminal law alone. Many aspects of domestic violence cannot be defined as crimes, nor do they fit into common categories of 'assault' under criminal law. For example, a woman who experiences infrequent physical or sexual assaults from her husband or partner may nevertheless find her daily life is controlled by such measures as having to seek 'permission' on a day-to-day basis to go out, to see her family or friends, to take up employment or education opportunities, and may often feel unable to do so for fear of the reaction. Many women in this situation will not have recourse to the criminal law, nor can the law effectively acknowledge the potential danger or escalation of abuse to which challenging this controlling behaviour may lead.

For women who have never lived or no longer live with their abuser, the introduction of new criminal offences for 'stalking', under the Protection from Harassment Act 1997, may provide more effective protection in these cases than has been available heretofore. Where a woman is being continually harassed or put in fear of violence, a prosecution can be made where there is evidence of a 'course of conduct', and a separate time-unlimited 'restraining order' can be attached on conviction.

Notwithstanding the inadequacies of the criminal justice system and the courts, a number of new developments to protect abused women and children have been piloted by police forces, from systematic new multi-agency approaches, for example in Fulham in London, or Killingbeck in Yorkshire, to the introduction of panic alarms, and 'cocooning' using community support systems. These new approaches are evaluated in the recent Home Office review of domestic violence carried out as part of the new Crime Reduction Programme Initiative, and discussed in Chapter 18.

Dealing with offenders: the probation service

The role of the probation service in supervising offenders where domestic violence is involved is set out in the Position Statement of 1992 (ACOP 1992, revised in 1996). This statement fully acknowledges the need to recognise the serious implications of domestic violence for the probation service.

Traditional ways of dealing with male offenders, including their strategies for rehabilitation, are based on the assumption that the sooner the offender returns to a settled family life (supported by his partner), the better the outcome will be. Where there has been domestic violence, however, this is tantamount to encouraging a repetition of the crime. The woman may feel unable to refuse, however, particularly when this is stipulated as a condition of parole.

The probation service is now rethinking their approach to men who abuse. Their traditional solutions for violent behaviour (such as anger management courses) do not tackle the root cause, i.e. the man's belief in his right to control 'his woman'. While anger management or alcohol dependency programmes may be ancillary, the key focus must be on education programmes based on changing both attitudes and behavioural patterns, as recognised in the Position Statement.

In this country, the development of programmes aimed at re-educating violent men has been fairly slow and sporadic. Programmes are divided between those which rely on voluntary self-referral and those which are court-mandated (and usually linked to the probation service). One of the problems of current provision of re-education programmes is that for resource reasons, they are normally available only to 'serious offenders'. It is important that attendance on

such a programme is not seen as an alternative to (and a diversion from) a custodial sentence, if that would be more appropriate. Domestic violence is not
only likely to be part of a history of abuse, but also likely to be repeated (see
Chapter 18) – if this were recognised by the criminal law as an *aggravating*
factor, then this would enable higher charges to be preferred, and more effective
sentencing, including referral to re-education programmes. Programmes cannot,
of course, guarantee an end to the violence; and in particular, attendance
should not be used to persuade the woman to remain in the relationship if she
would otherwise have decided to end it (see Dobash and Dobash 1992; Hague
and Malos 1993; see also Chapters 11, 16 and 17).

Probation officers must also ensure that abused women (whether they are
themselves offenders, or are the partners or ex-partners of offenders) have access
to independent advice agencies such as Women's Aid. There are now over 30
local Women's Aid groups working alongside perpetrators' programmes to
provide support to women survivors; many of these programmes are themselves
members of a national network which has developed good practice protocols.

The civil legislation

For the majority of women, the options provided by the civil legislation –
however inadequate – may be more appropriate to their needs than the criminal
process. The civil law can – at least, in theory – provide protection for women
and their children, help them with accommodation, property and financial settlements, and determine where the children should live, and the extent of
contact (if any) with the other parent.

One problem is that domestic violence legislation tends to be dealt with in
isolation from other legislation or policy changes affecting families. But
domestic violence cannot be treated as a discrete issue: social security changes,
divorce legislation, housing policies, child protection practices and changes in
the criminal justice system all have enormous impact on the relative ease (or
otherwise) with which women who are living or have lived in violent relationships can gradually begin to build new lives for themselves. Various pieces of
recent legislation – such as the Children Act 1989, the Child Support Act
1991, the 1996 Housing Act, and the establishment of the Social Fund in 1988
– have had adverse effects on women in this situation.

Protection from violence under the civil law: the new Family Law Act 1996

Part IV of the 1996 Family Law Act (which also incorporated the new divorce
legislation) rationalised and consolidated the existing mishmash of legislation
governing injunctions and protection orders. It is a comprehensive piece of legislation, based on the 1992 Law Commission White Paper, which is intended
both to remove anomalies and to make civil protection against domestic violence more effective.

Under Part IV, anyone who has been abused, threatened or assaulted by someone with whom they are living or have had a family-type relationship is able to apply, as an 'associated person' for an order prohibiting further molestation. They may also (depending on certain further criteria) apply for an order regulating the occupation of the home, including the exclusion of the offender. Unlike the previous provision, the non-molestation provisions not only apply to spouses, ex-spouses and (heterosexual) cohabitants, but also between siblings, parents and their adult children, or homosexual partners (where there is or has been cohabitation). Unfortunately there are still loopholes in eligibility as the legislation does not extend to those who have never lived with their abusers, except where there has been a formal promise of future marriage, or there is a child for whom both are parents or have parental responsibility. While other injunctive remedies are available under common law for women who are in this situation, they are not as effective as a power of arrest cannot be attached. Similarly a homosexual partner can only apply for occupation orders if s/he has existing rights to occupy the home (i.e. is a tenant or owner).

Nevertheless this legislation is a significant improvement in many respects: stronger powers of arrest to be attached to all such orders when made 'on notice', as a matter of course, except where this can be shown to be unnecessary. Such orders are now more readily enforceable by police if breached (as only those orders with powers of arrest are lodged at police stations). Other benefits include the removal of the need to prove actual bodily harm in some cases, the extension of the Children Act to allow social services to apply on a child's behalf for abusive fathers to be removed from the home, and new powers to transfer joint tenancies into one party's name, which now allow abused women who are afraid to stay in their former home area to exchange their existing tenancy for one in another area.

Unfortunately some potentially retrogressive amendments were also introduced during the passage of the Act. In particular, in relation to occupation orders, the conduct of the parties was re-introduced as a criterion. In relation to cases of domestic violence, it is worrying that conduct not related to matters of safety and protection from violence may be a factor when considering whether or not to make an order. Research since 1978 has consistently confirmed how violent men frequently cite the conduct of the non-violent partner (in relation to domestic services, mothering, or sexual fidelity) as 'provoking' or 'causing' the abuse. Such justifications have also been accepted by courts as reasons not to grant occupation orders (Barron 1990) or in more extreme cases within criminal law, as defences for killing wives or ex-wives on grounds of 'provocation'.

A second reference to conduct was also introduced into the 'balance of harm test' itself. Any 'significant harm' suffered by the applicant and any relevant child has to be 'attributable to the conduct of the respondent', whereas this is weighted against (any?) harm likely to be suffered to the respondent or any relevant child. The effect of this appears to change 'the balance of harm test' to favour the respondent (violent partner) as all forms of potential harm (defined as impairment of health or ill-treatment) may be considered on his part, whereas only harm attributed to his behaviour may be considered in relation to the applicant.

The improvements in protection will only be as effective as the ability of abused women to access them, and as their implementation in the courts. Recently, there has been increasing concern about the difficulties of accessing Legal Aid to pursue applications for injunctions. This follows the introduction of revised criteria in 1997 for applications for injunctive protection: these include the worrying requirement that a warning letter should have already been sent to the home, a measure that women might refuse for safety reasons. The new criteria also appear to be partly connected to an assumption that civil protection is only required if criminal law measures are not in place. User feedback on access to, and outcomes of, the new legislation is mixed; absence of formal research into its effectiveness makes its real benefits difficult to determine.

Finally, Part IV may allow new opportunities for a more holistic response to domestic violence, by linking action under the criminal law and protection for the future under the civil law more effectively. Section 60 allows the Lord Chancellor to make regulations to enable piloting of new powers by third parties to take out injunctions on behalf of abused women; for example, for police to take out orders on behalf of women at the same time as going before magistrates for criminal proceedings. Such measures have been used very successfully in Australia and the United States (with the woman's consent), and carry a number of advantages, for example, their speed, and the removal of problems associated with legal aid.

The new divorce legislation – Parts I, II and III of the Family Law Act 1996 – was due to be implemented by 1999 but, in fact, only Part I (the principles) and Part III (legal aid for mediation) have been implemented. Part II has been postponed indefinitely.

One of the unforeseen advantages of the addition of Part IV to the Family Law Act is that it was helpful in aiding Women's Aid and other activists to highlight concerns about domestic violence within the whole divorce process. Several key amendments, some drafted by Women's Aid, were successfully incorporated, with the result that some safeguards were built in. A new principle has been laid down in Part I, that any risk to the safety of the parties should be minimised or reduced by the court or other professionals; information about support and protection from domestic violence must now be provided in any divorce information sessions; parties have a right to separate meetings to receive information about mediation or other matters; and it is acknowledged that mediation, which is now voluntary, is inappropriate where there is fear of violence by either party. Despite this, however, concerns are now being expressed by some practitioners that the procedure for getting legal aid in family proceedings under Part III (in relation to arrangements for children under the Children Act, for example) does create a pressure to mediate in situations of domestic violence. There are no clear requirements under Part III for parties to be given full information about their rights to protection, and in the absence of information meetings to do this, some abused women, unless supported by a lay adviser, do not feel able to refuse mediation.

The Children Act

The Children Act 1989 is, in some respects, a positive piece of legislation. For example, the improvements to social services practices, the increasing partnership with parents, the increased emphasis on preventive work, and the requirement to consider the child's race, religion and other elements of her or his needs and identity were all welcome innovations. However, because of a failure to consider the specific issues surrounding domestic violence, the Act perhaps unintentionally presents difficulties and dangers for women and children leaving violent relationships. These are particularly evident in relation to orders for 'residence' and 'contact' under Section 8 of the Act (which effectively replaces the old arrangements for custody and access).

The Children Act is underpinned by two fundamental tenets: that children should, ideally, live at home with both their biological parents; and that if that is not possible, parents should try to make their own arrangements for the care of the children, a court order only being made as a last resort. The Children Act makes no mention of domestic violence. It assumes that parents are reasonable, loving and caring individuals, both to their children and to each other – even at the point of separation and divorce. The Act also assumes that, when parents do separate, the children will almost always benefit from continuing to have substantial and frequent contact with the non-resident parent (usually the father).

These assumptions are often unrealistic, and, where one parent is violent (whether or not he has directly abused the children), they can be dangerously mistaken. When a woman leaves home because of her partner's violence, she will usually take the children with her, and will probably wish to continue to care for them and make a home for them. Usually, this will also be in the children's own interests. In some cases, the children and the absent parent will wish to begin seeing each other regularly, and if this can be arranged without major problems, this is all well and good. But in many cases, especially where there has been risk to the children's safety in the past, the mother will be reluctant to have contact with her abusive ex-partner. Her very real fears may, however, be ignored by the court professionals who follow too narrowly the precepts of the Children Act, and believe, wrongly, that in so doing they are working in the best interests of the child.

Women's Aid's evidence to the Home Affairs Committee (Barron *et al.* 1992) highlighted the results of a postal survey of refuges, which showed that in a number of instances, orders were made inappropriately, with disastrous effects for the women and children concerned. A year later, a similar refuge survey came to equally worrying conclusions. Similarly, a study by Marianne Hester, Lorraine Radford and their colleagues found that out of 53 cases when contact orders had been made after relationship breakdown due to domestic violence, only seven did not result in further abuse or harassment of the mothers or children. They concluded that continued contact in such cases can lead to further abuse of women and children, and moreover that it can also, in some cases, draw the children into colluding in the abuse of their mother (Hester *et al.* 1995). Many of the women in the study did at first want their partners to have contact but found that it was untenable. Mothers who challenge contact to protect their children are often seen as 'implacably hostile' by the courts. A recent report, *Unreasonable Fears?*, based on a survey of over 200 domestic violence survivors, reveals how unsupervised contact was *more* likely to be granted where mothers raised concerns about their children's safety (Hester *et al.* 1997; Radford *et al.* 1999).

The process of determining where the best interests of the children lie can be traumatic for many women. Where there is no agreement on where a child should live, or how much contact (if any) the non-resident parent is to have, a court welfare officer (CWO) will usually be appointed to prepare a report on the child's circumstances and make recommendations to the court. There is a presumption in the Children Act that decisions about a child's welfare should be taken by both parents. This assumption is still interpreted to mean that joint meetings of both parents, together with the CWO, are necessary, and sometimes women are persuaded or pressured into attending. It is usually a terrifying experience for the woman to have to meet her abuser again face-to-face, and in many cases it has led to further threats and abuse.

This practice of joint meetings continues, especially at the court directions stage, despite the Position Statement on domestic violence issued by the Association of Chief Officers of Probation in 1992, which argued against it, and despite the recognition now being reflected in the national standards for the probation service. Marianne Hester and her colleagues pointed to a 'lack of regard for women's safety' which is prevalent among CWOs, lawyers and other professionals (Hester *et al.* 1994). Their research showed that these professionals deny or minimise the violence, and in any case tend to interpret 'the best interests of the child' as meaning contact with both parents at almost any cost. The patriarchal family structure under which domestic violence can flourish is therefore upheld even beyond divorce. In such circumstances, it is completely predictable that many men will continue to abuse, assault, or sometimes kill their ex-partners long after they have separated from them.

Following the development of the ACOP position statement on domestic violence in 1992, Women's Aid staff nationally and locally have had a continuing input into training seminars and conferences for probation court welfare officers both regionally and nationally to raise awareness and promote good practice. Pro-active approaches taken by some probation services to develop good practice guidance are clear signs that, in some areas, CWOs are now more aware of the issues and are consequently more cautious about recommending unsupervised contact when there has been domestic violence; but more work needs to be done (Neale and Smart 1997).

In Australia and New Zealand, growing awareness of these issues in recent years, highlighted by some particularly tragic cases, has resulted in changes to the equivalent legislation. In Australia, the Family Law Reform Act 1995 specifies that, in determining the best interests of the children (when, for example, residence of contact is disputed) the court must be aware of the need to protect them from physical or psychological harm, and must specifically look at all the issues of family violence. The New Zealand legislation goes further in stating that when a court is deciding custody or access, and is satisfied that a party to the marriage has used violence against a child or another party in the proceedings, neither custody nor unsupervised access should be granted until the court is satisfied that the children will be safe; and a list of criteria for assessing 'safety' has been developed. The onus is on the abuser to convince the judge that he can be trusted with the children (Kaye 1996).

The on-going campaign by Women's Aid to raise these issues and to amend the Children Act, citing many tragic cases in the UK which have ended in the deaths of mothers and their children, is finally beginning to bear fruit. New guidance is now being considered by the Lord Chancellor's Department, following a consultation by the Children Act Sub-Committee of the Family Law Advisory Board. In our view, further legislative changes may still be needed, but this guidance is a very positive step.

The Child Support Act

The patriarchal notions inherent in the Children Act are further reinforced by the Child Support Act 1991, which established a Child Support Agency to collect child maintenance payments from absent parents (usually fathers). As a result of concerns expressed during the passage of this bill, the Act does allow caring parents who felt that 'harm or undue distress' would result from any contact to the absent parent, to plead 'good cause' for refusing their authorisation to such contact. However, despite the 'good cause' provisions, since the legislation has come into effect, lone parents who claim Income Support, Family Credit or Disability Working Allowance have often felt pressured into making maintenance applications which are likely to put themselves and their children at risk of further abuse. These pressures have increased, following the enquiry into this area (Provan *et al.* 1996): the focus on fraudulent or collusive parents and the more stringent benefit penalties have led to more women authorising pursuit of child support from a potentially abusive ex-partner. In most cases, they receive no financial benefit and may even find themselves worse off, due to loss of entitlement to some benefits and the withdrawal of voluntary and informal support (Clarke *et al.* 1994; 1996).

Within the last year, lobbying by Women's Aid in relation to several problematic procedures has received a sympathetic hearing and has led to new guidance for CSA officers in relation to domestic violence, alongside new training procedures. However, it is difficult to assess the impact of changes on women not using Women's Aid support services, as those who do so have the benefit of Women's Aid advocacy roles and thus may experience fewer problems.

Domestic violence and homelessness

The need for both temporary and permanent secure accommodation for women and children who have left home because of violence must be paramount. Until 1996, under Part III of the Housing Act 1985, a woman who is experiencing violence from within the home was defined as homeless, and her local authority had a statutory duty to re-house her if she was in 'priority need' (which is often interpreted as having children with her). This law was interpreted inconsistently throughout the country: some local authorities have recognised the serious nature of domestic violence and consequent homelessness, and have developed good practice guidelines and domestic violence policies to govern their practice; others, however, take a much harsher view of the law, such that many women are left in insecure and dangerous situations (Malos and Hague 1993; Hague and Malos 1993; see also Chapter 13).

The 1985 Housing Act has now been superseded by the Housing Act 1996, Part VII of which contains the legislation relating to homelessness. Local authorities are now only able to offer permanent housing to those on their housing register, and homeless families, including women and children made homeless by domestic violence, will be placed in temporary accommodation only. The definitions of 'homelessness' and 'priority need' remain the same as under the 1985 Act, and recently 'homelessness' has been added to the list of categories (identified under s.167 of the Act) to which local authorities are required to give 'reasonable preference' when offering accommodation to those on the register. But unless women escaping violence ensure that they are included on the housing register, they may be repeatedly moved on from one temporary home to another. The legislation also allows local authorities to refuse accommodation to those whom they believe to have suitable available accommodation elsewhere. This provision particularly affects some women from minority ethnic groups who might be deemed to have access to accommodation in another country; and, as before, women who have no permanent right of residence in Britain, perhaps because they have stayed with their abusing partners for less than 12 months, have 'no recourse to public funds' and hence no assistance under the law. Research is currently being carried out on the effect of these changes on service users and refuge provision. However, the new Green Paper on Housing (May 2000), contains some provisions that may well improve the situation.

Government action on domestic violence

In response to the findings of the Home Affairs Select Committee Inquiry, the Conservative government established a Ministerial Sub-Committee on Domestic Violence, for which the lead department was the Home Office. They highlighted three areas where they would take work on domestic violence forward. Firstly, they supported the raising of public awareness, and, in the autumn of 1994, sponsored a low key awareness campaign, 'Don't stand for it'.

Secondly, the Government produced an inter-agency circular giving guidance to all statutory and voluntary agencies responding to domestic violence. Thirdly, there was a commitment to look at the funding of refuges and linked support services. Despite the publication of comprehensive research into refuge funding (Ball 1994), no further action was taken by the government of the day to look at the issue.

In May 1997 the Labour government came to power, having already made a number of pledges to tackle domestic violence in its manifesto and pre-election consultations with women's organisations, including the consultative conference 'Peace at Home'. While cross-departmental policy on violence against women was being developed by the Women's Unit, a number of practical measures were undertaken by Government departments, including publicising by the LCD of the (then) new provisions of Part IV of the Family Law Act. The Department of Health ran a series of regional multi-agency seminars on Part IV, developed in partnership with Women's Aid, published a new circular on the provisions of Part IV, and its implications for Health Trusts and Social Services departments, and also commissioned and disseminated 'Making an Impact', a major training pack on children and domestic violence with an accompanying definitive 'reader' on the issue (Hester *et al.* 1998). The Home Office also began a public awareness campaign, 'Break the Chain', the first stage of which was the production of a public information leaflet, drawing on existing materials produced by Women's Aid. The Home Office has also taken forward the issue of domestic violence in a number of criminal justice initiatives: work on vulnerable and intimidated witnesses, the Crime and Disorder Act, the crime reduction initiatives, as well as linked initiatives on sex offenders and rape.

To influence the formation of the Government's strategy on violence, Women's Aid, in consultation with local activists and survivors, produced a report, *Families Without Fear - the Women's Aid National Agenda for Action* (Harwin 1998 – see also Appendix 1). The report was widely circulated to all key agencies and attracted significant support from a diverse audience – from chief constables to the National Association of Women's Institutes (see also WNC 1996).

Finally in June 1999, the government launched *Living Without Fear*, an integrated approach to tackling violence against women, written by the Women's Unit, which set out a clear commitment for action by a range of government departments and by interdepartmental working groups. This included a summary of all work being undertaken so far and provides a useful marker for monitoring of government action. The report contained information about a range of 'good practice' initiatives being undertaken by voluntary and statutory agencies. Since then overall responsibility for violence against women has again reverted to the Home Office, and further initiatives have been taken forward including revised multi-agency guidance and forthcoming revised guidance to police.

While welcoming the work done so far by government, there are a number of areas within *Families Without Fear* that still remain to be addressed, across the criminal and civil law as well as within service provision, and in particular, the absence of any clear reference to the creation of a national funding strategy for refuge services. As noted earlier, a three-year programme for the implementation of a completely new funding system does not in itself hold the promise of further funding of hard-stretched services, and may seriously threaten existing achievements.

Recent multi-agency initiatives

Early attempts by Women's Aid groups to establish inter-agency co-operation, in order to improve statutory agency responses to women and children using refuge services, were often short-lived as relevant agencies often showed little interest. However, since the late 1980s, and partly linked to the development of radical changes in police policy, a new approach to community responses has been developing. Early projects such as those in Leeds, Nottinghamshire and Hammersmith and Fulham, showed how multi-agency work could improve awareness and practice responses to domestic violence as well as help initiate new and innovative responses. Since the publication of the National Inter-agency Report on Domestic Violence in 1992, there are now over 200 such initiatives across the United Kingdom, ranging from well-known and well-established multi-agency fora with paid co-ordinators often seconded from local authorities or statutory bodies, to small and struggling initiatives with few resources. Some fora have undertaken audits of current service provision and as a result, helped develop new resources, such as specialist outreach support for women and children or, for example, training packs for working with children (Hereford and Islington). Elsewhere specialist task groups have been set up to address particular aspects of domestic violence such as legal protection or children's needs.

Research into the effectiveness of multi-agency initiatives by Hague and Malos raised the question of whether such initiatives did result in real changes in the agencies' responses to women, or whether they merely constitute a 'talking shop'. Key factors in the development of appropriate responses seem to be the extent of participation by Women's Aid and the women's voluntary sector, as well as the extent to which agencies are prepared to review, develop or change their policies, and their willingness to take part in domestic violence awareness training. (For further discussion of these issues, see Hague and Malos 1996; Harwin, Hague and Malos 1999).

More recently, feminist activists, citing the multi-agency work in the criminal justice system of Ellen Pence and others in Duluth, have been promoting the concept of undertaking 'institutional audits' within multi-agency work, to examine the way individual attitudes, organisational ethos and existing procedures and protocols can interact to prevent an effective focus on women's safety or offender accountability (see Chapter 14). Recent changes in statutory agencies' awareness of domestic violence and the growth of multi-agency work means such approaches may now begin to be implemented (Harwin *et al.* 1999).

One popular response of some multi-agency fora, or local authorities taking up the issue, has been to run local public awareness campaigns, using the model developed by the Edinburgh Zero Tolerance Campaign, later the Zero Tolerance Trust, itself based on the Canadian campaign of the early 1980s (see Chapter 19). While the Campaign has had undoubted success in raising public awareness, such campaigns are no substitute for improvements in services to women and children, nor can they be effective unless significant changes take place in the responses of criminal justice and social welfare agencies.

For many activists, the advent of multi-agency work has been a mixed blessing (see Chapter 15). Undoubtedly recent years have seen a sea-change in the approach of statutory agencies to the issue, and the growth of multi-agency fora have enabled many Women's Aid projects to promote a feminist understanding of gender-based violence against women and improve awareness of the needs of women and children facing abuse in their homes. Nevertheless, the opportunity to participate in these developments has been hard fought in some areas, despite the key role Women's Aid activists have played in some of the more successful multi-agency initiatives. For many, the advantages of improved agency understanding are balanced against the dilemmas created by an increased workload, generated not only by rising referrals for help, advice and refuge, but also by the need to take time away from direct work with women and children to participate fully in work of the fora. Nearly 30 years of activism for better responses to domestic violence has seen a result, but in a context of shrinking funding and resources for many refuge services, competition for those resources by other agencies developing new initiatives can leave a bitter taste, especially when resources are redirected from voluntary into statutory (and different) services.

Conclusion

We have seen enormous changes in the last 30 years in both perceptions and responses to domestic violence; the issue has now been put firmly on the public agenda, witnessed by the frequency with which it now receives critical treatment within popular culture, for example, as a central plot-line in major soaps, and a regular feature of breakfast television. Despite the heartening signs of greater public awareness, a new focus by national government and widespread local multi-agency initiatives, the general picture within the legislative and social welfare framework is, unfortunately, still somewhat gloomy. This has been recently reaffirmed by the feedback on social policy from survivors in a ground-breaking Internet Consultation carried out as part of an E-democracy project by Women's Aid and the Hansard Society for the All Party Parliamentary Group on Domestic Violence (Bossy and Coleman 2000).

Not only does the issue of domestic violence tend to be looked at in isolation from all other related issues, it is also assumed that the majority of relationships – whether or not they are breaking down – are not violent or abusive in any way. So, on the one hand there are 'violent families' where certain measures (such as applying for an occupation order or a prohibited steps order) might be appropriate; on the other hand, there are 'normal families' in which two very civilised and reasonable parents can jointly come to agreement about how to bring up their children, with whom they should live, and so on, without any fear that undue pressure might be brought to bear on the weaker party or parties.

At worst, one can take the view expressed by Lynne Harne and Jill Radford (1994): that some legislation has been deliberately designed to 'redress the balance . . . and to re-establish patriarchal control over women and children' (p. 82). They argue that in particular the Children Act and the Child Support Act have had the effect of undermining mothers' rights while bolstering the traditional view of the father as an authority figure and provider (Harne and Radford 1994: 82). In a similar vein, Carol Smart and Bren Neale have argued that the non-interventionist principle of the Children Act combined with the emphasis of the courts on consensual parenting tends to bolster fathers' rights at the expense of those of mothers (1997).

At best, there is a recognition that at the point of separation or divorce, heightened emotions might for a time jeopardise rational behaviour. There is, however, a significant failure to understand that violence and abuse are extremely common features of many relationships and may not always be made evident; and where they occur, they will colour all other aspects of the relationship, including any attempt to negotiate over disputed issues.

Visions of a new egalitarian model of the family, where responsibilities for paid work, household duties and child-care are shared, have long been held by feminists, and are slowly beginning to have wider cultural acceptance, as part of improving the quality of family life. There is no doubt that new forms of fatherhood have at last begun to be accepted within popular culture. While, in the long term, such aims are admirable and essential, in the short term this emphasis runs the risk of ignoring the very grave danger facing women (and children) experiencing domestic violence, and can serve to buttress and support more orthodox views within current law and practice about men's 'rights' *vis-à-vis* their children. In some cases, where the relationship is abusive, the man's greater participation in those areas of family life which are traditionally seen as women's preserve may actually increase his control over his partner. We need to acknowledge the very real contradictions in attempting to pre-figure and support new egalitarian forms of social organisation while dealing with the inequalities and dangers of contemporary family relationships.

Despite the heightened awareness of domestic violence over the past decade, and the increasing seriousness with which it is addressed, particularly by the criminal justice system, there are still a number of issues of great concern. The legal protection available to women experiencing abuse is still very inadequate despite the 1996 Family Law Act. Legislation by itself can never be the complete answer. Domestic violence is a major social issue which has policy implications far beyond purely legislative change.

Our emphasis is in contrast with Government's perspective to date which (rightly) sees domestic violence as a crime, but has tended to downplay the fact that it is also a major social problem with enormous repercussions for family life and relationships generally. In our view, this approach side-steps the real issues which have implications far beyond the narrow focus on the criminal justice system. However, the recent emphasis by Government on cross-departmental and joined-up approaches to tackling social problems, including violence against women, will certainly be helpful in beginning to manage the contradictions between long- and short-term aims, between criminal justice and family policy, and to address some of the deeply rooted resistance to recognising and tackling woman abuse.

In our view there is still a need for a national task force to take forward a national strategy to tackle domestic violence across arbitrary bureaucratic divisions: a holistic approach that can promote safety and empowerment for the victim while making the offender accountable. This should involve key Government departments (Home Office, Health, Social Security, Education and Employment, and the Lord Chancellor's Department), and expert gender-sensitive representatives from relevant national statutory and voluntary bodies, such as the police, social services, health care, courts, probation, and the national network of Women's Aid.

For the foreseeable future, a key issue continues to be the provision of independent advocacy and support services for women and children: adequate refuge accommodation backed up by 24-hour helplines and outreach services which would enable any woman in any part of the country immediate access to support, advice and emergency accommodation whenever she needs it, for herself and her children. Yet despite virtually unanimous recognition of the need for refuge support services (for example among the statutory agencies responding to the Home Affairs Select Committee in 1992), there is as yet no national strategy to improve funding and support for refuge-based advocacy and support services.

Secondly, there is a desperate need for decent affordable housing, for a basic income, access to child-care facilities, job opportunities and retraining, to enable women leaving violent relationships to provide secure homes for themselves and their children. Criticisms of single-parent families, cuts in social security benefits, restrictive homelessness legislation and the shortage of social housing provision are all obstacles to women trying to rebuild their lives independently of violent ex-partners.

Thirdly, we should look at the possibilities for prevention. This needs to be two-fold. We need to challenge the widespread attitudes and social structures which endorse men's control over women's lives in and out of the family, and which provide the foundation for violence and abuse. Publicity as prominent as the Drink/Drive or HIV/Aids campaigns is required to generate a strong social message of the unacceptability of domestic abuse. We also need to promote new ways of managing conflict in interpersonal relationships, and of negotiating equality. Children and young people, in particular, would benefit from social education (along the lines of work currently being undertaken by Women's Aid) which emphasises equality and reciprocity in relationships, and which challenges the rigid division of roles and norms within the family. We need to move beyond traditional gender stereotypes and provide more positive models to create a non-violent future. There is still a long way to go.

References

Association of Chief Officers of Probation (ACOP)(1992) *Position Statement on Domestic Violence*, drafted by David Sleightholm; revised 1996, ACOP: London.

Ball, M. (1990) *Children's Workers in Women's Aid Refuges: A Report on the Experience of Nine Refuges in England*, London: National Council of Voluntary Childcare Organisations.

Ball, M. (1994) *Funding Refuge Services: A Study of Refuge Support Services for Women and Children Experiencing Domestic Violence*, Bristol: Women's Aid Federation of England.

Barron, J. (1990) *Not worth the paper. . .? The Effectiveness of Legal Protection for Women and Children Experiencing Domestic Violence*, Bristol: Women's Aid Federation of England.

Barron, J., Harwin, N. and Singh, T. (1992) *Written Evidence to the House of Commons Home Affairs Committee Inquiry into Domestic Violence*, Bristol: Women's Aid Federation of England.

Bird, R. (1996) *Domestic Violence, the New Law, Part IV of the Family Law Act 1996*, London: Family Law.

Bossy, J. and Coleman, S. (2000) *Womenspeak: Report of an Internet Consultation on Domestic Violence*, Bristol: Women's Aid Federation of England.

Bourlet, A. (1990) *Police Intervention in Marital Violence*, London: Open University Press.

Clarke, K., Glendinning, C. and Craig, G. (1994) *Losing Support: Children and the Child Support Act* (Barnados, Children's Society, NCH Action for Children, NSPCC and Save the Children) London: Children's Society.

Clarke, K., Craig, G. and Glendinning, C. (1996) *Small Change: The Impact of the Child Support Act on Lone Mothers and Children*, London: Family Policy Studies Centre supported by the Joseph Rowntree Foundation.

Cretney, A. and Davis, G. (1996) 'Prosecuting "Domestic" Assault', *Criminal Law Review*, 1996, pp. 162–74.

Cretney, A. and Davis, G. (1997) 'Prosecuting Domestic Assault: Victims Failing Courts or Courts Failing Victims?', *Howard Journal of Criminal Justice*, Vol. 36, No. 2, pp. 146–57.

Debbonaire, T. (1994) 'Work with Children in Women's Aid Refuges and After', in Mullender and Morley, *op. cit.*

Department of Health (2000) *Working Together to Safeguard Children*, London: HMSO.

Dobash, R. E. and Dobash, R. (1980) *Violence Against Wives*, London: Open Books.

Dobash, R. E. and Dobash, R. (1992) *Domestic Violence and Social Change*, London: Routledge.

Edwards, S. (1989) *Policing 'Domestic' Violence*, London: Sage.

Hague, G. and Malos, E. (1993) *Domestic Violence: Action for Change*, Cheltenham: New Clarion Press.

Hague, G. and Malos, E. (1996) *Against Domestic Violence: Multi-agency Approaches*, Bristol: Policy Press.

Hanmer, J. and Saunders, S. (1984) *Well-Founded Fear: A Community Study of Violence to Women*, London: Hutchinson.

Harne, L. and Radford, J. (1994) 'Reinstating Patriarchy: The Politics of the Family and the New Legislation', in Mullender and Morley, *op. cit.*

Harwin, N. (1998) *Families Without Fear: Women's Aid Agenda for Action on Domestic Violence*, Bristol: Women's Aid Federation of England.

Harwin, N., Hague, G. and Malos, E. (1999) *The Multi-agency Approach to Domestic Violence: New Opportunities, Old Challenges?* London: Whiting and Birch.

Hester, M., Pearson, C. and Harwin, N. (1998) *Making an Impact: a Reader on Children and Domestic Violence*, London: Jessica Kingsley Publishers.

Hester, M., *et al.* (1995) 'Child Contact in Circumstances of Domestic Violence', *The Magistrate*.

Hester, M. *et al.* (1994) 'Domestic Violence and Child Contact', in Mullender and Morley, *op. cit.*

Hester, M., Pearson, C. and Radford, L. (1997) *Domestic Violence: a National Survey of Court Welfare and Voluntary Sector Mediation Practice*, Bristol: Policy Press.

Home Affairs Committee (1993) Third Report: *Domestic Violence* Vol. I Report, Vol. II Memoranda of Evidence (HMSO).

Humphries, Cathy (1999) 'Avoidance and Confrontation: The Practice of Social Workers in Relation to Domestic Violence and Child Abuse', *Journal of Child and Family Social Work*, Vol. 4, No. 1, pp. 77–8.

Kaye, M. (1996) 'Domestic Violence, Residence and Contact', *Child and Family Law Quartely*, Vol. 8, p. 285.

Kelly, L. (1994) 'The Interconnectedness of Domestic Violence and Child Abuse: Challenges for Research Policy and Practice', in Mullender and Morley, *op. cit.*

Law Commission (1989) *Domestic Violence and the Occupation of the Family Home: A Working Paper*, London: HMSO.

Law Commission (1992) *Domestic Violence and the Occupation of the Family Home*, London: HMSO.

Malos, E. and Hague, G. (1993) *Domestic Violence and Housing*, Bristol: WAFE and the University of Bristol.

Mama, A. (1989) *The Hidden Struggle*, London: Race and Housing Research Unit.

Mullender, A. and Morley, R. (eds) (1994) *Children Living with Domestic Violence: Putting Men's Abuse of Women on the Child Care Agenda*, London: Whiting and Birch.

Neale, B. and Smart, C. (1997) 'Experiments with Parenthood?' *Sociology*, Vol. 3, No. 2, pp. 201–19.

Provan, B. *et al.* (1996) *The Requirement to Co-operate: A Report on the Operation of the 'Good Cause' Provisions*, Social Policy Research Unit, in-house report 14.

Radford, L., Sayer, S. and Amica (1999) *Unreasonable Fears? Child Contact in the Context of Domestic Violence*, Bristol: WAFE.

Saunders, A. *et al.* (1995) '*It Hurts Me Too*': *Children's Experiences of Domestic Violence and Refuge Life*, Women's Aid Federation, England, National Institute of Social Work and Childline.

Smart, C. and Neale, B. (1997) 'Arguments Against Virtue: Must Contact be Enforced?', *Family Law*, Vol. 27, pp. 332–6.

Smith, L. (1989) *Domestic Violence: An Overview of the Literature*, Home Office Research Studies No. 107, London: HMSO.

Stark, E. and Flitcroft, A. (1988) 'Women and Children at Risk: Feminist Perspectives on Child Abuse', *International Journal of Health Services*, 18 (1), pp. 97–118.

Taylor, J. and Chandler, T. (1995) *Lesbians Talk Violent Relationships*, London: Scarlet Press.

Victim Support (1992) *Domestic Violence: Report of a National Inter-Agency Working Party*, London: Victim Support.

Women's Aid Federation of England (1988) *Annual Survey of Refuges* (unpublished).

Women's Aid Federation of England (1999) *The Gold Book*, Women's Aid Directory of Domestic Violence Refuges and Helpline Services 1999, Bristol: WAFE.

Women's National Commission (1996) *In Pursuit of Equality: National Agenda for Action*, London: WNC.

Women's Unit and Home Office (1999) *Living Without Fear*, London: Cabinet Office.

13 Domestic violence and housing

Rebecca Morley

> If a violence-free home cannot be found, a woman cannot be free from violence.... The importance of housing cannot be overestimated. Along with economic independence and viability, it ranks as one of the crucial factors affecting women's ability to find viable alternatives to a violent relationship
>
> (Dobash and Dobash 1992: 93).

Introduction

Access to independent housing is crucial to enable women to overcome violent relationships. Studies of women's experiences of domestic violence have consistently shown that a major reason why women stay in, or return to, violent relationships is lack of safe, affordable, independent accommodation (e.g. Binney *et al.* 1981; Mama, this volume). Because women are systematically disadvantaged in their access to independent income, many women fleeing violence cannot obtain housing through the private market on the basis of ability to pay. Instead they must rely on social housing – housing provided by local authorities and, to a lesser extent, by housing associations – which is non-profit-making and ostensibly allocated according to need.

The feminist refuge movement recognised the importance of social housing from the beginning, and have campaigned vigorously to increase women's access to this vital resource. Their impact has been considerable. Domestic violence is recognised in law as a cause of homelessness. Central government policy documents encourage local housing authorities to give priority to women experiencing violence in their allocation of housing, and to work closely with refuges. Many refuge groups report good working relationships with their housing authorities. Some authorities have developed their own policies for dealing with domestic violence in consultation with refuge groups. Training provided by Women's Aid has undoubtedly raised the consciousness of many housing officers concerning the realities and needs of women escaping violence. The climate in which domestic violence is understood and responded to has been transformed since the early days of the movement. At the same time, women's access to social housing remains insecure. What is clear today, and has been from the beginning, is that the continuing presence of a strong, independent refuge movement is essential if women are to actualise their human right to live in violence-free homes.

Following a brief discussion of the importance of independent housing for women experiencing domestic violence, this chapter examines the changing responses of local and central government to abused women's need for social housing within the context of feminist political practice.

The importance of independent housing for women experiencing domestic violence

Access to independent housing is critical for women in violent relationships because ending violence very often requires that women lose their homes. This in turn is testimony to the failure of other possible solutions to violence.

Many women – initially at least – want to remain in the relationship but want the violence to stop. Although we do not have comprehensive data, it is clear that this is not often possible – being safe usually requires separation from the abuser. Remaining in the home, with the violent partner excluded, is theoretically an option, but this is often impossible in practice. Civil injunctions excluding the abuser have been available to women in some circumstances since the latter 1970s, but have been notoriously difficult to obtain and enforce (e.g. Barron 1990). Although the Family Law Act 1996, which replaced previous legislation, is stronger and more inclusive, there are still some circumstances in which women cannot apply for court orders – for example, if they have never lived with their abuser – and problems in obtaining and enforcing orders remain. In any case, court orders usually provide a short-term solution at best because they are typically time limited and do not alter property rights, which are more likely to favour men. And regardless of the availability of these or other legal options – for example, property settlements in matrimonial law – many women simply do not feel able to remain in their homes because of anxiety or outright terror at being potential targets of violent men who know where they live, or because the home is saturated with reminders of violence and degradation. In fact, the very act of involving the civil courts may invite violent reprisals from an angry abuser and/or abusive treatment – for example, removal of children, withdrawal of benefits or deportation – from other agents of the state (Morley 1993; see Mama 1989 for a discussion of these issues in relation to black women; see also Chapter 3).

Ultimately, the only way to be safe and feel secure may be to leave home, often to an unknown and distant location. Just as 'domesticity' is intimately linked with the experience of violence in the home, so it underlies the difficulties which abused women face in accessing alternative accommodation when they decide they must leave. Domesticity circumscribes women's employment patterns and income. Thus women without men are disadvantaged in access to housing (e.g. Pascall and Morley 1996). They are usually unable to afford owner occupation and are much more likely to rely on social housing.

Women can sometimes achieve owner occupation using the proceeds of a

property settlement with their ex-partner. However, this usually necessitates prolonged and often acrimonious negotiations involving court proceedings. For a
woman escaping violence, the contact this requires with the abuser – either directly
or through a solicitor – may be too dangerous. In any event, owner-occupation may
not be a viable long-term solution, given women's weak economic status.

The private rented sector is also problematic for women. Private lets are
increasingly prohibitively expensive and insecure, and landlords tend to be
reluctant to rent to benefit recipients or to people with dependent children.
Moreover, the physical condition of private rented housing is often poor and
lacking in physical security. Many women escaping violence report that they do
not feel safe in private tenancies. These safety concerns usually relate to the
abuser, but a number of studies suggest that women in private lets are at risk of
harassment from landlords (see Woods 1996: 74–5).

Given that women generally have difficulty in accessing independent housing
through the private market, and that women in violent relationships often need
to leave home, it is not surprising that domestic violence is strongly linked to
women's homelessness. Although we do not know what percentage of women
experiencing domestic violence become homeless, we have strong evidence that
women escaping violence constitute a substantial proportion of the homeless
population. Housing authorities keep statistics on the number of people they
accept for rehousing through the homelessness legislation, cataloguing the reasons
why the person lost her last settled accommodation. The proportion of people
accepted because of the breakdown of violent relationships is increasing and is
now the largest single category measured, constituting nearly one-fifth of *all*
homelessness acceptances, and over 70 per cent of acceptances resulting from
relationship breakdown (DETR 2000a: Table 4). This, of course, represents only
the tip of the iceberg. Not all women fleeing violence who are accepted will be
categorised as such – they may not have divulged their victimisation or they may
have escaped first to relatives or friends and so appear in the category
'relatives/friends no longer able or willing to provide accommodation'. They may
have applied as homeless but not been accepted for rehousing. Or they may not
have applied. Women without children have particular difficulty using the homelessness legislation. Recent evidence indicates that women escaping domestic
violence account for a significant proportion of single homeless women using
hostels and other direct access homelessness services (Jones 1999; Shelter 2000).

Women's lack of power to access independent housing in the private market
and consequent vulnerability to homelessness provide the context in which the
importance of social housing provision for women escaping violence must be
understood.

The response of the early refuge movement to women's housing need

The issue of housing was central to the emergence of the feminist refuge movement in 1971. The nascent women's liberation movement discovered a huge

and hidden need of women for a safe place to go to escape violent partners. The movement's core response to this need was 'the refuge' – safe houses, set up by local women's groups, where 'battered women' could run to in emergency, find safety, receive support from other women, and begin to take control of their lives.

Before refuges, women's options were grim. Jo Sutton, the first co-ordinator of the national coalition of feminist refuge groups – National Women's Aid Federation – wrote that 'battered women' unable to stay with friends or relatives would try to obtain emergency accommodation provided for homeless families under Part III of the National Assistance Act 1948. This accommodation usually excluded husbands and thus afforded temporary safety from violent men (Sutton 1977–8: 577). In 1966, the Government decided to admit husbands in the name of supporting family life, and women lost this sanctuary. 'Between 1966 and 1971 the only major safe places for battered women were with friends or relatives or in a prison, a hospital, or a mortuary' (*ibid.*). Refuges thus provided a powerful response to abused women's urgent need for temporary accommodation and support. But the movement also recognised the necessity of increasing women's access to resources from the state to meet other needs emanating from their lack of social power. These needs included permanent housing away from the abuser.

The publicity generated by the early refuge movement rapidly forced the issue onto the political agenda. A Parliamentary Select Committee on Violence in Marriage was announced in 1974 with a remit to examine the nature, extent and causes of domestic violence and to make recommendations for action. The Committee heard evidence from Government ministers, a wide range of professionals, Women's Aid, and 'battered women' themselves. Recommendations concerning housing featured prominently in the Committee's Report (1975), a testimony to the success of Women's Aid in arguing the case for housing as a key practical solution to the needs of abused women.

In the wake of the Report, again with vigorous lobbying from Women's Aid, Parliament passed two landmark pieces of civil legislation explicitly addressing the housing needs of abused women. The first, the Domestic Violence and Matrimonial Proceedings Act 1976, allowed people to apply to the courts for an injunction excluding the violent partner from the home. The second, the Housing (Homeless Persons) Act 1977, required local authorities to house homeless people, and defined domestic violence as a reason for homelessness.

Homelessness and domestic violence: law, policy and practice 1977–96

The Housing (Homeless Persons) Act 1977, later consolidated in Part III of the Housing Act 1985, was an important victory for the feminist refuge movement. It imposed a duty on housing authorities to secure accommodation for certain categories of people found to be 'homeless', and included domestic violence in its definition of homelessness: a person is homeless if it is probable that occupation of their accommodation will lead to violence, or threats of violence likely to be carried out, from someone else in that accommodation (s.1 (2)(b)). Thus the Act provided both official recognition that women have a human right to live in a violence-free home and tacit acknowledgement that they are disadvantaged in access to housing.

However the Act did not give 'homeless' people an unconditional right to housing, but required that they pass three additional 'tests': they must be in 'priority need', *not* 'intentionally homeless' and have a 'local connection' with the housing authority. Priority need categories included people with dependent children; pregnant women; and people 'vulnerable' due to old age, mental illness or 'handicap', physical disability, or 'other special reason' (s.2). Intentional homelessness was defined as deliberately doing, or failing to do, anything causing loss of accommodation that would have been 'reasonable' to occupy (s.17 (1)). People without a local connection (current or former residence, employment, or family ties in the local authority area) could be referred, at the authority's discretion, to another authority with which the person had a local connection. However the Act explicitly stated that a person with no local connection should not be referred to another authority if they would be at risk of domestic violence in that authority's area (s.5 (1)(a)(iii)); another powerful statement, this time acknowledging that the dynamics of violent relationships might require that women flee to a distant and unknown location to be safe.

The Act itself did not declare women fleeing violence to be in priority need or unintentionally homeless. However, the Code of Guidance first issued in November 1977 (DoE 1977) to advise authorities on implementing the Act clearly signalled an intention that 'battered women' should pass these tests. Although women would likely already be in priority need by virtue of having dependent children or being pregnant, the Code affirmed that 'it would be appropriate ... for authorities to secure whenever possible that accommodation is available for battered women without children who are at risk of violent pursuit or, if they return home, at risk of further violence' (para.2.12c.iii). It also forcefully asserted that 'a battered woman who has fled the marital home *should never* be regarded as having become homeless intentionally because it would *clearly not be reasonable* for her to remain' (para.2.16, my emphases). Further, while the Act itself did not define 'violence', the Code 'asked' authorities to 'respond sympathetically to applications from women who are in fear of violence' and stated that 'the fact that violence has not yet occurred does not, on its own, suggest that it is not likely to occur' (para.2.10b.). Finally, the Code recognised that whereas refuges provide an important source of temporary accommodation, a woman's residence in a refuge does not obviate the authority's responsibility to find permanent accommodation for her (para.A2.13). Taken together, then, the 1997 Act and Code ostensibly provided a policy framework capable of affording women fleeing domestic violence access to a core need: permanent accommodation away from the abuser.

However an early study, commissioned by the Department of Environment in 1977 and carried out by Women's Aid Federation England (Binney *et al.* 1981;

1985), clearly demonstrated that what seemed promised was not working well in practice. Of nearly 500 homelessness applications from women living in refuges in September 1978, almost half were refused. Fewer than half of the refuge groups thought the Act had improved women's housing prospects and some felt that getting re-housed had become even harder because 'authorities had tightened up their criteria in order to limit their responsibilities under the Act' (Binney *et al.* 1985: 175).

Although these findings might simply have reflected the teething problems of new legislation, similar outcomes were identified in subsequent studies throughout the 1980s and 1990s (e.g. Welsh Women's Aid 1986; Mama 1989; Thornton 1989; Bull 1993; Malos and Hague 1993; Charles 1994a, b; Cowan 1997). Women were often deemed not 'homeless' because they were not currently living with their abuser, they had accommodation in a refuge, or they had no proof of violence. Indeed, high levels of proof were often required, including signs of injury or corroboration from police, social workers, GPs, solicitors and even from the abuser. Women claiming to be in fear of violence or suffering non-physical abuse were often considered not 'homeless'. Women were sometimes told to seek injunctions, creating a 'no-win' situation where injunctions were required to prove violence and then were said to obviate the need for housing. Moreover, courts were not always prepared to grant injunctions if they were sought simply to satisfy housing authority requirements, creating another 'no-win' situation where women were unable to secure housing without an injunction and unable to obtain an injunction because they were seeking rehousing. Women without children often failed the test of 'priority need', even in cases where they had children who were not with them precisely because they were homeless – yet another 'no-win' situation: no housing without children, no children without housing. Some women were declared 'intentionally homeless' for leaving their home or for refusing to return home with an injunction. Finally, women with no 'local connection' in the area were often told to go home or were shunted back and forth between authorities with neither willing to take responsibility.

Moreover, the actual application process was often traumatic. Women frequently reported that housing officers were hostile and suspicious, asking detailed and intrusive questions. Many experienced long periods in temporary accommodation waiting for a decision, often with no information about what was happening. These and other obstructing and delaying techniques had the effect of dissuading women, often leaving them with no hope. Those who were accepted for rehousing frequently continued to wait for lengthy periods, sometimes two years or more, before being allocated poor quality accommodation. And for the many women not rehoused, the consequences could be disastrous:

> Most of the women ... who were not rehoused ... suffered traumatic life experiences as a result. In addition to exposure to renewed and sometimes extreme violence, the distressing catalogue of problems experienced by women included continued homelessness, continued transience in the

search for rehousing, further disruption to children's education and mental and physical health, psychiatric disturbances in children necessitating intervention by the statutory services, and high levels of anxiety, fear, depression and hopelessness for the women concerned. It was particularly troubling that some women who had left the home due to violence but were unable to secure permanent housing faced the loss of their children to their securely housed partners.

(Malos and Hague 1993: para.6.9).

But there were more positive outcomes. Research consistently noted large variations in practice both across authorities and between officers within authorities. Moreover, by the late 1980s, some authorities had developed enabling domestic violence policies (e.g. Malos and Hague 1993). These were commonly responses to pressure from local refuge groups, often in conjunction with local authority women's units and/or domestic violence forums in areas with strong grass-roots feminist organisations and feminist influence in local government. In many areas, policies represented genuine attempts by at least some parts of the housing organisation to respond positively to the needs of abused women. In other cases, policies could be more accurately described as attempts to remove pressure exerted by refuge groups without any commitment to meaningful change (e.g. Mama 1989).

Regardless of the existence of formal policies, many refuge groups were able to establish close working relationships with their housing departments ensuring that women from refuges received as good a service as possible. This might mean that the authority undertook to rehouse all women from the refuge. However good or poor the relationship, though, the support of refuge workers appeared to be a key factor in determining the service received. In some hostile authorities, only women with this active support stood any chance of success.

At national level, Women's Aid continued monitoring policy and campaigning for change using a variety of strategies including participation in national working parties and representations to the Department of Environment. Their influence can be seen in the substantially revised Code of Guidance issued in 1991 (DoE 1991). In addition to reiterating previous advice, this Code stated that victims of violence may be in 'considerable distress' and should be interviewed 'wherever possible' by same sex officers with training in domestic violence. It further clarified that authorities should not 'normally' ask for proof from the alleged perpetrator, should not 'necessarily' ask the applicant to return home with an injunction, should not 'automatically' treat applicants as intentionally homeless if they have not applied for an injunction, should consider people experiencing violence from outside the home as homeless, and should not delay permanently rehousing an applicant staying in a refuge 'in the hope that she might be "taken back" by her partner' (DoE 1991: para.13.2c).

The influence of feminist politics was also evident in the proceedings and report of the Home Affairs Committee on domestic violence which met in October 1992. While housing was outside the Committee's remit, the Report concluded:

We do not believe that we can ignore some of the wider issues. As WAFE pointed out, 'unless criminal justice measures are complemented by improved responses in other areas, the position of abused women and children will not improve overall, and may in some instances worsen.

(HAC 1993: para.128).

With respect to housing, the message was strong and unequivocal:

We recommend ... that local authorities be advised in the strongest possible terms to put an end to the nonsense where a victim fleeing domestic violence is deemed to have made herself intentionally homeless. We further recommend that an appropriate priority be given to rehousing victims of domestic violence.

(*ibid*. para.131).

In a survey of all housing authorities in 1994 (Mullins and Niner 1996), many reported having amended their practices in relation to domestic violence as a consequence of the revised Code. The survey report concluded with cautious optimism that homelessness practice generally was 'better and fairer' (para.1.25) since the issue of the new Code. In stark contrast, a study of decision-making under the homelessness legislation based on interviews with homelessness officers in 15 local authorities during 1994 concluded: 'Our fieldwork data suggest that there have been no significant advances from the earlier studies [of local authority responses to domestic violence]. Indeed, it might be suggested that, as practices had evolved, so they had regressed.' (Cowan 1997: 119).

Contexts of housing authority responses to domestic violence

Cowan's pessimistic conclusion probably undervalued the progress being made in some authorities. However, it is clear that while central government policy was steadily, if falteringly, reflecting greater sensitivity to the circumstances of abused women and their resulting housing needs, many authorities and/or housing officers were not embracing this guidance. Relationships between policy and practice were undoubtedly complex and linked to the variety of contexts in which policy was situated.

The 1977 Act represented an uneasy compromise between MPs and housing rights groups who wanted legislation giving homeless people an unconditional right to rehousing in recognition that homelessness is a *social* problem, and some Conservative MPs and local authorities who saw homelessness as an issue of personal inadequacy and feared that such legislation would provide the undeserving poor with an easy route into subsidised council housing. The concerns of the latter were not new, but originated in the nineteenth-century Poor Law principle of 'less eligibility' – the morally blameworthy poor must be offered charity at subsistence level only as a deterrent and to encourage self-sufficiency.

The 'tests' which homelessness applicants were required to pass were introduced to exclude the undeserving (see Robson and Watchman 1981). The test of 'homeless'(ness) required evaluating the reasons why the person lost her last home. 'Priority need' ranked the needs of certain groups of people – for example, families with children, over others – for example, single people. 'Intentional homelessness' was designed to appease concerns that an unconditional right to housing would lead to 'self-induced homelessness' by welfare scroungers, including young women who would get pregnant to acquire priority need status. 'Local connection' aimed to quell the fears of affluent local authorities that they would be over-run by disreputable outsiders.

Moreover, the language of the Act allowed authorities wide discretion in their interpretation of the 'tests' and in their decisions regarding whether individual applicants passed or failed. Duties under the Act only arose if the authority was 'satisfied', had 'reason to believe' or was 'of the opinion' that the applicant met the relevant criteria. And the criteria themselves were open to discretion. For example, 'A person is ... homeless ... if he [sic] has accommodation but ... it is *probable* that occupation of it will lead to violence...' (s.1 (2)(b)), (my emphasis). In its use of discretion, 'the Act signalled to those authorities which were hostile to the notion of extending housing "rights" to homeless people that they need house very few people, and then house those people only in the most unpopular accommodation' (Loveland 1995: 326). Although the Code of Guidance ostensibly spelled out how authorities should exercise their discretion, the Act merely said that the 'authority *shall have regard*' (s.12 (1)), (my emphasis) to the Code. This has been interpreted by the courts to mean that as long as they have 'regard' to it, authorities may depart from it (Arden and Hunter 1997: para.3.25) – that is, the Code too is discretionary. And, as illustrated in the previous section, the Code did not shy away from the language of discretion, with phrases such as 'wherever possible', 'not automatically', and the like.

Thus the legislation itself was steeped in the politics of exclusion, requiring that moral judgements be made to separate the deserving from the undeserving applicant. Because of successful intervention by the feminist refuge movement, the Act (and Code) clearly signalled that 'battered women' should be in the ranks of the deserving. The Code gave some guidance as to the meaning of this abstract category, as did local authority policies where they existed. But the problem for housing officers was deciding whether the actual woman standing before them exemplified this category, a task inviting the operation of the prejudices of individual officers. These included common-sense understandings of gender, race, and class, which were key factors related to whether the woman was recognised as a 'genuine case' of domestic violence deserving of housing or merely 'trying it on' (e.g. Mama 1989; Malos and Hague 1993). In discussing their decision-making strategies, officers often talked about the importance of 'gut feeling' and taking 'each case on its merits' (e.g. Bull 1993; Cowan 1997), suggesting that policy was not necessarily the major determinant of decision making.

Local refuge groups were often able to influence officers' use of discretion and their 'gut feeling'. 'Training officers to ... rid themselves of myths about beaten women' (Maguire 1988: 42) was an important strategy. However, officers did not necessarily translate their abstract knowledge into concrete recognition. Perhaps more importantly, therefore, refuge workers challenged concrete practices both of individual officers and of the organisation as a whole. And they often were able to confer the status of deserving on individual women for whom they advocated (see Chapter 7).

However, the decision making of housing officers was clearly constrained by wider economic and political contexts. These included the economics and politics of social housing supply (e.g. Cowan 1997; Malpass and Murie 1999). Council housing was the first target of Thatcher's 'welfare revolution': dismantling the comprehensive welfare state in favour of selectivity and market forces. The proportion of the population living in council housing decreased dramatically from 1979 when the first Thatcher government came to power. This residualisation was achieved systematically through three main strategies – right to buy legislation which required housing authorities to offer their properties for sale to tenants and attempted to make this an attractive proposition through sweeteners, large scale voluntary transfer schemes which encouraged authorities to voluntarily transfer their stock to housing associations and other registered social landlords, and restrictions on authorities' ability to use capital receipts from house sales to invest in new housing. By 1994 council house building had virtually stopped. The Government planned that the gap would be taken up by housing associations and the private rented sector. But this did not happen. The shortfall of housing stock became increasingly extreme, exacerbated by escalating levels of homelessness throughout the years of Conservative rule.

Thus it became virtually impossible for authorities to operate the homelessness legislation in an enabling way, and some authorities which had developed generous domestic violence policies were forced to revoke them. Moreover, the pressures on front line housing officers became more intense. In these circumstances the category of the deserving had to be drawn ever more tightly, with moral judgements becoming a crucial rationing devise. The high proportion of officer caseloads involving applicants alleging domestic violence undoubtedly fed suspicions of bogus claimants; 'common knowledge' held that alleging violence was the easiest route into social housing (e.g. Cowan 1997). Within this context, active involvement of feminist advocates – supporting individual applicants facing detailed questioning and enquiries, and challenging decisions on points of law and policy – often meant the difference between survival and defeat.

The Housing Act 1996 and New Labour

Many expected Thatcher to repeal the homelessness legislation. However it was the Major Government which took on the task of reform. A key motive was undoubtedly the crisis in council housing and the need to reduce demand, but the ideological tools were images of the undeserving – particularly single mothers. Peter Lilly, Social Security Secretary, told the Conservative Party faithful in 1992: 'I've got a little list ... [of] young ladies who get pregnant just to jump the housing list' (quoted in *The Guardian* 9.11.93). The following summer, John Redwood, Secretary of State for Wales, bemoaned the large numbers of single mothers on a Cardiff housing estate, prompting the Assistant Chief Constable to point out that many of these mothers had injunctions excluding violent partners. The 1993 Conservative Party Conference unveiled the infamous Back To Basics campaign which featured attacks on single parents and proposed changes to the homelessness legislation.

In 1994 the Government published its Consultation Paper (DoE 1994) proposing radical reform of the homelessness legislation. Single mothers were not mentioned explicitly, but remained a powerful subtext underlying the strong language of the deserving and undeserving. The Paper claimed that the homelessness legislation was being 'abused': it was a 'fast track' into social housing (para.1.1), creating a 'perverse incentive' for people to declare them-selves homeless (para.2.8). The government aimed 'to ensure *fairer* access ... and to ensure that subsidised housing is *equally* available to all who *genuinely* need it, *particularly* couples seeking to establish a good home in which to start and raise a family' (para.3.1, my emphases). The Paper proposed to break the link between acceptance as homeless and the duty to secure permanent accom-modation, replacing it with a duty to provide temporary accommodation for a period of six months to people who are 'in an immediate crisis that has arisen through *no fault* of their own' (para.3.2, my emphasis), and who have no accom-modation available (anywhere in the world) 'however temporary the tenure' (para.8.4). Persons from abroad with no recourse to public funds were to be excluded. 'However an authority would still be *required* to accept as in need of assistance someone escaping from domestic violence (*of whatever form*)' (para.8.3, my emphases) – a somewhat ironic undertaking, given that women escaping violence accounted for a very high proportion of lone mothers using the homelessness legislation. The Paper proposed that permanent housing be allocated through a single housing register where the homeless would compete on 'equal' terms with everyone else. Finally, it proposed that authorities make more use of the private rented sector in allocating housing.

The Consultation Paper elicited a barrage of hostile responses (see Shelter 1994), including from Women's Aid (WAFE 1994) and other feminist organi-sations. Fears were expressed that the proposed legislation would condemn women escaping violence to recurring cycles of homelessness with temporary periods in private rented accommodation or refuges, and would completely undermine the functioning of refuges.

In the event, the resulting Housing Act 1996 was not quite as draconian as expected. The main plank remained – separation of homelessness from the duty to secure permanent accommodation – but the six-month duty became a two-year renewable duty. The four 'tests' from the previous legislation were retained and one was added – 'eligibility for assistance' – designed to exclude certain cat-egories of person from abroad. However, another hurdle was also included. If the applicant passes all 'tests' but the authority 'is satisfied that other suitable accommodation (in the private rented sector) is available in the area', the authority only has a duty to provide her with advice and assistance 'reasonably required' for her to secure this accommodation. This effectively allowed authorities to side-step their rehousing duties altogether. All permanent housing must be allocated from a single housing register of 'qualifying persons', and the Act specified a number of categories of people who must be given 'reasonable preference' in allocation. Significantly, these included neither homeless people nor women escaping domestic violence. However the definition of domestic violence pertinent to the 'homeless' test was enlarged to include violence from any 'associated person', including former partners. Moreover, elsewhere in the Act, domestic violence was made a ground for seeking repossession of a tenancy. The Code issued with the new Act reiterated previous guidance on domestic violence but did not add appreciably to it.

Five months after the legislation came into effect, the New Labour Government was elected with a manifesto pledging to restore the right of homeless people to permanent accommodation and to tackle violence against women. The 1996 Act was amended almost immediately with secondary legislation requiring local authorities to give people owed a homelessness duty 'reasonable preference' on their housing register, partially restoring the pre-1996 Act situation. However, the rest remains intact, including the language of discretion and exclusion imported from earlier legislation.

At the same time, the public face of government commitment to the issue of domestic violence has reached new heights. The new Women's Unit of the Cabinet Office has consulted with women's organisations including Women's Aid and feminist researchers concerning its proposed strategy for tackling violence against women. In 1999, it published *Living Without Fear* (Cabinet Office/Home Office 1999) as a 'first step' in this project. Under the heading of housing, this document pointed to a new (draft) Code of Guidance (DETR 1999a) and a guide to relationship breakdown (DETR 1999b) which includes good practice examples and advice to local authorities about developing domestic violence policies. Elsewhere in *Living Without Fear*, the Government announced that people from abroad, normally required to return to their country of origin if they leave their marriage during their first year in the UK, are to be granted leave to remain in the UK (and therefore pass the 'eligibility for assistance' test for rehousing) if they can provide legal evidence of domestic violence.

The ESRC Domestic Violence and Housing Study[1]

A research team at the University of Nottingham is evaluating the impact of changing housing policy (including the Housing Act 1996) on women's vulnerability to violence. The research includes both questionnaire surveys of all refuge groups and housing authorities in England and case studies in four housing authorities involving in-depth interviews with women approaching the housing department because of violence and with local housing officers, refuge workers, and other agency workers. We are, at the time of writing, completing the data collection. However, preliminary analysis of the questionnaire survey of refuge groups (administered in March 2000) is suggestive.

Responses to the survey confirm *ad hoc* impressions from advocates in the refuge movement that the overall impact of the 1996 Act may be less dramatic than initially feared. Many refuges reported that their local authorities have not made any changes in practice towards women fleeing violence as a consequence of the 1996 Act. On the other hand, responses to other questions confirm that the Act has given authorities increased room to manoeuvre, allowing the worst ones to avoid their responsibilities altogether. At the most negative end, some authorities are not even providing temporary housing to fulfil the two-year duty, but are expecting women to secure accommodation for themselves in the private rented sector and/or insisting that they go back home with injunctions or pursue property rights.

However, most groups said that women from their refuges are usually accepted for rehousing. In some cases this is temporary accommodation, but most authorities are continuing to secure permanent accommodation. However, some authorities use the 1996 Act to allocate permanent housing in a way which adds an additional layer of insecurity for women who are already extremely vulnerable. The following comment was not untypical:

> Although our authority has taken up the responsibility to house our residents on a permanent basis, they always say this is temporary for two years and your case will be reviewed after this time. This will withdraw security from women.

In other cases, the situation is much more precarious:

> 70–80 per cent of women get accepted but are only offered the loan of a deposit to secure private rented accommodation. People have to live in the local authority for three years before they can put their names on the list for permanent accommodation.

Other groups mentioned that, since the Act, they have had to ask for reviews of decisions more often and to fight harder to secure appropriate accommodation.

Significantly, over half of refuge groups said that their housing authority's overall response to domestic violence is either good or very good. Moreover, the vast majority said that their working relationship with the authority is good or very good, usually representing an improvement over the past. A number of groups mentioned that they have 'partnership agreements' with their authorities which ensure that all women applying from the refuge are accepted for rehousing and/or that housing officers interview women in the refuge where they have the support of workers. Some mentioned the importance of good lines of communication and collaborative working.

Despite these positive relationships, however, some groups described attitudes and practices which reflect those found in previous research. For example:

> They usually want evidence from the police. They usually want married women to start divorce proceedings before she is accepted.

> Women are discouraged from applying to this authority.

> Currently officers try to find reasons not to rehouse.

> Women often feel they are not believed and have to talk about delicate situations which make them feel uncomfortable.

> They often appear to be very clear on what is not domestic violence rather than what is.

Perhaps the most striking finding concerns the importance of active refuge involvement in facilitating positive responses, even in authorities whose responses are rated as good:

> We rarely have women refused, although it does occasionally happen. If the authority looked as though they might refuse to accept a duty, we would argue. Mostly they would change their minds.

> It depends on whether the woman applying is seen as 'genuine' – i.e. hasn't left loads of times, has proof of physical violence, etc. Otherwise we would fight the case.

> We often have to support a woman through the process of proving she's not intentionally homeless.

> I'm not sure how good it would be if they didn't have to deal with us.... Occasionally we support a non-resident woman and they've usually been given awful advice.

> On the whole women are accepted – especially if we have been present.

Indeed, virtually all refuge groups said that their authority is more likely to accept a woman if she has refuge support than if she approaches on her own. Moreover, a number of groups commented that, in contrast to their own authority, neighbouring authorities – usually areas with no refuges – are poor at responding to domestic violence.

Finally, regardless of the quality of the authority's overall response, the survey suggests that housing outcomes are often bleak. Most groups said that women have access mainly or only to the less popular housing in their area and that the quality of accommodation offered is worse than that offered to applicants on the housing register who have not come through the homelessness route. It is clear that the concept of less eligibility still operates in the context of shrinking supply and rising demand for housing.

Conclusion

The history of government responses to the housing needs of women escaping domestic violence is full of contradictions. On the one hand, the impact of the refuge movement and feminist analyses has been immense. The official ideo-logical climate in which abused women are discussed has altered hugely. Domestic violence is condemned unreservedly in government documents and acknowledged to be an issue which disproportionately affects women due to inequality. It is seen as one form of 'violence against women'. The latest (draft) Code of Guidance to the Housing Act 1996 includes a separate section on domestic violence which is defined, for the first time, as 'any form of physical, sexual, or emotional abuse.... Authorities should be aware that domestic viol-ence can take a number of forms such as physical assault, sexual abuse, rape, threats and intimidation' (DETR 1999a: para.11.17). Also for the first time, authorities are told 'it is not good practice ... to expect evidence of violence' (*ibid.* para.11.9).

Many local authorities are continuing to respond positively to government guidance by developing their own policy and practice guidelines, supporting refuge services, and prioritising women fleeing domestic violence in allocation of housing. Initial analysis of the ESRC Study refuge questionnaires suggests that a large proportion of women in refuges applying as homeless are accepted and obtain permanent accommodation. Most refuges rate their relationship with their authority as positive and their authority's response to domestic viol-ence as good or very good. While there are still many examples of bad practice in housing departments, real progress has been made. At the same time, there are strong indications that outcomes can be much worse for women without the advocacy of refuge workers. Where the 'gut feelings' of housing officers are given unchecked expression, women are more likely to be excluded on the basis of judgements about the undeserving which are often linked to gender, race and class prejudices.

Moreover, the larger picture is one of uncertainty regarding the future of social housing. In April 2000, just weeks after the ESRC Study refuge question-naire was administered, the Government published its long-awaited Housing Green Paper (DETR 2000b), which proposes comprehensive reform of the homelessness legislation, including the extension of 'priority need' to people who are vulnerable because they are fleeing domestic violence and the end to the two-year temporary accommodation duty. It also proposes to strengthen the social rented sector, although it is not clear whether sufficient resources will be allocated to this aim. No money is going into new building in the local author-ity sector, stock transfers to housing associations are being encouraged, and some commentators predict that council housing will be all but extinct within the next 10 to 20 years. It remains to be seen whether housing associations and other registered social landlords will be able to meet the needs of a vulnerable section of society for social housing.

Finally there is the wider ideological and economic climate. There are contradictions running through the heart of New Labour's commitment to tackling domestic violence and its support for the married two-parent family and continuing, though less virulent, rhetoric about single parents and welfare scroungers. New Labour is doing little to discourage welfare residualisation and the ideologies which surround it. The proposed homelessness legislation will continue to be framed in terms of 'tests' which require moral judgements to exclude the undeserving.

Meanwhile Women's Aid groups continue to struggle to meet the demands for their services. And their future financial security is uncertain. However, they clearly do not have sufficient resources to meet the needs of all women seeking refuge, let alone those who, for various reasons, do not want to go to refuges but still need the help of strong feminist advocacy to enable them to access their right to social housing.

Abused women's ability to access resources required to 'determine their own futures' is clearly still precarious, pointing to the fact that the social transformation advocated by the feminist refuge movement is by no means complete (see Appendix 1). Women's Aid has much to celebrate, but there is still a long way to go.

Note

1 'The Impact of Changing Housing Policy on Women's Vulnerability to Violence', Rebecca Morley, Sarah-Jo Lee, Susan Parker, Gillian Pascall, is funded by the Economic and Social Research Council (ESRC). It is one of 20 projects in the ESRC Violence Research Programme.

References

Arden, A. and Hunter, C. (1997) *Homelessness and Allocations: A Guide to the Housing Act 1996 Parts VI and VII*, London: Legal Action Group.

Barron, J. (1990) *Not Worth the Paper …? The Effectiveness of Legal Protection for Women and Children Experiencing Domestic Violence*, Bristol: Women's Aid Federation England.

Binney, V., Harkell, G. and Nixon, J. (1981) *Leaving Violent Men: A Study of Refuges and Housing for Battered Women*, Leeds: Women's Aid Federation England.

Binney, V., Harkell, G. and Nixon, J. (1985) 'Refuges for battered women', in Pahl, J. (ed.) *Private Violence and Public Policy: The Needs of Battered Women and the Response of the Public Services*, London: Routledge and Kegan Paul.

Bull, J. (1993) *Housing Consequences of Relationship Breakdown*, London: HMSO.

Cabinet Office/Home Office (1999) *Living Without Fear: An Integrated Approach to Tackling Violence Against Women*, London: The Women's Unit, Cabinet Office.

Charles, N. (1994a) 'Domestic violence, homelessness and housing: the response of housing providers in Wales', *Critical Social Policy*, 14(2): 36–52.

Charles, N. (1994b) 'The housing needs of women and children escaping domestic violence', *Journal of Social Policy*, 23(4): 465–87.

Cowan, D. (1997) *Homelessness: The (In-)Appropriate Applicant*, Aldershot: Ashgate.

DETR (Department of the Environment, Transport and the Regions) (1999a) *Code of Guidance for Local Authorities on the Allocation of Accommodation and Homelessness* (Draft Consultation), London: DETR.

DETR (Department of the Environment, Transport and the Regions), Cabinet Office, and Department of Health (1999b) *Relationship Breakdown: A Guide for Social Landlords*, London: DETR.

DETR (Department of the Environment, Transport and the Regions) (2000a) *Information Bulletin*, 181, 15 March, London: DETR.

DETR (Department of the Environment, Transport and the Regions) (2000b) *Quality and Choice: A Decent Home for All*, The Housing Green Paper, London: DETR.

Dobash, R. E. and Dobash, R. P. (1992) *Women, Violence and Social Change*, London: Routledge.

DoE (Department of Environment) (1977) *Homelessness Code of Guidance for Local Authorities*, London: HMSO.

DoE (Department of Environment) (1991) *Homelessness Code of Guidance for Local Authorities* (third edition), London: HMSO.

DoE (Department of Environment) (1994) *Access to Local Authority and Housing Association Tenancies: A Consultation Paper*, London: Department of Environment.

HAC (Home Affairs Committee) (1993) *Domestic Violence*. Vol. I. Report together with the Proceedings of the Committee, London: HMSO.

Jones, A. (1999) *Out of Sight, Out of Mind? The Experiences of Homeless Women*, London: Crisis.

Loveland, I. (1995) *Housing Homeless Persons: Administrative Law and the Administrative Process*, Oxford: Clarendon Press.

Maguire, S. (1988) 'Sorry love': violence against women in the home and the state response, *Critical Social Policy*, 23: 34–45.

Malos, E. and Hague, G. (1993) *Domestic Violence and Housing: Local Authority Responses to Women and Children Escaping from Violence in the Home*, Bristol: Women's Aid Federation England and University of Bristol School of Applied Social Studies.

Malpass, P. and Murie, A. (1999) *Housing Policy and Practice*. 5th edition, Houndmills: Macmillan.

Mama, A. (1989) *The Hidden Struggle: Statutory and Voluntary Sector Responses to Violence Against Black Women in the Home*, London: London Race and Housing Research Unit.

Morley, R. (1993) 'Recent responses to "domestic violence" against women: a feminist critique', in Page, R. and Blacklock, J. (eds) *Social Policy Review 5*, Canterbury: Social Policy Association.

Mullins, D. and Niner, P. (1996) *Evaluation of the 1991 Homelessness Code of Guidance*, London: HMSO, Department of the Environment.

Parliamentary Select Committee on Violence in Marriage (1975) *Report from the Select Committee on Violence in Marriage*, London: HMSO.

Pascall, G. and Morley, R. (1996) 'Women and homelessness: proposals from the Department of the Environment I: Lone mothers', *Journal of Social Welfare and Family Law*, 18(2): 189–202.

Robson, P. W. and Watchman, P. (1981) 'The homeless persons' obstacle race', *Journal of Social Welfare Law*: 1–15, 65–82.

Shelter (1994) *Responses to the Consultation Paper – Access to Local Authority and Housing Association Tenancies*, London: Shelter.

Shelter (2000) *Shelterline One Year On*, London: Shelter.

Sutton, J. (1977–8) 'The growth of the British movement for battered women', *Victimology*, 2(3–4): 576–84.

Thornton, R. (1989) 'Homelessness through relationship breakdown: The local authorities' response', *Journal of Social Welfare Law*, 67–84.

WAFE (1994) *Access to Local Authority and Housing Association Tenancies: A Consultation Paper – Effects on women and children escaping domestic violence*, WAFE Briefing Paper.

Welsh Women's Aid (1986) *The Answer is Maybe – And That's Final. A Report About How Local Authorities in Wales Respond to the Housing Needs of Women Leaving Violent Homes*, Welsh Women's Aid.

Woods, R. (1996) 'Women and housing', in Hallett, C. (ed.) *Women and Social Policy: An Introduction*, Hemel Hempstead: Harvester Wheatsheaf.

Part V

Partnership approaches by statutory and voluntary agencies

14 Developing policies and protocols in Duluth, Minnesota

Ellen L. Pence and Coral McDonnell

The Duluth model's major contribution to the national legal reform effort (see Appendix 2) has been its method of negotiating agreements with community agencies that intervene in domestic violence cases. Included in this inter-agency effort are victim advocates, law enforcement officers and administrators, prosecutors, probation officers, court administrators, mental health providers, policy makers, and, in a limited role, judges. The model focuses on ensuring that practitioners respond to domestic violence cases in a consistent manner and that their response centralizes victim safety.

Although coordination is a method to achieve the overall goal of victim safety, it is not in itself the primary goal of the Duluth model. When reform efforts focus on coordinating the system rather than on building safety considerations into the infrastructure, the system could actually become more harmful to victims than the previously unexamined system.

If we measure success by counting increases in arrests, conviction rates, or a reduction of repeat cases entering the system, coordination may seem to be the key to an inter-agency effort. However, if we use the criteria of ensuring victim safety, holding offenders appropriately accountable for their violence, and changing the climate of tolerance for this type of violence, we see that coordination is merely a means to far more complex objectives.

Many cities adopt a strict mandatory arrest or a no-drop prosecution policy on domestic violence cases, as if apprehending and convicting batterers is the only goal of intervention. This course of action is short-sighted and ultimately fails because typically the victim is the biggest obstacle in convicting the abuser. The victim, who may or may not be helped by a conviction, is seen as the problem. From there, the reform effort shifts from a critique of the institution's ability to hold an offender accountable to a critique of the victim. Ineffective intervention strategies and structural problems with the law fade from view as objects of inquiry.

Examining and amending our policies and procedures to build in victim safety has been an on-going process at the Domestic Abuse Intervention Project (DAIP) in Duluth. In 1981, we negotiated agreements with nine key agencies to simultaneously enact policies directing practitioners to follow certain procedures when responding to domestic assault cases. It has been almost two decades since these policies were adopted, and we have continued the process of examination and change throughout this period.

Our primary task in intervening in domestic violence cases is to transform the way the system is structured to respond to domestic violence. Although existing procedures may serve the purpose of processing other misdemeanor crimes, they are often not effective in domestic violence cases. Several structural realities of the criminal justice system make processing domestic assault cases difficult. Problems with the structure include the slow processing of cases, victims being placed in an adversarial position to the offender, practitioners attending simply to single incidents instead of the overall use of violence, and texts (regulations, forms, procedures and reports) that are not designed to direct practitioners to give attention to victim safety and to the collective goal of placing controls on offenders. Another significant problem in the criminal justice system is its fragmentation. Each practitioner in the system is highly specialized and tends to pay attention to his or her own function rather than to the collective work of the entire process. Dispatchers or responding law enforcement officers must see the relationship of their work during the first hour of a case to the work of other practitioners who will later intervene in the same case. Prosecutors, sentencing judges, probation officers, rehabilitation specialists, protection order judges, and custody evaluators read initial police reports, looking for guidance on key decisions they must make in a case. Each practitioner needs to see how he or she is linked with others in the system.

Each practitioner is part of an organizational network. For the network to function properly, each player must be consistent in his or her actions and be aware of what others in the system are likely to do in certain circumstances. Although very little of what practitioners do is at their personal discretion, they do have discretion in whether to screen a case out of the system and to determine the appropriate level of intervention. Once those decisions are made, the practitioner typically complies with standardized procedures in processing the case.

For example, once a law enforcement officer decides to arrest a suspect, the procedures for arresting, transporting, booking, and filing a report are routinized. Consistency in carrying out these tasks is ensured through the use of administrative procedures, standardized forms, instructions, training programs, departmental policy or procedural guidelines, and employee supervision. To achieve consistency and attention to safety, institutional procedures must be linked together, and practitioners must be cognizant of the special problems these cases pose. When a practitioner's response is unpredictable, the best policies and procedures can still lead to failure. In designing an effective response, methods must be in place to ensure a high degree of practitioner compliance because, for a battered woman, an unpredictable system is like playing Russian roulette – a game with which she is already far too familiar.

Practitioners' actions are restricted by regulations, including federal and state laws, case law, insurance regulations, agency and department policies, and local inter-agency agreements. These regulations must be scrutinized relative to victim safety and offender accountability objectives. To centralize safety, the response must take into consideration the risk the offender poses to this and other victims. Therefore, a law, a policy, or a procedure must be constructed in a way that allows the practitioner to account for the probability that offenders who are batterers are likely to retaliate against their victims because of actions taken by the state or community. Policies need to account for the likelihood that most offenders will pursue another relationship in the future. The intervention approach must shift the burden of confrontation from the victim to the institution to whatever extent possible and without coercing victims into a certain course of action. Although the approach assumes that most offenders who batter will use coercion and force in any intimate relationship, responses must not be designed under the assumption that all assaults in intimate relationships constitute battering. Not every person who assaults his or her partner is engaging in an on-going pattern of coercion, intimidation and violence. To assess risk, the collective work of practitioners must be directed toward understanding the pattern and history of violence as well as the power differences between the victim and the offender. Because it is so important to understand how the violence is being used in a relationship, the task of documenting and assessing for levels of danger must be built into the work routines of practitioners and seen as the collective work of all interveners.

Some assumptions of Duluth's reform efforts

In Duluth, we work to hold batterers accountable. The term 'accountability' means to be held responsible for one's actions. This is a long and complicated discussion when used in relation to battering. We can only highlight some of the assumptions we use in the Duluth response to domestic violence cases.

First, we do not assume that all violence is the same. The person who is physically and sexually abused over a period of time and uses illegal violence as a way of stopping the violence is not doing the same thing as the person who continually uses violence to dominate and control a partner. Similarly, a person who engages in abusive behaviors, including grabbing and shoving his or her partner, is not to be treated the same as the person who threatens to kill his partner and uses actions to terrorize her. All of these parties should be held accountable, but the response must attempt to treat similar cases in a similar fashion. Therefore, policies and procedures should help standardize responses while allowing the system to respond to the specifics of a case.

To hold offenders accountable and protect victims, we need to understand how the violence is used by a person and how victims are affected by the violence. Harsh sanctions are not necessary with people who have used minimal force in a relationship, show potential for rehabilitation, and are entering the system for the first time. More jail time does not always mean more justice. On the other hand, we cannot be naive about how dangerous and deceptive many batterers can be. Offenders must be held accountable accordingly.

In Duluth, we assume that most victims of on-going abuse (intimidation, coercion and violence) are safer if the state or court has some level of control over the offender. For example, convictions and probation are preferred over deferred prosecutions, and two years of probation is recommended when abusers reach a level of abuse that indicates an escalating pattern of violence. Completely dropping a protection order is discouraged if a couple want to live together again. Dropping the exclusion order but keeping the restraining order gives the system leverage if the abuse resurfaces. Cases are processed so that the system can respond quickly to renewed violence. We assume that using violence against a child's parent adversely affects the child. Interventions must not pit the interest of the child against the interest of a parent who is an on-going victim of the violence. We continue to debate the role of the abused parent in providing safety for the children.

Some rules of policy making

In Duluth, policies evolved and developed over a long period time. The changes and some of the corresponding conflict came in phases, with many inactive periods between the more active periods of reflection and change. Policy making is as much about the process as it is about content. We have learned over the years that the process needs to be inclusive and based on dialogue, not debate. It must also be attentive to practitioners' knowledge, research findings and experiences of victims. Finally, the process must be open to scrutiny and evaluation. We list here some of the lessons we have learned during almost two decades of policy development in Duluth.

Mind your politics

In the early 1980s, we worked in an atmosphere of distrust, defensiveness and finger pointing. Shelter advocates challenged agencies and institutions, which often responded with hostility. Battered women's advocates were usually seen as 'pushy, single issue, and inherently biased outsiders.'

Internal conflicts existed within and among agencies: police thought prosecutors were dropping the ball, prosecutors pointed to the weak response of judges, judges claimed a lack of appropriate resources for sentencing, and clerks were tired of all the prima donnas in the system. Dispatchers were concerned about a pending decision to move from the police department into a countywide 911 system. Police officers were unable to agree over who should be appointed as the new police chief. Although most of these conflicts were not rooted in problems related to domestic violence cases, they were part of the political climate surrounding the domestic violence reform work in process.

Over the years, defensiveness to the criticism from outsiders in this case – activists in the battered women's movement – has diminished significantly.

Today, our system is not perfect; far from it. But now proposals for solutions are frequently raised by practitioners, rather than exclusively by advocates.

The number one rule of policy making in relation to domestic violence should be that the change must simultaneously deal with domestic violence while considering the political realities of the multi-agency response. Community members wishing to initiate successful institutional reforms should anticipate resistance, be inclusive rather than exclusive, and avoid slogans and rhetoric. They should create an atmosphere conducive to dialogue to sustain relationships through the difficult discussions. Advocates must give up the notion that only they care about battered women and that practitioners in the system are personally responsible for failures in the legal system. Practitioners need to give up the myth that they as professionals have been trained to be objective and fair (as opposed to advocates) and recognize that bias is built into their training and discipline. Finally, administrators must prioritize the protection of victims over the protection of the agency.

Assess current practices relative to the primary goals of intervention

The Duluth model owes much of its progress to the willingness of practitioners and policy makers to work with advocates and activists in the battered women's movement. These practitioners and policy makers relied on battered women's advocates to help identify problems in the system, participate in sessions to develop solutions, and evaluate the impact of new procedures. Visitors to Duluth are amazed at the extent to which agencies have been open to having their handling of cases be scrutinized by others. The attitude among agency directors in Duluth is that such scrutiny improves their services rather than hinders their ability to operate. A good system is refined by scrutiny; an ineffective system is replaced by it.

Initially, shelter workers drew up lists of obstacles that women faced when using the criminal and civil court for protection. These lists shaped the agenda for reform. Most of the reforms that came from the process between 1981 and 1984 were what we might consider macro-level changes. New policies were implemented in each agency that led to significant change in procedures – for example, dispatching policy required dispatchers to send a squad to all domestic assault-related calls and to give domestics involving assault the highest priority coding. Police policy required officers to make arrests when there was probable cause to believe that a misdemeanor-level domestic assault had taken place that had resulted in an injury to the victim. Police policy also required officers to write a report on every domestic-related call. Probation policy required probation officers to request a revocation hearing if an offender committed another assault on a victim. The agreement with the judiciary made it routine for judges to order pre-sentence investigations on all domestic violence-related offenses, no matter how seemingly minor. The agreement with counseling agencies requires that counselors work with offenders in groups or classes and not offer marriage counseling as a method of reducing violence. All of the policies required new methods of documenting cases and sharing information with other practitioners, including victim advocates.

Later policies were altered on a more micro-level as laws changed or experience highlighted problems. We conducted a series of low budget evaluations of specific aspects of the intervention process. We then used that data, as well as cases in which practitioners or advocates felt the system failed to protect victims, as the source for on-going refining of policies. From 1984 to 1994, we continued to make revisions but focused more on procedures than major policy changes. For example, criteria were established for police to distinguish between self-defense and assault. A protocol was developed for police clerical staff to provide victim advocacy agencies access to police reports on misdemeanor cases. We developed a curriculum for abuser classes and designed an inter-agency communication network that eventually became known as the Domestic Abuse Information Network (DAIN). We developed a program for victims of on-going abuse who had been arrested for assaulting their abusers. We opened a visitation center offering supervised visitation and exchange of children for parents in cases in which offenders were using visitation as an opportunity to continue the abuse. Native American activists reviewed each policy for its impact on Native American families and developed separate advocacy services and programming for the community.

In 1995, we began a new process for assessing our practices by employing the research methods of a Canadian sociologist, Dorothy Smith (1990), to investigate how procedures and daily routines in the system affected certain institutional goals (safety, accountability, and changing the climate of tolerance for violence). Based on her work, we developed a method for auditing our system that examined each step of case processing. From that audit, we uncovered many practices in our system that contributed to the inadequate outcome of cases and provided an agenda for change that will take another five years to fully implement.

The audit procedure is fully documented in a manual titled *Domestic Violence Safety and Accountability Audit* (Pence and Lizdas 1998). The audit process involves an inter-agency team that includes staff from the police department, probation department, prosecutor's office, court administrator's office, and a victim advocate. The team observes each processing point and interviews the practitioners involved. Such an audit provides a community with a full picture of where changes need to be made in the rules that guide practitioners' work and the daily routines used to carry out institutional objectives.

Build practice into everyday work routines

It is well known that large bureaucracies are coordinated by paperwork. Beginning with 911, most transactions and actions are textually mediated (paper driven). When a 911 call is made, the conversation between the caller and the dispatcher is guided by how the dispatcher is required to respond to and record the call. When a law enforcement officer arrives at the scene, he or she goes through certain steps to determine if an arrest is to be made and documents what happened in the incident. The strategy of reform has shifted over the years from 'change the attitude' to 'change the text.' Simply stated, if you expect a practitioner in a heavily burdened court system to consistently do something, look for something, or think about something, then request the information on the form that the practitioner uses to process the case. Do not leave safety or accountability to the whim, memory, or personal commitment of hundreds of people. During our audit, we found dozens of places in our system in which normal institutional practices failed to account for the safety needs of victims and left prosecutors in a weak position to obtain convictions even in serious cases. The following is an account from one of the workers involved in conducting the audit of our system. It graphically illustrates how a gap in the system is discovered in the audit process.

The little green frog story

While we were conducting an audit at the jail, a suspect was brought. I observed the jailer as he told the man to take off his bootlaces, belt, tie, and all the things he could possibly hang himself with. The jailer then told the man to take everything out of his pockets. Items in his pocket included $5.85, a tiny green plastic frog, a small Swiss army knife, a comb, and a few other items. The jailer put all these items in a plastic bag and wrote down everything that he took: the green frog, the Swiss army knife, the $5.85, the belt, and bolero tie. After writing down what had been put in the plastic bag, he told the inmate that he would put the bag in a box behind his desk and that he would get these items when he was released. The jailer then had the inmate sign a paper that stated what items had been taken from him.

You can see that the jailer was making it clear to the suspect that all his stuff was his, no one was going to take it, and that he would get it tomorrow. They documented everything to avoid a dispute later about what the man had with him when he was brought in.

This process is well thought through, particularly in terms of the potential for future lawsuits. The strange thing was that during the time they were going through this process, the guy was very angry and yelling and was threatening his wife, saying, 'Someday I'm going to kill that fucking bitch. She knew this would happen. I can't believe this. Every time I walk into the house she tells the kids to dial 911. She'll pay for this!' Then he was carted off to his cell. I told the jailer that I noticed he had recorded every item that he had taken from the man but I wondered if there were any place he recorded the threats that the man had made against his wife. He said no. I asked if there was a form for recording these kinds of threats. The jailer indicated that they did have an incident form on which they could report threats. I asked to see the form, and the jailer dug around and finally found the form. I asked him why, in this case, he had not recorded the man's threats. He said he was only obligated to report serious threats. I asked him how he knew the difference between a serious threat and a not very serious threat. He said that this guy had been in jail plenty of times and that he always blew off steam like that, so he knew it was not serious. I questioned the jailer more, and he asked me if I worked at a shelter or battered women's program, and I told him that I did. He asked me if women ever came to the shelter and told us that their husband had threatened to kill them. I told him they did. He asked if we called the police and told them that. I said we did. He then asked if we called the police every time a woman told us that her husband had threatened her, and I responded that we did not. He asked when we did call, and I told him we called when it was a serious threat. He asked how we knew it was a serious threat. I said, 'I just know.'

This example helped us see the need to carefully examine what seem to be perfectly adequate procedures. Two major tasks of an audit are to locate where safety and accountability can be built into the system and to translate safety and accountability into concrete practices such as a new jailer form or a new 911 response to a first call for help.

The following is a description of the first 24–hours of processing a misdemeanor domestic assault case in Duluth. Changes that have been built into the infrastructure of the system are in italics.

Victim calls 911 to report that her husband had assaulted her and violated the protection order. He had slapped her and grabbed the keys to her house. He left the house heading toward the east end of town in a blue 1985 Toyota pickup truck. The dispatcher gives the case a *priority call*, dispatching one squad to the house and alerting all other squads to the description of the vehicle and the alleged offender. The dispatcher *directly quotes the woman's* description of the assault on the CAD (computer-aided dispatcher) complaint report form.

Officers respond, and visit the house, conduct an interview *using a checklist format*, ask about *history of prior violence* by the suspect toward her or others, ask about *and document the involvement of children* in the incident *and overall abuse*, give her a *referral card* to the shelter/legal advocacy program, *and file a complete report*.

Two hours later, a second squad car pulls over a 1985 blue Toyota truck and identifies the woman's husband as the driver. After conducting an interview with him, officers determine they have *probable cause to make an arrest and do so*.

When the suspect is booked, he makes several threatening remarks toward the victim, *which are recorded on the jail incident form and turned over to the arraignment court* the next morning. After placing the suspect in his cell, the *jailer calls the shelter* and gives the name, phone number, and address of the alleged victim. The jail *holds the suspect* until arraignment court the next day.

The *shelter sends a trained on-call volunteer advocate* to the house to talk with the woman. The advocate provides advocacy and information on the shelter services, protection orders, and what might happen in court and asks for her permission to *forward information regarding the history of abuse to arraignment court*. *If the victim gives permission, the advocate fills out a history form and a state-*

ment *regarding the wishes of the victim regarding full, limited, or no contact with the offender. The advocate also obtains the name of a person who can reach the victim at any time.*

Domestic assault arrest police reports are given *priority by the word-processing department. A copy of each report is distributed to:*

- *the Domestic Abuse Information Network;*
- *the shelter advocate assigned to follow up on the case;*
- the probation officer and judge at pre-trial court;
- the court administrator;
- the detective bureau for follow-up on enhancing the charges;
- *the suspect's probation officer (suspect has a previous conviction);*
- *the domestic violence file.*

The next morning an employee of the city attorney and probation department prepares a file on the case that includes the arrest report, any past police arrest or investigative reports on this offender, CAD printout reports, a risk assessment form completed with a women's advocate, photos of victim injuries, copies of past and current protection orders, any pending court cases, probation information, past DAIN involvement, any prior victims known, and criminal history to be available in all future considerations of the case by the prosecutor, judge, probation officer, rehabilitation program, and so on.

The suspect is arraigned, and the probation officer appointed to this offender is sent the file to determine if he or she should ask for revocation of probation regarding the previous conviction.

All of these changes are the result of years of modification to the way our courts process these cases. Most changes represent many hours of discussion and debate. Others just seem to happen following one meeting on the subject. Effective policy development is a process that requires a commitment to the long haul.

Beware of categories

Several problems inherent to generalized policies and regulations often fail to account for the multiple social positions of those to whom the policy is being applied. For example, the arrest of an immigrant man who has recently arrived in this country could have devastating effects on him and his family. The use of a sentencing matrix that bases the decision to incarcerate an offender on past convictions rather than dangerousness to the victim will result in indigent men being sentenced differently for battering than wealthy men. Obviously, the threat of a conviction has a different meaning to men of different social classes and men from communities with different historical relationships to police and the courts.

Generalizing rules and regulations forces interveners to apply broadly defined rules to individual cases in which more effective responses could be made by verifying the specifics. Let us use the example of the Minnesota law, which divides assaults into two broad categories – felonies and misdemeanors. An assault becomes a felony if the assailant used a weapon or the assault resulted in permanent bodily harm or a broken bone to the victim. A misdemeanor is a less serious offense and is treated differently in several significant ways; most notably, a misdemeanor carries a lighter sentence. Judges often sentence misdemeanor cases without requesting pre-sentence investigations.

Statutes are a set of generalizing rules that tend to group different situations together and treat them as if they are the same or similar. Let us took at how victim safety was compromised in a case involving a double arrest in one Minnesota community. State intervention is based on the notion that felony assaults (assaults involving the use of a weapon or permanent bodily harm) are more serious assaults than misdemeanor assaults (no weapon and no permanent bodily harm). The following is an excerpt from a police report documenting the arrest of a woman who had been physically and sexually abused by her husband for seven years.

Developing policies and protocols

I asked Diane Winterstein to tell me what occurred, she said her husband Phillip had come home after drinking at the Y&R bar and was becoming very belligerent. She said he told her that people were 'reporting on her.' I asked what he might have meant by that and she said that he acts like everybody is his personal watch guard over her and that he makes up affairs she was supposed to have and then says his reporters saw her with someone. She went on to say that Phillip started pushing furniture around; I noted that a chair was pushed over in the dining room. She then went into the kitchen and got out a steak knife and threatened to 'poke his eyes out' if he didn't leave the house immediately. I asked her if she was in fear of grave bodily harm at this point and she said no, she thought he was going to leave. Then according to Diane he started to call her names like 'whore' and 'bitch' and 'cunt' at which point she lunged at him and 'poked him in the right hand with the knife.' She said when he saw the blood he started to cry and she called him a 'big baby,' at which point she says, 'he grabbed me by my hair, began pulling me toward the bathroom and kicking me.' She stated that he kicked her three or four times in the legs and right hip area. I asked her if there were any bruises. She showed me the area of her right hip which was red and swollen and beginning to bruise. I asked her if he did anything else to assault her and she stated that he threw her up against the wall and told her that this time she had gone too far. I asked her if she had been violent to him in the past and she said that she often threatens him to get him to leave her alone. . . . She said that he slapped her across the face twice and then spit in her face. . . . I conferred briefly with Officer Dickie and a decision was made to arrest both parties. I informed Diane that I was placing her under arrest for 2nd degree assault and took her into custody without incident. Officer Dickie placed Mr. Winterstein under arrest for 5th degree assault (see Officer Dickie's report for more details). . . . Officer O'Keefe took pictures of both parties' injuries. Both refused medical treatment. I placed a kitchen knife shown to me by Diane Winterstein as the one she used to stab her husband into evidence (Pence 1996: 123).

In this case, Diane Winterstein faced a prison sentence of 10 years. She eventually pled guilty to second-degree assault for 'stabbing her husband with a deadly weapon.' Because it was her first offense, she spent only 11 days in jail and was ordered to attend classes for offenders. The case against Phillip Winterstein was eventually dropped in exchange for his agreement to cooperate in the prosecution of the more serious case, the felony against Diane Winterstein.

It is the generalizing character of the law that impedes practitioners from intervening in this case in a way that will protect Diane from future assaults. In fact, it is quite possible that she actually has been made more vulnerable to her abuser by this state intervention than had the police never arrived at her door. Yet each practitioner in this case did his or her job.

Reformists must consider these potential problems when attempting to use generalizing rules, policies, laws, and regulations to enhance victim safety. Of course, it would be impossible to manage a large bureaucracy without these generalizing texts. The implementation team must pay close attention to how redrafts of regulatory texts can backfire on certain groups of people. There is no universal battered woman: race, class, age, and gender positions result in differing impacts of the same treatment.

Use policies to control the screening of cases

We have had to grapple with the difference between our rhetoric and the realities of people's lives. For example, consider the following:

- not every case of domestic violence is best resolved in a courtroom;
- every act of domestic violence does not necessarily lead to a serious attack on a victim;
- when victims call for help, they are not calling to activate a long, hostile criminal proceeding. They are usually calling to make something happen immediately;
- many individual victims will not be helped by a prosecution;
- some cases in which an assault did occur are almost unprovable in a courtroom using the standard of proof required in a criminal trial;
- most offenders who are arrested for assault will not be with the woman they abused after five years;
- with no intervention (sanction and/or rehabilitation), most offenders will continue to be violent for many years.

Who determines the significance of such 'facts'? Should the responding police officer decide which case should end up in a courtroom? If so, should the officer have full or only partial discretion to make that decision? The first question posed by a policy to which a practitioner can exercise discretion when a plan of action has been prescribed. The loss of discretion is the biggest source of staff resistance to inter-agency policy development. Policies should not turn practitioners into robots, mechanically applying a few predetermined actions to a case.

Instituting policies such as Duluth's mandatory arrest policy does not mean that officers stop thinking, evaluating, or making judgments. In fact, the opposite is true. The Duluth police policy states that the officer must decide when and if an arrest is appropriate, providing no injury has occurred. If the case has reached a level of violence in which someone has been injured and there is probable cause to believe that the suspect assaulted the alleged victim, the decision on whether to arrest is moot. This policy has increased officers' use of professional judgment and skills in these cases. In the past, if a case was difficult to sort out or the victim was reluctant to proceed with a criminal case, the officer simply advised and left a brief report or possibly no report. Currently, the officer is required to conduct a thorough investigation and question the parties at the scene to determine whether there is probable cause to arrest, to ascertain if any party was using self-defense, to document any action taken, and to gather evidence needed to prosecute these very difficult cases.

Change takes time

The changes we discuss here have been in process for almost two decades. Sometimes rigid policies are needed to change long-held beliefs and traditions in an institution. Eventually, the new practice becomes the routine. The policies can begin to give back a degree of discretion that may have been important to limit for the first five to ten years of reform, given the prevailing thinking about the problem.

Staff turnover affects change. For example, in the early 1980s, when we worked with police officers designing new policy, there was considerable resistance to changing long-held practices. Officers were opposed to giving up discretion on when to arrest. Currently, nearly all of the Duluth police officers comply with and are supportive of the arrest policy and report-writing guidelines because most of them became police officers after the policy was enacted. They were trained as rookies to use these methods of responding to domestic assault cases. Recently, when we introduced the notion of not making double arrests when there is a primary aggressor and two assailants, officers again resisted. Some of us thought the officers would appreciate the ability to use their discretion to determine which party to arrest, but instead officers argued strenuously for the application of existing arrest criteria in all cases.

Use policies to control for appropriate levels of responses

The criminal justice system cannot treat every assault as if it will become life threatening. Policies and protocols must guide practitioners in determining the level of response to cases based on their perception of the level of danger. With few exceptions, every practitioner has her or his own way of prioritizing these cases.

Policies should dictate the basis for which a practitioner should screen a case out of the system, respond as if it were an emergency situation, or take some action in between. Standard response has been established for domestic violence cases for all responders. Procedural checklists of actions to take on all domestic assault-related cases have been developed. For example, we recently developed a method for practitioners (i.e., prosecutors, probation officers, rehabilitation programs) to alert the sheriff's warrants division to cases that do or do not involve an immediate risk to the victims. The DAIN monitors the attendance of all offenders who have been court ordered to attend nonviolence classes. If an offender fails to attend court-ordered classes and is harassing or threatening the victim, the DAIN asks for a court hearing to find the offender in contempt of court. The sheriff's department is then notified that this is a high-risk situation. If, on the other hand, an offender fails to attend classes and the victim does not know where he is, has not heard from him, and is not aware of his whereabouts, the DAIN notifies the sheriff's department that this is not a high-risk situation. The sheriff's department then prioritizes the first case over the second in determining how aggressively to look to serve someone. This is necessary in situations in which the warrants division is too overburdened with warrants to look for a person beyond two or three attempts. We have agreed as a matter of principle not to use scales in determining levels of danger and corresponding levels of institutional action. Instead, in cooperation with practitioners, we discuss and think through the types of cases that would constitute a standard, elevated, or emergency response. An example of this is the sentencing recommendation matrix developed by the probation department in consultation with the shelter advocates and the DAIN staff. This matrix shows how probation officers use information gathered in their pre-sentence investigation, which includes a domestic violence supplement form, to make a decision about an appropriate sentence to recommend. The sentencing recommendation matrix is most effective when it is part of a coordinated community response to domestic violence (see Table 14.1).

Another example is the development of the emergency response team. In 1996, we organized a process by which any practitioner in the system can call an emergency response team meeting. If a practitioner feels that an offender poses imminent danger to a victim, he or she can call a meeting of all agents or practitioners involved in the case (e.g. child protection worker, police officer, shelter advocate, probation officer). Either a telephone conference call or an emergency meeting takes place to discuss a response to this case. The recent development of guidelines for jailers to use in alerting the shelter and victims about threats made by suspects in custody is another policy-driven procedure.

Use policies to link people together

The Duluth agencies have entered into a multi-agency agreement in regard to sharing information and documenting responsibilities on these cases. Every policy

Table 14.1 Domestic violence related misdemeanor sentencing recommendation matrix

	Category 1	Category 2	Category 3	Category 4
Offense	The offender commits an offense against the victim, but no evidence suggests that the offender is battering the victim. The offender has no history of battering.	The offender engages in battering behavior against the victim, but there is no indication that the battering is escalating in severity or frequency or that this offender has battered another person.	The offender has established a clear pattern of battering with this or past victims. The PSI indicates the battering will likely continue and possibly escalate in severity and frequency.	The offender's PSI demonstrates that the heightened, obsessive, or unrelenting nature of the battering poses a high risk of serious harm to this or other victims.
History of violence	This category may include offenders who commit an act uncharacteristic of their typical behavior. It may also include victims of battering who use illegal violence or activities to control or stop violence against them.	This category may include offenders who commit an act uncharacteristic of their typical behavior. It may also include victims of battering who use illegal violence or activities to control or stop violence against them.	This category may include batterers whose histories include multiple domestic violence related contacts with the police, demonstrated harassing behavior toward the victim, violation of an OFP, or repeated threats or assaults against this or other victims. The victim may be in fear of serious bodily harm.	This category includes offenders with histories similar to those of Category 3 offenders but also may include stalking behavior, threats to seriously harm or kill, use of weapons or threats to do so, and injuries that require medical attention.

Considerations	If the offender in this case is experiencing on-going battering by the person assaulted, the probation officer considers safety measures for both parties. Specialized programming is recommended, and the probation officer does not consider executed jail time unless the assault is severe.	Recommendations focus on victim safety and rehabilitation programming rather than sanctions.	Victim safety recommendations are combined with more sanction orientated sentencing, such as the maximum probationary period, some executed jail time, and rehabilitation programming.	Recommendations include the strongest victim safety measures possible, including working with child protection on children's safety. A substantial jail term and long term probation may be combined with programming if the offender is amenable.
Incarceration or other correctional programming	30 days stayed jail.	60 days stayed jail.	60 days stayed jail; 10 to 30 days executed jail/60 to 90 days stayed jail; 20 to 30 days executed jail.	60 to 90 days stayed jail; 20 to 30 days executed jail; 30 days stayed jail; 60 days executed jail; or 90 days straight time.
Gross misdemeanor incarceration or other correctional programming.	91 to 120 days stayed jail; 0 to 45 days executed jail.		91 to 120 days stayed jail; 45 to 120 days executed jail; 120 to 180 days stayed jail; 120 to 180 days executed jail.	120 to 180 days stayed jail; 120 to 180 days executed jail; 180 to 356 days stayed jail; 180 to 365 days executed jail.
Probation duration[a]	1 year.	1 year.	2 years.	2 years.

Source: Arrowhead Regional Corrections and Domestic Abuse Intervention Project, Duluth. Reprinted with permission.

Note: PSI = Pre-sentence investigation; OFP = Order for protection.

[a] Gross misdemeanor convictions routinely receive two years of probation.

should guide practitioners on how and when to share information. Figure 14.1 illustrates how we conceptualize each practitioner linking to others in the system.

This figure shows how the probation officer gets information from others in the system. A similar chart can be made with each of the other areas as focal points to see how each agency is linked to others in the system.

Provide training and follow-up

When developing procedures for handling cases, we recognize that most practitioners – whether advocates, probation officers, judges, or police officers – are average people. Forms, procedures, screening tools, assessment forms, and cur-

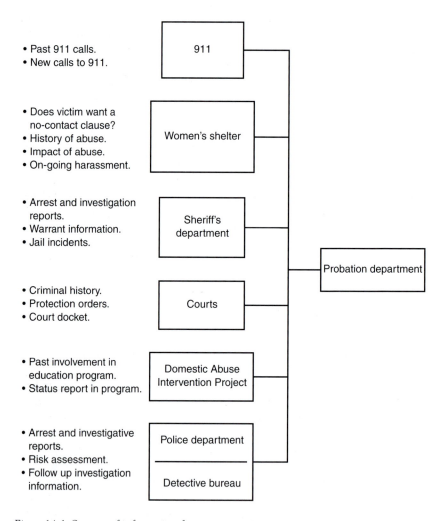

Figure 14.1 Sources of information for pre-sentencing investigations

riculums need to be user-friendly. Practitioners should not be overwhelmed trying to decipher what the tools require, or these recording devices will probably be tossed in the wastebasket and people will go back to using easier methods of dealing with the case.

Training on policies should focus on case examples so that practitioners can apply the guidelines or rules. The DAIP has developed a training curriculum for police officers, probation officers, rehabilitation providers, advocates, and other practitioners in the system. All of the training curriculums use case examples and apply policy and procedure to these case examples. For example, in the police training, there are a series of short videos of police officers responding to different cases. Each video is intended to elicit discussion with police officers about a particular aspect of investigating the case, such as identifying the primary aggressor, determining probable cause, distinguishing self-defense from an assault, recording the history of violence, and so on. Each of the training points is centered on actual case studies and practical dilemmas that practitioners face in their everyday work. Similarly, for probation officers, we provide a packet containing ten cases and ask probation officers to place each of these offenders on the sentencing recommendation matrix. Probation officers then discuss why they placed certain defendants at level one, two, three, or four on the matrix. In conducting training in this way, we come to an understanding together of how to apply written regulations and rules that we have collectively designed. This style of training has been very effective because it engages practitioners in a process that allows them to understand the intent behind each rule, regulation, and policy, as well as to understand the actual requirements on their part. It also leads to discussions that demonstrate how practitioners are linked to others in the system. It helps to identify the problems that practitioners will probably have in applying these procedures and provides them with an opportunity to enhance the process by discussing other information or resources needed to carry out a particular policy, regulation, or procedure.[1]

Recognize that victims and victim advocates are allies, not enemies

It is important to recognize that victim advocates, although they may sometimes seem unreasonable, biased, and maybe even hostile toward the court system, are in fact the most valuable allies that administrators can find if they are truly trying to improve their system's response. Victim advocates are obviously going to be your most vocal critics, but they can tell you where the problems in the system exist. It is important to incorporate ways to listen to the experiences of battered women who have looked for safety and justice from the court system.

In the Duluth system, we have been fortunate to have had a group of battered women who, from the beginning, volunteered to serve on a policy committee for the shelter, and the DAIR The Battered Women's Advisory Committee (BWAC) consists of 7 to 12 women who have used the system within the previous four years. The committee meets six or seven times each year to review and discuss any suggested changes that are being proposed in the system and ask how they believe those changes would have affected them when they were in the process of trying to use the legal system. The committee is made up of women whose class, background, ethnicity, personal history, and experience in the court system differ. Most of the BWAC's meetings center on a two-hour informal discussion and pizza dinner. Besides this input from victims' perspectives, victim advocates meet on a monthly basis to discuss issues in the legal system and frequently invite supervisors of different agencies to talk about problems in the system. We believe that without such input from victims and victim advocates, policy reform efforts would not achieve their goal of victim safety as effectively.

Conclusion

We end this discussion on policy making by providing a template we use as the outline for any new policy and a checklist we use when thinking through a policy. This template provides an overview of items that should be covered in a complete policy. It is provided with a warning: if you want practitioners to know what is in a policy, keep it brief and to the point. A policy should have two versions: the practitioner version and administration version. The practitioner version includes I and II. The administration version includes I, II, and III.

   I The intent and rationale for the policy.
  II Guidelines for processing cases:
     a what a practitioner should do and under what circumstances;
     b using procedures, forms, etc.;
     c what, when, and how information should be shared with others;
     d applicable laws, definitions, authority.
 III Supervision/monitoring:
     a how a policy will be monitored by an agency;
     b steps to ensure compliance;
     c record sharing for external monitoring (how, with whom).

The following checklist can help policy makers examine how a policy will organize workers to think about and act on the unique features of criminal cases.

- Focus on changing the institution, not the victim;
- balance between the need to standardize and the need to be attentive to the particulars of a case;
- focus on building cooperative relationships;
- focus on practices, not people;
- recognize that nobody owns the whole truth;
- build in methods of ensuring compliance with procedures in policy;

- link practitioners to those beyond the next worker in the system;
- account for the offender's level of danger;
- assume that a victim will be vulnerable to consequences if she or he participates in confronting the offender;
- assume that the offender is likely to batter in future relationships;
- document the pattern and history of abuse when and wherever possible.
- account for how:
  - categories help and hinder the understanding of a case,
  - practitioners will get around the intent of the policy,
  - offenders will get around the intent of the policy,
  - the policy or response will be used against victims of battering,
  - different levels of dangerousness and risk require different levels of response,
  - punishment or sanction will have an impact on the offender,
  - rehabilitation or programming could be used against the victim,
  - victims use violence against their abusers
  - slowness will affect victim safety,
  - children are affected by violence,
  - offenders could use children to control victims,
  - institutions send double messages about children's exposure to violence;
- determine who needs information, when, and how they will get it;
- distinguish between differing impacts of intervention depending on the social status of victim or offender;
- put it on the form – do not rely on memory;
- develop standardizing procedures that focus on safety (i.e., matrix, police report form, control log, dispatching screen);
- do not expect practitioners to be robots;
- provide training that focuses on why and how to carry out new practices by using case studies;
- focus the assessment of institutions on what frames a practitioner's response:
  - rules and regulations,
  - administrative forms and procedures,
  - resources and technology,
  - linkages to others in the system,
  - training and ways of thinking;
- make sure the policy covers the following:
  - what to do under specified circumstances,
  - guidelines to put cases into appropriate levels of response,
  - methods to ensure practitioner compliance (tracking),
  - guidelines for making exceptions to the policy,
  - how to document actions,
  - how and with whom to share information on a case.

If the policy is for the greater good, then it should be carried out in ways that protect the individual victim as much as possible.

Note

1   For information about any of the Domestic Abuse Intervention Project training programs, call or write to the National Training Project, 206 West Fourth Street, Duluth, MN 55806; phone: (218) 722–2781.

References

Pence, E. (1996) 'Safety of battered women in a textually mediated legal system', unpublished doctoral dissertation, University of Toronto, Canada.

Pence, E. and Lizdas, K. (1998) *Domestic Violence Safety and Accountability Audit*, Duluth: Minnesota Program Development.

Smith, D. E. (1990) *Texts, Facts and Femininity: Exploring the Relations of Rulings*, New York: Routledge Kegan Paul.

15 Enhancing multi-agency work

Davina James-Hanman

Partnership is simply a collection of agencies whose mutual hatred is subsumed by a collective desire for funding

(A domestic violence forum co-ordinator).

Throughout the 1980s, thanks to the campaigning work of Women's Aid and the wider women's movement, domestic violence moved on to and then steadily up the public and political agenda. Two factors in particular aided this process. Firstly, more agencies, both statutory and voluntary, were persuaded that domestic violence was an issue which they should be more effectively addressing. In some cases, this meant taking domestic violence on board as a new issue; in others, it meant recognising that their current response was ineffective. Secondly, there was an increasing focus on inter-agency approaches to preventing crime generally. As a consequence, improving service provision to women and children experiencing domestic violence[1] increasingly became identified as best achieved, or even *only* achievable, through increased inter-agency co-operation.

An inter-agency approach to domestic violence is not, of course, new. Refuges have worked for over 25 years with a range of agencies to improve the services used by their residents. Staff have campaigned tirelessly, often in the face of incredible hostility and disbelief, to bring to public and agency attention, both the issue of domestic violence and also the often conflicting operational and policy practices of relevant organisations.[2] It is, however, only relatively recently that such a style of working has been formalised.[3] The most common structure of this more formal approach has been, and still is, for a Borough-based Domestic Violence Forum to be established. There is now some form of inter-agency Forum in every London Borough (except the City) and over 200 across the country (Hague and Malos 1996).

The primary reason given by agencies and individuals for the promotion of inter-agency co-operation is because the services which women and children need are provided not by one agency, but by several. For example, a woman experiencing domestic violence may need access to housing, criminal and/or civil legal services, financial aid and emotional support, to name but a few (see Chapter 12).

Research has shown that, on average, a woman will make between five and twelve agency contacts before getting the help that she requires (McGibbon *et al.* 1989). Often this can be because she is receiving no help at all from the agencies she approaches, she is simply referred to another agency, or because the information or services which are given are contradictory or unhelpful.

There are many other reasons for seeking a co-ordinated response to domestic violence. Some of the more common ones cited include:

- to avoid duplication of services;[4]
- to promote a consistent rather than contradictory response;
- to increase awareness and understanding of domestic violence in both agencies and the general public;
- to identify gaps in service provision and work together to address these;
- to provide a more holistic intervention service.

Since the Labour Government was elected in May 1997, a co-ordinated response to domestic violence has also been given additional impetus. In the main, this has been local authority led, as part of an attempt by them to respond to the cry for 'joined-up thinking', and in recent months, as a response to the new statutory duties under the Crime and Disorder Act.

This new law has specific relevance for domestic violence in a number of key areas, although it has yet to be seen whether the potential will be fully exploited by the responsible authorities.[5] On the positive side, this is the first time police and local authorities have had to work together to reduce crime. Although this might appear to place inter-agency work on a statutory footing, there is no legal requirement to specifically address domestic violence. There has been, however, considerable encouragement from the Government that domestic violence be included in the activities required under the new legislation.[6]

Early indications are not, however, encouraging. One London Borough refused to include domestic violence in its main audit, leaving equalities staff to do it separately from the main process; another London Borough defined domestic violence as a 'nuisance' crime and another established a whole new structure which replaced an existing, voluntary sector led, multi-agency fora and replaced it with a statutory agency dominated group which actively supported projects that met council priorities over projects which made a difference to abused women and children.

One of the common obstacles in the auditing process has been the paucity of reliable data on domestic violence. In part, this is due to domestic violence being 'everywhere and nowhere'; in other words, no one agency has responsibility for collating statistics or for providing services. Those agencies who do collect some data rarely do so in a co-ordinated or consistent fashion. Comparisons are thus problematic, as different definitions are used and there is always the problem of 'double-counting' because women use more than one agency for help. Even the Government cannot agree; the Home Office published a (gender neutral) definition for the purposes of statistical data which focuses solely on 'partner violence'. Unfortunately, the Audit Commission also published a (gender neutral) definition for its domestic violence performance indicators which includes all violence 'between intimate partners or members of the same family'.

Nevertheless, some responsible authorities have used the new legislation to launch (or re-launch) a local Domestic Violence Forum and develop work pro- grammes. A review of London-based strategies shows lots of high ideals with little detail as to how they are to be achieved or, indeed, an understanding of the purpose of some activities. For example, almost all contain an objective of increasing reporting, but what difference will this make if the services are not meeting women's needs? Working in an inter-agency style has also been given impetus by other government initiatives. For example, the introduction of Best Value, the focus on Social Exclusion, Health Improvement Programmes and Education Action Zones are all government schemes with a clear link to domestic violence. At the current time, unfortunately, despite the obvious con- nections, inclusion of domestic violence has been patchy.

Inter-agency work, when done properly, can achieve a great deal. It can be an extremely effective method by which appropriate services can be provided; it can enable effective intervention and prevention work to take place and it can lead to the many unhelpful or inaccurate attitudes about domestic violence being challenged and changed.

These potential achievements are being proved by a growing body of evid- ence which suggests that, where a range of agencies do work closely together, domestic violence can be reduced and prevented. For example, at the Domestic Abuse Intervention Project in Duluth, Minnesota, their inter-agency strategy has significantly reduced the number of men who repeat acts of domestic viol- ence[7] as well as reducing the number of domestic violence murders (see Chapter 14). Indeed, this model has been duplicated in many other states and countries, and wherever it has been introduced it has reduced the domestic violence murder rate by a *minimum* of 50 per cent; in some cases, by much more. The key phrase above, however, is 'when done properly'. An inter-agency approach is also a style of working which is fraught with difficulties and which, when not done properly, can actually have the effect of worsening the situation.

For instance, many domestic violence inter-agency fora are little more than talking shops and act as smoke screens for agencies to disguise the fact that they are actually doing very little about domestic violence. It is relatively common to see agency Annual Reports state 'involvement in the local inter-agency domestic violence forum' as their 'evidence' that they are 'doing something' about domestic violence. Sadly, all it may mean in reality is that a member of staff is released once every couple of months to attend a meeting at which no decisions are made, no action is taken and no difference whatsoever is made to the lives of women and children experiencing domestic violence.

Furthermore, within many inter-agency fora, the style of working is far removed from inter-agency co-operation and consensus and is much closer to dictatorship. A common occurrence is for the powerful agencies, usually statutory bodies, to impose their definitions, their agendas and their solutions upon the less powerful agencies, usually voluntary sector groups. This is *despite* the fact that the direct knowledge of abused women's needs, together with a proven track record of meeting these needs, is far more often located within voluntary sector grass roots organisations than in the public sector. Nevertheless, due to the insistent promotion of inter-agency co-ordination as the way forward, the presumption that this is indeed the answer is rarely questioned. However, there is a case to be made, that due to the ineffectiveness of some (but by no means all) Domestic Violence Fora, that other approaches might be equally valid and potentially more effective. At the very least, several factors need to be in place before meaningful inter-agency co-ordination can take place.

For example, inter-agency work can only improve upon single agency responses. In many instances, inter-agency fora are trying to effectively co-ordinate a system of which the individual component parts are inadequate and unhelpful. Co-ordination *cannot* take the place of improvements needed in each individual agency. By properly clarifying the aim of inter-agency work, that is, what precisely it is meant to achieve, it often becomes clear that what is actually needed are changes *internal* to each organisation rather than changes *between* each organisation. Thus, when assessing inter-agency work on domestic violence, it must be acknowledged that some of the groups currently claiming to be operating in such a style are actually doing nothing of the sort. There is a clear need for a much wider discussion as to what criteria needs to be met in order for a group or project to 'qualify' as inter-agency. Such a definition needs to include criteria which go beyond simply having representatives from more than one organisation in the same room.

There are many factors that can affect the success of an inter-agency approach, some of which are discussed later, but as a summary, it should not be forgotten that Domestic Violence Fora are in the difficult position of attempting to address a sensitive and largely misunderstood issue

- by using a complex approach;
- with little guidance in structuring such an effort;
- with historically uncomfortable relationships between many of the participating agencies;
- within an environment of competing priorities;
- with few or no resources;
- with *either* overworked staff *or* inappropriate representatives *or* members who are not really agency representatives at all, merely interested individuals with no authority to implement change in their own organisations.

A belief in the power and value of co-ordinated activity is not necessarily erroneous but there now exists much evidence that the gap between this assumption and its translation into practice is neither an easy nor straightforward task.

Inter-agency co-ordination is a far more complex undertaking than has previously been realised. In March 2000, however, this was finally acknowledged by the Home Office who produced a detailed guide on addressing some of the common difficulties, included examples of good practice and set out a list of ten issues to be addressed by all agencies (see Appendix A) as well as issues for individual agencies[8] Moreover, this publication was accompanied by the announcement of a fund of £4.5m to be spent on inter-agency domestic violence projects.[9]

Hague and Malos, in their research, concluded that to be successful, multi-agency fora needed to monitor and evaluate their work in terms of:

- effectiveness in meeting and highlighting the needs of women and children experiencing domestic violence;
- effectiveness of the structures, decision making, organisational procedures and processes.

However, for a variety of reasons, effectiveness is hard to measure in terms of increasing safety, reducing the overall incidence and responding to the impact of domestic violence.

Hague and Malos's research found that factors which contributed to an effective forum included the following:

- active involvement of statutory agencies at both practitioner and policy-making levels with senior management support;
- full participation of Women's Aid and independent refuge and advocacy services, and concrete strategies to actively promote their central involvement;
- active participation of community, women's and grass roots organisations;
- active involvement of the voluntary sector at practitioner and management level;
- consistent, committed and active attendance and membership, preferably with members delegated to attend by their agency as an agreed part of their work duties or job description;
- stated commitment from member agencies, followed up by action, so that policy and practice changes can be taken up actively and implemented both within and between agencies;
- adoption of guiding principles and the development of common agreements about domestic violence;
- clear and well-developed aims and objectives, equal opportunities policies and other terms of reference;
- a workable structure enabling clarity and lines of accountability but avoiding unnecessary layers of bureaucracy;
- resources for activities, projects and co-ordination work and for servicing the Forum;

- if possible, the employment of a co-ordinator or development worker with administrative support;
- relating all activities to meet the needs, and increase the safety of, abused women and children and decrease domestic violence;
- the development of concrete initiatives and activities which are within the capabilities of the Forum;
- the integration of equalities issues into the Forum's work;
- the involvement of, and some form of informal accountability to, women survivors of domestic violence and their children;
- evaluation and monitoring in relation to work done and its effectiveness.[10]

If these criteria were met, useful and effective inter-agency work could take place. Unsurprisingly then, it is the lack of these which leads to ineffective inter-agency work and the common experience of degenerating into a 'talking shop'.

The criteria can be roughly grouped into the following areas, each of which will be explored further in the remainder of this chapter:

- membership;
- guiding principles/shared philosophy;
- an implementation strategy;
- a commitment to equalities issues;
- resources;
- a practical work programme which focuses on the needs of women and children experiencing domestic violence;
- a workable structure that avoids unnecessary bureaucracy.

Membership

Work by the Greater London Domestic Violence Project, mapping inter-agency work across London, has revealed huge variances in membership of Domestic Violence Fora in terms of which agencies attend, what level of seniority representatives have (and thus what changes in policy and practice they can agree to or what resources they can contribute) and whether or not members are indeed agency representatives or whether they are simply interested individuals. It is extremely difficult for a Forum to achieve an aim of co-ordinating an effective intervention system if they only represent half of the system that abused women and children are using! Although membership does vary, the following key agencies are commonly missing: Health professionals,[11] Social Services,[12] Education, the Benefits Agency, the Child Support Agency, and, with the exception of the police who are, in the main, consistent attendees at Domestic Violence Fora, all component parts of the Criminal Justice System although Probation are becoming more involved, especially in city based fora.

Furthermore, in many instances, people attend a Domestic Violence Forum because they are interested in the issue of domestic violence *not* because they have a prescribed and/or designated role as an agency representative, or the means to carry out such a role. Whilst this can undoubtedly lead to the formation of an effective and committed pressure group, this is not the same as inter-agency working. Rather, it is more comparable to a campaigning group that has access to some 'inside information'!

A further complication is that interested agencies are sometimes prevented from attending because insufficient account is taken of their ability or resource capacity to attend. Inter-agency work should *not* take place at the expense of direct service delivery to abused women and children. In one London Borough, where the refuge has only two paid workers, the number and frequency of meetings have effectively excluded Women's Aid from the process. If they were to fully participate in their Forum, it would, ironically, negatively impact on their ability to provide a quality refuge service. In many instances, public sector staff fail to realise the true level of under-resourcing of the voluntary sector. The lack of time, funding and staff, coupled with ever-increasing demands on service delivery, directly affects the ability of the voluntary sector to be true partners and to fully participate.

Some fora have begun to address this issue by developing membership criteria. For example, providing additional funding for refuge groups to employ locum workers so that the permanent staff can be fully involved in inter-agency work. In other fora, agencies might be required to attend a certain percentage of meetings to retain membership or before membership is granted, agencies might have to establish mechanisms for Forum decisions to be implemented. In this way, agencies can be held accountable and prevented from using the Forum as a 'smokescreen' to look good whilst not actually doing anything save sending a junior member of staff to a couple of meetings per year.

Developing guiding principles – a shared philosophy

Of all the problems involved in domestic violence work, this is perhaps the most difficult. As with many social problems, domestic violence is an arena full of myths ('men who abuse were abused themselves as children'; 'domestic violence is mainly caused by alcohol'), stereotypes ('domestic violence is more common in working-class families; 'domestic violence happens everywhere but it's much more brutal and accepted in Asian families') and misunderstandings ('if the violence was that bad she'd leave'; 'she probably doesn't know any better'). All of these are untrue, as has been proved by innumerable research studies, yet they continue to be common beliefs held by many individuals and agencies.

Thus the different agencies involved in Domestic Violence Fora are unlikely to share an understanding of either what the problem is (i.e., who is doing what to whom, and why) *or* the aim of inter-agency co-ordination. It is clear that agencies view the issue of domestic violence in different and often conflicting ways. The scope for effective inter-agency work can be severely undermined by differences in the definition of the problem together with differences in operational practices and organisational cultures.

The potential seriousness of such differing perspectives should not be underestimated. Although all participating agencies usually agree that domestic violence is an important issue, there is frequently disagreement about the precise nature of the problem and how it should be addressed. As well as the personal perspectives of each individual, organisational culture, political positions, existing policies and agency roles and responsibilities are also influential factors.

These differences between agencies have a *direct* influence on the types of change that are perceived as being needed and how such interventions or projects are subsequently structured. Much of the unhelpful or even dangerous practices which exist around domestic violence are because interventions are being informed by inaccurate information. Thus each misunderstanding and stereotype about domestic violence needs to be exposed and corrected before attitudes or practices will change. For example, if police officers believe that women will always withdraw charges, this affects their willingness to arrest. If staff in any agency believe that leaving a relationship will end the violence, necessary steps are not taken to maintain security measures such as keeping new addresses confidential. If judges or magistrates believe that men are violent when they lose control, rather than it being a deliberate and intentional act, anger management courses seem to be a reasonable intervention rather than dangerous and potentially lethal.

In many cases, shifting attitudes and increasing understanding of domestic violence appears to be an intractable problem. Presenting reputable research evidence and other factual information often has little effect. In part, this seems to be because individual members of any fora rarely come to this subject without some deep-seated emotions and beliefs which are fiercely defended. Domestic violence cannot help but address questions such as 'What does it mean to be a man? A woman? What are family values? What are relationships all about? When you want something and the other person doesn't, at what point does it become abusive?' These are issues with which we all struggle in our relationships and we bring this experience with us to Domestic Violence Forum meetings.

For example, it should be remembered that many non-violent but controlling forms of behaviour can be classified as part of a 'normal' relationship (whatever that is!) rather than as abusive. There remains a widespread acceptance within our society that women should take the major responsibility for childcare. The consequences of this are that many women with young children experience considerable amounts of social isolation – a feature common to abusive relationships. It is rare, however, for anyone to define this as abusive; it may be viewed as unfair or unreasonable, but to name it as abusive would be considered by many as being 'over the top'. The problem, then, is where does the line get drawn? When does a refusal to contribute to childcare inflict sufficient isolation that it is reasonable to name it as abusive?

Thus changing attitudes and understanding is rarely an easy task since it involves the delicate process of challenging individual people's beliefs and values, *as well as* the complex process of challenging organisational cultures, policies and practices.

An additional complication is that, in many people's thinking about domestic violence, the focus is often on the *responses to* or *consequences of* the violence rather than on the violence itself. Hence the most commonly asked question about domestic violence is still 'why do women stay?' and not 'why is he abusing her and why is he allowed to continue?'. Furthermore, in many instances, *responses* to the violence are incorrectly assumed to be *causes* of the violence. It is commonly assumed that women in violent relationships are weak and passive; if only they 'stood up to him', the violence would cease. This ignores that it is precisely the challenging of the abuser's (mistaken) assumption that he has the 'right' to control her which, for many women, leads to violence and abuse. An interim 'coping strategy' therefore, may be to *appear* to passively accept his exercise of control; but this is clearly a *consequence* of abuse and *not* a cause. Failure to comprehend this frequently leads to plans for assertiveness groups for abused women.

On the whole, people's response to the reality of domestic violence is one of extreme sadness and sympathy for the women and children, and of anger and despair towards the perpetrator and the lack of support to women and children from the systems which are meant to protect them.

This should be cheering news but, unfortunately, awareness training on domestic violence is conducted within a context of a society which accepts (and glorifies) violence as a 'natural' part of masculinity and which also systematically discriminates against and oppresses women. This means a sustained change in attitudes is difficult to achieve, however extensive the awareness raising/training initiative. What we need is constant reinforcement on the scale of, for example, public health anti-smoking campaigns or the anti-drink-driving campaign which is now some 30 years old.

In other words, what is needed is a public education campaign which is sustained over at least a generation and which consists of more than just posters, but is also accurately covered in a wide range of media on a regular basis (like the anti-smoking message). The aim would be to create an environment in which domestic violence is no longer tolerated, where it would be unthinkable for Paul Gascoigne to be selected to play for the England football team, for O. J. Simpson to be considered a suitable chat show guest, or for Sean Connery to ever dare to express his violent and misogynist views in public again. That's what we need; what we've actually got is a tentative commitment from the Home Office to run a one or two year poster campaign initially with a derisory budget commitment of only £60,000.[13]

Nowhere are the differences between agencies more acutely exposed than in the debates which rage over the definition of domestic violence. In order to get agreement, opting for the lowest common denominator is an unfortunate, but common, feature of inter-agency work. The following areas of contention are the issues which frequently expose the differences between agencies' understanding of the problem.

• The gendered nature of violence in the home

Despite the wealth of evidence which consistently shows that domestic violence is overwhelming committed by men towards women, actually stating this leads to near apoplexy for some agency representatives. In many cases, this results in a shared definition never being agreed. This may mean agencies continue to strive towards a shared definition whilst developing other areas of work or that some member agencies stop attending and those remaining are able to agree a definition, or, more commonly, a pragmatic course is followed, that is, a 'gender neutral' definition is adopted for the purposes of being able to progress. This is done despite the fact that this leaves a Forum existing to address a problem which it cannot, or will not, accurately define! Sometimes, the 'gender neutral' definition is softened by adding the following standard 'gendered explanation' paragraph:

> Domestic violence is overwhelmingly committed by men towards women. However, it can also occur in same sex relationships and in a minority of cases, by women towards men.

Even this compromise, however, is rarely reached easily.
   The next area of difficulty in reaching a shared definition is

• the gap between what women define as their abusive experiences and what the law – civil and criminal – acknowledges as abusive.

Direct service providers for abused women frequently find that women define the psychological effects of domestic violence as having a more profound effect on their lives *even where there has been life-threatening or disabling physical violence* (BMA 1998). Despite this, there is almost always pressure to define domestic violence *only* in terms of actual or threatened, physical violence since this is the aspect of domestic violence which clearly constitutes criminal behaviour. Even when emotional or psychological abuse is included in a definition, financial control/abuse and the imposition of social isolation/movement deprivation are often not included, despite these being extremely common aspects of abusive relationships.

   Furthermore, even when Domestic Violence Fora do adopt a more inclusive definition, (e.g., one that includes psychological abuse) individual agencies, and individual staff within these agencies, often still use a more narrow definition for their own operational purposes. It is rare, for example, for Housing Departments to accept psychological abuse alone as a reason to accept a homelessness application (see Chapter 13). Despite having separate units which deal with domestic violence, defined as including sexual abuse, it is rare that Police Domestic Violence Units deal with rape allegations against a current or former partner.

   There is also the danger in defining domestic violence so broadly in that it results in the inclusion of behaviours which are common to everyone, thus diluting the experiences of women who face life threatening or debilitating abuse. Furthermore, it permits men to claim that they experience domestic violence in equal numbers to women without the differences in power, impact and injury being given sufficient weight.

- The way domestic violence manifests itself includes a wide range of abusive behaviours which are essentially about the exercise of control and the misuse of power.

Although much of the current research and thinking on domestic violence now accepts that the desire to establish power and control is what underlies the use of abuse and violence, and even though individual agencies may pay lip-service to this definition, it is frequently not translated into practice. Hence, for instance, abused women are still labelled as uncooperative if they refuse offers of joint meetings with their abusers, rather than it being understood as a pointless exercise to enter into negotiations with someone whose idea of negotiating is them winning at any cost, up to and including using physical violence.

Understanding the power and control dynamic is crucial as it exposes the gap between conflicts common to most relationships and the life threatening or debilitating abuse experienced by thousands of women every year.

- An acknowledgement that defining abuse is not a scientific or objective activity; it is a political concept. As such, any definition needs to be the subject of continuous review, rather than set in stone.

As our knowledge and understanding of domestic violence has increased, the definition has also adapted and changed. Which behaviours are defined as abusive is clearly influenced by a political, social and to some extent, cultural, context. For example, the concept that a husband could rape his wife has only become accepted by most people in very recent years. It was assumed (and still is by many) that once a woman agreed to marriage, she had no right to deny sexual access to her body; indeed, she had a duty to allow unrestricted entry. As a consequence of a change in attitudes, brought about by an increase in women's social, economic and cultural autonomy, rape within marriage has now been added to the definition of abusive behaviour. Nevertheless, there is still not widespread acceptance of the idea that abuse cannot be conclusively defined, once and for all. This often leads to an atmosphere of resentment and/or impatience when individuals attempt to revisit or review the definition.

- And finally, a recognition of domestic violence as a form of abuse in its own right (i.e. adult men abusing adult women with whom they are in an intimate relationship).

There are frequently extended and heated debates about which forms of violence should be included within the definition of domestic violence. Is it only violence by one adult, usually male, against another adult, usually female? Does it also mean violence by women against men, or within lesbian and gay relationships, or are the dynamics so different as to be almost another issue, for which another name is required? Should sibling violence be included? Elder abuse? Child abuse? Violence by children towards parents? Is the 'test' a familial connection or the physical setting? How can the connections and overlaps be recognised, whilst still recognising domestic violence as a distinct form of abuse? Or indeed, is it a distinct form of abuse, or should it be viewed as inextricably connected to or entangled with either any of the above or as inextricably connected to all forms of violence against women and children? Or the use of violence within society in general? The debate continues.

An implementation strategy

In coming together, agencies are usually required to confront very real ideological differences, a history of mistrust, a lack of understanding about the operational and political constraints of other members and organisations. More detailed attention needs to be paid to the practical complexities of dovetailing varying agency objectives, incompatible operational procedures, the reality of scarce resources and varying staff skills, experience and authority; all of which affect the likely success of inter-agency work.

Failure to address the issues outlined above means that, in the absence of clarification as to what the consequences might be of participation, individual agencies on the Forum are rarely prepared to enthusiastically embark upon any radical changes; indeed they may be unwilling to implement any changes at all.

Related to the issue of failure to attend to the *process* of how the Forum members work together, is a lack of sufficient attention to the implementation of any new initiatives. It cannot be emphasised enough that the implementation of any projects or changes in policy upon which a Domestic Violence Forum may embark needs to be planned *as carefully* as the framing of the project. There is often an assumption that projects will be implemented as proposed but as many fora have found to their cost, the reality is often very different.

Project or policy implementation should include:

- clarity of the project/policy intent;
- defining each stage of implementation;
- identifying the likely constraints of each affected agency;
- identifying where influences outside of each agency might affect organisational change;
- identifying those responsible for implementing each component part;
- how, and by whom, each of the above stages will be monitored.

The work of both developing, and then implementing, any initiatives which the

Domestic Violence Forum may devise, needs the involvement of staff with experience and skills who can do this work. All too often, an agency will be represented by a member of staff who has expressed an interest in domestic violence rather than by an appropriately skilled person. Moreover, representatives need to be actively supported by their agencies rather than, as frequently occurs, being marginalised. For instance, representatives are often not allocated sufficient space within their work programmes to develop any initiatives. Nor are they permitted to be publicly critical of their agency. Nor are they given sufficient authority to either agree to new inter-agency initiatives or to implement change within their own agencies. Indeed, in many instances, agency representatives are not monitored by their own organisations nor is guidance given to them as to their precise remit (see, for example, Plotnikoff and Woolfson 1999).[14]

Agency representatives need to be in sufficiently senior positions within their agencies to both take decisions regarding fora proposals and to commit resources *or* they need to have clear access to the individuals who can make such decisions.

A clear and active commitment to equalities issues

Given that domestic violence affects all sections of the community, it is necessary to make sure all sections are represented in the planning of any strategy. However, it is equally important that the consequence is not, for instance, an all white forum with only one black worker whose only role is to provide specialist information on 'cultural issues'. This is becoming more common since the emphasis on membership increasingly focuses on obtaining more senior representation, where Black[15] staff are frequently under-represented, especially in the more powerful (statutory) agencies.

A lack of commitment to equalities issues within the respective agencies can also powerfully impact on levels of trust in a Domestic Violence Forum. For example, if an agency is well known for harassment or victimisation of its female or Black staff, other agencies may then be mistrustful of their ability to fully understand or successfully contribute to other issues.

It is also important that all equalities issues are considered in any project upon which a Forum may embark. It is not enough to provide the same service to everyone as this does not guarantee equal access. For example, women with young children may be able to attend advice sessions but will they really want to talk openly and honestly in front of them? Or is it really a good idea to hold advice sessions at 3.30 in the afternoon when many women are collecting children from school? Is information accessible for everyone? What about women whose first language is not English? Or who have literacy difficulties? How many services can be used by women with 'no recourse to public funds'? In order to develop an effective strategy, all of these issues must be an integral part of the planning process.

Resources

Even the most cursory assessment of Domestic Violence Fora clearly shows that the overwhelming majority of those fora which have achieved substantial change are those with access to resources, *especially* those with a paid member of staff. The reality for most fora is that they are made up of members with extremely heavy workloads who simply do not have the time available to progress any projects. For some organisations, even taking the minutes of meetings, typing them up and mailing them out is a task with too many resource implications, let alone progressing any new initiatives.

In some fora, joint funding strategies are now being developed, most commonly, this is between any combination of police, social services, health and occasionally, other local authority departments such as Community Safety Units. In other fora who have established themselves as charities, applications are made to trust funds or the National Lottery Charities Board.

For smaller scale, discrete projects, private financing is sometimes raised. For example, local solicitors are often prepared to sponsor the production of leaflets outlining women's legal rights.

The lack of resources is almost always identified as the primary obstacle to fora being more effective. The consequence of these limits is that fora tend to develop what can be funded rather than what might most be needed.

A practical work programme which focuses on the needs of women and children experiencing domestic violence

Domestic Violence Fora often lose sight of their purpose of being. For example, many become much more concerned about producing a glossy referral directory which quickly becomes out of date than in addressing the practical needs of women experiencing domestic violence, such as who will house the family pet whilst in a refuge? Who will provide childcare whilst at the solicitors? How will she move her furniture? What will she live on if she has no recourse to public funds? This is not to say that a referral directory is necessarily an inappropriate activity, but many such directories do little more than make agencies feel they are doing something about domestic violence whilst the directories themselves gather dust on office shelves. There is also the problem that directories tend to outline the policy of an organisation which may be a very idealised version of their actual practice.

The easiest way to avoid this is to relate all activities to the needs and experiences of abused women and children, with particular reference to increasing safety. Yet despite all the years of action around domestic violence, it still seems to be a revolutionary concept to actually listen to abused women and children and then to develop services based on their needs. Of course, there is still a great deal of silence on the subject of domestic violence but this is emphatically not because abused women are silent; it's because they are silenced by being ignored, patronised and treated dismissively. For example, often when women seek help they meet an expectation from agencies that they should behave like a 'proper victim'. This means appearing grateful for the opportunity to live in one room in a bed-and-breakfast or face accusations of the violence not being serious or real. It means not objecting to the suggestion of joint sessions to make arrangements for future contact with the children or being labelled 'implacably hostile'. It means crying in court to avoid being seen as vindictive. It means never being angry or others may assume you 'had it coming'. It means appearing weak, passive and submissive simply to get services and protection.

Forcing women to behave like 'victims' is one of the many ways in which society colludes with the abuser and further punishes women for experiencing domestic violence. By expecting a woman to behave in this way we add to her sense of shame for not coping better (whatever that is), we add to her humiliation at having to wash her dirty linen in public, we add to her sense of failure for having picked the wrong man and we add to her sense of embarrassment at having to ask for help in these individualistic times. And then we produce posters urging women to 'break the silence' or as the previous Government did in their public education campaign, tell women 'Don't stand for it'.

Of course, the silence which surrounds violence against women in the home is far from absolute. Women do resist and they do speak out. Women do complain and they do take action against violent men and demonstrate enormous courage in doing so, given that they are usually doing this in a climate of disbelief and hostility.

Asking survivors how to improve services has been given much encouragement by the Government, especially under the Crime and Disorder Act but also under several other initiatives, such as Best Value. Despite this, very few fora have established mechanisms for doing this with some notable exceptions. In many instances, the fact that voluntary sector agencies who work directly with abused women are Forum members is considered to be sufficient. Whilst in some instances this may be adequate, this does not allow for the fact that voluntary agencies may be reluctant to criticise agencies who are also their funders, does not provide for information to come to light about poor practice within voluntary sector agencies and nor does it allow for the views of women and children to be heard directly; they are always filtered through a 'professional lens'.

A workable structure which avoids unnecessary bureaucracy

In part, this relates to the issues above on proper agency representation, but it also means that a Domestic Violence Forum should not just keep a list of work done but should also attempt to evaluate their effectiveness without becoming unnecessarily tied up in paper exercises. Producing leaflets and holding meetings certainly have the *potential* to be useful activities but if they make no difference to the lives of women and children experiencing domestic violence, they are a waste of time and other resources. If they make no difference to the almost unbelievable prevalence of domestic violence, they are a waste of time. If abusive and violent men are left unaccountable for their behaviour and free to abuse again, they are a waste of time.

Evaluating initiatives can sometimes throw up unexpected results which can help shape future interventions. The evaluation of the Domestic Violence Intervention Project in Hammersmith, for example, revealed that the main achievement was not, as might have been expected, a sustained and fundamental change in abusive men's behaviour (Burton *et al.* 1998). Rather, the programme created a window of opportunity for the female partners to plan safer responses to the violence and abuse. Thus this evaluation has proved that concurrent partner support services are an essential, core element of violent men's re-education projects rather than an optional extra.

As Domestic Violence Fora become more established, so the attendant bureaucracy grows. Although some method is undoubtedly needed to keep the information flowing, it is also important that creativity does not become stifled. Within all work undertaken by multi-agency fora, it is essential that the focus remains on a vision of a world where violence and abuse no longer occurs. It is within the capacity of all of us, including men, to change and this process of change *can* be influenced and hastened by statutory and voluntary sector organisations, as well as individuals, nationally and locally, working towards a common vision of a world where domestic violence no longer happens. This is not an easy task but in the absence of any other emerging strategy for addressing this issue, it seems that we must continue to find new ways to make inter-agency work more effective.

APPENDIX A: EXTRACT FROM 'MULTI-AGENCY GUIDANCE FOR ADDRESSING DOMESTIC VIOLENCE', HOME OFFICE, 2000

Basic points for all agencies

The following basic points are for consideration by all agencies which may have to deal with domestic violence and its survivors.

1 All agencies must be fully aware of the level and nature of domestic violence, of the need for their policies and practices to address it, and of its possible presence in cases they have to deal with. Importantly, this includes those cases which originally come to their attention for other purposes.
2 Domestic violence training is important for staff at all levels.
3 When dealing with individual cases, the priority for agencies must be the client's safety. They should themselves undertake such emergency action as they can.
4 As employers, agencies should develop appropriate responses to members of staff who may be experiencing or perpetrating domestic violence.
5 Agencies should ensure that information about both statutory and volun-

tary domestic violence services is available to staff and the public in an accessible format.

6   Participation with local inter-agency domestic violence fora is desirable where such fora exist, but must be seen as a means to an end, not an end in itself.

7   Agencies should work to create a safe and supportive environment which encourages people to report domestic violence.

8   Services must be fully accessible to all. Agencies must be aware of the needs of women from ethnic minorities, those with disabilities, elderly people, those with drug or alcohol dependency, people with mental health problems and those in same sex relationships.

9   The success of any initiative to reduce domestic violence depends on a careful implementation strategy and needs to be confirmed by thorough evaluation and monitoring.

10   Agencies should consider the importance of information sharing (section 115 of the Crime and Disorder Act) as a valuable part in the co-ordination of their client-based services.

Notes

1   This includes holding abusers accountable for their behaviour.

2   Given this history of inter-agency work, albeit informal, it is surprising to see the amount of literature which incorrectly attributes the development of domestic violence inter-agency work solely to the 1995 Home Office circular on the issue, especially since many of the formal inter-agency fora were established prior to this date.

3   The longest running Domestic Violence Fora were established in the mid to late 1980s.

4   This is a commonly cited reason for inter-agency work although, in reality, service provision is so scarce that duplication is rare.

5   Responsible authorities are defined in the Act as the local authority and the local police, working together, in partnership, with other local agencies who may vary according to local circumstance.

6   Amongst others, this has included specifying domestic violence in the guidance issued by the Home Office, statements in the House of Commons and a letter from Paul Boateng MP circulated to all responsible authorities.

7   Morton, F. (1994) *Community Safety and Justice for Women*, London Action Trust.

8   Home Office (2000) *Multi-Agency Guidance for Addressing Domestic Violence*, London: Home Office.

9   Whilst this funding is welcomed, it should be noted that the total Crime Reduction Budget is £250m.

10   Extract from Hague, G. and Malos, E. (1996) *Tackling Domestic Violence: A Guide to Developing Multi-agency Initiatives*, Bristol: Polity Press.

11   If health professionals are involved, it is commonly a health visitor rather than a GP (despite the latter being the people to whom women experiencing domestic violence most often initially report), hospital staff, midwives, dentists or public health education staff; all of whom have an important role to play. This is, however, a situation which may rapidly change following the publication of guidance from the Department of Health in March 2000.

12   If Social Services are involved, it is commonly a representative from the Children and

Families part of Social Services, not the Vulnerable Adults side. This is one of the reasons why issues relevant to abused disabled women are so inadequately addressed.

13 In 1994, the now defunct Association of London Authorities ran an awareness campaign on domestic violence in 13 London boroughs on a budget of around £100,000.

14 This is not meant to imply that other organisations are any better organised.

15 Whilst acknowledging the limitations of such a definition, I am using Black here in its political context to include all black and minority ethnic communities.

References

British Medical Association (1998) *Domestic Violence: A Health Care Issue?*, London: BMA.

Burton, S., Reagan, L. and Kelly, L. (1998) *Supporting Women; Challenging Men*, Bristol: Polity Press in Association with The Joseph Rowntree Foundation.

Hague, G. and Malos, E. (1996a) *Multi-agency Work and Domestic Violence: A National Study of Inter-agency Initiatives*, Bristol: Polity Press.

Hague, G. and Malos, E. (1996b) *Tackling Domestic Violence: A Guide to Developing Multi-agency Initiatives*, Bristol: Polity Press.

Home Office (2000) *Multi-agency Guidance for Addressing Domestic Violence*, London: Home Office.

McGibbon, A., Kelly, L. and Cooper, L. (1989) *What Support?*, Community Safety Unit, London Borough of Hammersmith and Fulham.

Morten, F. (1994) *Community Safety and Justice for Women*, London Action Trust.

Plotnikoff, J. and Woolfson, R. (1999) *Policing Domestic Violence: Effective Organisational Structures*, London: Policing and Reducing Crime Unit, Home Office.

Part VI

Decreasing the violence
of men

16 Confronting violent men

Russell P. Dobash, R. Emerson Dobash,
Kate Cavanagh and Ruth Lewis

The violent physical abuse of women in the home is now recognised in many countries and by a number of human rights organisations as a significant human rights issue requiring urgent attention (Heise 1994). While developments have been geared to assisting and enabling women, the source of the problem – the violent male – has remained an obscure spectre, rarely subjected to systematic scrutiny and often ignored in public debates regarding 'what is to be done about domestic violence'. But what about men, particularly those who perpetrate violence? Is the development of more challenging and effective responses possible and worth the effort, or is it a wasteful expenditure of scarce resources? Are men to be considered as beyond redemption or reform? Further, if we are to challenge men, what are the best methods and avenues of influence? Is it through voluntary participation in therapeutic treatment programmes, or is the justice system the only way forward? And if men are to be considered, what role will feminist insights and methods play in these efforts?

Whatever the political and pragmatic concerns, many recent developments particularly, though not exclusively, within the civil and criminal justice arenas, have directly or indirectly included efforts to deal with violent men. Enhanced injunctions, including the powers of arrest and exclusion, an increasing emphasis in some locations on arrest and occasionally prosecution, are the most obvious of these innovations. Of particular importance in North America, Australia and New Zealand are innovative pro-feminist programmes for violent men. Though sparsely represented in Europe, men's programmes have recently emerged in Scandinavia and Britain. This chapter considers the nature of criminal justice interventions in domestic violence and therapeutic and pro-feminist programmes for violent men. We pay particular attention to two British programmes and present the results of a three-year research evaluation of these two programmes.

Domestic Violence Units, arrest and injunctions

In Britain apparently well-intended efforts to deal with violence against women through the creation of Domestic Violence and Women and Children Units in police forces have had mixed results (Grace 1995; Hoyle and Sanders 2000).

Domestic Violence Units often emphasise assistance and support over arrest and prosecution (Grace 1995). The most important limitations of these units is that they rarely challenge violent offenders. In the United States, though less so in Britain, arrest has become a more common response to violence against women in the home (Buzawa and Buzawa 1992; Dobash and Dobash 1992; Sherman 1992; Berk 1993). In some locations in the United States 'mandatory arrest' has been introduced as a means of encouraging more assertive action by police officers.

In the early 1980s, an experimental field model in Minneapolis, Minnesota required police officers when responding to an incident of domestic violence to randomly allocate three types of disposition: arrest, or offering advice, or asking either the man or woman to leave the household (Sherman and Berk 1984; Sherman 1992). The results of this study offered strong support for the assumption that, all things being equal, arrest of a man who was violent toward his partner was more likely than the other two responses to reduce violence. Sherman and Berk (1984) argued that men who were arrested for incidents of domestic violence were deterred from committing subsequent acts of violence because of the fear of re-arrest. They implied that fear of arrest was a significant means of protecting women from future assault. Once completed, the Minneapolis study provoked a rash of interest, receiving national prominence when a pro-arrest strategy was endorsed by the Attorney General's Task Force on Family Violence (Fagan 1992).

The research community responded with scepticism to the claims of the Minnesota arrest study (Fagan 1992; Dobash and Dobash 2000). Apparently ignoring the ethical issues associated with such research, and in an attempt to overcome the technical limitations of the initial arrest experiment, the National Institute of Justice (NIJ) embarked on an extensive research programme aimed at replicating the Minneapolis study. Studies using a similar, though not identical, experimental design were carried out in Kansas City, Missouri; Colorado Springs, Colorado; Dade County, Florida; Charlotte, North Carolina; Atlanta, Georgia; and Milwaukee, Wisconsin (see, for example, Dunford, Huizinga and Elliott 1990).

Results of these investigations have been less clear cut than those of the initial study. Some commentators urged, counter-intuitively, that those violent men who were least responsive to arrest because they were the most criminalistic should not be arrested for violence against their partner (Sherman 1992). Other commentators involved in these various evaluations offered other conclusions, suggesting that arrest on its own is not effective because more rather than less criminal justice intervention is required to generate an effect (Berk *et al.* 1992). North American feminists and criminologists continue to debate the efficacy of arrest in domestic violence cases, although many argue that arrest is an appropriate and effective method for deterring subsequent incidents of domestic violence, not least because of the wider societal message conveyed by a criminal justice response that such violence is a criminal offence (Berk 1993; Pence and Paymar 1993; Stark 1993).

Recent research in Britain indicates that, despite new policies and practices, only a small proportion of call-outs (two per cent in one study) result in arrest and prosecution (Edwards 1989; Wright 1995; see also Chapters 8 and 18). The most frequently employed justice intervention in most jurisdictions is the use of civil injunctions (Dobash and Dobash 1992). In the 1980s, a number of British studies investigated the use of these measures and revealed that enforcement of injunctions and the use of the attached powers of arrest were often inconsistent and inefficient (Homer *et al.* 1984; Faragher 1985; Barron 1990). According to these early research reports injunctions were often ineffective; with only a minority of women judging them as useful. In the United States, however, women who used injunctions were likely to say they found them useful and to endorse them as a means of support (Grau *et al.* 1985; Horton *et al.* 1987; Fagan 1989; Chaudhuri and Daly 1992; Ptacek 1999).

Recent evidence gathered in Great Britain supports these positive assessments in spite of women's reports showing that violent men often continue to abuse and harass them while the injunction is in force, and courts and police sometimes fail to respond to these abuses (Lewis *et al.* 2000). The evidence from Britain suggests that some women are able to use the civil law as a resource in their attempts to deal with violent men. Research and experience in the United States indicates that injunctions are probably most useful in cases where the man does not have an extensive criminal record and where there is criminal justice commitment to improved effectiveness (Finn and Colson 1990; Chaudhuri and Daly 1992; Keilitz *et al.* 1996). In jurisdictions where the judiciary provide clear and explicit admonitions regarding the violence and harassment, and other justice personnel are prepared to enforce these messages, injunctions can be effective. Willingness to apply sanctions when violent men breach the civil order is also important.

Therapeutic approaches to violent men

Partly because of the failures and limitations of traditional criminal justice interventions and as a result of the continual pressure of women's groups, more and more men are participating in 'treatment' programmes. In the United States and Canada a vast array of programmes exist to deal with violent men: some are extremely orthodox, building upon the theoretical positions and practices associated with traditional psycho-dynamic notions while some break new ground in offering pro-feminist programmes which seek to re-educate violent men (see Chapter 17). Until recently, traditional therapeutic notions seemed to predominate in North America where it is claimed these developments have occurred primarily through the process of defining violence as 'a clinical condition' (Schlesinger *et al.* 1982: 148).

The majority of existing approaches are based on the assumption that such men have unique traits causing violent behaviour. Men who use violence are described as suffering from inadequate and impaired 'ego functioning' and 'antisocial' and 'pre-morbid' personalities resulting from 'rejection and inadequacy' in childhood (Powers and Kutash 1982: 44). Deschner (1984), for example, thinks that violent men are the youngest sons in families where they have all experienced or witnessed violence. The 'uncontrollable anger' of a violent man emanates from 'unresolved conflicts' with his parents resulting in 'displacement of anger and aggression onto the most convenient targets in his life – his wives and girl friends' (Schlesinger *et al.* 1982: 163). Psycho-dynamic approaches to violent men also emphasise the influences of stress, drug and alcohol dependency, the inability to play, lack of self control, co-dependency and the 'imbalance of roles brought about by the women's liberation movement' (see for example Elbow 1977).

One of the highly influential approaches in the United States and elsewhere constitutes violence as the product of an interacting couple or, more abstractly, the family. The director of counselling at the Tyler [Texas] Family Preservation Project claims, 'many couples have mutual hostility and resentment against the world. They find each other, they form a bond or a symbiosis so that it's "Us against the world"' (quoted in Shupe *et al.* 1987: 36). In such a family system, 'likes do attract likes' with each partner bringing the same weaknesses to adult relationships, 'emotional dependence, childlike insecurity, and a generally low self-image' (Shupe *et al.* 1987: 61). It seems that the coming together of two people who suffer 'a general emotional immaturity' and 'mutual obliviousness to interpersonal processes' leads inexorably to 'a violence prone system, and once an incident of abuse is consummated, a battering system' (Weitzman and Dreen 1982: 261). Family systems of this nature are apparently very different from non-violent ones where, 'normal relationship rules are negotiated, each spouse has the prerogative, alternating control occurs and a symmetrical posture develops' (Weitzman and Dreen 1982: 261).

Treatment within this systems approach predictably involves intervention in the whole family 'system': 'We will never really make progress in resolving family violence if we do not consider the family as the unit to be helped' (Shupe *et al.* 1987: 31). Family systems counselling conceives of the problem as emerging from sick, malfunctioning and violent-prone communication systems, with violence solely or primarily understood as a result of 'interactional behavior sequences between the partners' (Shapiro 1984: 119). Consequently there are no victims or abusers. In such work, 'neither partner has an exclusive right to either term' (Neidig 1984: 475) and both are seen as 'equally culpable and victimized' (Shapiro 1984: 119). Therapy involves altering interaction by overcoming 'communication problems' and 'skills deficits'. Accordingly, each member of the family must accept responsibility for change, yet therapists may encounter resistance as the 'two parties join in collusion to avoid changes' (Geller 1982: 205). In the face of such obstacles some therapists believe that the best route to overcoming resistance may be to 'discuss and expose the system's characteristics' and 'escalate conflict in order to locate the couple's threshold for change' (Weitzman and Dreen 1982: 264).

Despite their apparent diversity, psycho-dynamic approaches to violent men have a number of common elements. Whether they stress bio-chemical, neurological or physical disorder; transference of aggression; displacement of needs; or situational factors such as stress and alcohol abuse; the basic assumption is that the fundamental cause of violence is faulty personality or some sort of personality disorder 'intrafamilial violence is primarily considered a psychological and social disease' (Flanzer 1982: 136). Motivations, values, and intentions play no role in these explanations and interventions, nor do notions of guilt and responsibility. Characterising people in this way means that it is impossible for them to play an active role in transforming their own behaviour. In allocating responsibility for violence against women, men are seen as having no role to play because the explanations of their actions involves the behaviour of women, the family (women), or other factors beyond their control.

Confronting violent men

Traditional psycho-dynamic conceptions of violence and violent men have been challenged by alternative perspectives and practices rooted in feminist research, the experience of those working with women who have been abused and new cognitive-behavioural interventions directed at offenders. Pro-feminist and feminist programmes for violent men were first developed in the United States, some of the first and most influential of these are Emerge in Boston, Massachusetts (see Chapter 17), the Duluth Abuse Intervention Programme (DAIP) in Minnesota (see Chapter 14), and the Man Alive Programme in Marin, California (Sinclair n.d.; Adams 1988; Ptacek 1988; Pence and Paymar 1993). Pro-feminist men's programmes have been created to challenge men's violence. A fundamental principle is to hold men responsible for their violence.

Based on the knowledge and experience of nearly two decades of work in the battered women's movement, pro-feminist men's programmes take a more direct and pragmatic approach, focusing on men and seeking to increase men's insight into their own behaviour and emotions and helping them to end their violent behaviour. Traditional therapeutic technologies are sometimes employed but always within the context of more encompassing forms of reaction and critical feminist interpretations. Confrontational group work is the preferred technology for seeking personal change. According to Ann Ganley (1987: 156), '*Appropriate use of confrontation* is crucial to alter the client's characteristics of minimization, denial and externalization' (emphasis in original). Confrontation involves attempts to convince men to acknowledge their violent behaviour and to accept responsibility for actions and for the need to change.

The focal point in pro-feminist men's programmes is the violence. Reflecting feminist interpretations of male violence (e.g., Dobash and Dobash 1979), pro-feminist perspectives consider violence as intentional behaviour chosen by men as a tactic or resource associated with attempts to dominate, control and punish women (see also Dobash and Dobash 1999; Dobash et al. 2000). The violent and controlling behaviour of men becomes the major and concrete focus in pro-feminist programmes, not something to be skirted over and ignored. It is a retributive starting point, a continual referent for reminding men of their responsibility and of the harm they have inflicted on their partners and children. The past is continuously linked to the present by communicating disapproval of violence and emphasising its impact on others and the wider community. Men should not forget how their acts have affected the women who have been abused and the children who may have witnessed this abuse. Beginning from this retributive starting point leads more clearly to reparative and reformative goals for personal behaviour. Making amends and remedying wrongs is a fundamental part of the reformative process (Tavuchis 1991). We think this process of 'respectful retribution' – a phrase we developed through Martin Luther King's discussion of appropriate responses to those who perpetrate racially motivated violence – is a critical foundation and continuing touchstone for the creation of alternative thinking and action.

Reconstructing violent events is also important in increasing men's awareness of their own intentions and motivations (Edleson 1984; Ptacek 1988). Locating interventions in actual behaviour is an important means of building and modelling new forms of conflict resolution. Concrete approaches make it possible, for example, to follow the event through to consider the immediate and long-term impact on women and children. An event-focused approach may help increase empathy and to confront the denial and minimisation associated with men's accounts of their own violence (Cavanagh *et al.* 2001). Focusing on the violence in the context of a group of men also provides a forum for examining the social, cultural and political issues associated with wife abuse and relating these to individual behaviour. Group discussions can deal with the many myths and justifications which are intricately linked to men's violence and domination. This makes it possible for men to recognise their inflexible and distorted beliefs and expectations, such as those associated with sexual jealousy and various forms of possessiveness (Dobash and Dobash 1999; Wilson and Daly 1998). Recognition of these rigid, authoritarian beliefs may be an important step in altering them and avoiding many of the confrontations and conflicts associated with violence. Few traditional approaches explore the links between individual behaviour and the wider society; even fewer are sensitive to gender and power.

Pro-feminist programmes see violence as one end of a continuum of male domination. The widely used 'Power and Control Wheel' developed at DAIP by Ellen Pence and Michael Paymar (1993), which incorporates various forms of domination, is the most explicit exemplar of this concentration on power. Constituting the physical violence as one of a number of forms of power enables men to confront a wide range of abuses, including economic and emotional abuse. In the Duluth model (see Appendix 2) the abusive and controlling acts incorporated into the Power and Control Wheel are to be supplanted by non-violent methods of negotiation, responsibility and trust represented in an Equality Wheel (Pence and Paymar 1993; Dobash *et al.* 1995). The overall goal is the elimination of male dominance within the family and society.

A model criminal justice based community programme

The most successful of the community and criminal justice based programmes operating in the United States is the DAIP, created in 1980 in Duluth, Minnesota, a small city with a population of around 100,000 and a small police department of approximately 100 uniformed officers (Dobash and Dobash 1992; Pence and Paymar 1993; see also Chapter 14). The size of the city, combined with an established pattern of progressive community action and skilled feminist activists, have coalesced to produce what is generally acknowledged to be one of the most successful criminal justice based pro-feminist projects for violent men anywhere in the world.

A major strategy of the project is to attempt to *protect women* by reducing men's violence through an educational programme aimed at convincing violent men that they are accountable and responsible for their violent behaviour and for its elimination. The method for achieving this goal is to treat the violence as a crime and ensure effective processing and sanctioning by the justice system in ways that focus on the elimination of future violence rather than on the 'punishment' of a given offence.

British programmes for violent men

By comparison to North America, there are proportionally very few British programmes for violent men. One of the main reasons for this is the under-developed nature of clinical psychology in contrast to institutional social work. In North America, much of the therapeutic work with men who physically and sexually abuse their partners is done by independent psychologists and counsellors who 'treat' men in privately owned and financed clinics. There is very little of this sort of organisational structure in Britain, consequently the current interventions with violent men are run on a voluntary basis by community groups or they are incorporated into probation work with offenders (Scourfield and Dobash 1999).

CHANGE and the Lothian Domestic Violence Probation Project

The first two dedicated criminal justice programmes for violent men in Britain were created in Scotland in 1989: CHANGE in the Central Region of Scotland and the Lothian Domestic Violence Probation Project (LDVPP) in Edinburgh. Neither programme developed out of a men's group, the establishment of CHANGE was preceded by four years of foundation work involving Women's Aid, researchers, a prominent Sheriff (magistrate), a solicitor and others (Dobash *et al.* 1995). The LDVPP was conceived through the foundation work of CHANGE and generated as a result of women's representation on the local authority.

The two pro-feminist programmes were very similar in their basic philosophy and approach, but operated on a somewhat different basis. CHANGE was funded by Urban Aid and provided probation court services to Central Region Courts and Social Work (Morran and Wilson 1994; 1997). Operating independently of statutory institutions, programme staff assisted in the compilation of Social Enquiry Reports for the Courts but did not hold the probation orders on the offenders sentenced to the project. CHANGE not only operated a programme for men but, like DAIP, it sought to work on a wider community basis, by linking with, and providing information and training to, a number of voluntary and statutory agencies. It aimed to raise the profile of domestic violence as a criminal justice concern throughout the Central Region. Although the LDVPP was also linked to the community, its location within the Lothian Social Work Department meant it was primarily oriented to operating the men's programme. Staff conducted initial Social Enquiry Reports for the Courts and held the probation orders of the programme participants. Thus, they had a wider range of criminal justice responsibilities than CHANGE. From their inception and throughout their operation, both the LDVPP and CHANGE maintained important contacts with local Women's Aid groups.

While there was variation in the shape of the respective programmes delivered to men, this was more a matter of the detail of delivery than overall content or philosophy. Like their North American counterparts, these two Scottish programmes focused specifically on the offender and his violent behaviour. They did not accept voluntary referrals; men participating in the programmes had been found guilty of an offence involving violent behaviour toward their partner and, having been assessed as appropriate for the programme, participated as a condition of a probation order. The core of the intervention involved 'challenging' group work conducted on a weekly basis for a period of 24 (CHANGE) to 27 weeks (LDVPP). A wide range of techniques were used in the group work, including (see Dobash *et al.* 2000 for a fuller description):

- the re-enactment of specific violent events and the use of videos depicting violent events in order to increase self-awareness;
- the use of continuous forms of self-assessment and monitoring such as anger and control logs between the weekly group sessions as a means of reinforcing group work;
- group training in non-violent forms of conflict resolution which were meant to be practised between sessions;
- the teaching of cognitive techniques for recognising the sequence of events and the nature of emotions associated with the onset of violence;
- didactic methods aimed at enhancing offenders' understandings of the nature of violent behaviour to women and its social and cultural supports.

Both programmes attempted to maintain contact with women, to keep them informed of the work with men, and to either facilitate or, in exceptional circumstances, to provide support when it was requested. For example, LDVPP's initial information leaflets for men and their partners included explicit expectations about the mandated nature of the man's attendance, made no promises to keep the relationship together, and rejected alcohol abuse as a 'cause' of violence. Information provided in the leaflets indicated to the woman that the court was considering placing her partner on the programme because of his offence involving violence to her, and stressed that she was not responsible for his violence. Information provided to women also indicated that the programme was for men only, that the focus was on the violence and ways of stopping it, that her safety could not be guaranteed as a consequence of programme participation and therefore she should continue with safety plans involving interdicts (injunctions) and the use of resources such as the police, friends, neighbours and Women's Aid (Dobash *et al.* 2000).

A research evaluation of British programmes for violent men

In 1991, with the support of the Scottish Office and Home Office, we set out to conduct a comprehensive evaluation of these two programmes by comparing their impact to other criminal justice sanctions (Dobash *et al.* 1995; 1999a; 2000). Prior to the completion of this project no substantial research had been conducted on programmes for violent men in Britain, although considerable research had been carried out in the United States and Canada on similar interventions. While a number of these North American studies reported a reduction in violence – 50 per cent to 80 per cent of the men are reported to be non-violent 6–12 months after intervention – as a result of programme participation, most suffered from serious limitations in design and implementation (for critical reviews see Eisikovits and Edleson 1989; Tolman and Bennett 1990; Gondolf 1991; 1997; Dobash *et al.* 1995).

The evaluation of the LDVPP and CHANGE was designed to minimise methodological problems. The study used a longitudinal panel design to compare the impact of a number of sanctions at three time periods; immediately after the imposition of the criminal justice sanction (time one), three months after the initial assessment (time two) and 12 months after the initial assessment (time three). At time one, men and women were involved in separate face-to-face interviews. At times two and three, men and women were sent separate postal questionnaires. The results of the follow-up questionnaires were used to assess the impact of criminal justice interventions over a period of 12 months.

Men involved in this study were arrested, charged and convicted of an offence involving violence against their partners. Charges ranged from breach of the peace, to serious assault. Sample populations were drawn from the cases of all men who were sanctioned for an offence involving violence against their partner in Sheriff's Courts in Edinburgh and Central Region during the fieldwork period. The final design included five sample groups:

1   CHANGE;
2   LDVPP;

3   other court (fines, admonishment, etc.);
4   probation;
5   prison.

Men and their partners were included in each sample group. For the purposes of the research, two naturally occurring comparison groups were created: the Programme group comprised of cases from CHANGE and the LDVPP and a second group, Other CJ (criminal justice), included cases in which men received another type of sanction (probation, fine, prison, etc.).

Methodology and methods

We explicitly employed a context-specific, feminist-inspired methodology, locating the violence and other controlling acts in the overall context of women's lives (Dobash and Dobash 1983; 1992: 251–84; Longino 1994). At time one, systematic, in-depth forms of interviewing were combined with quantitative forms of data collection to obtain fulsome accounts of violence and the experiences of women. In previous research by Dobash and Dobash (1979; 1983) interviews with women focused on specific violent events – the first, the worst and the last before a woman went to a refuge. This contextual form of 'event analysis' yielded a wealth of qualitative and quantitative data (Dobash and Dobash 1979; 1984). In this way women's interpretations are linked to concrete lived experiences, making the interviews and the resulting data more meaningful.

In the initial in-depth interviews in the present study, event analysis was used to explore the first violent event in the relationship and the one that resulted in criminal justice intervention; women and men were also asked about the nature of the violence throughout their relationship. The series of items pertaining to any particular violent event began with a question such as, 'Can you tell me what happened during the incident which led to the court case?' When interviewing women, a question such as this would elicit a wealth of information regarding the sequence of events preceding the violence, the violence itself and resulting injuries and reactions. Most men were rather less forthcoming. In order to facilitate the disclosures of men and to increase the probability of obtaining systematic results over time, we also asked men and women to respond to pre-prepared indices of violent acts, injuries and controlling behaviours after asking them to provide their own accounts.

As constant critics of the most widely used methods of measuring violence between intimates (Dobash and Dobash 1992; Dobash et al. 1992) we considered it necessary to construct new methods for assessing violence, injuries and other controlling and coercive behaviour. The Violence Assessment Index (VAI), Injury Assessment Index (IAI) and Controlling Behaviour Index (CBI) were created and used in interviews and postal questionnaires to gather systematic quantitative data about the nature, range and frequency of abusive behaviours used by men (Dobash et al. 2000). The VAI included 26 distinct types of violence, ranging from a slap inflicted on the arm to a kick directed at the head. A number of distinct types of injury was measured through the IAI index, including bruises, cuts, black eyes and internal injuries. Men who use persistent violence against their partners often employ other methods of control, such as physical threats and intimidation. These controlling behaviours involve direct overt types of intimidation as well as more subtle types of coercion; the CBI assessed 21 distinct forms of control and coercion. In contrast to the widely used and often criticised Conflict Tactic Scales (Straus and Gelles 1990), these indices were embedded in the context of conflicts and aggression and used in the research to assess the impact of criminal justice sanctions over time.

Postal questionnaires used at times two and three were intended to assess changes in the behaviour and orientations of men and the predicament of women at two periods of time – three months and twelve months after interview. Fundamental issues explored through follow-up questionnaires were: the nature and extent of contact between the man and woman; current levels of violence, injury and intimidation; and the perceived impact of the criminal justice sanction on the relationship. The above-mentioned indices were used to assess these orientations and behaviours. An additional measure included in the final questionnaire was the Quality of Life Index (QLI) which aimed to assess perceived changes in the quality of life for men and especially women at the end of the evaluation period.

The research evaluation is based on evidence gathered at interview (time one) from a sample group of 256 subjects, made up of men (122) and women (134), and follow-up questionnaires obtained from 83 per cent of the Programme group and 71 per cent of the Other CJ group at time two (three months after interview) and 62 per cent of the Programme group and 55 per cent of the Other CJ group at time three (12 months after interview). The reports of men and women were used in the evaluation to assess changes in men, but the accounts of women are given prominence because we consider them more valid and because they provide a more conservative and stringent test of the success of the innovative programmes than self-reports of men (Dobash *et al.* 1999b).

Changes in violence and other controlling behaviours

The research evaluation assessed change over time in various ways. Data from the postal questionnaires allowed us to measure the incidence, frequency and severity of violence during the follow-up period; to assess the maintenance or reduction in the controlling and coercive behaviours associated with violence; and to determine the improvement or deterioration in the predicament and orientations of the women who had been the victims of violence. A traditional measure of outcome was also employed. Using court records, we were able to determine differential rates of subsequent additional criminal charges in the two groups. The fundamental questions were: are women whose partners have been on one of the two programmes more likely than women with partners in the Other CJ group to experience less violence, fewer incidents of violence, reduced severity, a reduction in controlling behaviours and an improvement in their quality of life and relationships?

According to court records, only a small minority of men (7 per cent of Programme men and 10 per cent of Other CJ men) failed by re-offending and experienced a subsequent charge associated with violence against their partner during the 12–month period following initial arrest and prosecution. On the basis of these sorts of results, we might conclude that arrest and prosecution have an extraordinary effect on subsequent incidents of violence and that the innovative Programmes are only slightly more successful in reducing levels of violence than other criminal justice sanctions. The results of follow-up postal questionnaires tell a different story and show that, on a range of measures, men participating in the innovative programmes are much more successful in reducing their violent and intimidating behaviour than men who have been fined, admonished, placed on probation or sent to prison (Other CJ group). According to the reports of women, three months after the initial interview, 62 per cent of men in the Other CJ group had perpetrated at least one incident of violence while only 30 per cent of men in the Programme group had been violent. Twelve months after the initial interview at time three, 70 per cent of men in the Other CJ group had committed at least one violent act against their partner, while only 33 per cent of the men in the Programme group had acted violently. These differences are important and statistically significant.

Women's reports were also used to assess the *frequency* of violence at times one, two and three. At interview, time one, 31 per cent of women in the Other CJ group and 26 per cent in the Programme group reported five or more incidents of violence in the year preceding interview. Three months after interview at time two, no women in the Programme group reported frequent violence, whereas 16 per cent of women in the Other CJ group said they experienced five or more incidents of violence. At time three, a year after interview, 37 per cent of women in the Other CJ group reported frequent violence whereas only 7 per cent of women in the Programme group indicated they experienced frequent violence. The proportional differences in the two groups at both follow-up periods were highly statistically significant (Dobash *et al.* 1999a).

The results indicate that the majority of men who fail by committing a violent act do so very shortly after the imposition of a criminal justice sanction and that those men who fail do not seem to change the severity of their violence whatever the criminal justice intervention, though there is some indication that men who have been on one of the programmes use less severe violence. It is important to note that although men in the Programme group were more likely than men in the Other CJ group to have stopped their violence over the 12–month period of follow-up, about a third of the men in the Other CJ apparently did not commit a violent act during the follow-up period. These results suggest that concerted criminal justice response involving arrest and prosecution may affect the subsequent violence of men.

If men's programmes are more successful in reducing violence than other criminal justice sanctions, we would also expect a proportionately greater reduction in associated acts of coercion and intimidation. It could be argued that sustaining patterns of non-violence beyond 12–months will be dependent upon changes in these associated behaviours, thus making it important that they are evaluated alongside explicit acts of physical and sexual violence. In order to conduct a valid assessment of possible changes in controlling behaviours in the two groups over a 12–month period, we compared the prevalence and frequency of controlling behaviours at times one and three for each of the two groups. If the programmes are effective we would expect a greater reduction in the prevalence and frequency of controlling behaviours from men who have participated in one of the programmes than men who did not participate.

The comparative data on changes in controlling behaviour derived from the CBI index for the two groups tell a consistent story. In contrast to women in the Other CJ group, women living with men who participated in one of the programmes report statistically significant reductions in both the incidence and frequency of a range of controlling behaviours after programme completion (Dobash *et al.* 2000: 120). These results cast doubt on the often repeated claim that men who participate in such programmes may reduce their violent acts but are then more likely to engage in various intimidating and coercive behaviours. The evidence leads to the conclusion that, in comparison to other criminal justice sanctions, participation in one of the programmes is more likely to reduce the incidence and frequency of violence and associated controlling behaviours.

Changes in quality of life

The Quality of Life indices were used to allow men and women to report whether their lives had improved, worsened or remained the same during the 12–month period of follow-up. On average women living with partners who participated in the LDVPP or CHANGE were much more positive about their quality of life than women living with men who experienced other types of criminal justice intervention. The general picture is one of far more positive changes for the women whose partners have been on one of the innovative programmes and negative changes for women in the Other CJ group (see Dobash *et al.* 2000, Chapter 7 for details).

The programmes encourage men to accept responsibility for their violent and controlling behaviours and to be more aware of their partners' views and feelings. A significant proportion of women in the Programme group report that 12 months after interview and their partners' participation on one of the programmes, their partners were more likely to see their point of view, to be aware of their feelings, and to respect them. An overwhelming majority of women in the Programme group also report that their partner is less likely to restrict their life and a majority indicate that he is more likely than in the past to take responsibility for his violence. Only small proportions of women in the Other CJ group report positive changes on the same indices and many report significant deterioration. At the end of a 12–month period, the results of the evaluation reveal that the men who participated in CHANGE or the LDVPP are likely to be more sympathetic toward their partner, less self-centred and to take greater responsibility for their violence.

The evidence on violence, controlling behaviours and quality of life from the evaluation project shows that criminal justice sanctions can make a difference, and this is especially true for men participating in one of the innovative programmes. Although the research reported here has, like all existing evaluations, some limitations, such as small sample size at time three, the results across a wide variety of qualitative and quantitative assessments suggest that men who have 'graduated' from CHANGE or LDVPP have, in contrast to men sanctioned in other ways, significantly reduced the prevalence and frequency of their violence and significantly suppressed the range and frequency of their controlling and coercive behaviours. These changes have been sustained months after the completion of the programme and, although multi-variate analysis of the results shows that other factors may affect the incidence of violence (particularly type of relationship), Programme participation still has an important 'value-added' effect on successful reduction in violence (Dobash *et al.* 2000). The female partners of these men report important improvements in the behaviours and orientations of the men; changes that have significant effects on their own quality of life.

Abuser programmes and criminal justice interventions

Programmes for violent men, even pro-feminist ones such as CHANGE and the LDVPP, have generated an enormous amount of political debate and controversy within the battered women's movement (Dobash and Dobash 1992; Hague and Malos 1994; Mullender 1996). In the past decade, men's programmes have been one of the most contentious issues facing the Women's Aid movement in Britain. Although the movement has sometimes provided impetus for the development of men's programmes (particularly in the United States) they are sometimes treated with scepticism and concern. There is, for example, the problem of the relationship between the movement and its adversaries. Are men's programmes allies in efforts to seek social change or potential adversaries against the movement and social change? Do such programmes offer meaningful alternatives to the status quo of accepting and supporting male violence? A continual concern is the possibility that programmes for men will divert energy, resources and public attention away from the urgent needs of abused women and their children. There is the danger that those who run such groups may inadvertently collude with batterers by supporting, or failing to reject, common notions that deny or diminish the violence and/or men's responsibility; thus, deflecting blame and generally shifting attention away from the violence and the man. Programmes may also increase the risks to women by giving them false hopes that their partners will be transformed through this work, and thus provide another mechanism for entrapping women in violent relationships. As with other criminal justice innovations, there is always the danger of race- and class-based forms of discrimination. The creation of court mandated men's programmes may disproportionately increase the number of working-class and ethnic-minority men processed by the criminal justice system. Programmes for violent men must be attuned to the intersections of masculinity, ethnicity and class (Crenshaw 1993), sensitive to the possibility of alternative cultural patterns and interpretations, though this should never be reduced to the position that intervention is impossible and that women from certain backgrounds should 'endure' the burden of violence as a cultural imperative. It appears that programmes for violent men will continue to present the battered women's movement with difficult questions and the movement will continue to confront dilemmas and contradictions regarding engagement with these programmes.

Criminal justice based programmes for violent men such as CHANGE and the LDVPP appear also to present a number of dilemmas for certain feminist accounts of justice (Smart 1990; see Dobash and Dobash 1992: 213–50 for a review). Paralleling many of the arguments of European and American abolitionists, some feminists have indicated that women's sense of justice is radically different from men's, consequently this 'different voice' leads to an ethic of care based on the premise 'that no one should be hurt' (Gilligan 1982). Other feminist discourses stress the importance of justice based on 'outrageous love' and principles of healing and forgiveness (Harris 1987; Davidson 1985). Still others link with 'republican criminology' and opt for models of justice based on idealised conceptions of communitarian responses rooted in kinship-based societies (Braithwaite and Daly 1994). Basing their arguments on the premise that it is relatively simple to invoke guilt, shame and thus a sense of responsibility in violent men, communitarians eschew arrest and prosecution. They propose 'community' conferences as solutions for physical and sexual violence against women, arguing that through this communitarian process 'increasing numbers of men would be made accountable for their violence against women' (Braithwaite and Daly 1994: 202). These proposals ignore evidence which suggests that one of the most powerful impediments to women's attempts to seek assistance and justice is the continuing threats and coercion they experience at the hands of their partners (Hoyle and Sanders 2000; Lewis *et al.* 2000). It is unlikely that a 'community conference', even a series of such meetings, will successfully challenge and re-direct the aggression and violence of men (see Stubbs 1997 for a critique of conferencing). Evidence from a wide variety of sources suggests that community based interventions are very unlikely to be successful in dealing with long-standing forms of abuse such as domestic violence (see Dobash and Dobash 1992).

Whatever the reservations about criminal justice based programmes for violent men, they are becoming increasingly popular. The British research discussed in this chapter provides important evidence regarding the utility of a certain type of intervention. The two criminal justice based programmes evaluated in the three-year study delivered direct services to violent men based on a structured, systematic and pro-feminist approach to challenging violent behaviour and associated attitudes, and to developing more positive methods of dealing with conflicts. Paralleling recent evaluations conducted in North

America, the research reported here shows that well-managed criminal justice based projects delivering a programme focusing on the offender and the violent offending behaviour are more likely than other forms of criminal justice interventions to reduce or eliminate violence and intimidating behaviour (Bersani *et al.* 1988; Hamm and Kite 1991; Dutton 1995; Gondolf 1999). It is important to note that not all men participating in one of the programmes were successful in reducing their violence, and not all women reported significant changes in associated controlling behaviours and their quality of life. Some women remain wary and apprehensive, adopting a 'wait and see' approach; most have seen somewhat similar, albeit more short-term changes before. The significant issue is whether these changes can be sustained, whether they are permanent. We might be rather more optimistic, like some of the women participating in the research, because men who reduced their violence also altered a range of associated coercive and controlling behaviours and orientations.

While positive changes have been achieved through programme participation, evidence collected in this study and elsewhere points to the importance of criminal justice sanctions for serious and escalating violence (Fagan 1989; 1992; Ford 1991a, b). Research shows that, while programmes based on voluntary participation may be worthwhile for a small number of men – the most highly motivated – they usually have high rates of attrition and may send unfortunate messages regarding violence (Gondolf and Foster 1991). Those who run programmes in North America report that men who enter voluntary counselling because they want their partners to return or because they fear they will leave them, drop out once they have secured their 'co-operation'. The process of being arrested, charged, prosecuted and sentenced to one of the programmes apparently provided a lever, an 'incentive' for men interviewed in this evaluation study to participate in CHANGE and the LDVPP. So too, did the fear of an escalation of sanctions. It should be noted that, through weekly attendance at group sessions, recounting of violent events, and self-monitoring of current behaviour, the men's programmes not only provide 'treatment' and re-education but also constitute a form of social control and 'surveillance'. Practices such as these reinforce the view that wrongs have been committed and that arrest and prosecution are consequential. Locating programmes for men within the criminal justice system creates clear costs for using violence, and these and other costs are reinforced within the context of programme participation. Abuser programmes reinforce these messages and offer positive alternatives for violent men.

Communitarian and some feminist commentators reject the use of criminal justice interventions in domestic violence, including court mandated abuser programmes. We would suggest that solutions to men's violence will not be associated with efforts that seek to deflect or divert men away from civic and criminal justice interventions, nor will such efforts 'empower' women in their struggles to end the violence and coercion they experience. Certainly, criminal justice intervention and court mandated abuser programmes are not a panacea, but we suggest that the way forward is to treat violence against women as a crime and to follow the principles set out many years ago by those who created the Duluth intervention project. These principles and the practices associated with them attempt to shift responsibility for dealing with the violence away from the victim and onto the state, to hold men accountable for their violence and to provide support for women in their efforts to obtain safety and security through civil and criminal justice interventions.

References

Adams, D. (1988) 'Treatment models of men who batter: a pro-feminist analysis', in Yllo, K. and Bograd, M. (eds) *Feminist Perspectives on Wife Abuse*, Beverly Hills: Sage, pp. 176–97.

Barron, J. (1990) *Not Worth the Paper . . .?*, Bristol: Women's Aid Federation England.

Berk, R. A. (1993) 'We can do no better than arrest', in Gelles, R. and Loseke, D. R. (eds) *Current Controversies on Family Violence*, London: Sage.

Berk, R. A., Campbell, A., Klap, R. and Western, B. (1992) 'The deterrent effect of arrest in incidents of domestic violence: a Bayesian analysis of four field experiments', *American Sociological Review*, 57, 698–708.

Bersani, C., Chen, H. J. and Denton, R. (1988) 'Spouse abusers and court-mandated treatment', *Crime and Justice*, Vol. 11, 43–59.

Bolton, F. G. and Bolton, S. R. (1987) *Working With Violent Families*, Newbury Park, CA: Sage.

Braithwaite, J. and Daly, K. (1994) 'Masculinities, violence and communitarian control', in Newburn, T. and Stanko, E. A. (eds) *Just Boys Doing the Business?*, London: Routledge, pp. 189–213.

Buel, S. M. (1988) 'Mandatory arrest for domestic violence', *Harvard Women's Law Journal*, 11: 213–26.

Buzawa, E. and Buzawa, C. (eds) (1992) *Domestic Violence: The Changing Criminal Justice Response*, Westport, Conn: Auburn House.

Cavanagh, K., Dobash, R. E. and Dobash, R. P. (2001). 'Remedial work': Men's strategic responses to their violence against intimate female partners', *Sociology*, in press.

Chaudhuri, M. and Daly, K. (1992) 'Do restraining orders help? Battered women's experiences with male violence and legal process', in Buzawa, E. and Buzawa, C. (eds) *Domestic Violence: The Changing Criminal Justice Response*, Westport, Conn: Auburn House.

Crenshaw, K. W. (1993) 'Race, gender, and violence against women,' in Minow, M. (ed.) *Family Matters: Readings on Family Lives and the Law*, New York: New Press.

Davidson, H. S. (1985) 'Community control without state control: issues surrounding feminist and abolitionist approaches to violence against women', *Canadian Criminology Forum*, Vol. 7, no. 2, 92–101.

Deschner, J. P. (1984) *The Hitting Habit: Anger Control for Battering Couples*, New York: Free Press.

Dobash, R. E. and Dobash, R. P. (1979) *Violence Against Wives*, New York: Free Press.

Dobash, R. E. and Dobash, R. P. (1983) 'The context specific approach', in Finkelhor, D. et al. (eds) *The Dark Side of Families*, Beverly Hills, CA: Sage, pp. 261–76.

Dobash, R. E. and Dobash, R. P. (1984) 'The nature and antecedents of violent events', *British Journal of Criminology*, Vol. 24, 269–88.

Dobash, R. E. and Dobash, R. P. (1992) *Women, Violence and Social Change*, London and New York: Routledge.

Dobash, R. E. and Dobash, R. P. (1999) 'Violent men and violent contexts', in Dobash, R. E. and Dobash, R. P. (eds) *Rethinking Violence Against Women*, Beverly Hills, CA: Sage, pp. 141–68.

Dobash, R. E. and Dobash, R. P. (2000) 'Evaluating criminal justice interventions for domestic violence', *Crime and Delinquency*, Vol. 46, no. 2, pp. 252–70.

Dobash, R. P., Dobash, R. E., Cavanagh, K. and Lewis, R. (1995) 'Evaluating programmes for violent men', in Dobash, R. E., Dobash, R. P. and Noaks, L. (eds) *Gender and Crime*, Cardiff: University of Wales Press.

Dobash, R. P., Dobash, R. E., Cavanagh, K. and Lewis, R. (1999a) 'A research evaluation of programmes for violent men', *Journal of Social Policy*, Vol. 28, no. 2, pp. 205–33.

Dobash, R. P., Dobash, R. E., Cavanagh, K. and Lewis, R. (1999b) 'Separate and intersecting realities: a comparison of men's and women's accounts of violence against women', *Violence Against Women*, Vol. 4, no. 4, pp. 382–414.

Dobash, R. P., Dobash, R. E., Cavanagh, K. and Lewis, R. (2000) *Changing Violent Men*, Beverly Hills, CA: Sage.

Dobash, R. P., Dobash, R. E., Wilson, M. and Daly, M. (1992) 'The myth of sexual symmetry in marital violence', *Social Problems*, Vol. 39, pp. 402–32.

Dunford, F. W., Huizinga, D. and Elliott, D. (1990) 'The role of arrest in domestic assault', *Criminology*, Vol. 28, no. 2, pp. 183–206.

Dutton, D. G. (1995) *The Domestic Assault of Women: Psychological and Criminal Justice Perspectives*, Vancouver: UBC Press.

Edleson, J. L. (1984) 'Working with men who batter', *Social Work*, Vol. 29, no. 3, 237–42.

Edwards, S. S. M. (1989) *Policing Domestic Violence*, London: Sage.

Eisikovits, Z. and Edleson, J. (1989) 'Intervening with men who batter: a critical review of the literature', *Social Science Review*, Vol. 37, no. 3, 385–414.

Elbow, M. (1977) 'Theoretical considerations of violent marriages', *Social Casework*, Vol. 58, 515–26.

Emerge (1981) *Emerge: A Men's Counselling Service on Domestic Violence*, Boston: Emerge.

Fagan, J. (1989) 'Cessation of family violence: deterrence and dissuasion', in Ohlin, L. and Tonry, M. (eds) *Family Violence*, Vol. 11, Crime and Justice Series, Chicago: The University of Chicago Press, pp. 377–425.

Fagan, J. (1992) 'The social control of spouse assault', in Adler, F. and Laufer, W. (eds) *Advances in Criminological Theory, Volume 4*, New Brunswick: Transaction Publishers, pp. 187–235.

Faragher, T. (1985) 'The police response to violence against women in the home', in Pahl, J. (ed.) *Private Violence and Public Policy*, London: Routledge.

Finn, P. and Colson, S. (1990) *Civil Protection Orders: Legislation, Current Court Practice, and Enforcement*, Washington DC: National Institute of Justice, US Department of Justice.

Flanzer, J. (1982) 'Alcohol and family violence: double trouble', in Roy, M. (ed.) *The Abusive Partner: An Analysis of Domestic Battering*, New York: Van Nostrand Reinhold, pp. 136–42.

Ford, D. A. (1991a) 'The preventive impact of policies for prosecuting wife batterers', in Buzawa, E. and Buzawa, C. (eds) *Domestic Violence: The Changing Criminal Justice Response*, Westport, Conn: Greenwood.

Ford, D. A. (1991b) 'Prosecution as a victim power resource: a note on empowering women in violent conjugal relationships', *Law and Society Review*, Vol. 25, 313–34.

Ganley, A. L. (1987) 'Perpetrators of domestic violence: an overview of counseling the court-mandated client', in Sonkin, D. J. (ed.) *Domestic Violence on Trial*, New York: Springer, pp. 155–73.

Geller, J. (1982) 'Conjoint therapy: staff training and treatment of the abuser and the abuse', in Roy, M. (ed.) *The Abusive Partner: An Analysis of Domestic Battering*, New York: Van Nostrand Reinhold pp. 201–5.

Gilligan, C. (1982) *In A Different Voice*, Cambridge: Harvard University Press.

Gondolf, E. W. (1991) 'A victim based assessment of court mandated counseling for batterers', *Criminal Justice Review*, 16, 214–26.

Gondolf, E. W. (1997) 'Batterer programs: what we know and need to know', *Journal of Interpersonal Violence*, Vol. 12, 63–74.

Gondolf, E. W. (1999) A comparison of four batterer intervention systems: do court referral, program length, and services matter?, *Journal of Interpersonal Violence*, Vol. 14, 41–61.

Gondolf, E. W. and Foster, R. A. (1991) 'Pre-programme attrition in batterer programmes', *Journal of Family Violence*, Vol. 6, 337–50.

Grace, S. (1995) *Policing Domestic Violence in the 1990s*, Home Office Research Study No. 139, London: HMSO.

Grau, J., Fagan, J. and Wexler, S. (1985) 'Restraining orders for battered women: issues of access and efficacy', *Women and Politics*, Vol. 4, no. 3, 13–28.

Hague, G. and Malos, E. (1994) *Domestic Violence, Action for Change*, Cheltenham: New Clarion Press.

Hamm, M. S. and Kite, J. C. (1991) 'The role of offender rehabilitation in family violence policy: the batterers anonymous experiment', *Criminal Justice Review*, 16, 227–48.

Harris, M. K. (1987) 'Moving into the new millennium: toward a feminist vision of justice', *The Prison Journal*, Vol. 67, 27–38.

Heise, L. L. (with Pitanguy, J. and Germain, A) (1994) *Violence Against Women: The Hidden Health Burden*, Washington, DC: The World Bank.

Homer, M., Leonard, A. and Taylor, P. (1984) *Private Violence: Public Shame*, Cleveland, England: Cleveland Refuge and Aid for Women and Children.

Horton, A. L., Simonidis, K. M. and Simonidis, L. L. (1987) 'Legal remedies for spousal abuse: victim characteristics, expectations and satisfaction', *Journal of Family Violence*, Vol. 2, no. 3, 265–79.

Hoyle, C. and Sanders, A. (2000) 'Police response to domestic violence: from victim choice to victim empowerment', *The British Journal of Criminology*, Vol. 40, no. 1, 14–36.

Keilitz, S. L., Hannaford, P. L. and Efkeman, H. S. (1996) *Civil Protection Orders: The Benefits and Limitations for Victims of Domestic Violence*, Executive Summary, Washington, DC: National Center for State and National Courts.

Lewis, R., Dobash, R. E., Dobash, R. P. and Cavanagh, K. (2000) 'Protection, prevention, rehabilitation or justice?: women's use of the law to challenge domestic violence', *International Review of Victimology*, Special Issue on the Law and Domestic Violence Vol. 7, 1–3, 179–205.

Longino, H. E. (1994) 'Essential tensions – phase two: feminist, philosophical, and social studies of science', in Antony, L. M. and Witt, C. (eds) *A Mind of One's Own: Feminist Essays on Reason and Objectivity*, Oxford: Westview Press, pp. 257–72.

Mettger, Z. (1981) 'Help for men who batter: an overview of issues and programs', *Response*, Vol. 5/6, 1–2.

Morran, D. and Wilson, M. (1994) 'Confronting domestic violence: an innovative criminal justice response', in Duff, A., Marshall, S., Dobash, R. E. and Dobash, R. P. (eds) *Penal Theory and Practice: Tradition and Innovation in Criminal Justice*, Manchester: Manchester University Press, pp. 216–30.

Morran, D. and Wilson, M. (1997) *Men Who Are Violent to Women: A Groupwork Practice Manual*, Lyme Regis, Dorset: Russell House.

Mullender, A. (1996) *Rethinking Domestic Violence*, London: Routledge.

Neidig, P. H. (1984) 'Women's shelters, men's collectives and other issues in the field of spouse abuse', *Victimology*, Vol. 9, no. 3/4, 464–76.

Pence, E. (1983) 'The Duluth Domestic Abuse Intervention Project', *Hamline Law Review*, Vol. 6, no. 2, 247–75.

Pence, E. (with Duprey, M., Paymar M. and McDonnell, C.) (1989) *Criminal Justice Response to Domestic Assault Cases: A Guide for Policy Development* (revised), Duluth, MN: Domestic Abuse Intervention Project.

Pence, E. and Paymar, M. (1993) *Education Groups for Men Who Batter: The Duluth Model*, New York: Springer Publishing.

Pence, E. and Shepard, M. (1988) 'Integrating feminist theory and practice: the challenge of the battered women's movement', in Yllo, K. and Bograd, M. (eds) *Feminist Perspectives on Wife Abuse*, London: Sage, pp. 282–98.

Powers, R. J. and Kutash, I. L. (1982) 'Alcohol, drugs, and partner abuse', in Roy, M. (ed.) *The Abusive Partner: An Analysis of Domestic Battering*, New York: Van Nostrand Reinhold, pp. 39–75.

Ptacek, J. (1988) 'Why do men batter their wives?', in Yllo, K. and Bograd, M. (eds) *Feminist Perspectives on Wife Abuse*, Beverly Hills: Sage, pp. 133–57.

Ptacek, J. (1999) *Battered Women in the Court Room: The Power of Judicial Response*, Boston: Northeastern University Press.

Schlesinger, L. B., Benson, M. and Zornitzer, M. (1982) 'Classification of violent behavior for the purposes of treatment planning: a three-pronged approach', in Roy, M. (ed.) *The Abusive Partner: An Analysis of Domestic Battering*, New York: Van Nostrand Reinhold, pp. 148–69.

Scourfield, J. B. (1995) *Changing Men: UK Agencies Working With Men Who Are Violent Towards Their Women Partners*, Monograph 141, Social Work Monographs, University of East Anglia: Norwich.

Scourfield, J. B. and Dobash, R. P. (1999) 'Programmes for violent men: recent developments in the UK', *The Howard Journal*, Vol. 38, no. 2, 128–43.

Shapiro, R. J. (1984) 'Therapy with violent families', in Saunders, S., Anderson, A. M. and Hart, C. A. (eds) *Violent Individuals and Families*, Springfield, Ill: Charles C. Thomas, pp. 112–36.

Sherman, L. W. (1992) *Policing Domestic Violence: Experiments and Dilemmas*, New York: Free Press.

Sherman, L. W. and Berk, B. A. (1984) 'The specific deterrent effects of arrest for domestic assault', *American Sociological Review*, Vol. 49, 261–72.

Shupe, A., Stacey, W. A. and Hazelwood, L. R. (1987) *Violent Men, Violent Couples*, Lexington, MA: Lexington.

Sinclair, H. (n.d.) *The MAWS Men's Program and the Issue of Male-Role Violence Against Women, A Training Manual*, Marin, CA: Marin Abused Women Services.

Smart, C. (1990) *Feminism and the Power of Law*, London: Routledge.

Stark, E. (1993) 'Mandatory arrest of batterers. A reply to its critics', *American Behavioral Scientist*, Vol. 36, no. 5, 651–80.

Straus, M. A. and Gelles, R. J. (eds) (1990) *Physical Violence in American Families*, New Brunswick: Transaction Publishers.

Stubbs, J. (1997) 'Shame, defiance, and violence against women: a critical analysis of 'communitarian' conferencing', in Cook, S. and Bessant, J. (eds) *Women's Encounters With Violence: Australian Experiences*, Thousand Oaks, CA: Sage.

Tavuchis, N. (1991) *Mea Culpa: A Sociology of Apology and Reconciliation*, Stanford, CA: Stanford University Press.

Tolman, R. M. and Bennett, L. W. (1990) 'A review of quantitative research on men who batter', *Journal of Interpersonal Violence*, Vol. 5, 87–118.

Weitzman, J. and Dreen, K. (1982) 'Wife beating: a view of the marital dyad', *Social Casework*, Vol. 63, no. 5, 259–65.

Wilson, M. and Daly, M. (1998) 'Lethal and nonlethal violence against wives and the evolutionary psychology of male sexual proprietariness', in Dobash, R. E. and Dobash, R. P. (eds) *Rethinking Violence Against Women*, Thousand Oaks, CA: Sage.

Wright, S. (1995) 'The role of the police in combating domestic violence', in Dobash, R. E., Dobash, R. P. and Noaks, L. (eds) *Gender and Crime*, Cardiff, Wales: University of Wales Press, pp. 410–28.

17 The Emerge program

David Adams

Until Emerge's founding in 1977 as the world's first batterer intervention program, notions of men taking responsibility for their own and each other's violence toward women were untested. The initial emphasis of the battered women's movement had been on calling attention to domestic violence, re-defining it as a crime against women, and promoting safety and justice for victims. But many victim advocates argued that men must join women in this fight, not only to communicate the message that violence against women was a human rights issue of equal importance to men but also that men had a unique role to play in educating and confronting men who batter. Ideally, men would join this fight without usurping women's leadership or undermining the feminist analysis that battering is a problem with roots deeply embedded in sexism and patriarchy. Historically, there was good reason for such concerns given the male domination in previous social change movements.

Emerge was established at the behest of women who had set up the first bat-tered women's programs in Boston. Hotline staff at Transition House and Respond were receiving an increasing number of calls from batterers; some requesting information about their partner's whereabouts and others requesting help for their violence. Since it was not their mission to work with batterers, staff from both programs publicized a request for men to establish a program for batterers. Nearly all of the ten men who attended the first planning sessions of Emerge were friends or relatives of workers at Transition House or Respond. While most of the founders were social workers or counselors, others included a teacher, a community organizer, a lawyer and a cab driver.

A year of study

After several meetings with battered women's advocates, it was decided that prior to formulating a counseling program for batterers, Emerge should devote 6–12 months to learning about domestic violence. A review of the literature revealed that very little had been written about domestic violence. Several art-icles and books had been published which specifically addressed men who batter but nearly all put forth theories which mitigated men's responsibility for viol-ence. In 'The Wifebeater's Wife: A Study of Family Interaction', published in

1964, the authors concluded that the majority of the 37 battering husbands they interviewed were 'provoked' or otherwise incited to become violent by 'manipulative', 'domineering', 'irritating' or 'sexually frigid' wives (Snell *et al.* 1964).

At least three separate articles about batterers were published in 1977 and all three advanced the notion that batterers were not fully responsible for their violence. Faulk (1977) found that the most prevalent type of batterer was a 'dependent, passive' type who 'characteristically gave a good deal of concern and time trying to please and pacify his wife, who tended to be querulous and demanding'. Geller and Walsh (1977) concluded that battering will not stop 'unless both partners are involved in counseling'. Shainess (1977) asserted that men 'lash out from frustration' and typically exhibit 'poor ability to tolerate frustration'.

By 1979 however, several published articles legitimated the view of battered women's advocates that men's violence toward women was not irrational behavior but served as an instrument of control (Martin 1976; Warrior 1976). In studying actual cases of domestic violence, Dobash and Dobash (1979) concluded that the use of violence against wives is 'an attempt to bring about a desired state of affairs. . . . When a husband attacks his wife he is either chastising her for challenging his authority or for failing to live up to his expectations or attempting to discourage future unacceptable behavior.'

As edifying as these readings were, the most critical sources of information for the founders of Emerge were battered women themselves. Staff at the three battered women's shelters in the Boston area encouraged victims to speak to Emerge about their experiences, and dozens did so. From this testimony arose an understanding of battering as a pattern of coercive behavior which included physical, sexual, psychological, verbal and economic abuse. Just as compelling as the actual abuse which the women related was the 're-victimization' they'd experienced at the hands of police, courts, medical centers and social service agencies. From this testimony, it became apparent that, by ignoring domestic violence and by discouraging or blaming victims who sought help, mainstream institutions colluded with batterers. Findings of social and cultural collusion bolstered the feminist analysis that the sexist attitudes and expectations of individual men who batter merely reflected those of mainstream institutions (Schechter 1982).

The Emerge group model

The originators of Emerge were unified in the belief that battering men should be educated to accept complete responsibility for their violence and to learn non-violent and non-coercive behavior. However, there were no existing models for how to do so. This notwithstanding, Emerge's conception of battering as a learned behavior, as opposed to a mental illness, suggested several key features to the developing model. As can be seen from the following description of these characteristics, the Emerge model has evolved considerably over the past 23 years. Due to space limitations, the following is not intended as a complete description but rather as a selective summary of key features.

Group education

While individual psychotherapy tended to reinforce the perception of domestic violence as a private and essentially psychological problem, Emerge believed that a group format would best promote recognition of battering as a socially-learned behavior. Only in groups could an individual man who batters recognize that he was not the only one with the problem. A group process would better enable men to critically re-examine common attitudes and expectations which lead to violence toward women. Emerge also believed that a group format was essential because of the opportunity it provided for peer support and confrontation. The group model had been successfully employed in addressing other behaviors, such as alcoholism and gambling, which had been re-defined as socially undesirable.

Emerge believed that an educational approach would be more familiar and less threatening to the majority of men than a psycho-therapeutic one. While very few men participate in therapy, nearly all have attended school. In school, it is also more readily accepted that there are concrete standards for advancing or failing to advance, whereas criteria for advancement in therapy tends to be more vague and subjective.

Contact with victims

From the beginning, Emerge staff have attempted telephone contact with each of our client's victims and/or current partners. The purpose of this contact was to:

1   inform victims about services for battered women, including emergency shelter, support groups, child visitation centers, legal options, and other services;
2   inform victims about the Emerge program, including the limitations of batterer intervention programs. Information about the program is given to counteract the tendency of many batterers to misrepresent the goals or requirements of the program to their partners. Information about the limitations of batterer interventions is given to minimize any false hopes victims may have about their partner's likelihood of changing;
3   request information from the victim about her partner's past and current patterns and types of abuse. This information helps Emerge to determine the level of dangerousness of each client and the extent to which the batterer is minimizing his abuse.

Following the initial contact, which is made by a battered women's advocate, follow-up contacts are made by group leaders to solicit her feedback about the batterer's progress. To minimize any risk of retribution, victims are assured confidentiality, not only in terms of what Emerge reports to the batterer but also in terms of what Emerge reports to the court. Only information that the victim wishes to be repeated to her partner is repeated. Victims' wishes about this vary from wanting nothing revealed to her partner, to having bits of information repeated, to having her perspective summarized by the group leaders.

Regardless of how much, if any, is revealed to the batterer, information from victims guides Emerge's work with men. Emerge group leaders attempt follow-up telephone contact with each client's partner every eight weeks. However, victims are encouraged to initiate contact if there are problems, and many do so. This continued contact with victims has several benefits. First, victim contact has been found to be validating and empowering to victims. In 1993, Emerge conducted a survey of 20 women whose partners had attended Emerge at least two years previously. The purpose of this survey was to learn more about the impact of partner contacts on partners. All 20 of the women interviewed said that the partner contact had been helpful. The most frequently cited benefits were that it made women feel more safe, it helped them to recognize that the abuse wasn't their fault, it enabled them to better recognize on-going abuse, and that it generally felt validating of their perspective. Many women attributed their decision to seek support services to encouragement they received from Emerge. Many of the women who had left their partners said that Emerge's feedback that their partners were not making sufficient progress was instrumental in their decision making. Others said that just the process of being asked about various kinds of abuse by their partner helped them to become more critically aware of abusive behavior and to have higher expectations of their partners.

The second benefit of contact with victims has been the perspective it brings to group leaders at Emerge. Victims' accounts of abuse, as well as their overall perspective, typically varies a great deal from those of the batterer. In groups, batterers naturally attempt to present information about their relationships in a manner which arouses sympathy from others. Most batterers come across as quite charming and likeable and it is therefore easy for those who have not witnessed these men's violence to forget, downplay, or excuse their violent side (Adams 1989). For this reason, group leaders at Emerge have found periodic contact with victims to be invaluable as a way of continually keeping the victim's perspective in mind and minimizing the batterers ability to manipulate sentiments in the group.

Male-female co-leadership

To promote the idea of men's responsibility for change, the groups that Emerge originally provided were co-facilitated by men. This emphasized Emerge's belief that non-battering men have much in common with battering men since they share a common social and cultural heritage. Since all men grew up in a sexist and patriarchal society, no men were completely free of sexist beliefs or controlling behaviors. Controlling behavior was conceptualized as a continuum which ranged from physical violence and intimidation to overt psychological and economic abuse to more subtle forms of psychological control such as 'interrupting', 'not listening', 'claiming the truth' and 'withholding of affection'. Initially, male group leaders at Emerge disclosed their own controlling behaviors as a means of promoting trust and modelling critical self-examination. Perhaps naively, Emerge group leaders sought to create an alternative male peer culture in which battering men would repudiate abusive and competitive behaviors, develop less rigid sex roles and develop greater empathy and respect for women. Group members were encouraged to acknowledge and express feelings other than anger to their partners as well as to each other. Men were asked to recognize ways in which they expected unilateral emotional support, domestic services, childcare and respect from their partners. Finally, men were supported and confronted to give up controlling behaviors and to strive for equality in their relationships.

Despite the theoretical merits of the male co-facilitation model, Emerge found that in actual practice, it was difficult to assess men's progress when both group leaders were men. Consistently, battering men exhibit different, more respectful behavior toward men than toward women. Many men who participated exceptionally well in groups were not exhibiting the same positive behaviors toward their partners. There was a growing perception that battering men's underlying negative attitudes toward women were not being recognized in group due to their more positive interactions with other men in the groups. As a result, group members as well as group leaders tended to over-estimate men's progress. Moreover, there was a growing concern that male group leaders could not sufficiently represent women's perspective. Despite the good intentions of the male co-facilitators, women's perspective about men's attitudes and behavior was being replaced by men's interpretation of that perspective. In too many instances, this interpretation was wrong.

Because of these problems, Emerge began experimenting with male-female group co-facilitation in 1987. The most immediate finding was that battering men responded very differently to their female group leaders. Men were much more likely to interrupt, challenge, and ignore their female co-leaders; even when female group leaders were making exactly the same points made by their male counterparts (Cayouette 1996). This differential reaction to female group leaders was particularly pronounced in the early stages of the program. Some group members literally could not let their female group leaders finish sentences. Others would avoid eye contact with female group leaders and address their comments solely to the male group leader. At worst, some men would become extremely belligerent toward women group leaders while others would communicate sexual interest in their female co-leaders.

The clear advantage of having female group leaders was that battering men's true attitudes and behaviors toward women were more likely to be revealed. The addition of female co-leaders at Emerge provoked a re-examination about the role of male group leaders and which behaviors should be modeled for abusive men. Whereas previously, male co-leaders modeled a more sensitive kind of man, this modeling occurred in a setting devoid of women. When groups were co-facilitated by a man and woman, however, a very different kind of modeling was required of male group leaders. Male co-leaders were now modeling how to share leadership, solve problems, negotiate time and co-operate with women. With this understanding, male-female co-facilitation became one of the cornerstones of the Emerge model. Today, nearly all groups are co-led by a man and a woman.

Promoting men's responsibility

By trial and error, Emerge sought to find the right balance of support and confrontation which would provide the maximum motivation for battering men to abandon abusive behaviors and to treat their partners with empathy and respect. It became clear early on that support and encouragement alone would not induce battering men to give up abusive behaviors. In fact, supportive encouragement, without confrontation and consequences, seemed only to reinforce battering men's self-centered expectations and abusive behaviors, given that most already felt entitled to unilateral support and appreciation from their partners. Creating a democratic group in which group leaders modeled self-disclosure and non-coercive forms of interaction also seemed to backfire. When group leaders called attention to on-going abuse, group members would manipulatively accuse them of being 'hypercritical', 'judgmental' or 'controling'.

Ultimately, it was found that education for batterers must be accompanied by consistent limits and consequences for on-going abuse. There must also be clear consequences for such other common behaviors as poor attendance, insufficient or disruptive group participation, or failure to acknowledge abuse. Without consistent standards, it was found that groups operated at the level of the lowest common denominator. In the first ten years of Emerge's existence, virtually none of its clients were court-mandated. Without court sanctions, most battering men failed to remain in the program long enough to achieve lasting benefits. While some completed the program and appeared to do well, others made only cosmetic changes which seemed primarily designed to manipulate their partners into continuing the relationship or discontinuing any legal recourses. Presently, about 75 per cent of Emerge's clients are court-mandated. Approximately half complete the program which has a minimal duration of 40 sessions. To be eligible to complete the program, clients must have ceased all violent or intimidating behaviors for a minimum of 20 weeks. Clients must also have accepted responsibility for past violence. Accepting responsibility is operationally defined in the following ways:

1   stop minimizing your violence;
2   stop blaming your partner for your violence or for any steps she took in response to your violence;
3   recognize how your abuse has adversely affected your partner and children.

Approximately one-quarter of Emerge clients who have attended the minimum 40 sessions are found to have made insufficient progress in one or more of the above goals and therefore additional time is recommended to the court. As will be discussed in more detail later, the court's response to this recommendation varies from court to court and judge to judge.

Besides specifying that men who attend Emerge must become non-violent and accept responsibility for their violence, Emerge also requires men to recognize a responsibility to each other in their group participation. Men are expected to hold each other to the goals and higher standards that are specified by the program. Support for excuses or lesser levels of abuse are not permitted. Each man is expected to establish, with the group's endorsement, individual goals which relate to his past and current patterns of abuse. Goal-setting for each group member is a process which is done in the group. Prior to establishing individual goals in the group, each man is expected to do a relationship history in which he describes, in sequential fashion, each of his relationships with women. This history includes a detailed account of his abusive behavior toward past partners as well as his current or most recent partner. After hearing this history, fellow group members are asked to help the individual to establish goals which relate specifically to his past abuse. Examples of these goals are:

1   I will stop all jealous and possessive behavior toward Jane;
2   I will listen to Jane;
3   I will respect Jane's opinions;
4   I will take equal responsibility for the care of my children;
5   I will not pressure Jane in any way to drop the restraining order or to reconcile with me.

Once an individual's goals are established, they are posted on the wall of the group room during sessions. This gives each group member an easy point of reference for their week-to-week feedback to each other. Feedback is intended to help group members to recognize any on-going abusive or controling interactions with their partners or children and to help them to assess the degree to which they are adhering to their posted goals (Emerge 2000). In groups, Emerge clients are required to refer to their partners by name rather than as 'my wife', or 'my partner'. This serves to promote greater recognition of their partners as people as opposed to possessions.

Emerge has found that battering men do not give each other constructive feedback as a matter of course. Without active engineering on the part of the program, battering men's feedback to each other tends to be superficial at best, and at worst, is reinforcing of excuses for abuse. Therefore, expectations of active and constructive group participation are clearly articulated and enforced. Beyond this, group members are continually given feedback about the quality of their feedback to others.

Ideally, this feedback comes from fellow group members as well as group leaders, as illustrated by the following example.

GEORGE: I had a close call the other day. Mary did something stupid, really stupid. But it didn't get physical. I guess the program is working for me.

JIM (GROUP LEADER): Can you explain what happened?

GEORGE: Well, Mary blew a tire on our car by driving it against the sidewalk. I got a little mad about it but it was contained.

JANICE (GROUP LEADER): What did you do?

GEORGE: Nothing. I was quiet. She could tell I was angry.

JANICE: Before you were quiet, did you say anything?

GEORGE: I might have yelled a little. Yeah, I might have swore a little. Not at her, just out of frustration.

JIM: Does anyone in the group have any feedback to George about this?

MARTY: I can understand your feelings, man. Tires are expensive.

JANICE: Before we continue with George, does anyone have any feedback to Marty about what he just said?

PHIL: Man, you really threw out the life preserver!

CARL: Yeah, I think you really let George off the hook. I mean, he's still yelling and swearing at her, isn't he?

ANDY: It was an accident! I don't see how you [to George] can get mad about an accident.

JIM: Yes, but before we get back on what George did, let's stay with Marty a bit. Let me ask the group, how do you think Marty's feedback would influence George?

ANDY: Oh it would make George feel more justified in the future.

JANICE: Justified about what?

ANDY: About yelling and carrying on about nothing. Just an innocent mistake!

CARL: And blaming her.

JIM: Is George still being abusive to Mary?

PHIL: Oh yes, I'd say so.

JIM: Did Marty recognize this?

MARTY: Well, now maybe but I just wanted George to know I understood his feelings.

JANICE: But was Marty helping George?

PHIL: No!

ANDY: No way!

JIM: Do you have anything to say to George now, Marty?

MARTY: I'm sorry I didn't jump all over you, man!

(Laughter from group)

JANICE: Seriously?

MARTY: Yeah, I guess I let you [George] down . . . by not expecting more.

Though the focus eventually shifted back to analyzing George's actions, the initial focus of group leaders was on Marty who was the newest member of the group. Such feedback is essential in order to help group members to clarify how they can best help each other. When confrontation comes solely from the group leaders, group members settle into a passive role and fail to internalize the values and higher standards of the program. In the case above, the value being articulated was acceptance and respect for one's partner; a higher standard than simply refraining from physical abuse.

Maintaining high standards also helps to avoid manipulation and bargaining by men who batter. Men who batter, much like substance abusers, will often attempt to bargain with others (particularly their partners and their counselors) to retain as much of their abuse as possible (Adams 1989). Bargaining often takes the form of the batterer making adjustments in his abusive behavior rather than abandoning it altogether. By making adjustments rather than more qualitative changes in behavior and attitude, batterers are learning to become 'better batterers'. Group leaders sometimes become unwittingly complicit with this manipulation when they praise clients who have apparently 'taken a step in the right direction' by exhibiting a lesser level of abuse.

Emerge's overarching expectation of its clients is that they treat their partners and ex-partners with empathy and respect. Simply abstaining from abuse does not necessarily communicate either empathy or respect. As operationally defined by Emerge, empathy means recognizing and caring about the feelings and concerns of one's partner or ex-partner. Respect means recognizing her independence and rights, including the right to self-determination. From Emerge's perspective, having empathy and respect for one's partner or ex-partner does not mean that the batterer must love his partner or remain involved with her. Practically speaking, empathy is expected more for those men who are still involved with their partners, whether they are living together or living apart but still co-parenting their children. Men who have more limited contact are expected to minimally treat their partners with civility and respect, regardless of whatever disagreements or differences exist. Realistically, the development of empathy and respect for one's partner or ex-partner are not requirements for program completion since feelings and attitudes cannot be dictated. Rather, empathy and respect are aspirational goals which are articulated throughout the program. In theory, those clients who learn to respect, rather than to merely tolerate others, seem most likely to maintain any changes they've made while in the program.

Documentation of abuse

Various outcome studies of batterer intervention programs have found that, on average, approximately half of batterers complete batterer intervention programs (Tolman and Bennett 1990; Gondolf 1997). And even though program completers have a lower rate of recidivism compared to non-completers, substantial numbers still revert to physical and psychological abuse. Recognizing these realities, Emerge views its primary mission as building accountability, as opposed to changing batterers. While change is clearly possible for some batterers, accountability is potentially achievable for all batterers, independently of their ability or willingness to change.

For this reason, Emerge attaches a great deal of importance to documentation of men's violence as well as documentation of non-compliance. For all its clients, independently of whether they are court-referred, Emerge maintains written documentation of the abusive behavior that they acknowledge as well as violence that has been reported by sources other than the victim, such as police reports, criminal records and child welfare records. It is not uncommon for batterers to disavow any violence once they have completed or been terminated from a batterer intervention program; even violence which they had previously acknowledged while attending the program. The written record is made available to all victims and partners upon their request. Women whose partners are contesting divorce, seeking child custody, or seeking to gain more liberal child visitations have found Emerge's records to be very helpful since these narrative reports also identify any problems that Emerge has identified in terms of the batterer's level of dangerousness, acceptance or responsibility, parenting, abuse of substances, or mental health problems. These reports are often the only documentation of the batterer's problems which is independent of the victim's allegations.

Developing cultural competence

Emerge was one of the first batterer intervention programs to provide services in Spanish and was the first to develop services in Vietnamese and Khmer. Emerge also provides African-American men the option of being in all-African-American groups during the second phase of the program. Reflecting the racial diversity of its clients, half of Emerge's group leaders are African-American, Latino or Asian. Aside from its language-specific groups, all groups at Emerge are racially-mixed. Since 1996, Emerge has provided groups for lesbians who batter. Emerge is currently developing a program for gay men who batter.

When establishing services for previously unserved communities, Emerge has undertaken to learn as much as possible about the new communities. This learning process is one aspect of developing 'cultural competence' (Williams 1994). One useful step in this learning is the establishment of advisory groups composed of members of the new community. When developing a program for Vietnamese and Cambodian men, for instance, Emerge established an advisory group which was made up primarily of Vietnamese and Cambodian service providers and community activists. This group not only helped Emerge to develop culturally appropriate services but also assisted in recruiting bi-cultural staff, promoting the program, and developing a community education component. One key recommendation of this group was that, because older people are revered in Asian culture, group leaders should be middle-aged or older. Another cultural adaptation is that groups for Cambodian men are small, with 2–4 member each. Prior to their placement in a group, Cambodian men are seen individually for 3–5 sessions. Individual intakes and smaller groups more easily fit Asian cultural values which eschew personal disclosure to strangers or large groups. To engender community awareness and support, program staff in Emerge's Latino, Cambodian and Vietnamese programs devote half their time to community outreach and education. For instance, the Cambodian community educator is a monthly guest on a Cambodian call-in show about domestic violence which airs on a Cambodian radio program. The Vietnamese community education worker has been working with victim advocates to produce an educational video about domestic violence which is in Vietnamese.

Building accountability

Approximately half of Emerge's clients fail to complete the program. The most common reasons for program termination are continued acts of violence or harassment, poor attendance, poor levels of program participation, failure to admit abuse, or failure to take responsibility for abuse. As mentioned earlier, however, the court's response to these program terminations varies greatly. Judges who have become educated about domestic violence have routinely sanctioned men for being terminated. Common sanctions include incarceration, increasing the term of probation or requiring the perpetrator to re-enrol with the warning that additional problems will result in a jail sentence. At least one study has found that routine judicial monitoring of men's participation in batterer intervention programs increases attendance and participation and decreases recidivism (Gondolf 1998).

Presently, the biggest frustration for Emerge, as well as many other batterer intervention programs, is judges who fail to sufficiently sanction men who are terminated from batterer intervention programs. In the United States, many victim advocates and batterer intervention staff have perceived a backlash on the part of courts because of the dramatically increased numbers of domestic violence cases now coming before the court. Some judges have criticized established batterer intervention programs for terminating such a high proportion of their clients. Some of these judges have stopped referring to these established programs and started referring the majority of batterers to shorter 'anger management' programs which tend to have less stringent criteria for program completion. Most anger management programs do not make contact with victims and base their evaluations of the batterer's progress strictly on the men's group participation. To counteract this trend, many states have established certification standards for batterer intervention programs. As of March 1997, at least 24 states had certification standards and an additional 20 were in the process of creating standards. Typically, state certification standards require batterer intervention programs to have a specified minimum duration of sessions as well as specific criteria for program completion. Minimum program durations in the states with certification standards currently range from 12 sessions in Arizona to 52 in California. The majority of states which specified minimum program durations required at least 24–26 sessions (Austin and Dankwort 1997). The majority of states also specify that batterer intervention programs must attempt contact with victims, minimally to warn them of danger and refer them to services. In Massachusetts, certified programs are additionally required to advise victims of the limitations of batterer intervention programs and to inquire about the batterer's history of violence. Programs in Massachusetts as well in other states are required to maintain the confidentiality of victims.

Though state certification standards have served to improve the safety and accountability of batterer intervention programs, judges in most states are not required to refer to the certified programs. Judges in many states have continued to favor the shorter and less stringent 'anger management' programs. One of the unfortunate results of this backlash on the part of courts is that a significant number of the certified programs in the United States have ceased operations due to lack of court referrals. Other certified programs have lowered their standards in order to insure continued court referrals and co-operation. To reverse this trend, victim advocates and batterer intervention workers in many communities have forged alliances with prosecutors, probation officers, police officers, members of the media, and progressive judges to urge stronger and more consistent sanctioning of batterers. Co-ordinated community responses, pioneered in Duluth, Minnesota (see Chapter 14) and Quincy, Massachusetts, have helped to identify and to rectify gaps in the criminal justice and overall community response to domestic violence. Emerge staff participate in at least six such municipal coalitions, called 'community roundtables'. In some communities, court watch projects have served to call attention to case dismissals and otherwise weak sanctioning of batterers (NCJW 1997). Finally, a growing number of states have created state-wide commissions or task forces on domestic violence. In Massachusetts, the Governor's Commission on Domestic Violence created standards for police officers, prosecutors, child visitation centers, and batterer programs. This Commission was responsible for developing progressive new standards for police, prosecutors, child visitation centers and batterer intervention programs.

Conclusion

Since Emerge's founding in 1977, a great deal has been learned about how to educate and motivate men who batter to take responsibility for their violence. Despite this, the vast majority of batterers don't seek help unless ordered to do so, and even many of those who do remain resistant to change. Emerge, as well as the many other batterer intervention programs, will continue to tinker with and refine our approach. However, we must also recognize that batterer intervention programs, by themselves, are inherently limited in their ability to change batterers. We are still a long way away from consistent and co-ordinated social and criminal justice sanctions against men's violence toward women, despite the improvements. In recent years, domestic violence activists have had to fight to maintain these changes amid the current backlash which has been fueled in part by a more organized men's rights movement in the United States. Emerge has endeavored to use the credibility gained from working with batterers to promote increased accountability for batterers as well as justice and empowerment for victims. Without this, many men will continue to decide that the benefits of violence toward women outweigh the costs.

References

Adams, D. (1988) 'Stages of anti-sexist awareness and change for men who batter', in Dickstein, L. and Nadelson, C. (eds) *Family Violence*, Washington, DC: APPI Press, pp. 63–97.

Adams, D. (1989) 'Treatment models of men who batter: a profeminist analysis', in Yllo, K. and Bograd, M. (eds) *Feminist Perspectives on Wife Abuse*, Beverly Hills, CA: Sage, pp. 176–99.

Adams, D. (1989) 'Identifying the assaultive husband in court: you be the judge', *Boston Bar Journal*, July/August, 23–5.

Austin, J. and Dankwort, J. (1997) 'A review of standards for batterer intervention programs'. Unpublished. Available though VAW Net: Electronic resources for those working to end violence against women. www.vaw.umm.edu/bip.asp

Cayouette, S. (1996) 'Safety issues for female group leaders'. Unpublished. Available through Emerge, 2380 Massachusetts Ave, Cambridge, MA.

Dobash, R. E. and Dobash, R. P. (1979) *Violence Against Wives: a Case Against the Patriarchy*, New York: The Free Press, Macmillan.

Emerge (2000) 'Program Manual for Second Stage Groups'. Available through Emerge, 2380 Massachusetts Ave, Cambridge, MA.

Faulk, M. (1977) 'Men who assault their wives', in Roy, M. (ed.) *Battered Women: a Psycho-sociological Study of Domestic Violence*, New York: Van Nostrand Reinhold, pp. 121–2.

NCJW (National Council of Jewish Women) (1997) 'Nine steps to establishing a court watch program in your community'. Pamphlet available through The NCJW Office, 1250 Bardstown Rd, Louisville, KY 40204.

Geller, J. and Walsh, J. (1977) 'A treatment model for the abused spouse', *Victimology: An International Journal*, 2, no. 3–4, 630.

Gondolf, E. (1997) 'Multi-site evaluation of batterer intervention systems: summary of a 15–month follow-up'. Report submitted to Centers for Disease Control (CDC), Atlanta, GA (November 1997).

Gondolf, E. (1998) 'The impact of mandatory court review on batterer program compliance: an evaluation of the Pittsburg Municipal Courts and Domestic Abuse Counseling Center (DACC)'. Unpublished. Available through Mid-Atlantic Addiction Training Institute, Indiana University of Pennsylvania, Indiana PA 15705.

Martin, D. (1976) *Battered Wives*, San Francisco: Glide Publications.

Schechter, S. (1982) *Women and Male Violence: the Visions and Struggles of the Battered Women's Movement*, Boston: South End Press, pp. 19–27.

Shainess, N. (1977) 'Psychological aspects of wifebeating', in Roy, M. (ed.) *Battered Women: a Psycho-sociological Study of Domestic Violence*, New York: Van Nostrand Reinhold, pp. 114–15.

Snell, J., Rosenwald, R. and Robey, A. (1964) 'The wifebeater's wife: a study of family interaction', *Archives of General Psychiatry II* (August 1964): p. 109.

Tolman, R. and Bennett, L. (1990) 'A review of research on men who batter', *Journal of Interpersonal Violence*, Vol. 5, no. 1, March 1990, 87–118.

Warrior, B. (1976) *Wifebeating*, Somerville, MA: New England Free Press.

Williams, O. (1994) 'Partner abuse programs and cultural competence: the results of a national survey', *Violence and Victims*, 9 (3) 327–39.

18 Policing repeated domestic violence by men

A new approach*

Jalna Hanmer and Sue Griffiths

Introduction

This chapter describes a new operational model for policing domestic violence. This new operational model was developed in order to implement systematically the existing force policy on domestic violence, that is, to pro-actively respond to perpetrators and to protect those who are victimised. As responding effectively to crime and implementing Force policy on victim protection requires the prevention of future repeat offending, the model is based on the concept of 'repeat victimisation'. When repeat violence is likely, responding effectively to perpetrators incorporates both immediate and long-term safety considerations for those who are victimised. The model is, first and foremost, based on the understanding that protecting women from home-based violence requires effective responses to abusing men. Effective responses to perpetrators are central to achieving short- and long-term safety for those who are victimised by known others and for the reduction of domestic violence. The model is a strategic approach to reducing domestic violence from men to women.

This model was implemented in a West Yorkshire Police Force division over a 12–month period. It incorporated multiple interventions. The effectiveness of the model was statistically evaluated and the analysis allowed for identification of factors that influence domestic violence offending. Women who required police attendance were interviewed for their views on the interventions. Both theoretical and practical advances were made in policing domestic violence. The model and its evaluation are presented in this chapter, beginning with the development of the concept of repeat victimisation and how this theory was applied to domestic violence. The model, its operation, findings and a discussion of the relevance and importance of arrest then follow.

Repeat victimisation

The term 'repeat victimisation' comes from criminology and first appeared in the 1970s (Farrell and Pease 1993). The first use of repeat victimisation as an approach to crime reduction took place in the UK in 1986 with a burglary project in Kirkholt (Pease 1998). In 1994 the British Home Office hosted a repeat victimisation conference and in 1996 repeat victimisation was designated a key performance indicator for policing in England and Wales. It is a relatively new phenomenon in terms of tackling crime.

The idea of repeat victimisation emerged from a growing recognition that a few victims were being subjected to an inordinate proportion of crime. Using data from the 1992 British Crime Survey, Farrell and Pease (1993) demonstrated that 4 per cent of the respondents suffered 44 per cent of the offences reported. Pease (1998) went on to explore the possibility that repeat victimisation rates may vary between crime types. Using British Crime Survey data for the years 1982 to 1992, he found that 2 per cent of property crime victims (excluding car crime) suffered 41 per cent of reported crimes. This figure was worse when personal crime (primarily violent crime) was examined: 1 per cent of victims suffered 59 per cent of personal crime. From our work on the West Yorkshire police project we know that almost one-third of the perpetrators (31 per cent) generated just under two-thirds (60 per cent) of police attendances to domestic violence incidents over a 12–month period (Hanmer, Griffiths and Jerwood 1999).

As a strategy, repeat victimisation has been applied to a number of crime types. Racial crime in East London (Sampson and Phillips 1992; 1995); burglary and car crime in Kirkholt and Huddersfield (Forrester, Chatterton and Pease 1988; Anderson, Chenery and Pease 1995); and domestic violence in Merseyside and Killingbeck (Lloyd, Farrell and Pease 1994; Hanmer, Griffiths and Jerwood 1999). This approach to crime continues to be developed through the Home Office Crime Reduction Programme. New projects in response to domestic violence and rape and sexual assault by known perpetrators are being funded for 2000–2002. The Policing and Reducing Crime Unit of the Home Office is producing publications on domestic violence, both briefing notes and a book (Taylor-Browne 2001). In West Yorkshire, as part of the Home Office targeted policing initiative, the domestic violence model is currently being rolled out across all divisions and applied to two other crime types – racially motivated and homophobic crime.

There are numerous benefits to a repeat victimisation approach to crime. It concentrates resources on high crime areas; targets prolific offenders; focuses on victims at greatest risk of repeat victimisation; fuses the historically separate roles of victim support and crime prevention; improves information gathering; increases consistency in service delivery.

Applying the theory to domestic violence

The original model was a burglary and car theft project from another British town, Huddersfield. The Huddersfield project linked crime prevention with detection, deflection and victim support. It was premised on routine activity theory where crime is conceptualised as comprising three elements: victim suitability, lack of capable guardianship, and a motivated offender. Removal of one or more of these elements is theorised as the means of reducing the likelihood of repeat victimisation (Cohen and Felson 1979). The strategy used in the Huddersfield project was a three-stage model of progressive interventions. In essence, the three response types employed were to property target harden through the provision of locks, alarms and other security devices.

The West Yorkshire project built on this incremental intervention model. The emphasis on detection in the Huddersfield model shifted to the gathering of evidence as domestic violence, by definition, means the perpetrator is always known. The activity shifts to obtaining sufficient evidence to charge and convict. The target hardening approach to property in the Huddersfield project became an 'offender constraint hardening' strategy. This strategy, offender constraint hardening, is applied directly to the offender rather than indirectly to the offender's target (which, with burglary, is the property). This is achieved through the application of progressive measures that act to constrain the offender's future actions through early, direct interventions and, if persistent, through progressively increasing interventions. In the language of this theory, target hardening reduces victim suitability by demotivating the offender. Victim suitability is also reduced by direct support to those who are victimised. This dual approach increases capable guardianship; that is, the interventions of the police become more relevant and consistently applied.

Whilst police intervention forms the key element of the proposed model, the involvement of other agencies is also important. Two agency areas were identified, both statutory and voluntary welfare agencies that work with victimised women and criminal justice agencies responding to offenders. The welfare agencies provided advice and practical interventions involving legal, welfare and housing support. The criminal justice agencies included the Criminal Justice Support Unit, Crown Prosecution Service, the probation service and magistrates.

An effective repeat victimisation strategy focusing on domestic violence is not just about targeting a small number of offenders who commit a large percentage of offences. It is also about preventing escalation into repeat offending. When women or a neighbour or another person calls the police to a domestic incident, it is very unlikely that it will be the first assault or disturbance. A widely-quoted study suggests women will, on average, have been assaulted 37 times prior to the first police attendance (McGibbon, Cooper and Kelly 1989). Positive intervention by the police at the earliest possible stage is important for maximising impact and, ultimately, for reducing ongoing resource implications. Utilising resources as effectively and efficiently as possible is an ultimate aim of all organisations as these ensure better services for those who need them.

Introducing a new model of police interventions was facilitated by previous responses to domestic violence. In 1985 the West Yorkshire Police agreed to research being undertaken on policing of violence against women (Hanmer and Saunders 1987). The recommendations of the research report were accepted by the Chief Constable in 1988, when changes to policy, training, information processing on crimes against women, advice to victims, liaison with other

agencies, and the setting up of specialist units for sexual offences, domestic violence and child protection were announced (West Yorkshire Police Authority
1988). The central aims of these changes were to ensure that officers enforced
the law when an assault took place within the domestic environment exactly as
they would in the case of stranger-assaults outside the home, and to be responsive to the safety needs of women.

With the new policy came a new information database for domestic violence
incidents. The Domestic Violence Index was established in 1989 to record all
police attendances to incidents involving family members, neighbours and,
more recently, racial incidents. This database now holds ten years of information on the domestic violence histories of individuals. It records police attendances, irrespective of whether the attendances resulted in arrests or criminal
charges. With the political will to support domestic violence initiatives and an
existing infrastructure logging attendance at incidents, the West Yorkshire
domestic violence model could be both implemented and evaluated.

Central to the model was the abolition of the 'No Further Action' police
response. All police attendances during the pilot year of the project would result
in action; simply logging the attendance on the Domestic Violence Index
ensured that the case was referred and project interventions implemented. The
West Yorkshire model was aimed at women who were victimised and men who
were perpetrators, as they account for 90 per cent of domestic violence police
attendances in West Yorkshire.[1] These incidents differ in important respects
from the remaining 10 per cent, which include both same-sex violence and
women's attacks on men.

Repeat victimisation approaches to domestic violence may appear easy to
understand and to implement, but there are methodological issues to be considered:

- under-reporting of domestic violence is high – conservative estimates put it
  at 80 per cent (Mayhew, Aye Maung and Mirrlees-Black 1993);
- even when reported, there are patchy incident (rather than crime) logging
  systems in operation;
- identifying a repeat incident varies: household addresses, victim's name,
  offender's name;
- calculating the time period for repeat victimisation varies: a week, a month,
  a year;
- focusing solely or primarily on the victim means the perpetrator is never
  directly confronted with the unacceptability of his behaviour.

These issues were confronted in developing the West Yorkshire Domestic Violence Repeat Victimisation pilot project. Under-reporting is a major reason for
evaluating the success of the project in terms of prevalence, that is, the increase
or decrease in the number of women experiencing domestic violence reported
over time. Repeat victimisation incidents to the same woman attended by the
police vary from the non-criminal to the criminal. Logging systems require

standardisation and consistency in identifying attendances to domestic incidents as many domestic calls do not result in sufficient evidence to warrant arrest and subsequent action for criminal offences. Recording criminal incidents only does not permit vulnerable victims to be fully identified. Databases become more valuable over time because domestic violence may be repeated over many years. With domestic violence, all attendances should be recorded in three ways: by the household address and by the names of the victim and the offender. This is necessary because women and men may move location, and men may attack more than one woman either serially or at the same time. Being able to identify perpetrators is a vital element in providing protection to those who are victimised.

Operation of the West Yorkshire model

For this project repeat victimisation status was defined by the man's history of police attendances to *any* women recorded on the Domestic Violence Index over the previous 12 months. With repeat attendances the level of intervention moved from Level 1 to 2 to 3. Incidents where the men involved were not attended within the past year were dealt with at Level 1, with one attendance in the past year at Level 2 and with two or more attendances in the past year at Level 3. The automatic increase in interventions with each attendance was of major importance in demotivating perpetrators and in supporting victims. Increases in activity with each attendance reinforced the message that the police were both willing and able to respond to domestic violence. This message is crucial as the two most frequently cited reasons for not informing the police of domestic abuse are the beliefs that the police are either unwilling or unable to respond effectively. A graded response that increases incrementally with each attendance actively demonstrates these beliefs to be unfounded.

Police discretion was not eliminated and, on rare occasions, a combination of other factors could influence the final decision on intervention level allocation, such as the nature of previous incidents; whether the man was living with or separated from the woman (or women); the frequency of previous police attendances; previous police actions; the existence of injunctions and/or related bail conditions; information given by the woman to attending officers about previous reported or unreported incidents, although officers did not know the level of intervention of any call for assistance. The level of intervention was allocated subsequently and prior allocations to repeat attendances were recorded separately. The model was flexible enough to allow for interventions at a higher level if circumstances called for this. For example, the police attended an incident in which a man was released recently from prison for attempted murder on a previous partner. While this was his first offence against his current partner, he was subsequently entered at Level 3. This example also illustrates why repeat victimisation should be established by the perpetrator's history of attendance and not that of the victim.

Table 18.1 lists the operational interventions at each level for the perpetrator and for the victimised woman of both common law (primarily breach of the peace) and criminal offences. The interventions at all levels, including Level 1, involved a greater police response than that offered prior to the project's implementation.

Letters were sent at each level and these explained the policy and actions that could or would be taken, including support for the victimised woman. The letter to the victimising man explained that his behaviour was unacceptable and listed any further action that might be taken. The woman was offered a copy of the letter sent to him if useful for any civil action she might be pursuing, such as obtaining an injunction, divorce or in relation to access to children. At Level 2, a community constable called on the woman and offered to set up a 'Cocoon Watch'. A Cocoon Watch, similar to neighbourhood watch, requests the help and support of neighbours, friends and/or family and relevant agencies in further protecting the woman by contacting the police immediately if further incidents occur. A Cocoon Watch would only be implemented with the informed consent of the woman, and the perpetrator was made aware of this action. At Level 2 or 3 Police Watch was introduced to provide a visible police presence to both the victimised woman and the offender. This involved police patrols within the vicinity of the incident on a twice weekly basis for a period of four to six weeks immediately following reported incidents.

The model required continuing input from officers who attend calls and who process the outcome of attendances. The Domestic Violence Officer (DVO) had overall responsibility for implementing the specific aspects of the model. Having assigned the level of intervention, s/he ensured that letters were sent out to victimised women and perpetrators tailored to the type of offence and level. At Level 2 the DVO ensured that Police Watch requests were made when required, and that community constables visited victimised women. The DVO visited women at Level 3 and liaised with other agencies that became involved. While superficially simple, the process of implementing the model required systematic and thorough follow-up to ensure the interventions were implemented and implemented correctly for each incident.

The work of police officers on patrol was not changed. On the initial call-out, they were to respond to incidents as required by the policy of the Chief Constable and to identify the incident as domestic for recording purposes. Project interventions were then initiated by the DVO on the following day. Officers responding to domestic violence calls were to provide information both to the victim and the perpetrator, and arrest where possible. With common law and criminal offences the perpetrator was arrested and removed from the home. When arrest was possible for criminal offences, police also involved the other criminal justice agencies. Additional responses are possible when a woman is living independently, as the man has no automatic right of entry into her home. This permitted interventions identical or similar to those undertaken for burglary and other property offences when there is an attempted or forced entry.

Table 18.1 The domestic violence repeat victimisation model

Intervention level	Victim	Perpetrator (common law offences[1])	Perpetrator (criminal offences)
Level 1	• Gather information; • Information letter 1; • Police Watch.[2]	• Reiterate Force policy; • First official warning; • Information letter 1.	• Magistrates – conditional bail/checks; • Police Watch; • Information letter 1.
Level 2	• Information letter 2; • Community constable visit; • Cocoon[3] and Police Watches; • Target harden property.[4]	• Reiterate Force policy; • Second official warning; • Police Watch; • Information letter 2.	• Magistrates – bail opposed/checks; • Police Watch increased; • Information letter 2; • CPS file jacket and domestic violence (DV) history.
Level 3	• Information letter 3; • Police Watch; • Domestic Violence Officer visit; • Agency meeting; • Panic button/vodaphone.	• Reiterate Force policy; • Third official warning; • Police Watch; • Information letter 3.	• Magistrates – bail opposed/checks; • Police Watch increased; • Information letter 3; • Crown Prosecution Service (CPS) file jacket and DV history and contact CPS.
Emergency intervention	Implement – log reasons for selection.	Not applicable.	Implement and log level of action undertaken.

[1]Common law offences were primarily breach of the peace.

[2]Police Watch provides a visible police presence to both the victim and the offender and involves police patrols within the vicinity of the incident on a twice-weekly basis initially for a period of six weeks immediately following reported incidents.

[3]Cocoon Watch requests the help and support of neighbours, family and relevant agencies in further protecting the victim by contacting the police immediately if further incidents occur. A Cocoon Watch is only implemented with the informed consent of the victim, and the perpetrator is made aware of the action.

[4]Target hardening of property refers to additional security measures that can be applied to women's homes when living separately from violent/abusive men.

Did the model reduce repeat attendance?

To assess the model's effectiveness, the level of domestic violence attendances in 1997 was compared with a three-month period in 1996 before the project began. The aim of the project was to reduce the number of attendances at Levels 2 or 3 while not reducing the number of requests for attendance to women. Table 18.2 confirms that the numbers of men entering the project at Levels 2 and 3 significantly decreased during the project period. This means that the Level 1 intervention, or early intervention, was more effective than the previous way of responding to domestic attendance requests. Table 18.2 demonstrates these findings. During April to June 1996, the pre-project period, Level 1 entries were less frequent and Levels 2 and 3 are more frequent than during the project period. The change at each level is progressive over each quarter of 1997. This reflects growing understanding of the model and improvements in police operational systems to implement it.

Prior to the project each attendance was treated separately and unconnected with previous attendances, although officers were told of any previous logged incidents on the way to the incident. Further follow-up was unlikely unless an arrest was made. While each call for assistance must be responded to in relation to the specific situation, the subsequent actions introduced by the DVO meant that the sequence of attendances, whatever the outcome at the time, such as requiring the man to leave home for the night or walk around the block or arrest, would also form part of the policing response.

Interviews with women responded to at Level 1 were particularly positive about police intervention in relation to themselves and to their previous or current partners. The letters established that the police were willing to intervene to restrict the behaviour of the perpetrator and served to back up the physical attendance of officers. As a result men occasionally rang the DVO to argue that they were not violent. The DVO would explain what domestic violence is

Table 18.2 Entry level of men by quarterly time periods

Time Periods	Level 0*	Level 1	Level 2	Level 3	Totals
Pre-project Apr-June 1996	- -	216 (66%)	69 (21%)	44 (13%)	329 (100%)
Project Jan-Mar 1997	71 (22%)	192 (60%)	38 (12%)	21 (6%)	322 (100%)
Project Apr-June 1997	75 (26%)	185 (63%)	29 (10%)	4 (1%)	293 (100%)
Project July-Sept 1997	46 (15%)	236 (78%)	16 (5%)	6 (2%)	304 (100%)
Project Oct-Dec 1997	38 (13%)	239 (85%)	2 (1%)	2 (1%)	281 (100%)
$(p < 0.001)$					

*Level 0 refers to attendances that did not receive any project interventions

and how the police were responding which often resulted in agreement on the part of the man that the new approach was worthwhile in relation to him as well as others. The new approach was not simply an externally applied mechanism of social control, but could also positively engage the individual in an educational process.

Table 18.2 establishes that for each quarter of 1997:

- Project entry at Level 1 increased relative to entry at Levels 2 and 3. 60% of entries were at Level 1 in the first quarter, rising to 85% in the last quarter, while Levels 2 and 3 accounted for 18% in the first quarter, dropping to 2% in the last quarter. These findings are the result of two outcomes. Firstly, when the new approach began the Leeds division in which the project was located had a number of men being repeatedly attended. These chronic cases were gradually reduced over the year by interventions at Levels 2 and 3. The success of Level 1 intervention meant men who were previously unknown to the division were less likely to require repeat attendance.
- The total number of men entering the project varied in each quarter, but there was no evidence to suggest that these fluctuations are statistically significant. This demonstrates that new women were continuing to contact the police for assistance or, put more negatively, that there are sufficient abusing men in the community to provide a steady stream of offenders. This programme of actions is responsive to demand for assistance. In reducing repeat domestic violence it prevents crime, but other programmes and initiatives are required to reduce the need for the first attendance.
- Accuracy in Domestic Violence Index (DVI) recording of domestic violence attendances increased as Level 0 entries, the result of non-logging of attendances on the DVI at the time of attendance, decreased. Over time the number of logging errors were reduced. The amount of time taken to establish a logging error meant that interventions could not be implemented in the entries classified as Level 0. Very high levels of correct coding are required to operate repeat victimisation approaches.[1]

Table 18.3 provides further information on the progression between levels. This table can be read horizontally and diagonally. Horizontal reading shows the number and proportions of attendances at each entry level. For example, 230 men received no interventions, 852 received Level 1, 85 received Level 2 and 33 received Level 3 interventions. Diagonal reading shows the progression of men requiring repeat attendances for each entry level. For example, 210 of the Level 1 entrants required a second attendance (25 per cent of the original 852), and of these 75 required a third attendance (9 per cent of the original 852) and so on.

Early intervention

Table 18.3 shows that early intervention achieves the greatest reduction in repeat attendances. For all entry levels the number of men requiring repeat

Table 18.3 Repeat attendance of men by entry level January–December 1997

	Level 0	Level 1	Level 2	Level 3				Totals
1st call	230	852	85	33				1200
	100%	100%	100%	100%				100%
2nd call		85	210	39	21			355
		37%	25%	46%	64%			30%
3rd call			36	75	27	13		151
			16%	9%	32%	39%		13%
4th call				16	31	12	9	68
				7%	4%	14%	27%	6%
5+					7	11	9	6	33
					3%	1%	11%	18%	3%
(p<0.001)							Total attendances: 1870	

attendances gradually decreases with each repeat attendance. Level 1 entrants have the lowest proportion of attendances for each repeat attendance required. For those who experienced no project interventions at the point of entry into the project, i.e. Level 0, their subsequent progression to Level 2 and beyond is significantly higher than those who entered at Level 1. Repeat attendance increases with entry level from 1 to 2 to 3. Table 18.3 confirms that early intervention is particularly effective in reducing repeat attendance. Level 1 entrants performed better than any other entry with 75 per cent not requiring a second attendance during 1997. The percentage of Level 1 entrants requiring two or three or more attendances was consistently less than those at the other levels.

Offenders with a history of police attendance for domestic violence were allocated an entry level of 2 or 3. Subsequently, they are not as likely to be demotivated as Level 1 entrants. This indicates that introducing the first intervention at Level 2 or 3 is not as effective as a first intervention at Level 1. The most likely reasons for this are either that the offender has become desensitised or has concluded that the police do not object to his behaviour or both. Women interviewed about the police interventions confirmed these interpretations.

Chronic offenders

Table 18.3 records both the number of men and the number of attendances and allows the individual identification of chronic repeat offenders. To be effective the model calls for a rational response from an offender, i.e. the recognition that the actions taken in relation to him, and the support given to his victim, mean that it will become progressively more difficult to continue with his behaviour without the likelihood of some negative consequences to himself, and/or his behaviour will become less effective in relation to his victim. This message was not received by everyone, as 33 men (3 per cent) were attended five times or more during 1997.

If overall failure of the programme is defined as the entry of an offender into Level 4, then the overall observed failure rate for 1997 was 6 per cent. The failure rate was highest among the decreasing number of Level 2 and 3 entrants. Once the model becomes established, advanced entry will become a rare occurrence. With all entries at Level 1, the failure rate drops to 4 per cent.

The three-tiered model is a robust system of intervention and rational decision making is occurring, although a minority of men, easily identified through their individual repeat pattern, were not demotivated. Those not demotivated required further assessment. Police interventions can be tailored to meet specific situations and begin with one or more individuals, although the involvement of other agencies may be required for some men. Chronic offenders, or the 'failures', differed significantly. There could be issues of mental health or educational ability or severe drug and other addictions as well as repeated criminal behaviour across a range of crimes. There is no single type of domestic violence perpetrator. In taking these differences into account other agencies and services, particularly health, may have a major role to play in controlling acts of domestic violence by men.

The model's effectiveness measured by intervals between repeat victimisation

Another way of measuring the effectiveness of the West Yorkshire model is by examining the time intervals between police attendances. Previous work on domestic violence in England showed that, after a first police attendance, 35 per cent of households required a second attendance within five weeks (35 days), and 45 per cent of these households need a third attendance within five weeks (35 days) (Lloyd *et al.* 1994).

In West Yorkshire, within five weeks, nine per cent who entered at Level 1 were attended again; and of those entering at Levels 2 and 3, 15 per cent and 26 per cent were attended again within five weeks. Survival analysis was used to chart how long an offender 'survives' before being attended again by the police. Survival time, the number of days between calls, is defined as a period of temporary demotivation of an offender which is terminated by a repeat attendance. The outcome of a single attendance during the year is either a totally demotivated offender or someone who may require another attendance after the project's closing date. Obviously men who entered the project near the final date of 31 December 1997 had less time in which a repeat attendance could occur. As each man required a repeat attendance, the percentage surviving was systematically reduced.

In Figure 18.1, the Level 1 line shows when each of the 210 (25 per cent) men required a repeat attendance. The gradual decline in this line shows that these are well-separated events over time.

The Level 2 line represents the Level 2 entrants (85) plus the Level 1 entrants who required a repeat attendance (210). The decline is steeper than at Level 1, showing that the interval between repeat attendances is shorter.

The survival pattern at Level 3 shows an even more rapid decline. This

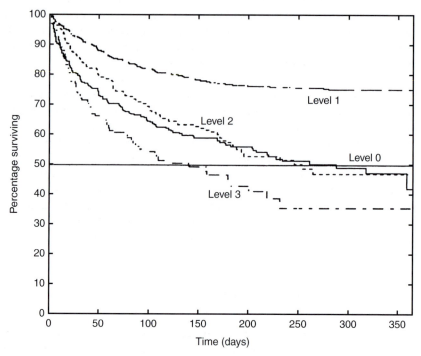

Figure 18.1 Number of days between attendances by intervention level

represents the relatively shorter periods between attendances to men receiving Level 3 interventions as they progress to Level 4.

The survival pattern for Level 0 (those who did not receive project interventions) suggests these men are a combination of Level 2 and Level 3 men as their profile crosses both these lines.

Figure 18.1 also shows the median survival time, i.e. the time in which 50 per cent of all the men at each intervention level required a repeat attendance. The median survival time at Level 1 is well over a year; at Level 2 it is 270 days; and at Level 3 it is 150 days.

The question is, given a longer period of time, what are the proportion of offenders who are likely to have been totally demotivated?

Using split-population proportional hazards survival model of analysis, the survival data were analysed to predict the proportion of men who would require a repeat attendance at some point in the future and those who would not. This analysis also identified the factors significant in re-offending.

For Level 1 men it was predicted that 61 per cent would be totally demotivated and 39 per cent would require a repeat attendance. 25 per cent did so during the project period and a further 14 per cent would do so in the future. Factors identifying repeat offenders were previous police attendances, arrest, and the level of crime in the area in which the victim lived.

At Level 2 it was predicted that 42 per cent of offenders would be demotivated and 58 per cent would require further attendances; 46 per cent during the project period and 12 per cent would do so after this period. No factors were identified as significant in this cohort of men, suggesting a mixed set of characteristics and patterns with little commonality.

For Level 3, the most chronic and persistent offenders, it was predicted that only 36 per cent would be demotivated and 64 per cent would receive repeat attendances. In fact, the 64 per cent repeated during the project period and by the end of the project period Level 3 entrants were almost non-existent. These men are quick to re-offend and the median survival time of 150 days is accurate. The factors associated with their repeat offending were previous police attendances, the crime-levels of the areas in which the victim and the perpetrator were living, and the age difference between the victim and the perpetrator. When the offender is older the likelihood of re-offending reduces by 5 per cent per year of difference. When the offender is younger the likelihood of re-offending increases by 6 per cent per year of difference.

Other potential explanations – leaving home

Looked at from the actions of victimised women, the most common response to repeat domestic violence is to leave their homes temporarily or permanently. Could this explain the positive results of this project? Whether the women were living with or separately from the perpetrators was not found to be significant. Although there was a slight increase in the percentage of women living separately by Level 3 attendances, the differences were not statistically significant. 58 per cent of the Level 1 attendances were living together, 55 per cent of the Level 2 and 48 per cent by Level 3. This is further evidence that it is the repeat victimisation model of interventions that made the difference in reducing repeat attendances.

What was statistically significant was the variation in police actions between men and women who lived together and those living separately. Police were more likely to arrest when women were living with the men, possibly because the men were more likely to be present on these occasions. Variations in outcomes after arrest were also strongly associated with living arrangements. Release within hours of arrest was more likely when women lived with the perpetrator and, if there were further proceedings after arrest, these were more likely to be for the misdemeanour offence of breach of the peace. Criminal charges were more likely if the couple were separated. This suggests that more serious offences were being committed against women who were separated at the time of the police attendance. This interpretation is supported by women's experiences of leaving home at a time of increased violence and severity of violence. The reduction in repeat offending achieved by the introduction of this new approach is not a result of women separating from perpetrators.

The role of arrest in repeat victimisation

The experimental work on arrest and domestic violence by Sherman and Berk (1984) in Minneapolis had a major influence on legislation and police operations in the US. Despite criticisms of the methodology and interpretation of results, and despite dissimilar findings from other studies, arrest continues to dominate criminological work on domestic violence in the US (see Chapter 16). Sherman acknowledges that the interpretation that arrest causes further violence is problematic, but he suggests that 'the weaker the suspect's social bonds, the more likely it appears to be that arrest will backfire by causing increased violence'. He defines weaker social bonds as non-marriage and male unemployment.

In the West Yorkshire study, arrest was identified as a significant factor in men's repeat victimising. Arrest increased the risk of re-attendance by 51 per cent. This would seem to support the findings of American studies. But the progressive interventions approach of the West Yorkshire study allows a different analysis of the relationship between arrest and repeat offending.

Table 18.4 shows that there was no significant variation in arrest rates between the different intervention levels, apart from Level 0. Neither was there any variation in percentages arrested for the misdemeanour offence of breach of the peace. If arrest were a causal factor of repeat offending, one would expect the arrest rate for Level 1 attendances to be lower, as this group of men generated significantly fewer repeat attendances.

Variation occurs after arrest with 'release without charge' greatest for men at Level 1 (62 per cent) but progressively reduced as men moved from Level 1 to 2 to 3. Conversely, the proportion of men facing criminal charges increased as the level of intervention increased; from 20 per cent of the Level 1 men to 48 per cent of the Level 4 men. The systematic patterns of release and charging after arrest suggest that men who behave more violently progress to higher levels of intervention.

From this analysis arrest and repeat attendance is understood as a statistical correlation, not a causal relationship. Arrest is a means of identifying men who are more violent and likely to require further police interventions. It is interpreted as another indicator that violent men differ in their willingness to use violence against women in the home. The causal connection is between the man himself and his behaviour, and not external environmental and other factors.

Work on the impact of arrest on repeat victimisation is in its infancy and raises a number of issues. First, there is the issue of quantifying the percentage of arrests in domestic violence attendances. The West Yorkshire figures show that 27 per cent of attendances resulted in arrest. Kelly (1999) found only 14 per cent of reported incidents resulted in arrest but this percentage increased to 37 per cent if the base rate was incidents recorded as crimes. The Local Government Act 1999 introduced a new duty of Best Value. This Act led to a new performance indicator for repeat domestic violence in which arrest rates are to be calculated as a 'percentage of reported domestic violence incidents where

Table 18.4 Arrests and outcomes by intervention level January-December 1997

Level	No. of attendances	No. of arrests (% of attendances)	Breach of the peace (% of arrests)	Released (% of arrests)	Criminal charges (% of arrests)	Other* (% of arrests)
0	371 (20%)	59 (16%)	8 (14%)	18 (31%)	23 (39%)	10 (17%)
1	886 (47%)	268 (30%)	39 (15%)	165 (62%)	54 (20%)	10 (4%)
2	299 (16%)	77 (26%)	13 (17%)	38 (49%)	21 (27%)	5 (6%)
3	160 (9%)	52 (33%)	10 (19%)	22 (42%)	19 (37%)	1 (2%)
4**	154 (8%)	46 (30%)	7 (15%)	17 (37%)	22 (48%)	0
Total	1870 (100%)	502 (27%)	77 (15%)	260 (52%)	139 (28%)	26 (5%)

*includes arrest on warrant and unknown outcomes
**repeat of Level 3 interventions

there was a power of arrest, in which an arrest was made relating to the incident'. The impact of this indicator is that arrest rates will appear to rise in relation to domestic violence attendances.

A second issue concerns the mono-causal view of arrest and its impact on repeat victimisation. Arrest is the beginning of a process that has a number of possible outcomes. Arrest may result in immediate release from custody, or release after a very short period of time or charging. In turn, charging can result in a number of actions including not proceeding with cases and non-guilty findings as well as convictions. Focusing solely on arrest ignores these variables, any one of which (or multiples) may be of even greater importance to further repetition (or not) of violence by individual men than arrest itself.

Arrest and subsequent outcomes remain to be fully investigated for their significance in relation to chronic offending. This aspect of arrest will be explored in a new evaluation of domestic violence repeat victimisation in West Yorkshire when the model is rolled out across the Force.

Conclusion

This research demonstrates that it is possible to demotivate men, that is, to curtail their willingness to continue to abuse current and past female partners, by systematically implementing a graded response based on increasing police interventions with each police attendance. Interviews with women attended by the police confirmed that early pro-active interventions were effective in reducing repeat victimisation. This was borne out in the project's finding that calls for assistance to individual women increased over the year while the number of repeat attendances decreased.

The evaluation of this operational programme furthered our understanding of the factors that influence repeat offending; it developed new statistical analyses of repeat attendances; and it demonstrated the effectiveness of early and targeted interventions. Most men were not arrested and did not require a repeat attendance which suggests that a focus on the differences between abusing men is as important as a focus on their similarities. An operational programme that is effective with both men who do and who do not require repeat police attendance, that is, across differences in male behaviour, offers greater protection to women. Implementing this new model achieved the aims of improving the consistency and efficiency of service delivery both to those who victimise and who are victimised and the effectiveness of policing domestic violence.

Note

* This chapter draws on previously published work by the authors (see Hanmer, Griffiths and Jerwood 1999).
1   Being vulnerable to victimisation does not imply passivity on the part of the woman. This chapter uses the terms 'victim' and 'perpetrator/offender' to clarify where responsibility lies for violence, in this project from men to women.
2   Accurate logging of domestic violence attendances is difficult, but essential. When the project began at the West Yorkshire division, recording accuracy was 50%. This meant that only 5 out of every 10 attendances were being properly recorded and only

2.5 of both attendances. It is not possible to operate a repeat victimisation model with this degree of inaccurate recording. If 90% recording accuracy can be obtained then 1 out of every 10 first attendances will not be recorded and both attendances will not be recorded for almost 2 out of 10 attendances. Achieving 100% accuracy is necessary for the full implementation of the model. This requires checking of incoming calls for assistance for correct coding on a regular basis and must be accepted as an integral part of the operational programme.

References

Anderson, D., Chenery, S. and Pease, K. (1995) *Biting Back: Tackling Repeat Burglary and Car Crime*, Police Research Group, Crime Detection and Prevention Series Paper No. 58, London: Home Office.

Cohen, I. E. and Felson, M. (1979) 'Social change and crime rate trends: a routine activity approach', *American Sociological Review*, Vol. 44, 608–88.

Farrell, G. and Pease, K. (1993) *Once Bitten, Twice Bitten: Repeat Victimisation and its Implications for Crime Prevention*, Police Research Group, Crime Prevention Unit Series Paper No. 46, London: Home Office.

Forrester, D., Chatterton, M. and Pease K. (1988) *The Kirkholt Burglary Prevention Project, Rochdale*, Crime Prevention Unit Paper No. 13, London: Home Office.

Hanmer, J., Griffiths, S. and Jerwood, D. (1999) *Arresting Evidence: Domestic Violence and Repeat Victimisation*, Police Research Series Paper No. 104, London: Home Office.

Hanmer, J. and Saunders, S. (1987) *Women, Violence and Crime Prevention*, West Yorkshire Police Authority (also published by Avebury 1993).

Kelly, L. (1999) *Domestic Violence Matters: An Evaluation of a Development Project*, Home Office Research Study 193, The Research Development and Statistics Directorate, London: Home Office.

Lloyd, S., Farrell, G. and Pease, K. (1994) *Preventing Repeated Domestic Violence: A Demonstration Project on Merseyside*, Police Research Group, Crime Prevention Unit Paper No. 49, London: Home Office.

Mayhew, Pat, Aye Maung, Natalie and Mirrlees-Black, Catriona (1993) *The 1992 British Crime Survey*, London: HMSO; Home Office Research Study 132.

McGibbon, A., Cooper, L. and Kelly, L. (1989) *What Support? An Exploratory Study of Council Policy and Practice, and Local Support Services in the Area of Domestic Violence within Hammersmith and Fulham*, London: Hammersmith and Fulham Community Safety Unit.

Pease, K. (1998) *Repeat Victimisation: Taking Stock*, Crime Detection and Prevention Series Paper No. 90, London: Home Office.

Policing and Reducing Crime Unit (2000) *Reducing Domestic Violence . . . What Works? Briefing Notes*, London: Home Office.

Sampson, A. and Phillips, C. (1992) *Multiple Victimisation: Racial Attacks on an East London Estate*, Police Research Group, Crime Prevention Unit Series Paper No. 36, London: Home Office.

Sampson, A. and Phillips, C. (1995) *Reducing Repeat Racial Victimisation on an East London Estate*, Police Research Group, Crime Detection and Prevention Series Paper No. 67, London: Home Office.

Sherman, L. W. and Berk, R. A. (1984) 'The specific deterrent effects of arrest for domestic violence', *American Sociological Review*, Vol. 49. pp. 261–72.

Taylor-Browne, J. (2001) *Reducing Domestic Violence . . . What Works?* London: Research and Statistics Directorate, Home Office.

West Yorkshire Police Authority, Agenda Item No. 17, 25 November 1988.

19 The Zero Tolerance campaigns

Evelyn Gillan and Elaine Samson

> It is difficult to verbalise the emotional response to seeing a billboard saying simply No Man Has The Right. One woman on seeing the Edinburgh campaign said she stood there and simply said 'Yes'. How can you convey the sense of power – the power to name, power to object, power to reject male violence, power to be? 'Yes' encapsulates the fist raised in defiance, the spirit raised in hope and the voice raised in accord with women
>
> (Cosgrove 1996, p. 196).

Zero Tolerance was the first initiative in Britain to use public education via the mass media to directly challenge male violence against women and children. Zero Tolerance makes the links between the different forms of violence including rape, child sexual abuse and domestic violence. The first campaign was launched in Edinburgh in 1992 with a clear strategic aim – to move the issue of violence against women and children up the public and political agenda. The campaign uses posters, adshels, billboard, bus and cinema advertising to challenge the norms, beliefs and values which give rise to and sustain male violence.

Following the success of the campaign in Edinburgh, Zero Tolerance was taken up throughout the UK and ran in New York and South Australia. The Zero Tolerance Charitable Trust was established in 1995. The Trust is primarily concerned with the prevention of male violence and works in partnership with statutory and voluntary agencies throughout Europe to develop innovative policies which address the root causes of male violence.

This chapter will:

- outline the policy context within which the campaign was developed;
- illustrate how Zero Tolerance succeeded in creating a space which allowed the potential for change;
- examine the impact that Zero Tolerance has had on policy and practice.

National context

Second-wave feminism had made explicit the significance of male violence in the exercise of power and control over women. The three goals of the refuge movement identified in 1974 were:

- assisting victims;
- challenging male violence;
- changing women's position in society.

The election of a right-wing Conservative government in Britain in 1979 led to a policy focus which promoted the traditional nuclear family and a strong law and order agenda. Hague (1999) notes that the endemic nature of violence in the home by men against women runs contrary to the myth that the heterosexual nuclear family is the best social environment for all and that domestic violence presents a contradiction to policies bolstering the traditional family.

The late 1980s saw a convergence of the two policy agendas – families, and law and order – with the emergence of the police response to domestic violence and the growth of Domestic Violence Units in police forces. Although broadly welcomed by the refuge movement, some feminists questioned the real motivation behind this policy response given the concern about 'oppressive policing' and the inner city riots of the early 1980s (Mama 1989; Radford and Stanko 1996). Whilst the pioneering work done by organisations like Women's Aid and Rape Crisis had succeeded in making male violence against women and children visible, the focus of Government policy gave much cause for concern (see Chapters 10 and 12). Both the Home Office and the Scottish Office had developed policy initiatives on violence against women under the crime prevention/community safety agenda. The *Positive Steps* initiative produced leaflets and posters targeting women which offered women advice on how to stay safe. Women were advised to stay away from dark, unlit streets and to 'keep an escape kit at the ready'.

Hester *et al.* (1996) note how the Home Office attempted to redefine the problem of men's violence as one of women's excessive and irrational fear of crime. They quote the British Crime Survey which asked women how safe they felt walking alone in their neighbourhoods after dark and compared the findings to the lower numbers of women who disclosed incidents of crime. The Home Office concluded that women's fear of crime was excessive, and therefore, irrational. 'This reinterpretation of the problem led to crime prevention policies aimed at reducing women's fear of crime, rather than attempting to reduce men's perpetration of it' (Hester *et al.* 1996: 10). The outcome has been a re-definition of the issues within a non-feminist discourse, producing woman-blaming policies of individual responsibility for personal safety (Stanko and Radford 1999).

Local context

The crime prevention/community safety agenda of the national government was being promoted by local authorities and others at a local level. In Edinburgh and other areas of Scotland, police authorities were joining forces with local authorities to run *Women's Fear of Crime* courses. These courses followed the model established by Central Government – they targeted women and adhered to an individualised, problem-solving approach. Women were shown how to fit locks on doors, taken on a visit to the local police station and offered classes in self-defence. The emphasis was on gender-neutral crime prevention which was in keeping with the Government's promotion of itself as the government of 'law and order'. Bacchi (1999) highlights the importance of analysing the way that problems get represented in policy proposals as every policy proposal contains within it an explicit or implicit diagnosis of the 'problem' which she refers to as the 'problem representation'. The problem representation of both national and local policy initiatives to address male violence against women was clear – women were responsible for male violence. Although it was men's behaviour which was creating the problem, it was women who had to change their behaviour in order to bring the problem under control.

In the mid-1980s, the Labour administration of Edinburgh District Council established the second Women's Unit in Scotland (the first was established by Stirling District Council) with three Principal Officer Posts – one of which was dedicated solely to campaigns and promotions. The Women's Committee instructed the Women's Unit to undertake a consultation exercise with women in Edinburgh to identify the issues that most concerned them. Safety emerged as one of the issues that most concerned women. Concern about the *problem representation* and gender-neutrality of the crime prevention agenda coupled with the results of the women's consultation survey, led to the Women's Unit's Campaigns Officer beginning to formulate an idea about developing a campaign to address male violence.

Background

The Women's Unit's Campaigns Officer had taken the opportunity to visit a number of women's projects whilst on holiday in Canada. The Federal Government of Canada had implemented an ambitious family violence initiative in the late 1980s which included a mass media campaign. The Ontario Women's Directorate had also developed an integrated campaign to challenge violence against women. Pat Marshall, the Federal Government official responsible for the Canadian Panel on Violence had first come across the term 'zero tolerance' in relation to quality control in business. Although the term was used in the supporting campaign material it did not form a major element of the Canadian initiative. The idea of developing a campaign around the concept of Zero Tolerance began to develop in the Women's Unit of Edinburgh District Council.

However, in order to persuade the politicians in Edinburgh to put resources into such a campaign, more evidence would be needed. The Women's Unit proposed to the Women's Committee that they carry out a research study into the attitudes of young people in Edinburgh on the issue of violence against women. The Women's Committee agreed and a study was carried out in three secondary schools involving over 300 young people aged between 12 and 16 years. The study found that:

- boys were more accepting of violence against women than girls;

- violence against women was more acceptable when the perpetrator was married to the victim;
- a significant number of boys said that they thought they might use violence in future relationships.

The research also showed that being exposed to information about violence against women had the effect of reducing tolerance of violence. Following the results of the research, the Women's Committee agreed to run a high-profile mass media campaign to raise awareness about violence against women and children. There was no indication at that time that the campaign would remain anything other than local and Edinburgh-based.

Analysis

The creative team[1] began by defining the politics of the campaign. Building on the pioneering work undertaken by the refuge and rape crisis movement, Zero Tolerance emphasised the second two goals of the refuge movement – challenging men and changing women's position in society, but did not restrict the focus to domestic violence. It is perhaps significant that, whilst drawing on the social action tradition of second-wave feminism, the campaign did not come out of the front-line women's organisations. By the early 1990s, the front-line women's organisations had found themselves operating in an increasingly hostile policy environment. Lack of adequate funding meant that they were already struggling to provide services to women. Not surprisingly, most of their energy went into assisting women, leaving little time or resources for campaigning. The local authority Women's Units on the other hand, at least had some guaranteed funding (albeit limited in the context of local authority budgets) and did not have the same pressure to provide front-line services.

Zero Tolerance was informed by a feminist analysis of male violence, and making the links between the different forms of violence was seen as an essential component of the campaign. Guberman and Wolfe (1985) note that looking at different forms of violence in a piecemeal way makes them seem unconnected, whereas placing them side-by-side reveals common themes. Kelly's description of the 'continuum' of violence (1988), in which 'typical' and 'aberrant' male behaviour shade into one another, was a critical influence on the development of the campaign. Zero Tolerance made the point that all forms of violence against women and children were linked and share the same underlying causes. The problem was not about mad, bad or sad men but about power and control, and Zero Tolerance sought to make the connections.

Zero Tolerance had a clear strategic aim – to move the issue of male violence against women and children up the public and political agenda and, in doing so, to inject gender-specificity into the gender-neutral crime prevention policy agenda. The campaign rejected the dominant view that women were responsible for male violence. Defining the problem differently, Zero Tolerance located male violence within the context of structural inequality and called for action to address root causes. The campaign developed a new approach which, although building on the social action tradition of second-wave feminism in the 1970s, adopted new methods of communicating which used 'the tools of the powerful to communicate the campaign's counter-hegemonic messages' (Gillan 1999).

An important factor in the development of Zero Tolerance was the combination of skills which were brought to bear on the campaign. The creative team had a clear theoretical perspective informing the campaign, but were also skilled in visual communication, public relations, media and political lobbying. The creators of the campaign were clear from their own experiences, both as activists and as professionals working within the political structures, that the only way to move the issue of male violence up the public and political agenda was to build a broad base of support which would create the conditions for change. By directly harnessing public support, Zero Tolerance would in effect go over the heads of politicians and policy makers and build a consensus for change. Nevertheless, it was important to secure the support of key politicians in the Council in order to get the campaign into the public domain. The support of the chairperson of the Women's Committee – Margaret McGregor – and the leader of the Council – Mark Lazarowicz – was critical in this.

Prevention, provision, protection

Consultation with the front-line women's groups in Edinburgh was an essential part of the planning process. The front-line organisations understandably had some initial concerns that the campaign would put additional pressure on their already overstretched resources. Whilst the Labour administration of the Council had taken a number of steps to increase the refuge provision for women experiencing domestic violence since they had come to office, the local Rape Crisis centre did not have any full-time staff and was offering a limited service. It was agreed that the Women's Unit would assist Rape Crisis in attempting to secure additional funding for Rape Crisis before launching the campaign. A successful urban aid application saw a significant increase in the local Rape Crisis staff resource. The campaign organisers argued that moving the issue up the public and political agenda would make it easier for the front-line groups to lobby for increased resources in the long term. Consultation with the front-line women's groups led to the development of the 'three Ps' approach. In recognition of the fact that public education is only one component of an overall strategy, Zero Tolerance called for action to address violence to incorporate:

- active prevention of crimes of violence;
- adequate provision of support services for women and children;
- appropriate legal protection.

Eight years on, the governments in London and Edinburgh have incorporated the three Ps into their strategies to address violence.

PR strategy

Given the potentially controversial nature of the campaign, much of the strategic planning went into developing a wider public relations strategy. This included looking critically at strengths, weaknesses, opportunities and threats – a standard SWOT analysis. Zero Tolerance used the principles of public relations theory to ensure that the campaign had broad-based support weeks before the first poster appeared. All of the political parties represented on the Council offered their support. Organisations that had not previously supported action to address male violence were approached in advance and asked for their support. A number of high profile representatives from the churches and the local police force attended the launch of the campaign.

This tactic was adopted by other local authorities that later took up the campaign. Katie Cosgrove, the co-ordinator of the Strathclyde campaign, writing in *Women in a Violent World*, talks of the inclusion of men as a shrewd, strategic element of the campaign. 'Men have not been asked to validate what we say, nor to co-opt this issue or to take credit for the achievements of the women's movement – but to accept the centrality of their role in ending male violence.' (Cosgrove 1996: 196).

In the early SWOT analysis, the role of the local media was identified as a potential threat. Although support had been secured from key politicians, we were aware that negative publicity could seriously weaken their resolve as well as giving ammunition to others who did not want to see the campaign succeed. However, the media was also identified as a potential opportunity in that it could play an important role in getting the campaign's messages over to a wider audience. The campaign was being developed on a shoestring budget with a relatively small number of media outlets in comparison to most mass media campaigns. In developing our media strategy, we sought to transfer a potentially negative situation into a positive one.

A primary media outlet was identified which was read by a large percentage of the population as well as the vast majority of politicians – the local newspaper, the *Evening News*. One woman journalist who would be sympathetic to the campaign was identified and the proposal was put that the newspaper come on board as a sponsor of the campaign. Two women journalists, Jean West and Nicola Barry, were responsible for persuading the Editor to support the campaign. The newspaper ran lead articles three times a week for the duration of the campaign (six months). There is no doubt that the support of the *Evening News*, along with the effort of the two journalists, were critical factors in the subsequent success of the campaign.

Developing the creatives

All the creative decisions in developing the campaign material were informed by the overall analysis. The campaign is designed to challenge men but not at the expense of women. Zero Tolerance recognises that if we are serious about addressing male violence in the long term, women need to feel empowered by the campaign. This rules out the use of victim imagery. Instead, the visual imagery is used to challenge many of the myths concerning violence against women. The campaign highlights the different ways in which men abuse to enable us to understand the continuum of male violence. Zero Tolerance unequivocally names the gender of the problem as male and the use of the strapline *Male Abuse of Power* clearly locates male violence in the context of structural inequality between men and women.

As the campaign was inviting change, the first step was to raise public awareness about the extent and nature of male violence against women and children. Early campaign material focused on prevalence with a series of posters addressing rape, child sexual abuse and domestic violence. The posters are linked together with the slogan *No Man Has The Right*. The core message of the early campaign was that violence against women and children is a crime and should not be tolerated. The criminalisation message was a strategic response to the high policy priority that the Conservative Government had given to law and order.

All the images in the original campaign were shot indoors to challenge the myth that women were more at risk from strangers outdoors. The rape poster features a grandmother and a young child to challenge the myth that rape is about sex. The posters depicted middle-class settings to challenge the myth that violence occurs in one specific social class. The images all focus on domestic situations to highlight the prevalence of violence against women and children which occurs in their own homes. The imagery used is visually appealing and reflects people's notions of comfort and security. This contrasts sharply with the message of the text. The effectiveness of this iconography has been noted in evaluations of the campaign. Four of the posters are shown on pages 351–4.

Later campaign material examines the causes of violence and continues to dispel myths, i.e. that alcohol causes men to be violent. The *Justice* campaign takes the concept of abuse of power further by linking individual abuse of power to a wider, social and legal abuse of power. *Justice* calls on the criminal justice system to take responsibility for protecting women and children who experience violence. The *Respect* initiative goes further into the causes of male violence, specifically targeting young people and challenging the gender socialisation which creates the conditions for violence in intimate relationships. *Respect* encourages young people to develop relationships based on trust, respect and equality.

Evaluation

Since it was first launched in 1992, Zero Tolerance has been taken up across the UK. At the time of writing, approximately 80 per cent of the Scottish population live in areas where the campaign has run and Zero Tolerance has appeared in many of the major cities in the UK. The Zero Tolerance Trust has produced over a hundred mass media public education campaigns for use locally. The campaigns have been led by a wide variety of organisations including local authorities, multi-agency forums, community safety partnerships, health boards and voluntary sector women's organisations. There have been a number of evaluations conducted by universities, market research companies and individual researchers. Whilst there are some differences from area to area, all of the evaluations report broadly similar findings:

- over 80 per cent of the respondents believe that the public as a whole do not know enough about violence;
- over 80 per cent believe that Zero Tolerance is good for the Council's image; showing the Council to be innovative, forward-thinking and concerned for its women citizens;
- over 80 per cent believe that money spent on Zero Tolerance is money well spent.

Effect on policy

Both the European Parliament and the Council of Europe have called on member states to adopt the Zero Tolerance approach. The European Commission issued a call for proposals under the *European Campaign to Raise Awareness About Domestic Violence* in 1999. When Trust staff phoned up to request further information they were told that the programme was based on the Zero Tolerance model. Zero Tolerance has inspired preventive public education initiatives throughout the world. In one month in 1999 the Trust had 20 requests for information from outside Europe. One overseas visitor to the Trust's office told staff that Zero Tolerance had 'transformed women's lives in Kenya'. The level of international interest is all the more remarkable when you consider that the Trust receives no statutory funding, raises all its income itself and has no marketing or promotions budget.

The Government produced the policy document *Living Without Fear* which incorporates the three Ps of prevention, provision and protection although there is no acknowledgement of source. Zero Tolerance is listed as a model of good practice in the document. In England, the term 'zero tolerance' has been *appropriated* by politicians and policy makers to the extent that it is not associated with male violence against women. The Prime Minister, the Home Secretary, Chief Constables, and the Drugs Tzar have all invoked the term in relation to petty crime, drug abuse, bad teachers. Moreover, not only has the term been *appropriated* but it has been used in policy contexts which are diametrically opposed to the original use of the term. Where Zero Tolerance of violence against women is radical, zero tolerance of petty crime is reactionary. Bea Campbell, writing in the *Guardian*, challenged Tony Blair's misuse of the term and called on the Prime Minister to pay tribute to Zero Tolerance's radical roots. Radford and Stanko (1996) observe the contradiction facing feminists when feminist work is appropriated but without the feminist commitment which gave it meaning.

Following the high profile that local authority Zero Tolerance campaigns had in Scotland, the Scottish Office developed its own mass media campaign in 1994 but did not consult with Zero Tolerance. The campaign perpetuated many of the myths that Zero Tolerance sought to challenge. Zero Tolerance ran bus campaigns with the slogan *Drunk or Sober – there is no excuse*, whilst the Scottish Office ran a television advertisement on domestic violence set in a pub. By locating the ad in a pub, the Scottish Office sent an implicit message which linked domestic violence to alcohol abuse. Zero Tolerance depicted middle-class domestic environments to scotch the myth that violence against women was associated with a specific social class, while the Scottish Office used tattooed fists in a billboard advert. The qualitative evaluation of the Scottish Office campaign did, however, confirm that Zero Tolerance had some success in challenging these myths as both the pub setting and the association with one social class were criticised by the public.

After five years of sustained campaigning, the Zero Tolerance effect could be seen in other policy forums in Scotland. Her Majesty's Inspectorate of Constabulary, the Scottish Forum for Public Health Medicine and the Convention of Scottish Local Authorities (COSLA) all produced policy reports on domestic violence. It is worth noting that, even although Zero Tolerance consistently made the links between the different forms of violence, it was domestic violence and not rape or child sexual abuse that was taken up by policy makers.

When the Scottish Parliament was established in 1998, it identified confronting the problem of violence against women as a key priority. In the space of one year, there have been two debates in the Parliament, one on domestic violence and the other on rape and the criminal justice system. The Scottish Executive has released £3 million pounds to establish a domestic abuse service development fund with local authorities being asked to match funds, and Scottish Homes putting in £2 million for capital expenditure on refuge provision. The Scottish Executive have also run a mass media campaign on domestic abuse. Once again Zero Tolerance was not involved in the campaign which, like the previous campaign, was produced by an advertising agency. The Scottish Partnership on Domestic Abuse has produced a Workplan which has been approved by the Parliament.

Zero Tolerance has also impacted on local policy and procedure. A recent report by the Scottish Executive outlined the extensive work undertaken by local authorities on violence against women. Over two-thirds of the local authorities surveyed indicated that they were undertaking public-awareness raising locally with the most common participants (organisations involved) found to be the Zero Tolerance Charitable Trust (Workplan 26). Strathclyde Police Authority, the biggest force in Europe, has undertaken the *Spotlight Initiative* which aims to drive tolerance of domestic abuse out of the Force. Greater Glasgow Health Board has pioneered innovative work on policy and practice in relation to domestic violence and primary health care settings.

Conclusion

> Zero Tolerance does not say that there is a deep-seated quality in all men that makes them abuse. It says there is a problem with male socialisation and that large numbers of men can be affected by it. It grasps the issue that male violence is rooted in male power and control over women. The underlying background to this is a historical belief that men have the right to that power and control
>
> (Malcolm Chisolm MP).

Zero Tolerance has clearly impacted on policy at international, national, and local level. However, Bacchi (1999) reminds us that achieving social problem status for one's cause is not in itself a sign of success or a commitment to important change. Rather, it depends upon the way in which the problem is represented.

Key elements of the Zero Tolerance approach have been appropriated into mainstream policy making in Scotland: the adoption of the three Ps, the acceptance of the gender-specificity of violence against women, the link between male violence and women's subordinate position in society, the use of the mass media to challenge violence. However, other elements have, to date, not been taken up. Although Zero Tolerance specifically challenged the myth that women were responsible for male violence and sought to put responsibility onto men, the first draft of the Scottish Executive's strategy document cited the main objective of government action as 'encouraging women to challenge abuse'. Gordon (1988) notes that women, as the focus of analysis, become the problem, while male behaviour goes under-analysed and under-problematised. There is a real concern that, by making women the major focus of policy proposals, the governments in both London and Edinburgh will shape the problem of male violence in ways which limit the possibilities for change (Bacchi 1999).

Zero Tolerance pioneered the three Ps of prevention, provision, and protection, and argued for government strategies to encompass all three elements. However, out of 92 items listed for action in the Scottish Executive's Workplan, less than a quarter deal with prevention.[2] The policy focus is very much on the first goal of the refuge movement 'assisting women' rather than the more radical goals of 'challenging men' and 'changing women's position in society'. Whilst there is clearly a pressing need to establish adequate levels of service provision, there is a need to ensure that strategies aim to prevent violence before it happens, as opposed to simply dealing with the consequences. Kelly (1998) has commented on a loss of vision about the possibility of ending violence against women and prevention being the central goal which has led to a focus on service provision and an unwillingness to challenge men.

The Scottish Executive's strategy document does make the link between male violence and women's subordinate position in society, and clearly sets out new action that the Government can take. *Living Without Fear* has been criticised for not being a strategy at all but simply a reference list of good practice. However, the Scottish Executive's Workplan has been criticised for only focusing on domestic violence whilst *Living Without Fear* makes the links between the different forms of violence.

There are undoubtedly some concerns about the way that politicians and policy makers are taking up the issue of violence against women. However, it is fair to say that we are in uncharted waters in that it is the first time that a government has been elected on a manifesto which puts a high priority on addressing violence against women. Feminist activists, campaigners and academics who have struggled to make male violence visible deserve the credit for the current policy focus. There are some encouraging signs. The Scottish Executive's Workplan, if implemented in full, outlines an ambitious programme and the service development fund has been established with new (albeit limited) funding. The Parliament's Justice Committee will be considering legislative changes to ensure greater protection for women experiencing violence and opposition Member of the Scottish Parliament Gil Paterson has established a cross-party group to address male violence against women and children, and monitor the Executive's progress on the issue. The Home Office's Crime Reduction Programme is providing funding never previously available for development projects, albeit the sum allocated (£6.3m) represents a tiny percentage of the overall crime reduction budget (£250m).

Bacchi (1999) concludes that, despite the contradiction facing feminists when reform proposals get taken up, feminist campaigners still have a role in continuing to analyse and deconstruct problem representations and their programmatic outcomes, as these representations shape an issue in ways which limit possibilities for change. Feminist campaigners will continue to analyse and deconstruct policy initiatives to ensure that they maximise the potential for change. Zero Tolerance, building on the pioneering work done by the refuge and rape crisis movements, put the essential truths of male violence into the public domain and helped to create a consensus for change. The challenge now is to ensure that policy reform is not restricted to a narrow focus on service provision, but works towards the elimination of male violence against women and children. Tackling the root causes of male violence means developing policy which aims to prevent violence before it happens, as opposed to simply dealing with the consequences.

Note

1 The original creative team comprised Evelyn Gillan, Franki Raffles and Susan Hart. The creative team since 1995 has been Evelyn Gillan and Elaine Samson.
2 The Scottish Executive's National Strategy launched by the First Minister on 29th November, 2000, now includes a much stronger focus on prevention. This is as a direct result of the Zero Tolerance Trust's membership of the Group who prepared the strategy.

END

THE MALE

PROTECTION

RACKET

Justice Z for women and children
ZERO TOLERANCE

From three to ninety three,

women are raped.

Z

ZERO TOLERANCE

HUSBAND, FATHER, STRANGER – MALE ABUSE OF POWER IS A CRIME

She lives with a successful businessman,
loving father and respected member of the community.

Last week he hospitalised her.

Z

ZERO TOLERANCE

EMOTIONAL, PHYSICAL, SEXUAL – MALE ABUSE OF POWER IS A CRIME

When they say no, they mean no.

Some men don't listen.

Z

ZERO TOLERANCE

References

An Evaluation of the Scottish Office Domestic Violence Media Campaign (1995) Central Research Unit, Scottish Executive, pp. 62–3.

Bacchi, C. L. (1999) *Women, Policy and Politics: the Construction of Policy Problems*, London: Sage.

Cosgrove, K. (1996) 'No man has the right', in Corrin, C. (ed.) *Women in a Violent World*, Edinburgh: Edinburgh University Press, pp. 186–203.

The Development of the Scottish Partnership on Domestic Abuse and Recent Work in Scotland (2000) Scottish Executive, p. 26.

Domestic Violence, Scottish Needs Assessment – A National Approach (1997) Scottish Forum for Public Health Medicine.

Final report of Activities of the Group of Specialists for Combating Violence Against Women (25th June 1997) Council of Europe.

Gillan, E. (1999) *All Due Respect*, In Concept Volume, no. 3, Edinburgh: Community Learning Unit.

Gordon, L. (1988) *Heroes in Their Own Lives: The Politics and History of Family Violence, Boston 1880–1960*, London: Virago.

Guberman, C. and Wolfe, M. (eds) (1985) *No Safe Place: Violence Against Women and Children*, Toronto: Women's Press.

Guidance on Preparing and Implementing a Multi-agency Strategy to Tackle Violence Against Women (1998) COSLA.

Hague, G. (1999) 'Domestic violence policy in the 1990s', in Watson, S. and Doyal, L. (eds) (1999) *Engendering Social Policy*, Buckingham: Open University Press.

Hester, M., Kelly, L. and Radford, J. (eds) (1996) *Women, Violence and Male Power*, Buckingham: Open University Press.

Hitting Home – A Report on the Police Response to Domestic Violence (1997) Her Majesty's Inspectorate of Constabulary.

Kelly, L. (1988) *Surviving Sexual Violence*, London: Polity Press.

Kelly, L. (1997) *Briefing Document on Evaluations*, Edinburgh: Zero Tolerance Trust.

Kelly, L. (1998) 'Resisting violence against women: experiences from Britain, Northern Ireland and former Yugoslavia', in *Workshop on Violence Against Women Report*, Calcutta: The British Council.

Kitzinger, J. and Hunt, K. (1993) *Evaluation of Edinburgh District Council's Zero Tolerance Campaign*, Edinburgh: Edinburgh District Council.

Living Without Fear (1999) Home Office.

Mama, A. (1989) *The Hidden Struggle: Statutory and Voluntary Sector Responses to Violence Against Black Women in the Home*, London: London Race and Housing Research Trust.

Private Trouble – Public Issue: An Inter-agency Strategy on Domestic Violence, (1997) Department of Public Health, Greater Glasgow Health Board.

Report to the Women's Committee, Edinburgh District Council (May 1992) *Adolescents' Knowledge About, and Attitudes to, Violence Against Women*.

Session Document, European Parliament (16th July 1997).

Stanko, E. and Radford, J. (1999) 'Violence against women and children: the contradictions of crime control under patriarchy', in Hester, M., Kelly, L. and Radford, J. (eds) *Women, Violence and Male Power*, Buckingham: Open University Press.

Workplan: Scottish Partnership on Domestic Abuse (1999) Scottish Executive.

20 Gendering domestic violence
The influence of feminism on policy and practice

Catherine Itzin

Introduction

In June 1999 the Government published a policy document entitled *Living Without Fear: An Integrated Approach to Tackling Violence Against Women*, setting out their 'long term goal to prevent the terrible crime of violence against women' by 'providing timely support and protection ... to improve women's chances of a decent life' and by 'bringing perpetrators to justice' (Cabinet Office/Home Office 1999: 4–5). In support of this policy, the Government was committing £6m for projects to reduce crime against women and £6.3m for the agency 'Victim support to assist victims through the legal process'.

The fact that these have become the Government's policy objectives is largely if not wholly as a result of the influence of feminist activism and scholarship over the previous three decades in the UK and USA. This chapter considers, with reference to the material in this book, the nature of this feminist influence and what the Government has still to take on board if the objective of 'prevention' defined in terms of 'stopping abusers abusing' is to be achieved (Kelly *et al.* 1991; Itzin 2000).

The nature, extent and gender of domestic violence

Prevalence

Living Without Fear includes current Government statistics on violence against women (p. 7):

- one woman in four experiences domestic violence at some stage in her life and it is estimated that between one in eight and one in ten has experienced domestic violence in the past year (British Crime Survey 1998);
- every week two women are killed by their current or former partners (Homicide Statistics 1998);
- every day thousands of children witness cruelty and violence behind closed doors. More than a third of children of domestic violence survivors are aware of what is going on and this rises to a half if the women have suffered repeat violence (British Crime Survey 1998)

- domestic violence accounts for one-quarter of all violent crime (British Crime Survey 1998);
- domestic violence often starts and/or escalates during pregnancy (British Medical Association 1998);
- reported rape has increased by 165 per cent in the last 10 years; the conviction rate has dropped from 24 per cent to 9 per cent (Home Office 1999).

These data show that violence against women occurs on a very substantial scale. At the same time, there is a consensus view that available data represent an underestimation of the nature and extent of this violence (Mooney 1994 and Chapter 2; British Medical Association 1998). The policy of the Women's Aid Federation (England) has been to recognise that any woman is at risk and that many women are victims (Harwin and Barron, Chapter 12).

Concepts and definitions

One contribution of feminism to domestic violence prevention has been to research its nature and extent. This is important because how violence is conceptualised and defined will determine what is visible and seen and known; how it is understood and explained; and what is and is not done about it through policy and practice (Itzin 2000b). Prevalence rates for domestic violence will, therefore, vary according to the concepts and definitions used. Most commonly domestic violence is conceptualised as physical violence or 'battering'.

Mooney, however, in a methodologically sophisticated study of a random sample of 571 women and 429 men in the borough of Islington in north London used their experiences to define domestic violence (1994 and Chapter 2). This approach produced five categories of violence:

- mental cruelty, which included verbal abuse (e.g. the calling of names, being ridiculed in front of other people), being deprived of money, clothes, sleep, prevented from going out;
- threats of violence or force;
- actual physical violence, which included being grabbed or pushed, or shaken, being punched or slapped, kicked, head-butted, attempted strangulation, hit with a weapon/object;
- physical injuries which included bruising or black eyes, scratches, cuts, bites, broken bones, being burned with cigarettes, scalded, knocked unconscious, and experiencing miscarriages as a result of an assault;
- and rape, defined as being made to have sex without consent involving actual violence and/or its threat.

The study found all these forms of domestic violence were common occurrences, experienced by one-quarter to one-third of women in their lifetimes and ten per cent of women in the previous 12 months, with a high rate of frequency for each type of violence.

The methodology of the study was designed to generate data on the attitudes and behaviour of men as well as the experiences of women. It was based on the four main sources of conflict identified by Dobash and Dobash (1979, and Chapter 11) as leading to violent attacks by men: their possessiveness and jealousy; their expectations concerning women's domestic work; a sense of their right to punish 'their' women for perceived wrong-doing; and the importance to men of maintaining or exercising their position of authority.

The study found that, by their own account, nearly two out of three men admitted they would use violence on their wives or women partners in 'conflict situations' defined as: being confronted with infidelity, being 'nagged', a partner arriving late home without explanation, a heated row, or when expectations over housework or childcare are not met. Nearly one in five men said they would react violently every time. A similar number said they would resort to violence in at least two of those situations. One in five (19 per cent) admitted to actually having used violence against women in at least one of the situations. Only 37 per cent of men questioned said they would never use violence.

These data were corroborated by the women who said they would expect their men to use violence against them in at least one of these 'conflict situations', and consequently they had developed strategies to avoid these situations occurring. This study evidences empirically the violence and abuse used by ordinary men routinely on a very substantial scale against the women with whom they live and share their lives. The readiness of large numbers of men to admit to using violence against women in these ways suggests that it is regarded as a normal part of their behaviour, and illustrates how normalised it is in the gendered relations between men and women.

Hanmer's study of 60 women in West Yorkshire (see Hanmer 1998, and Chapter 1) produced data which brought sharply into focus aspects of men's controlling and coercive behaviour as forms of domestic violence and abuse. Hanmer categorised these as:

- men's 'jealousy motivated strictures on what their women wear and how they look' (p. 136);
- restrictions on women's movements outside the home (in some cases 'so extreme that women never leave the house without his accompanying her' (p. 137) or being 'commanded to keep their heads down and look straight ahead' (p. 133));
- men's multiple extra-marital sexual relationships (as causing 'great unhappiness to women'(p. 133));
- sexual activity both forced (rape) and denied;
- both the creation (through forced pregnancy) and denial of new life (through forced abortion or miscarriage as a result of battering during pregnancy);
- financial exploitation (having money such as wages or benefits taken from them);

- domestic servitude (having to maintain excessive and unreasonable standards of housekeeping).

Helena Kennedy (in Quaid and Itzin, Chapter 9) also identifies the abuse of women's domestic labour as a form of domestic violence.

Importantly, Hanmer used women's accounts to conceptualise domestic violence in terms of men's negative feelings, and the 'pattern of [their] emotional response . . . to hold women responsible for [their] feelings' (Hanmer 1998: 132; see also Chapter 1). Adams (Chapter 17) illustrates this with the man on the Emerge domestic violence intervention programme who described himself as 'getting mad' and yelling and swearing at his wife for 'doing something stupid, really stupid' (she'd had a flat tyre), and then going 'quiet', but knowing 'she could tell I was angry'. This man was priding himself on not having resorted to violence because, as he put it, 'it didn't get physical', and his anger was 'contained'.

A characteristic of all forms of men's violence is the exercise of power and control. It is important for domestic violence prevention to see men's controlling behaviours as a continuum, at one end of which are 'interrupting, not listening, claiming the truth and withholding affection' (Adams, Chapter 17), along which are the range of behaviours identified above, at the other end of which are the behaviours experienced by women whom Helena Kennedy has represented in court, of being so terrorised and controlled that even when they had killed their husband, they couldn't believe he was dead (Quaid and Itzin, Chapter 9).

Co-occurrence of domestic violence, intra- and extrafamilial child sexual abuse and rape

Another contribution of feminism has come from identifying the connections between physical and sexual violence and abuse against women and children in the home, extrafamilial child sexual abuse and exploitation, and rape. The links between domestic violence and child abuse were recognised initially amongst children in refuges with their mothers. The Women's Aid movement conceptualises domestic violence *as* child abuse in the form of emotional damage inflicted on children who are caught up in living with the abuse of their mothers (Harwin and Barron, Chapter 12; Hague *et al.*, Chapter 7). Research has now established a very high co-occurrence of domestic violence and child abuse of 40–60 per cent (see McGee, Chapter 5 and Hester, Chapter 6).

Farmer and Owen (1998; 2000) found, in a study of 44 child protection cases, domestic violence in two-fifths of the child sexual abuse cases, and three-fifths of the physical abuse, neglect and emotional abuse cases, and cited findings in other studies as high as 70 per cent. Hester (Chapter 6), in research conducted with the NSPCC, found that of the 111 cases of child abuse accepted for service in a randomly selected period of time, three-quarters were for child sexual abuse, and of these two-thirds also involved domestic violence, almost always

violence against the mother by her male partner. This study found 'that the perpetrator of the domestic violence and the abuser of the child/ren was likely to
be the same individual, usually the child's natural father'. Research cited by
Harwin and Barron (Chapter 12) has shown that between 45 per cent and 70
per cent of children whose mothers are abused are themselves being directly
abused, usually by the same man (Stark and Flitcroft 1984; 1988; Kelly 1994;
Mullender and Morley 1994).

Lees (Chapter 4) found an overlap between marital rape and domestic violence, and marital rape and murder, and 'no evidence that rapists can be divided
into distinct groups on the basis of whether or not they rape strangers, acquaintances or sexual partners or wives'. She describes it as 'a myth that different
types of men rape their wives than rape strangers' and considers it likely that
many rapists do both. Eldridge (1998; 2000), citing sex offender studies, found
an overlap between intrafamilial and extrafamilial child sexual abuse and rape:
in a study of rapists, one-third admitted child sexual abuse (Weinrott and
Saylor 1991), and in two studies of child sexual abusers, nearly one in five were
also found to be rapists (Abel *et al.* 1988; Becker and Coleman 1988). Itzin
(1996; 1997a, b), using survivor data, found an overlap between intra- and
extrafamilial child sexual abuse and exploitation, as well as evidence from
various sources that, in many cases, 'the sexual abusers of children are ordinary,
heterosexual men often with wives and children' (Itzin 2000b: 446). Altogether
there is evidence of a very substantial overlap between domestic violence, child
abuse and rape perpetrated by men against their wives or women partners and
their children, as well as sexual violence and abuse against other women and
other people's children.

Gendering the power relations of domestic violence

Male violence and male dominance

One of feminism's major contributions to domestic violence policy and practice
has been to identify men as primarily the perpetrators of domestic violence and
child sexual abuse (Hanmer and Saunders 1984; Kelly 1988; Dobash and
Dobash 1992; Itzin 2000); and to conceptualise this as a problem of men's violence in the context of social power relations gendered in terms of male dominance and female subordination (Patel 1998, and Chapter 10; Hanmer 1998,
and Chapter 1; Itzin 2000). This is articulated in various ways in this book.

Dobash and Dobash (Chapter 11) have found that 'the predominant pattern
of violence between spouses is one of male violence directed at a female
partner.' This includes homicide in the home, which regardless of the gender of
the victim 'is based on a history of quarrels, usually about sexual jealousy and
possessiveness . . . the end point in a series of conflicts . . . the final event following a history of male violence'. Dobash *et al.* (Chapter 16) refer to the 'accumu-
lating knowledge and systematic research [showing] that many men who assault
their wives are habituated to such acts' and the evidence that 'violence [is]

intentional behaviour chosen by men as a tactic or resource associated with attempts to dominate, control and punish women' (see also Dobash and Dobash 1999; Dobash *et al.* 2000).

Harwin and Barron (Chapter 12) attribute domestic violence crucially to 'the man's belief in his right to control the women in his family'. Dobash and Dobash (1992 and Chapter 11) describe this as 'traditionally a prerogative of men who were given authority over and granted the right within … marriage to use physical force and violence' to exercise control over their women and children. They describe 'the use of violence and its threat [as] how ordinary men establish and maintain control in their relationships with their women partners'. They conceptualise 'male violence as one end of a continuum of male domination.' Like child sexual abuse, domestic violence is something that men do 'because they want to, because they can and because largely they can get away with it' (Itzin 2000a, b).

Emerge believe that 'non-battering men have much in common with battering men since they share a common social and cultural heritage … since all men grow up in a sexist and patriarchal society' (Adams, Chapter 17). Harwin and Barron (Chapter 12) are concerned about conceptualising 'violent families' and 'normal families' as mutually exclusive categories, and the 'significant failure to understand that violence and abuse are extremely common features of many relationships and may not always be made evident'. They stress the importance of seeing domestic violence 'within a social and structural context of unequal power relationships between women and men'. The public education work of the Zero Tolerance Charitable Trust (see Gillian and Samson, Chapter 19) is premised on the understanding of men's violence against women as an abuse of male power in the context of structural inequalities. They have 'named the gender of the problem as male', and use as a strapline on their campaign posters 'male abuse of power is a crime'. There are illustrations of these posters in Chapter 19.

The Duluth Domestic Violence Intervention Project developed a model to illustrate how men use power to exercise control over women. This includes using intimidation, emotional abuse, isolation, male privilege, economic abuse, coercion and threats, and by minimising and denying the abuse or blaming women for it. The Duluth Power and Control Wheel with its examples of these abuses is reproduced in Appendix 2.

Hanmer (1998, and Chapter 1) argues that 'men have advantages that come from being male, from being sons, husbands and fathers' (p. 129) and that men gain both 'intangible and tangible benefits… from the abuse of women' (p. 130). She sees violence as 'how individual men maintain their socially superior position and the basis for the extraction of all other benefits men make from women' (p. 129). She argues that 'the advantages men gain from violence have been known for some time as "women's oppression" rather than the personal and social benefits to men'. She concludes that women's accounts reveal men as 'a primary force in the construction of social life characterised by degradation, humiliation and personal harm', and the necessity, therefore, of 'dismantling the male privileged position over women and children in the family' (p. 131).

The 'intersectionality' of race, ethnicity, religion, class and gender

Mama (1989, and Chapter 3) conducted a milestone study in the 1980s in London in collaboration with the women's refuge movement and community organisations of over 100 black women from 21 different countries and found no difference between black women's and white women's experience of domestic violence except black women had the additional burden of the effects of racism. This involved having to contend with stereotypes about black families. There was a particular fear of deportation, and Mama found that 'in all cases the police appear more ready to investigate immigration status than to respond to domestic violence in black communities'. It would be interesting to replicate this study now, to see how much this might have changed in response to developments in policing over the past decade.

Patel (1998, and Chapter 10) sees 'the family' as a site of 'power relations,' where 'race, gender and class lock men and women into varying subordinate and dominant positions'. Culture and religion in all societies, she argues, 'act to confer legitimacy on gender inequalities 'and on gendered violence'. The black 'struggle' is based on the myth of homogeneity amongst minority communities in the UK without the 'recognition that culture and religion also perpetuate class, caste and gender inequalities'. In this context, she sees multi-culturalism functioning to shift the focus away from the subordination of women and men's violence within the family and the ethnic community, and in particular away from the control over the sexuality and fertility of women imposed by the patriarchal tenets of religious fundamentalism.

Hanmer's study of 60 women in West Yorkshire, half of whom were of Asian origin and half white of local origin, found that whatever the cultural differences, the women had in common 'devastating relationships with men': that whatever the race, culture, religion or ethnicity, they 'do not produce fundamentally different gendered experiences of violence' (Hanmer 1998, p. 129–30 and Chapter 1). Thus, for example, women from all cultural groups are subject to the whole range of domestic violence as defined earlier in this chapter. In the view of Mama (Chapter 3) and Patel (Chapter 10), it is necessary to separate gender oppression from race and religion oppression, in order to see 'the violent male', and to grasp as a fundamental and overarching 'home truth' that 'racism', as Mama puts it, 'does not take up the hand of the black man and oblige him to beat up his partner'.

Why women stay with violent men

Mooney (1994, and Chapter 2) found 27 per cent of women saying they had stayed with violent men for reasons of economic dependence; 27 per cent in the hope he would change; 26 per cent because they had nowhere to go; 20 per cent concerned about the effect on the children of breaking up the family home; and 19 per cent out of fear of further violence. These data are corroborated and elaborated in various ways in the book.

One reason women stay is the responsibility they feel for the violence taking place. It is a characteristic of violent men to blame women for their violence and women may respond by feeling they deserved it and turning blame into self-blame (Mooney 1994, and Chapter 2; Hanmer 1998, and Chapter 1). Kennedy (in Quaid and Itzin, Chapter 9) describes women feeling shame and often hiding the evidence of violence and giving false accounts. She describes men 'destroying a woman's self worth so that she ends up believing it is her own fault and she deserves no better'.

Domestic violence has characteristics in common with methods of torture: 'Isolation, humiliation and degradation followed by protestations of love and acts of kindness with the threat of returning to the degraded state if some type of compliance is not obtained' (Brown 1987: 125, cited in Lees, Chapter 4). As with torture, the victimised woman may 'reinterpret his violence as caring for her' or 'proof of the man's positive feelings' (Hanmer 1998: 132, and Chapter 1). Abused women may have a tendency to minimise the nature and scale of the violence and its harm (Lees, Chapter 4; Kennedy in Quaid and Itzin, Chapter 9). Although the abuse they experience may be severe, it might not be regarded by them as such. Swann (2000), for example, describes girls being introduced into prostitution by pimps who use methods of extreme degradation which the girls interpret as evidence of being loved.

Various contributors describe the effects of domestic violence on women as: 'grinding down and self-diminishment' (Griffiths, Chapter 8); denial, disbelief, shock, confusion, fear, powerlessness, vulnerability, loss of control (Lees, Chapter 4); depression, hopelessness, learned helplessness, heightened vigilance in anticipating the violence, and terror (Kennedy in Quaid and Itzin, Chapter 9). These are all effects associated with trauma, and with Post Traumatic Stress Disorder (PTSD), and as such, provide some explanation why women might feel powerless to leave violent men.

Another reason why women find it difficult to leave violent men is the fear that he will keep or take the children. Hanmer (1998, and Chapter 1) found that 'both contact and residence orders can be made in favour of men who have violently abused both women and children' (1998: 138; see also Armstrong 2000 and Itzin 2000b). In other cases, men abused or rejected women's children from previous relationships, for example, forcing her to put them into the care of a local authority for their protection and 'as a way of maintaining marital harmony'. Statutory agencies may also force women to make a choice between their husband and their children in cases of domestic violence and child sexual abuse (Hanmer 1998: 140; Farmer and Owen 1998; 2000).

Mama (Chapter 3) found the lack of alternative housing to be a key factor in black women's choice to leave violent men. Dobash and Dobash (Chapter 11), Harwin and Barron (Chapter 12) and Morley (Chapter 13) also identify the lack of affordable independent housing as a major obstacle in the way of women escaping domestic violence. Providing 'refuge' housing for women and their children in immediate danger when leaving violent men has been the first and foremost objective of the Women's Aid movement in the UK (see Harwin and

Barron, Chapter 12; Hague *et al.*, Chapter 7), and the battered women's movement in the USA (see Dobash and Dobash, Chapter 11).

This provision has been of such over-riding importance because of the evidence that men become most violent and dangerous to women when they try to
leave. Lees (Chapter 4) cites research findings that 'ending a relationship with a
violent man puts a woman at particular risk for her life'. Browne (1987) found
that 'ninety percent of women subjected to violence in the family thought the
abuser could or would kill them' (p. 115) and that 'many women stay in violent
marriages because they believe their partner would retaliate against an attempt
to leave him with further violence' (p. 113). Finkelhor and Yllo (1985, cited in
Lees, Chapter 4) found 'wife rape most likely to occur during and after the
break up of a relationship'.

Lees (Chapter 4) has found that women whose husbands have been charged
or convicted of marital rape may retract their evidence or visit their husbands in
prison because they believe their lives are in danger and they fear retribution or
retaliation, especially if they testified against their husbands. Browne (1987)
concluded from her study that: 'She is theirs. She cannot leave and refuse to
talk to them. They may nearly kill their mates, but they do not want to lose
them' (p. 115).

It is not so much a question of why women stay with violent men, but a
matter of wonder that many women are able to leave at all. Of primary importance from a public policy perspective, however, is that women leaving violent
men does nothing to prevent domestic violence, or to stop men from using violence against women. It only protects a particular woman from violence perpetrated by a particular man at that particular moment in time. As Hanmer has
observed (1998: 142, and Chapter 1): 'when women succeed in leaving, men
often form another relationship and have further children, continuing the
pattern of violence and control'. To have any meaningful impact on domestic
violence prevention, men who use violence against women must be seen as
'serial abusers' and policy developed that takes this into account.

The use of violence by women against men

Dobash and Dobash (1979 and Chapter 11) have found that when women
'respond to men's violence with counter-violence' they are usually acting 'in
self-defence and/or retaliation' for abuse that, (citing Saunders 1988) involves
'a narrow range of acts . . . not usually intended to inflict injury.' The analysis by
Griffiths (Chapter 8) of data from her study of women who fought back against
or killed violent partners illustrates this.

Griffiths has categorised women's responses to violence as 'reactions, resolutions and resistance'. In reaction to a man's violence, a woman may initially
walk out (and then return), or directly challenge the men with physical retaliation. Women stop 'fighting back', when they find this triggers a worsening of
the man's violence both in terms of frequency and severity. Confronted by the
man's greater physical strength and ability to overpower, they fear the repercus-

sions of trying to hit back. Women in this position have to shift their responses to preventing or lessening the likelihood of the man using violence.

A number of women in Griffith's sample had left and all returned, some on more than one occasion. Hanmer found that leaving temporarily and leaving permanently involve different 'internal resolutions', and women often return as 'the conflict of feeling generated by leaving becomes too intense for them to remain away' (p. 133). Men can also 'vary their strategies when the limits to [their] acceptable violence are reached' and 'women begin to leave', by apologising, for example, and promising to stop the violence (Hanmer 1998: 130, 141, and Chapter 1).

Women may go to great lengths to maintain a relationship, using appeasement and efforts to please the man, or more damagingly, as Griffiths found, through the use of 'tranquillisers, or alcohol, or illicit drugs as a means of blocking – and blanking – out the effects of the violence.' Her study showed that often women will continue to seek 'resolution' in this way unsuccessfully, endangering themselves in an environment of worsening violence. 'Women kill,' says Kennedy (in Quaid and Itzin, Chapter 9) 'when all her usual strategies for coping will not sustain her.' Jones (1991) found that 'women kill when violent men won't quit'. The women Griffiths studied didn't mean to kill, but 'to bring about a cessation to the men's violence.' Dobash and Dobash (Chapter 11) cite findings that 'women usually kill men in acts of self-preservation when their situation has reached a desperate state'.

In Chapter 8, Griffiths argues that 'a new defence to murder is required, one that acknowledges women's experiences of and responses to domestic violence in the same way that self defence or provocation acknowledges men's experience of imminent attack or provocation'. She explains how, historically, the existing defence of provocation reflects men's right to 'angered retaliation'; the entitlement of men to respond in anger to the injury of verbal or physical abuse or its threat, with a 'sudden loss of control' that may be lethal in consequence. By contrast, she argues, women are denied the defence of provocation because their anger and its effects are cumulative, 'slow-boiling' rather than sudden. This, she thinks, is better reflected in the concept of 'self-preservation' than provocation, and argues that it should be added to existing defences to murder (see Dobash and Dobash, Chapter 11 and Kennedy in Quaid and Itzin, Chapter 9).

Gendering domestic violence interventions

Women helping women

This Reader contains chapters on the development of services provided by the Women's Aid movement in the UK for women and children in need of a place to go to escape violent men (Harwin and Barron, Chapter 12; Hague *et al.*, Chapter 7; see also Pahl 1985). Locally, these have included refuge accommodation, support, advice and information on accessing statutory services. Nationally, Women's Aid has provided an overview of law and policy and co-ordinated responses to government and statutory agencies. Moreover, Women's Aid has pioneered work with child victims of domestic violence and abuse, developing specialist children's workers in three-quarters of its refuges, and influencing child protection policy, with the recognition that the protection of women can be the most effective form of child protection. Listening to women and children and believing what most people without experience of domestic violence find unbelievable has been central to Women's Aid policy, often in the face of hostility and disbelief.

The focus is on the safety of women and on holding men responsible for their violence and abuse. Women's Aid operate an 'open door policy': no woman is turned away and, in recognition of the dangers for women leaving violent men, all women are found a safe place to go. This is particularly important given that, on average, women contact ten different agencies, many of them more than once, before receiving effective help (Hanmer 1995). Dobash and Dobash (Chapter 11) believe that the 'importance of housing cannot be over-estimated'. This is iterated and elaborated by Morley in Chapter 13.

Dobash and Dobash (1992, and Chapter 11) describe the women's refuge movement as a driving force for change, assisting victims, challenging male violence and changing women's position in society. They describe the refuge as a 'transformative experience' for individual women, and a 'living laboratory of social change'. This is true. They describe the women's movement as a social movement which has 'achieved recognition throughout the world of male violence and the physical abuse of women in the home as problems of importance, and a legitimate concern of government, and placed this on the agendas of social and political change.' This is also true.

The influence of the refuge movement in the UK is illustrated in this book in Harwin and Barron's chapter (12) which charts the history of Women's Aid activism and influence on developing government policy on domestic violence over the past 30 years. This is reflected most recently in the government policy document *Living Without Fear* (1999) which borrowed from the Zero Tolerance campaign the crucial issues of Provision, Protection and Prevention to conceptualise and structure its policy objectives. A substantial portion of the document is dedicated to providing examples of good practice. These number 70, at least half of which have been developed and provided by feminist organisations, with many more having been influenced by feminism. Pressure from Women's Aid was instrumental in creating the impetus behind the Home Affairs Committee on Domestic Violence and its recommendations in 1993. Women's refuges working with statutory and voluntary sector agencies in localities provided the model for the Home Office Inter-agency Circular in 1995. The establishment of local Domestic Violence Fora was built on the foundations of years of Women's Aid work, as have the establishment by the London Metropolitan Police and other forces, of Domestic Violence Units and the employment of Domestic Violence Officers. The Crime and Disorder Act 1998 placed a mandatory requirement on localities to develop multi-agency plans for crime prevention which included domestic violence. The full programme of necessary measures that are still required to protect women and children from violent men is set out in the Women's Aid Federation (England) policy document *Families Without Fear* in Appendix 1. This represents the agenda for developing government policy over the next decade, a priority being 'a national strategy to improve funding and support for refuges' (Harwin and Barron, Chapter 12)

The influence of feminism and the Women's Aid movement can also be seen in the 'mapping of services working with families where there is domestic violence' (Humphreys *et al.* 2000). This surveyed all refuges affiliated to the Women's Aid Federations of England, Wales, Northern Ireland and Scotland; the four children's charities NSPCC, NCH Action for Children, Barnardos, and the Children's Society; projects working with perpetrators of domestic violence; each social service department in England, and health trust in Northern Ireland, together with an audit in Scotland. It found 326 Women's Aid projects, 449 projects provided by the children's charities, patchy provision in the statutory sector, with comprehensive services in some areas, participation in Domestic Violence Fora in 90 per cent of local authorities, mention of domestic violence in 65 per cent of Children's Services Plans, but only 26 per cent with plans for service provision, 20 per cent of local authorities with no designated services, and 47 per cent with no designated member of staff responsible for domestic violence policy and practice. The survey found only 19 projects providing specialist provision for perpetrators, but also found it 'impossible to ascertain what proportion this represents of actual projects' (p. 6).

Altogether, much has been achieved by the influence of feminism and women's movement activism, what Dobash and Dobash (1992) describe as the 'great mobilisation of women'. Much remains to be done, in particular in the area of domestic violence prevention, defined as taking effective steps to stop men using violence against women and children in the home (Itzin 2000a, b).

Holding men responsible for using violence and stopping it

This Reader also contains five models of programmes of intervention which focus primarily on individual men and their violence. This section focuses on what can be learned from them for purposes of domestic violence prevention. Three programmes work with men, all or most of whom have been convicted of domestic violence offences. These are Emerge in Boston (see Adams, Chapter 17) and two programmes in Scotland, CHANGE and Lothian Domestic Violence Probation Project (Dobash *et al.*, Chapter 16). There are two projects which involve a co-ordinated community approach to policing and other agency responses: the Domestic Abuse Intervention Project (DAIP) in Duluth Minnesota (Pence and McDonnell 1998, and Chapter 14); and the Repeat Victimisation Policing Programme in West Yorkshire (Hanmer and Griffiths, Chapter 18).

The fundamental principles in each case are to ensure the safety of abused women and their children, and to hold men responsible and accountable for their violence, seeking to 'increase men's insights into their own behaviour and emotions and helping them to end their violent behaviour [in recognition of] the harm they have inflicted on their partners and children' (Dobash *et al.*, Chapter 16). Each has been influenced by the women's refuge movements and what is known from feminism about men's violence and women's experience of it. Each has been subject to an evaluation of its effectiveness, and the lessons to be learned from these models about the gendered nature of domestic violence are important to domestic violence policy and practice in the USA and UK, and crucial to domestic violence prevention.

The men's programmes

Emerge was the world's first batterer intervention programme, founded in 1977. Currently 75 per cent of its clients are court mandated. In order to successfully complete the 40–session-20–week minimum programme, the men have to stop battering; stop minimising their violence; stop blaming their partner for their violence or for any steps she took in response to their violence; and recognise how their abuse has adversely affected their partner and children. The programme makes and maintains contact with each client's victim, providing them with information about the programme and, for purposes of monitoring the man's progress, requesting information about their partner's previous and continuing abuse (Adams, Chapter 17).

The CHANGE project in central Scotland and the Lothian Domestic Violence Probation Project (LDVPP) in Edinburgh involved four years of foundation work with local Women's Aid groups. Men participating in the programmes had been found guilty of an offence involving violent behaviour toward their partner, and having been assessed as appropriate for the programme, were participating as a condition of a probation order. The Scottish Office/Home Office evaluation compared the outcomes of the two programmes with other criminal justice interventions, which consisted of being fined, admonished, placed on probation or sent to prison.

Like Emerge, both Scottish programmes maintained contact with the men's women partners to keep them informed of the work. LDVPP produced leaflets for the men and their partners with 'explicit expectations about the mandated nature of the man's attendance and the focus of the programme on his violence and ways of stopping it; with no promises to keep the relationship together; rejecting alcohol as a "cause" of violence; stressing that she was not responsible for the violence; and telling her that her safety could not be guaranteed and she should continue with safety plans, e.g. injunctions, police, friends, neighbours, Women's Aid' (Dobash *et al.*, Chapter 16).

Findings

Emerge have found that 'supportive encouragement without confrontation and consequences does not induce battering men to give up abusive behaviours', and can have the opposite effect. Only about half of the men complete batterer intervention programmes. The most common reasons for 'programme termination' are 'continued acts of violence or harassment ... failure to admit abuse, or failure to take responsibility for abuse'. Completers have a lower rate of recidivism, but 'substantial numbers still revert to physical and psychological abuse'.

A feature of the programme is 'documentation of the men's violence, as acknowledged, reported and recorded', but it is 'not uncommon for batterers to disavow any violence once they have completed or been terminated from a batterer intervention programme ... even violence they had previously acknowledged while attending the programme'. Emerge have found that 'the vast majority of batterers don't seek help unless ordered to do so, and even many of those who do remain resistant to change'.

The evaluation of the Scottish programmes found that, based on police records over a 12–month period, only seven per cent of the men on the programmes and ten per cent of the men receiving the other criminal justice sanctions had re-offended. Dobash *et al.* (Chapter 16) observe that, on this evidence, they might have formed the view that 'arrest and prosecution have an extraordinary effect on subsequent incidents of violence and that the innovative programmes are only slightly more effective in reducing levels of violence than other criminal justice sanctions.' However, data collected from the men's partners presented a very different picture. They reported a much higher incidence of violent behaviour: 33 per cent, not seven per cent for men on the programmes, and 70 per cent not ten per cent for men with the other criminal justice sanctions. Importantly, however, less than one-third of the men from the programmes had used violence as compared with nearly two-thirds of the men with other criminal justice sanctions. Re-offending was not a reliable measure of recidivism.

Women whose partners had participated in the programme, reported that the quality of their lives had improved and that their partners were 'more likely to see their point of view, to be aware of their feelings and to respect them; less likely to restrict their lives; and more likely than in the past to take responsibility for their violence' (Dobash *et al.*, Chapter 16, also 2000). This provides another illustration of the importance of women's accounts in developing policy – and practice – responses to domestic violence.

Conclusions

In the USA research has found that 'routine judicial monitoring of men's participation in batterer intervention programmes increases attendance and participation and decreases recidivism' (Gondolf 1998, cited in Adams, Chapter 17). In Emerge's experience, 'judges who have become educated about domestic violence have routinely sanctioned men for being terminated ... [through] incarceration, increasing the term of probation or requiring the perpetrator to re-enrol with the warning that additional problems will result in a jail sentence'. However, Adams reports (Chapter 17) that judges are referring batterers to 'anger management' courses with less stringent criteria for completion, and not informed by the experience of abused women in the ways that have been shown to be crucial to domestic violence prevention.

The evaluation of the Scottish programmes, for example, found that 'in comparison to other criminal justice sanctions, participation in one of the programmes had significantly reduced the prevalence and frequency of [the men's] violence and significantly suppressed the range and frequency of their controlling and coercive behaviours'. Dobash *et al.* (Chapter 16) concluded from their study and research in the USA, 'that well-managed criminal justice projects delivering a programme focussing on the offender and the violent offending behaviour are more likely than other forms of criminal justice interventions to reduce or eliminate violence and intimidating behaviour ... and associated coercive and controlling behaviours'; that 'the process of being arrested, charged, prosecuted and sentenced to one of the programmes ... provided a lever, and an "incentive" for men to participate', as did 'the fear of an escalation of sanctions'; and that, in addition to treatment and re-education, the programmes also operated as 'a form of social control and surveillance'. It appears to be the combination of criminal justice sanctions and men's programmes influenced by a feminist analysis of men's violence that produce the best outcomes in domestic violence prevention. At the same time, Dobash *et al.* (Chapter 16) found that criminal justice system sanctions on their own were also effective in reducing the incidence of violence reported by one-third.

The community based multi-agency policing programmes

The Domestic Abuse Intervention Project (DAIP) – or the 'Duluth Model' as it is known – began in 1980 in Duluth, Minnesota as a community based interagency initiative based on negotiating agreements with all relevant agencies 'simultaneously to enact policies directing practitioners to follow certain procedures when responding to domestic violence assault' (see Chapter 14 and Appendix 2). The Duluth approach also involves a process of continual scrutiny of all relevant agency policies and procedures, and the development of new policies and protocols, supported by the use of an audit methodology. Change is managed and monitored through these administrative processes.

Pence and McDonnell (1998, and Chapter 14) emphasise that 'in designing an effective response, methods must be in place to ensure a high degree of practitioner compliance because for a battered woman, an unpredictable system is like playing Russian roulette' (p. 43). In the Duluth model, there is a requirement that a 'law, a policy, or a procedure must be constructed in a way that allows the practitioner to account for the probability that offenders who are batterers are likely to retaliate against their victims because of actions taken by the state or community'. At the same time they believe that the 'intervention approach must shift the burden of confrontation from the victim to the institution to whatever extent possible' (pp. 42–3), and they have found that 'victims are safer if the state or court has some level of control over the offenders' (p. 45).

The West Yorkshire Repeat Victimisation Policing Project is an operational model for policing domestic violence implemented and evaluated during 1997 in a Division of the West Yorkshire Police Authority in the UK. It has adopted a strategic approach to mainstreaming domestic violence policy in the context of existing policing policy and procedures for targeting resources on 'repeat victimisation' for burglary and car theft. Previous work with the West Yorkshire police had identified a similar pattern for domestic violence crime. This suggested that domestic violence might also be reduced by adopting a 'repeat victimisation' approach (Hanmer *et al.* 1999). This project was based on the understanding that protecting women from home-based violence requires effective responses to abusing men. It focused on gathering evidence to charge and convict, and on making early interventions to prevent escalation into repeat and continued offending.

Arrest

The Duluth model operates a mandatory arrest policy subject to individual practitioner's judgement and discretion. At the macro level, a mandatory arrest policy is critical for victim protection and offender accountability. At a micro level, however, 'victims may or may not be helped by [an arrest or] a conviction' (Pence and McDonnell 1998: 42, and Chapter 14) for various reasons:

- not every case of domestic violence is best resolved in a courtroom;
- every act of domestic violence does not necessarily lead to a serious attack on a victim;
- when victims call for help, they are not calling to activate a long, hostile criminal proceeding. They are usually calling to make something happen immediately;
- many individuals will not be helped by a prosecution;
- some cases in which an assault did occur are almost unprovable in a courtroom using the standard of proof required in a criminal trial.

At the same time 'with no intervention (sanction and/or rehabilitation), most offenders will continue to be violent for many years' (Pence and McDonnell 1998: 54, and Chapter 14). Understanding the paradox of the need for a mandatory arrest policy, which may only be used in particular cases, is crucial to an effective public policy response to domestic violence.

West Yorkshire Police have a policy for both responding to the safety needs of women and for enforcing the law when an assault takes place within the domestic environment exactly as it would in the case of stranger assaults outside the home. The policy also requires police to report domestic violence incidents 'irrespective of whether the attendances result in arrests or criminal charges' because only a proportion of domestic violence results in arrest and prosecution, and 'records of criminal incidents only [do] not permit vulnerable victims to be fully identified' (Hanmer and Griffiths, Chapter 18). As in Duluth, police discretion has not been eliminated in the handling of particular domestic violence cases.

The repeat victimisation project found that 27 per cent of attendances resulted in arrest, and that 'most men were not arrested and did not require a repeat attendance'. Moreover, this study found that arrest produced an escalation of violence, and increased the risk of re-attendance by 51 per cent. Hanmer and Griffiths conclude, like Pence and McDonnell, that arrest is not appropriate in many cases; when it is, it is a means of identifying men who are more violent and likely to require further police interventions (see Chapters 14 and 18). Dobash *et al.* (Chapter 16) discuss findings from research in the USA on the effectiveness of arrest as a deterrent against domestic violence.

Surveillance and social control

The repeat victimisation project focused on individual perpetrators and their history of police attendances for violence to any woman. Each attendance was recorded by household address, by victim name and by offender name, because 'women and men may move and men may attack more than one woman either serially or at the same time' (Hanmer and Griffiths, Chapter 18). The programme focused on demotivating perpetrators and supporting victims through staged interventions involving letters to perpetrators and victims, arranging neighbourhood and police watches, and visits from a Domestic Violence Officer. Like Duluth's, this is a paper-driven procedural intervention which standardises responses and ensures consistency independent of any particular individual practitioner's knowledge and views about domestic violence.

The project demonstrated the effectiveness of early and targeted interventions by the police to demotivate men and to curtail their willingness to continue to abuse current and past female partners. The Home Office has now funded the roll out of a three-year programme of implementation of the repeat victimisation model throughout the West Yorkshire Police Authority.

Distinguishing between violence used by perpetrators and victims

The Duluth programme makes clear distinctions between violence used by perpetrators and violence used by victims:

> To hold batterers accountable and protect victims we need to understand how the violence is used by a person and how victims are affected by the violence ... First we do not assume that all violence is the same. The person who is physically and sexually abused over a period of time and uses illegal violence as a way of stopping the violence is not doing the same thing as the person who continually uses violence to dominate and control a partner. Similarly, a person who engages in abusive behaviours, including

grabbing and shoving his or her partner, is not to be treated the same as the person who threatens to kill his partner and uses actions to terrorise her

(1998: 44, and Chapter 14).

As a consequence, the programme uses criteria to distinguish between self-defence and assault, and victims who have assaulted their abusers are conceptualised in terms of a 'primary aggressor and two assailants' (p. 55). Police are trained to identify the primary aggressor, to determine probable cause, to distinguish self-defence from an assault, and to record the history of the violence. In the USA, the Duluth Model has been implemented and used by the military in its response to domestic violence offenders amongst its personnel.

Societal tolerance as an obstacle to domestic violence prevention

The Zero Tolerance Trust do not believe there is a deep-seated quality in men that makes them violent and abusive, but rather a problem with male socialisation that affects large numbers of men (Gillan and Samson, Chapter 19). Their emphasis, therefore, is on long term solutions that address gender socialisation. A survey conducted in 1992 by the Zero Tolerance Charitable Trust on the attitudes and beliefs of secondary school children found that one in two boys and one in three girls thought that there were some circumstances when it was okay to hit a girl or force her to have sex; a significant minority of boys (36 per cent) thought they personally might force a girl to have sex; more than one in two young people thought women provoked violence in a range of contexts; and at least half knew someone who had been hit by a male partner and someone who had been sexually abused (Zero Tolerance Charitable Trust 1992, and Gillian and Samson, Chapter 19). A subsequent survey conducted by Burton, Kitzinger, Kelly and Regan (1998) found what the government policy document *Living Without Fear* (1999) described as a 'worryingly high acceptance of sexual violence by young men' (p. 46).

This climate of acceptance and tolerance of domestic violence was illustrated in 1996 when Paul Gascoine the England footballer was discovered to have battered his wife shortly before a key match was to be played. The coach decided he deserved a second chance despite pictures in the press of his wife with a bruised face and bandaged hand. Women's groups at the International Conference on Violence Abuse and Women's Citizenship taking place that week made the point that if he'd assaulted his coach, he would have been dropped from the England squad.

Zero Tolerance promote a criminalisation message that physical violence and rape are crimes, but often have not historically been seen as such when they occur in a domestic environment. This continues to be the case. Reports regularly in newspapers make it clear that crimes of violence against women by known men are regarded as being of a lesser order than the same crimes perpetrated against male or female others: i.e. as being 'just a domestic'. In the

Independent on Sunday's brief 'round up' of short news items (3 August 1997), located alongside the winning lottery numbers, the weather prediction for boat racing at Cowes, and a new ride at a theme park in Derbyshire, under the heading 'Woman Dies After Being Set Alight', was an item about a woman doused in petrol and set on fire at her home in what police described as a 'domestic incident', as if that woman's murder warranted no further comment or concern, and indeed was of no more importance than the other news items. This is not uncommon in the reporting of serious crimes of violence by men against 'their' women.

The judicial response to marital rape (which became a crime in 1991) illustrates the extent to which men's sexual violence against their women partners is tolerated. Lees (Chapter 4) found that all Court of Appeal marital rape cases between 1991 and 1995 involved previous violence by the man, but it has been 'at the judge's discretion whether or not domestic violence can be put in front of the jury'. The courts do not take into account the fact that women are in greatest danger when leaving violent men; and at the point of separation or divorce, most vulnerable to being killed. Nor do they take into account the connections between marital rape and murder. As Lees points out, even in cases of the victim becoming unconscious through strangulation, the charge is not attempted murder.

Lees (Chapter 4) uses sentencing as an example of the cultural tolerance of domestic violence. In 1986 new sentencing guidelines were issued in an effort to increase the length of sentences for rapists. Their impact was short lived: there was an increase from 42 per cent in 1985 to 79 per cent in 1987, but a decrease then from 1987. Moreover, the Court of Appeal has reduced sentences in even the most appalling and serious of cases, as for example a woman who was raped and buggered in front of her children. Marital rapists get shorter sentences than stranger rapists, but none of them are out of circulation for long. Lees observes that theft is treated more seriously than rape.

Taken together, as two ends of a spectrum of attitudes about men's violence against women, the Zero Tolerance schools' survey and Lees' study of Appeal Court judges, offer some insight into the nature and scale of the re-education and re-socialisation interventions that will be required if domestic violence prevention is to become a reality.

Gendering the language of domestic violence

The problem of gender-neutral policy

The language used to describe domestic violence determines what is seen and known and done about it in policy and in practice (see Itzin 2000b). In the use of ungendered language, men are invisible as primarily the perpetrators of domestic violence. 'Domestic violence' is itself ungendered and functions to shift the focus away from what is primarily men's violence against women in the home. Hearn (1998) argues that 'the notion of [gender] neutral knowledge is not tenable' (p. 88, cited in Cowburn and Pringle 2000). Kennedy (in Quaid and Itzin, Chapter 9) does 'not think the legal norm can be made gender neutral' and has come to believe that 'gender neutrality is unachievable because it does not exist'.

In the USA, however, the dominant academic discourse has been influenced by the widespread use of the Conflict Tactic Scales, a methodology which has produced what look to be scientifically robust data showing that wives are about as violent as husbands, and even that husbands are more likely than wives to be victims of acts of severe violence (see Dobash *et al.* 1992: 72–3). However, 'evidence from police and court records, and national crime surveys and victim surveys continue to confirm the asymmetrical pattern of domestic violence' as being predominantly men's violence against women (Dobash and Dobash, Chapter 11). The semblance of symmetry occurs, I believe, as a result of a theoretical artefact, that is the failure to recognise the paradigm of gendered power as it is reflected in every domain of gender relations, including gender-based violence and abuse (see Itzin 2000b for an explanatory framework that elaborates this).

The Duluth model *does* take gendered power relations into account in the distinctions it makes between perpetrator violence and victim violence as reflected in the concept of 'a primary aggressor and two assailants', in the knowledge that domestic violence *is* gendered, and that responding appropriately to this is crucial to domestic violence prevention. However, nowhere in the Pence and McDonnell paper (1998, and Chapter 14) is the language of domestic violence gendered or the gender of the problem identified as male, reflecting perhaps an orthodoxy in the USA based on a presumption of gender symmetry in domestic violence. Given this, it is likely that Pence and McDonnell's use of gender neutral language is a strategy adopted to accommodate that orthodoxy in order to promote a domestic violence prevention model which is effective. Paradoxically, the Duluth model is effective precisely because it takes account of the gender asymmetry of domestic violence.

In developing a methodology for the Scottish Office/Home Office evaluation of the criminal justice system programmes for convicted batterers, Dobash *et al.* (Chapter 16) took into account the gendered nature of domestic violence, and the need, in contrast to the Conflict Tactic Scales, to design gender-sensitive instrumentation for assessing 'violence, injuries and other controlling and coercive behaviours'. This involved producing four instruments: a Violence Assessment Index (VAI) with 26 distinct types of violence ranging from a slap inflicted on the arm to a kick directed at the head; an Injury Assessment Index (IAI) including bruises, cuts, black eyes and internal injuries; a Controlling Behaviour Index (CBI) with 21 distinct forms of control and coercion; and a Quality of Life Index (QLI) for assessing perceived changes in the quality of life for both men and women following the men's programmes' interventions.

Looking behind the use of ungendered language it is possible to see that the notion of gender neutrality in contexts of domestic violence is not really tenable. From a materialist perspective, it is counter-intuitive. Most men (even little men) are bigger and stronger than most women. In any physical conflict, therefore, most men will outmatch most women. You don't have to be a feminist to see that a woman hitting a man will, generally speaking, not have the same effects as a man hitting a woman; that the degree of risk and damage will be mediated by men's greater physical powers and capacity to overpower women. Every time a man strikes a woman, he is using these physical powers to abuse.

This is, in part – simply, literally, materially, and, one would think, uncontentiously – what feminism has conceptualised as 'male abuse of power', set in a wider context of empirically evidenced and quite undisputable gender inequalities. This, in turn, is what feminism has – naturally, one would have thought – used, in part, to theorise power relations gendered in terms of male dominance and men's use of violence to maintain the benefits these bring (see Hanmer 1998, and Chapter 1; Itzin 2000b). To maintain a view of gender symmetry in men's and women's use of violence in domestic conflict, when there is such empirical, analytical and theoretical evidence to the contrary, suggests a very high level of dissociation, denial, accommodation and normalisation of men's routine use of violence against women culturally in the US and amongst the academic community which takes the Conflict Tactic Scale findings at face value (see Strauss 1999).

The invisibility of 'men the abusers' in UK government policy on domestic violence is constructed somewhat differently, but to similar effect. Thus, *Living Without Fear: An Integrated Approach to Tackling Violence Against Women* (Cabinet Office/Home Office 1999) does *not* state that in the vast majority of cases men are the perpetrators and women the victims. Instead it states equivocally that 'Domestic violence affects both men and women . . . [with] 15 per cent of men saying that they have been physically assaulted by a current or former partner at some point in their lives' (p. 7). It then goes on to cite the government statistics I have cited at the beginning of this chapter that identify women as primarily the victims and on a very substantial scale. By then adopting the convention of calling the victim a woman, but largely not calling the perpetrator a man, *Living Without Fear* also contributes to constructing the invisibility of men as primarily the perpetrators of domestic violence.

Dobash and Dobash (1992 and Chapter 11) point out that in the absence of an explicitly gendered perspective, 'the source of the problem – the violent male – has remained an obscure spectre, rarely subjected to systematic scrutiny and often ignored in public debates regarding what is to be done about domestic violence'. As a consequence, in policy and practice in both the UK and USA 'the violent male is elusive . . . male violence is invisible, and the violent male is rarely the focus of intervention'.

The problem this poses in practice is illustrated by Hanman (Chapter 15) writing about her experience as a Domestic Violence Forum co-ordinator. Although domestic violence is overwhelmingly perpetrated by men, she finds that 'actually stating this [in meetings] leads to near apoplexy for some agency representatives'. This leads to a shared definition never being agreed, and a gender-neutral definition being adopted for purposes of being able to progress work, leaving a Forum existing to address a problem which it cannot or will not actually define.

Conceptualising domestic violence prevention in terms of men stopping their use of violence against women

This absence of 'the violent male' in domestic violence policy creates an insurmountable obstacle to domestic violence prevention. Aid to women in the form of assistance and support, such as Women's Aid has provided, even with sufficient refuge and temporary and permanent housing, paramount though this is, will not prevent domestic violence (see Dobash and Dobash, Chapter 11, Harwin and Barron, Chapter 12, Morley, Chapter 13 and Gillan and Samson, Chapter 19). The Domestic Violence Fora in every London borough and the 200 elsewhere in the country, together with even the very most effective multi-agency working, essential though this is, will not prevent domestic violence (see Harwin and Barron, Chapter 12 and Hanman, Chapter 15). The 60 Domestic Violence Units in the London Metropolitan Police Authority, welcome though these are, will not prevent domestic violence (see Dobash *et al.*, Chapter 16). Arrest (mandatory or otherwise), prosecution, conviction, probation and prison, important though these are in relevant cases, will not prevent domestic violence (see Pence and McDonnell 1998: 41–2, and Chapter 14).

These can only be regarded as damage limitation and harm minimisation interventions, the means to very crucial ends in providing for and protecting abused women and their children, but falling very far short of domestic violence prevention. The primary objective of domestic violence policy at government level must be to reduce the incidence and prevalence of domestic violence. Hanmer (1998, and Chapter 1) has pointed out, 'there is no evidence at the moment of violence against women diminishing in frequency or intensity' (p. 128), and Dobash and Dobash (Chapter 11) have found that 'to date, the overwhelming majority of men have not given up violence or managed to live without further harassment or intimidation of their female partners'. In this context, domestic violence prevention can only be meaningfully defined in terms of men stopping their use of violence against women.

We know that the most effective interventions are those which target individual men who are violent against women using a combination of criminal justice system sanctions and intensive cognitive behavioural individual and group work based on what is known from women's experience of men's violence. However, this will only ever apply to the very small proportion of men who are arrested (27 per cent in West Yorkshire) and convicted (two per cent in the London Borough of Hammersmith and Fulham) of domestic violence (see Hanmer and Griffiths, Chapter 18; Kelly 1999). This leaves the very large proportion of normal, ordinary men who routinely use violence against their women partners: that is, to at least a quarter of all men according to official figures, or higher using the hidden figures of Mooney's study previously cited, which found only 37 per cent of all men saying they would not use violence against their women partners (1994 and Chapter 2).

I think we must be very pessimistic indeed about the potential of government policy in the USA or in the UK to reduce the incidence and prevalence of domestic violence very much or at all until the problem is defined as men's violence and abuse of male power. The overarching message from the women's aid and battered women's movements, reflected in the effectiveness of the interventions discussed in this chapter, has been to identify the problem as men's violent, abusive, coercive and controlling behaviour, and to focus interventions on individual men. Likewise, government policy, if it is to have any chance of meeting its 'long term goal to prevent the terrible crime of violence against women', must recognise the problem of domestic violence as a 'men-thing', evidenced empirically as what normal, ordinary men do routinely on a very substantial scale because they want to, because they think they have a right to, and because nothing effective is done to stop them. This recognition is crucial to the success of domestic violence prevention at the level of the state, just as it has been shown to be at the level of the individual. Violence against women by known men will only end when the men who do it decide to stop, and the men who don't decide to stop the men who do. This is unlikely to happen without concerted intervention by the state.

References

Abel, G. G., Becker, J. V., Cunningham-Rathnew, J., Mittelman, M. and Rouleau, J. L. (1988) 'Multiple paraphilic diagnoses among sex offenders', *Bulletin of the American Academy of Psychiatry and the Law*, 16 (2), 153–68.

Armstrong, L. (2000) 'What happened when women said incest' in Itzin, C. (ed.) *Home Truths About Child Sexual Abuse: Influencing Policy and Practice*, London: Routledge pp. 27–49

Becker, J. V. and Coleman, E. M. (1988) 'Incest', in van Hasselt, V. B., Morrison, R. L., Bellack, A. S. and Jersen, M. (eds) *Handbook of Family Violence*, New York: Plenum, pp. 187–205.

British Medical Association (1998) *Domestic Violence: A Health Care Issue*, London: BMA.

Browne, A. (1987) *When Battered Women Kill*, New York: Free Press.

Burton, S., Kitzinger, J., with Kelly, L. and Regan, L. (1998) *Young People's Attitudes Towards Violence, Sex and Relationships*, Edinburgh: Zero Tolerance Charitable Trust.

Cabinet Office/Home Office (1999) *Living Without Fear: An Integrated Approach to Tackling Violence Against Women*, London: Cabinet Office Women's Unit.

Cowburn, M. and Pringle, K. (2000) 'Pornography and men's practices', *Journal of Sexual Aggression*, Vol. 5, No. 3, London: Whiting and Birch.

Dobash, R. E. and Dobash, R. P. (1979) *Violence Against Wives*, New York: The Free Press.

Dobash, R. E. and Dobash, R. P. (1992) *Women, Violence and Social Change*, London: Routledge.

Dobash, R. E. and Dobash, R. P. (1999) 'Violent men and violent contexts', in R. E. Dobash and R. P. Dobash (eds) *Rethinking Violence Against Women*, California: Sage pp. 141–68.

Dobash, R. P., Dobash, R. E., Cavanagh, K. and Lewis, R. (2000) *Changing Violent Men*, Beverly Hills, Calif: Sage.

Dobash, R. P., Dobash, R. E., Daly, M. and Wilson, M. (1992) 'The myth of sexual symmetry in marital violence', *Social Problems*, 39, 1, 402–32.

Eldridge, H. (1998) *Therapist Guide for Maintaining Change: Relapse Prevention for Adult Male Perpetrators of Child Sexual Abuse*, Thousand Oaks, Calif: Sage.

Eldridge, H. (2000) 'Patterns of sex offending and strategies for effective assessment and intervention', in Itzin, C. (ed.) *Home Truths About Child Sexual Abuse; Influencing Policy and Practice*, London: Routledge, pp. 313–35.

Farmer, E. and Owen, M. (1998) 'Gender and the child protection process', *British Journal of Social Work*, 28, 545–64.

Farmer, E. and Owen, M. (2000) 'Gender and the child protection process', in Itzin, C. (ed.) *Home Truths About Child Sexual Abuse: Influencing Policy and Practice*, London: Routledge pp. 353–372.

Finkelhor, D. and Ylo, K. (1985) *The Dark Side of Families*, London: Sage.

Gondolf, E. (1998) *The Impact of Mandatory Court Review on Batterer Program Compliance: An Evaluation of the Pittsburg Municipal Courts and Domestic Abuse Counselling Center (DACC)*, Indiana PA: Mid-Atlantic Addiction Training Institute.

Hanmer, J. (1995) *Policy Development and Implementation Seminars: Patterns of Agency Contact with Women*, Research Unit on Violence, Abuse and Gender Relations, Bradford: University of Bradford, Research Paper No.12: ISBN 1-85143-III-X

Hanmer, J. (1998) 'Out of control: men, violence and family life', in Popay, J., Hearn, J. and Edwards, J. (eds) *Men, Gender Divisions and Welfare*, London: Routledge.

Hanmer, J. and Saunders, S. (1984) *Well-Founded Fear: A Community Study of Violence To Women*, London: Hutchinson.

Hanmer, J., Griffiths, S. and Jerwood, D. *Arresting Evidence: Domestic Violence and Repeat Victimisation*, Police Research Series, Paper 104, London: Home Office.

Hearn, J. (1998) 'Theorising men and men's discursive practices in men's theorising of men', *Theory and Society*, 27, 781–816.

Home Office (1997) *The Processing of Rape Cases by the Criminal Justice System*, London: Home Office Research, Development and Statistics Directorate.

Home Office (1998) *The 1998 British Crime Survey*, London: Home Office Research, Development and Statistics Directorate.

Home Office (1999) *Homicide Statistics*, London: Home Office Research, Development and Statistics Directorate.

Humphrey, C., Hester, M., Hague, G., Mullender, A., Abrahams, H. and Lowe, P. (2000) *From Good Intentions to Good Practice: Mapping Services Working with Families Where There is Domestic Violence*, Bristol: The Policy Press.

Independent on Sunday (1977) 'Woman dies after being set alight', 3 August, p. 7.

Itzin, C. (1996) 'Pornography and the organisation of child sexual abuse', in Bibby, P. (ed.) *Organised Abuse: The Current Debate*, Aldershot: Arena, pp. 167–97.

Itzin, C. (1997a) 'Pornography and the organisation of intrafamilial and extrafamilial child sexual abuse: a conceptual model', in Kantor, G. K. and Jasinski, J. L. (eds) *Out of the Darkness: Contemporary Perspectives on Family Violence*, Thousand Oaks: Sage, pp. 58–80.

Itzin, C. (1997b) 'Pornography and the organisation of intrafamilial and extrafamilial child sexual abuse: developing a conceptual model', *Child Abuse Review*, Vol. 6, no. 2, 84–94.

Itzin, C. (ed.) (2000) *Home Truths About Child Sexual Abuse: Influencing Policy and Practice – A Reader*, London: Routledge.

Itzin, C. (2000a) 'Child sexual abuse and the radical feminist endeavour: an overview', in Itzin, C. (ed.) *Home Truths About Child Sexual Abuse: Influencing Policy and Practice*, London: Routledge, pp. 1–25.

Itzin, C. (2000b) 'Child protection and child sexual abuse prevention: influencing policy and practice', in Itzin, C. (ed.) *Home Truths About Child Sexual Abuse: Influencing Policy and Practice*, London: Routledge, pp. 405–49.

Jones, A. (1991) *Women Who Kill*, London: Victor Gollancz.

Kelly, L. (1988) *Surviving Sexual Violence*, Cambridge: Polity.

Kelly, L. (1994) 'The interconnectedness of domestic violence and child abuse: challenges for research policy and practice', in Mullender, A. and Morley, R. (eds) *Children Living With Domestic Violence: Putting Men's Abuse of Women on the Child Care Agenda*, London: Whiting and Birch.

Kelly, L. (1999) *Domestic Violence Matters: an Evaluation of a Development Project*, Home Office Research Study 193, London: Home Office.

Kelly, L., Regan, L. and Burton, S. (1991) *An Exploratory Study of the Prevalence of Sexual Abuse in a Sample of 16–21 Year Olds*, London: Child Abuse Studies Unit, University of North London.

Kennedy, H. (1992) *Eve Was Framed*, London: Chatto and Windus.

Mama, A. (1989) *The Hidden Struggle*, London: Runnymede Trust

Mooney, J. (1994) *The Hidden Figure: Domestic Violence in North London*, London: Islington Council and Islington Police Crime Prevention Unit.

Mullender, A. and Morley, R. (1994) *Children Living with Domestic Violence: Putting Men's Abuse of Women on the Child Care Agenda*, London: Whiting and Birch.

Pahl, J. (1985) 'Refuges for battered women: ideology and action', *Feminist Review*, no. 19, March, 25–43.

Patel, P. (1998) 'Third wave feminism and black women's activism', in Mirza, H. S. *Black British Feminism*, London: Routledge, pp. 255–68.

Pence, E. L. and McDonnell, C. (1998) 'Developing policies and protocols', in Shepard, M. F. and Pence, E. L. (eds) *Coordinating Community Responses to Domestic Violence: Lessons from Duluth and Beyond*, Thousand Oaks, CA: Sage, pp. 41–64.

Saunders, D. G. (1988) 'Wife abuse, husband abuse, or mutual combat', in Yllo, K. and Bograd, M. (eds) *Feminist Perspectives on Wife Abuse*, California: Sage

Stark and Flitcroft (1988) 'Women and children at risk: feminist perspectives on child abuse', *International Journal of Health Services*, 18 (1), pp. 97–118.

Straus, M. (1999) 'The controversy over domestic violence by women: a methodological, theoretical, and sociology of science analysis', in Arriaga, X. B. and Oskamp, S. (eds) *Violence in Intimate Relationships*, Thousand Oaks, CA: Sage.

Swann, S. (2000) 'Helping girls involved in prostitution: a Barnardos' experiment' in Itzin, C. (ed.) *Home Truths About Child Sexual Abuse: Influencing Policy and Practice*, London: Routledge, pp. 277–90.

Weinrott, M. R. and Saylor, M. (1991) 'Self report of crimes committed by sex offenders', *Journal of Interpersonal Violence*, 6, (3) pp. 286–300.

Zero Tolerance Charitable Trust (1992) *Adolescents' Knowledge About and Attitudes to Domestic Violence*, Report to the Women's Committee Unit, Edinburgh: Edinburgh District Council.

Appendix 1

Families without fear: Women's Aid agenda for action on domestic violence[1]

Nicola Harwin

Introduction

Domestic violence is not a new problem. Throughout history, and across divisions of class, race and culture, it has always been a feature of family life, and part of a wider problem of violence against women. What is new is that domestic violence is no longer acceptable.

Domestic violence can be seen as any form of physical, psychological or sexual violence that takes place within an intimate or family-type relationship. However, statistics, research and the experience of helping agencies show, both in the UK and across the world, that it is usually women and their children who are the main victims and survivors of domestic violence, and men who are the perpetrators.

Just 100 years ago it was legal for a man to beat his wife provided he used a stick no thicker than his thumb. Up to 25 years ago, 'wife-battering' was still seen as a private matter; a hidden and largely ignored problem. A woman living with a violent and abusive man could expect no protection from the law, and little help from welfare services. In response to this, from the early 1970s, the Women's Aid movement set up refuges and helplines across the UK and lobbied for changes to laws, policy and practice.

Women's Aid is proud of the successes that it has achieved in developing services and putting domestic violence on the public agenda, and welcomes the significant improvements in responses by many agencies that Women's Aid has seen in the last decade, but there is still much to be done. Last year over 54,000 women and children stayed in refuges in England, and 145,000 sought advice and help from Women's Aid services. A series of reports in the last few years, including most recently one by the British Medical Association, have drawn attention to the fact that the lives of as many as one in four women may be affected by domestic violence.

What has not changed in these last 25 years is the pain, fear and loneliness of the women and children who live with domestic violence. Similarly, those men who do abuse still believe, at some level, that they have the right to control the members of 'their' household and to expect domestic and sexual services from their partners or wives, believing that it is acceptable to use intimidation, threats, abuse and violence to achieve these things. And so, women continue to suffer, abusive men fail to take responsibility for their violence, and children continue to live in families where their well-being and safety is threatened.

In the last decade, Women's Aid has seen a number of initiatives to tackle domestic violence at both local and national level, including radical changes in police responses to domestic violence, and the development of over 200 multi-agency domestic violence forums in the UK. While local multi-agency initiatives have enabled a more co-ordinated response in many areas, this in itself is limited by the absence of a coherent national strategy to tackle domestic violence. This is needed to ensure that central government laws, regulations and guidance encourage, and do not hinder, effective action at a local level.

Therefore, in this context, Women's Aid welcomes the Government's recognition of the serious and endemic nature of domestic violence within contemporary society, and the commitment that has been made to develop a national strategy to tackle this. Women's Aid is aware that the strategy will be published for consultation later this year and welcomes this opportunity to indicate priorities for action. Consultation with the Women's Aid membership of local refuges and other domestic violence services has identified numerous suggestions for practical changes, not all of which are able to be included in this document for reasons of space. *Families Without Fear: Women's Aid Agenda for Action on Domestic Violence* offers key recommendations for the development of an effective, multi-agency strategic response to create a future where all family members can live without fear.

Women's Aid agenda for action on domestic violence

Vision

The primary aim of a national strategy against domestic violence must be to end violence and abuse in personal relationships in order that there can be true equality within all aspects of family life. A national strategy must:

- promote the *protection* of women and children at risk of violence and harm through beneficial changes to law, policy and practice, and hold violent men accountable for their abusive behaviour;
- ensure the *prevention* of interpersonal and gender-based violence in the short and long term through public awareness and education of children and the general public, as well as through an effective legal framework;
- develop the *provision* of effective services to meet the needs of all abused women and children.

Approach

A co-ordinated multi-agency approach is needed at all levels of government (local and national) involving all key criminal justice and social welfare agencies. Independent women's advocacy and refuge organisations must be involved centrally in reviewing the law and planning and delivering appropriate services.

Unless laws, regulations and practice are changed, and a lead taken by government in terms of co-ordination and setting policy priorities in this area (the Home Office, the Lord Chancellor's Department, the Department of Health, the Department of the Environment, Transport and the Regions, the Department of Social Security, as well as the new Women's Unit), the improved response of many individual agencies and multi-agency forums will only have a limited effect, despite the enormous commitment of many individuals working within them.

Establishing a framework for action

1 Establish a government task force to co-ordinate the work of developing and implementing a national strategy over a five- to ten-year period. This should involve all relevant government departments with representation from key national statutory and voluntary agencies within the criminal and family justice system, including Women's Aid. This would also create a central point to which local activists and professionals could give information and evidence about successful initiatives and continuing problems.

2 Establish a justice system task group (with representation and 'ownership of the problem' by the judiciary and legal professionals and enforcers, as well as representation from women's advocates) to review the civil and criminal law in relation to domestic violence, hear evidence, and make recommendations for practice changes to improve the safety and protection of survivors.

3 Review the operation of current law, policy and practice including instigating research into how current law, policy and practice helps or hinders prevention, protection and provision in relation to domestic violence. Monitor and evaluate how the implementation of Part IV of the Family Law Act 1996, proceedings under criminal law, the operation of Section 8 the Children Act 1989 (arrangements for children in relationship breakdown), and (when it comes into force in 1999) the operation of Parts 1–3 of the Family Law Act 1996, are working in practice.

4 Develop a co-ordinated national strategy for the provision and funding of refuges, helplines, outreach, counselling and other specialist services for women and children who are survivors and victims of domestic or sexual violence to meet a wide range of support needs, including those of black and ethnic minority women, women with disabilities, lesbians and older women. This strategy should be developed in conjunction with national Women's Aid federations and local authority bodies.

5 Issue circulars and guidance from all government departments to policy makers and fund-holders in each service area. For example, within the field of health, to require all Regional NHS Management Executives to make

domestic violence a priority in Purchasing and Planning guidelines, in the development of Health Action Plans, and in delivering funding for training and on-call support services to be developed by Accident and Emergency Departments and GP surgeries, in partnership with Women's Aid.

6   Require 'institutional audits' to be undertaken by local government bodies, national and local criminal justice agencies, health and social welfare agencies, housing organisations and other public, private and voluntary sector bodies to assess where changes to policy, operational guidelines, organisational values and staff training need to be implemented in order to deal effectively with domestic violence.

7   Develop and promote an on-going national public awareness campaign to improve understanding of the nature and impact of domestic violence. This needs to be carried out in conjunction with other measures to develop effective policy and service responses.

8   Provide domestic violence awareness training to all agencies likely to be approached by women experiencing domestic violence, including magistrates, judges, police, prosecutors, housing officers, social workers, doctors, nurses, health visitors, midwives and DSS officers. Both single agency and inter-agency training is crucial to develop understanding of domestic violence, as well as to promote better implementation of specific agency responsibilities. It is now widely recognised that, in practice, most effective domestic violence awareness training is undertaken by, or in liaison with, experienced Women's Aid staff both locally and nationally.

9   Establish a central monitoring body for the collection of statistics on domestic and gender-specific violence. All relevant agencies, particularly local authority housing departments, social services, and health authorities should also keep easily accessible information on the numbers of clients approaching them for help with problems of domestic violence.

More detailed recommendations on key policy areas

1   Access to information and help: agency responses

1.1   All statutory and relevant voluntary agencies should have clear and publicly available written policies on domestic violence. They should develop appropriate minimum standards and good practice guidelines with clear monitoring mechanisms.

1.2   Agencies should take a visibly anti-violence stance by displaying posters and making information about legal rights to protection and help with all forms of violence available in a range of community languages.

1.3   Women should be offered the choice of talking to female staff in any agency and specialist provision should be available to meet the needs of specific groups, including black and ethnic minority women.

1.4   All agencies, including police, courts, solicitors, social services, housing departments and voluntary agencies should have straightforward access to non-familial interpreters.

1.5   All agencies should respect the right to confidentiality of any woman seeking help because of abuse. Any limits to this confidentiality, for example, in relation to child protection, should be clearly stated at the outset. Abused women should not be referred on to any other agency without their explicit consent.

1.6   Key points of first contact, such as health services, should be required to develop domestic violence policies and protocols. Early intervention and prevention can reduce costs throughout the rest of the social welfare and criminal justice system. Full information should be given to abused women about their rights to protection and help at all stages of primary health care, and accident and emergency intervention. Training for front-line staff, GPs and consultants (especially obstetricians) should be developed and delivered as part of routine medical training.

2   Specialist refuge and advocacy services

2.1   A range of appropriate specialist advocacy and refuge services should be available for any woman and her children who have experienced domestic violence.

2.2   Funding of existing local refuge and ancillary support services should be urgently secured. Existing mechanisms for funding must be co-ordinated and rationalised. Resources should be ring-fenced by central government for maintaining the existing network of refuges and developing new services.

2.3   An on-going funding source for the Women's Aid National Helpline should be identified to enable the continuation and development of existing services to respond to the continuing increase in calls from women survivors.

2.4   A long-term strategic plan for the development and funding of local and national refuge, outreach and helpline services should be drawn up by government in consultation with the Women's Aid federations, based on a national mapping exercise of current provision and unmet service needs, to deliver carefully targeted and appropriate services. A funding strategy should include rationalisation of funding streams to create a level playing field between housing association and local authority tenures across England and Wales. A unified funding system could be established on a per capita basis, and monitored by one agency either regionally or nationally, which would help to end the wasteful, time-consuming and costly duplication caused by multiple levels of monitoring by different funding sources.

2.5   Local Social Services Departments should recognise that children who have experienced domestic violence are 'children in need' and should contribute to funding for children's support staff in refuges through s.17 of the Children Act 1989, again calculated and distributed on a per capita basis

2.6   A funding source should be identified for the development of women's advocacy, outreach, and support services including helplines, drop-in advice centres for women in all towns and cities, and support for women going through the civil or criminal legal process. These services should be provided by or in conjunction with Women's Aid.

3   Criminal law

3.1   The Home Office should make domestic violence a notifiable offence and a top priority for policing. The provisions of the 1990 Circular to Chief Constables should be reviewed, updated, monitored and enforced.

3.2   Local and national government should pilot and develop co-ordinated community responses along the lines of the Duluth (see Appendix 2) and San Diego models in the United States.

3.3   Police response should be further improved, including: strengthening pro-arrest policies, improving evidence collection, and stopping the routine release of the offender on bail.

3.4   Specialist police Domestic Violence Officers should be retained either within specialist Domestic Violence Units or within other Community Safety or Vulnerable Persons Units.

3.5   The Crown Prosecution Service should pilot the introduction of specialist trained prosecutors along the lines of successful examples in the United States to improve effective prosecution and outcomes.

3.6   The Home Office and Crown Prosecution Service should review the policy on Charging Standards in relation to domestic violence to prevent the routine downgrading of charges by prosecutors (so that serious offences are processed in the Crown court instead of being downgraded to the magistrates court).

3.7   Information and support services to women should be improved through, for example: access to specialist, independent victim advocacy and support; the creation of 'privileged communication' between the 'victim' and women's support advocate; full information about rights and options; and prior notice of discharge of violent partner by police or prison authorities.

3.8   There should be a rebuttable presumption that victims of domestic violence are defined as 'vulnerable or intimidated witnesses' in any new guidance or legislation.

3.9   The process of attending and giving evidence at court should be completely overhauled to make it more user-friendly and safe. Within the court, separate waiting rooms and children's care resources should be provided.

3.10   Stronger sanctions should be introduced against violent partners. Probation services and other agencies should be encouraged to continue and extend the provision of perpetrators programmes using cognitive/behavioural re-education techniques on the Duluth model (see

Appendix 2) with separate support services for women to ensure accountability. Prison sentences should be a routine option if violent men re-offend or fail to complete programmes. There should be no access to the telephone for perpetrators on remand, so as to prevent on-going harassment of ex-partners. Duluth-style perpetrators programmes should also operate in prison.

3.11 The Home Office should consider making it an offence for a violent ex-partner approaching a women's refuge to harass or intimidate a resident. (Prison sentences of up to ten years have proved effective in the USA in helping to reduce attacks on women and children in refuges.)

3.12 The Home Office should consider introducing a new offence for any agency or individual (e.g. bounty hunters) to track down, for financial gain, someone who is fleeing from domestic violence.

3.13 The gender anomalies in the homicide law in relation to women who kill violent men must be addressed to end the discrepancy in defences for manslaughter available to both men and women and the inequalities in sentencing outcomes.

3.14 Following the implementation of the Crime and Disorder Act, the Home Office should issue specific detailed guidance to police and local authorities on appropriate mechanisms for carrying out crime audits in relation to domestic violence, given its private and hidden nature, and on the need to work in close co-operation with specialist agencies like Women's Aid.

4 Civil law

4.1 Civil protection remedies must also dovetail and work together with the criminal law: emergency and interim court orders under Part IV of the Family Law Act and the Children Act 1989 should be available alongside action under the criminal law to ensure the safety of women and children at risk.

4.2 Section 60 of the Family Law Act 1996 should be brought into force to allow applications for injunctions by third parties such as the police.

4.3 The criteria for eligibility for Legal Aid in relation to injunctions should be amended to enable all women who need protection from domestic violence to use Part IV of the Family Law Act 1996.

4.4 A National Register for all injunctions should be established to enable a more effective multi-agency response by police, probation, social services and the courts to secure the safety and protection of abused women and children.

4.5 Injunctions should be more strictly enforced and any breach should be treated severely by both police and the courts.

4.6 The Government should introduce legislation to enable breaches to be made a criminal offence, in cases where there is a history of physical violence, to allow the courts to deal with violence effectively.

This would bring the Family Law Act 1996 Part IV more in line with civil remedies under the Protection from Harassment Act 1997. Referral to probation programmes for perpetrators could then be used by the courts alongside other measures for disposal.

4.7   Discrimination in remedies for protection under the civil law between married and unmarried women, heterosexual and homosexual couples should be removed.

5   Divorce and court proceedings

5.1   The implementation of Parts 1, 2 and 3 of the Family Law Act 1996 should be monitored and evaluated to assess whether new arrangements for divorce and mediation are putting women at risk of domestic violence.

5.2   Other forms of proof of violence should be added to the divorce legislation as well as the existence of an injunction (e.g., an undertaking, or criminal proceedings) so that abused women do not have to wait 18 months to get divorced, as this is likely to delay access to permanent safe accommodation for themselves and their children, and to increase disruption to family life.

5.3   Court procedures must be changed to prevent women being pressured to meet with their abusers and agree arrangements at the court directions stage. Information should first be sought in private about any history of violence, or any evidence of this that may be held by other agencies.

6   Housing provision

6.1   The Housing Act 1996 should be repealed or amended to improve provision for women fleeing violence. A right to permanent accommodation should be reinstated for homeless applicants; eligibility rules for people from abroad should be changed so that women fleeing violent men can return to this country; and local authorities should be prevented from introducing widespread exclusions in their allocation policies.

6.2   Introductory tenancies should be reviewed so that local authorities cannot use them to remove tenants who have rent arrears or defects charges, as this impacts unfairly on abused women who frequently have to pay off rent arrears or damage charges incurred by their violent partners.

6.3   The Code of Guidance on Homelessness should be made mandatory to improve local authority responses to domestic violence. This should: ensure help for all those at risk of physical, psychological and sexual abuse, including single women; prevent victims being defined inappropriately as 'intentionally homeless' if they refuse to apply for an occupation order and return home when it is not safe to do so; and ensure that the lack of 'local connection' is not used to penalise women forced to flee violence from their home area.

6.4   The Department of the Environment, Transport and Regions should issue a circular to require housing authorities to recognise domestic violence as a problem which needs a national as well as a local response, to fast track procedures for referrals between local authorities, emergency transfers and the use of the mobility scheme, and to take account of the individual needs of abused women and work in partnership with local refuge services to develop strategic approaches to the provision of emergency and temporary accommodation and housing advice.

7 Implementation of the Children Act 1989

7.1 Government guidance on good practice regarding domestic violence should be drawn up to accompany the Children Act for use in all court proceedings under the Act. It will not always be known to the court that domestic violence is involved, and so any good practice guidelines should apply to all cases. This guidance should also highlight the need to support the parent who is willing to provide everyday care for the child and to ensure that court orders do not endanger the safety of that parent or set conditions which make it impossible for that parent to lead a normal life.

7.2 The Children Act 1989 should be amended to include a rebuttable presumption of no contact until it can be shown to be safe for all parties, if there is evidence of a history of violence to either the child or the other parent. (Tragic homicides of women and children during contact arrangements have led, in the USA, Australia and New Zealand, to legislation that contains a rebuttable presumption that residence or contact where the father is violent is not likely to be in the best interests of the child.) In such cases perpetrators should not be allowed to make repeated applications for contact until they can submit professional evidence to prove that their behaviour will no longer present a threat to those whom they have abused, including the other parent or adult carer. When considering what is in the child's best interest, the child's wishes and well-being should always be taken into consideration but safety should be the main consideration.

7.3 The Lord Chancellor's Department should investigate mechanisms for monitoring child contact arrangements in cases of domestic violence to ensure that abuse does not re-occur.

7.4 Seek and find orders (under s.33 of the Family Law Act 1986) should not be pursued in cases of domestic violence, and court procedures should be altered to ensure that the addresses of abused women and children remain confidential and that abusive men are not given any indication of the area in which they are living.

7.5 All Social Services Departments should develop guidance and training for social workers to enable them to improve responses to abused women and children in an empowering way. This should examine the possibility of domestic violence whenever child abuse is suspected and consider the impact of this at every stage of investigation and intervention, and assist women and children to escape from a violent man by providing cash or other practical help with travel and getting into a refuge.

7.6   Social Services Departments should recognise that supporting the non-abusing parent is the most effective child protection resource to help her make safe choices for herself and the children. They should work separately with each parent where domestic violence is a factor; in particular, ensuring separate representation and attendance at meetings and case conferences to enable the abused woman to speak freely without fear of retribution.

7.7   Social Services should recognise the value of Women's Aid as an effective monitoring and child protection resource which helps to keep non-abusing family members together and also enables children who have lived with domestic violence to come to terms with their experiences.

8   Welfare benefits and related issues

8.1   The Government should safeguard the crucial role played by the Benefits Agency in enabling women and children fleeing violence to access emergency services, live safely in temporary accommodation and rebuild their lives afterwards.

8.2   Specific guidance should be developed for the Benefits Agency so that women fleeing domestic violence are entitled to payment in an emergency, and are not prevented, by arbitrary district-led funding structures and cutbacks in out-of-hours services, from accessing safe emergency accommodation and support.

8.3   The Social Fund guidance should be altered so that claimants who have lost their possessions, and often their homes and their jobs, due to fleeing domestic violence are specified as a priority group for community care grants, whether or not they have children, as the repayment of loans can leave them in extreme poverty.

8.4   Abused women are often in no fit state to work and need time to recover from the trauma of domestic violence, especially if they have young children. The lone-parent premium should be restored for single parents who have children under school age and for those who are unable to work for medical or social reasons such as domestic violence.

8.5   Evidence of identity rules within legislation on benefits system fraud should take account of the difficulties faced by people who have left home in a hurry without supporting evidence to enable a claim for benefit to be processed, so that women fleeing violence are neither forced to return home, nor made ineligible for housing benefit rental income which is then lost to the refuge service that is supporting them.

8.6   Women must not be forced to stay in a violent relationship because they are economically dependent on their husbands or partners.

Where women have left violent relationships, but would not normally be eligible for Social Security benefits because of their immigration status, exception should be made to the 'no recourse to public funds' rule. This would enable them to claim income support for themselves and their children, housing benefit for emergency accommodation, and Legal Aid to obtain protection from their abuser.

8.7   Current safeguards within the Child Support Act in relation to domestic violence should not be withdrawn or weakened.

9   Immigration laws

9.1   There should be a recognition of domestic violence in immigration law. The Home Office must recognise the dangers of domestic violence and must take this into account in dealing with applications to remain. Women must not be forced to remain in violent situations in order to stay in the UK.

9.2   There must be a recognition of gender discrimination. The Home Office must also take into consideration the very real problems that divorced and separated women face in some countries, where they will be discriminated against and prevented from supporting themselves or living in dignity. This may amount to persecution, or inhuman and degrading treatment, on grounds of gender. This must be recognised as a legitimate claim for asylum.

10   Education

10.1   Local authorities should be encouraged to work with Women's Aid and other domestic violence services to raise awareness of domestic violence in schools and youth clubs through discussion groups, special activities and the development of training packs. As part of this, awareness training should be provided and guidelines developed to enable teachers and youth workers to deal sensitively with the disclosure of abuse while addressing issues of confidentiality and safety. Ideally this should be included both within the main national curriculum and within PHSE.

10.2   Schools should receive guidance stressing the urgent need to offer places promptly to children living in women's refuges and to ensure that children who join the school after the beginning of the academic year receive an adequate needs assessment and to make resources available to enable these children to be fully integrated into everyday school life.

10.3   Local authorities should be encouraged to offer classes in child development which are mandatory for both teenage boys and girls as a means of promoting better care and understanding of the needs of children and more responsible attitudes to parenting.

Note

1   Previously published in 1998 by Women's Aid Federation of England, Bristol.

Appendix 2

The Duluth domestic abuse intervention project power and control wheel

Index